George W. Alexander
and Castle Thunder

ALSO BY FRANCES H. CASSTEVENS
AND FROM McFARLAND

*The 28th North Carolina Infantry:
A Civil War History and Roster* (2008)

*Tales from the North and the South: Twenty-Four
Remarkable People and Events of the Civil War* (2007)

*Edward A. Wild and the African
Brigade in the Civil War* (2003; paperback 2005)

*The Civil War and Yadkin County,
North Carolina* (1997; paperback 2005)

*"Out of the Mouth of Hell":
Civil War Prisons and Escapes* (2005)

*Clingman's Brigade in the
Confederacy, 1862–1865* (2002)

AND FROM ARCADIA

*Yadkin County, North Carolina:
The First One Hundred Years* (1996)

George W. Alexander and Castle Thunder

A Confederate Prison and Its Commandant

FRANCES H. CASSTEVENS

McFarland & Company, Inc., Publishers
Jefferson, North Carolina, and London

The present work is a reprint of the illustrated case bound edition of George W. Alexander and Castle Thunder: A Confederate Prison and Its Commandant, *first published in 2004 by McFarland.*

LIBRARY OF CONGRESS CATALOGUING-IN-PUBLICATION DATA

Casstevens, Frances Harding.
  George W. Alexander and Castle Thunder : a Confederate prison and its commandant / Frances H. Casstevens.
      p.   cm.
  Includes bibliographical references and index.

  ISBN-13: 978-0-7864-3730-6
  softcover : 50# alkaline paper ∞

  1. Castle Thunder Prison (Richmond Va.)   2. Alexander, George W., Captain.   3. Prison wardens — Virginia — Richmond — Biography.   4. Prison wardens — Confederate States of America — Biography.   5. United States — History — Civil War, 1861–1865 — Prisoners and prisons, Confederate.   6. Prisoners of war — Confederate States of America — History.   7. Prisoners of war — Virginia — Richmond — History — 19th century.   8. Sailors — United States — Biography.   I. Title.
  E612.C34C37   2008
  973.7'71'092 — dc22   2004006353

British Library cataloguing data are available

©2004 Frances H. Casstevens. All rights reserved

No part of this book may be reproduced or transmitted in any form or by any means, electronic or mechanical, including photocopying or recording, or by any information storage and retrieval system, without permission in writing from the publisher.

On the cover: Castle Thunder, Richmond (Library of Congress, Washington, D.C., LC-B8171-3160). Captain George W. Alexander, from Loreta Janeta Velazquez, *The Woman in Battle* (Richmond: Dustin, Gilman & Co., 1876)

Manufactured in the United States of America

McFarland & Company, Inc., Publishers
  Box 611, Jefferson, North Carolina 28640
    www.mcfarlandpub.com

To Brad Hively, a modern-day *provost marshal* re-enactor and Yadkin County law enforcement officer;

and to my son
Timothy T. Casstevens
(March 9, 1962–November 21, 2003),
who shared my love of history.

Acknowledgments

J. E. Brown, photographer, Yadkinville, North Carolina; Lewis Brumfield, researcher, Yadkinville, North Carolina; Caren Casstevens, artist, Yadkinville, North Carolina; Jim Dowdy, researcher, Stevensville, Maryland; Duke University, Durham, North Carolina; Michael D. Gorman and his "Civil War Richmond" site on the Internet; Library of Congress, Washington, D. C.; Library of Virginia, Richmond, Virginia; Cathy Millward, genealogical and historical researcher, Durham, North Carolina; Museum of the Confederacy, Richmond, Virginia; National Archives, Washington, D. C.; Prince George's County Historical Society, Riverdale, Maryland; Rowan County Public Library, Salisbury, North Carolina; Scott S. Sheads, historian, Fort McHenry National Monument and Historic Shrine, Baltimore, Maryland; Mabry Tyson and his site on naval history; Virginia Historical Society, Richmond, Virginia; Valentine Museum, Richmond, Virginia; The Salisbury Confederate Prison Association, Salisbury, North Carolina; United States Navy Department Library, Washington Navy Yard, Washington, D.C.; Glenn Helm; John A. Wyman, Elkton, Maryland; Wake Forest University, Winston-Salem, North Carolina; and the librarian and staff of Yadkin County Public Library, Yadkinville, North Carolina.

Contents

Acknowledgments vi
Introduction 1
Chronology of Alexander's Military Career in the Confederacy 5

1. Around the World with the United States Navy — 7
2. Sailing for the Confederacy: The Capture of the *St. Nicholas* — 17
3. Escape from Fort McHenry — 26
4. Assistant Provost Marshal Alexander — 32
5. New Prison Opened in Richmond — 46
6. The Lighter Side: Alexander — Poet, Dramatist and Actor — 55
7. Life Within the Castle: The Dark Side — 61
8. Spies, Traitors and Hostages — 74
9. General Hospital No. 13, "The Lunatic Hospital" — 84
10. Escape Attempts — 88
11. Cruel and Unusual Punishment vs. Standard Fare — 97
12. The Congressional Investigation — 107
13. The Verdict — 119
14. The Washington Adventure: Alexander Plays at Spying — 125
15. Under Fire Again — 128
16. 1864: Charlotte, Danville and Salisbury — 132
17. The Final Months of the War, 1864–1865 — 144

18. After the Surrender	153
19. 1870–1890	160
Epilogue	165
Appendix 1—Partial List of Inmates at Castle Thunder	169
Appendix 2—Transcript of Court Martial of Private John R. Jones	203
Appendix 3—List of Prisoners Sent from Camp Holmes in September 1863	207
Appendix 4—Morning Report of Captain G. W. Alexander, September 18, 1863	209
Appendix 5—The Military Prison Keepers of the Late Southern Confederacy, in the Van of the Democratic Party	213
Notes	219
Bibliography	257
Index	265

Introduction

The American Civil War was fought by brave and courageous men on both sides of the conflict. Many of those men distinguished themselves on the battlefield and, if they lived, were rewarded with medals and promotions.

On the other side of the coin, many soldiers, both Union and Confederate, deserted. Citizens on both sides of the Mason-Dixon line were arrested on suspicion of disloyalty or of treasonous acts. Spies and counterspies abounded. Both governments took steps to arrest suspicious persons, and deserters who were caught were sentenced by court martial to terms in confinement. Prisons were established and provost marshals were appointed to arrest, confine, and care for prisoners.

Some of the prisons became notorious for the treatment the prisoners received while confined inside their walls. Andersonville and Salisbury in the South, and Johnson's Island on Sandusky Bay of Lake Erie and Camp Douglas near Chicago in the North, gained notoriety for the conditions and treatment of prisoners within their confines.

Although George Washington Alexander was known for his courage and heroism, his reputation was stained by his association with the Confederate prison system. George W. Alexander and the history of Castle Thunder will be forever intertwined. Castle Thunder was, according to A. F. Ryden, "a dark house with a dark history"—a history so dark that the Confederate Congress launched an investigation into the treatment and "disappearance" of prisoners from within its walls.[1]

The "dark" aspects of Castle Thunder were enhanced by the appearance of its first commandant, Captain George Washington Alexander. A medium-sized man, Alexander stood only 5 feet, 8 inches, but his body was well-toned and muscular. As a provost marshal, Alexander presented a frightening sight in his tight-fitting black trousers, black stockings, and black shirt. With his black eyes shining, his black hair and black beard flowing in the wind, Alexander galloped through the streets of Richmond on his huge black horse, followed by his massive black Bavarian boar hound.[2] The trio struck terror in the hearts of all that saw them.

Captain George W. Alexander, from Loreta Janeta Velazquez, *The Woman in Battle* (Richmond, Va.: Dustin, Gilman & Co., 1876).

A picture of Alexander was reproduced in the autobiography of Loreta Janeta Velazquez, *The Woman in Battle*.[3] The stern look on his face is enhanced by a trim beard and moustache. Below a receding hairline, his dark brows are knitted together in a frown above piercing black eyes. This picture of a mature George W. Alexander is a far removed from the energetic, handsome young officer who served in the United States Navy. The only other image available is a poor quality sketch published in a newspaper along with an account of his death.[4]

George Washington Alexander was once "one of the most conspicuous, notable men in Richmond during the war." He was a unique individual, a "controversial man living in controversial times."[5] He lived a life of excitement and adventure matched by few of his contemporaries. His was honored as a hero, and condemned as a cruel prison superintendent.

After serving for 13 years in the United States Navy, and being a member of Commodore Matthew Perry's expedition to Japan in 1861, Alexander resigned his position as an assistant engineer and joined the Confederacy. One of his first acts was to lead a group of volunteers in June of 1861 to capture the U. S. Navy steamer *St. Nicholas*. Encouraged by their success, the group went on to capture several more ships for the Confederacy before being recognized. Alexander and some of his men were captured and confined at Fort McHenry near Baltimore, Maryland. Disguised in a Union uniform brought to him in prison by his wife, Alexander made a daring escape.[6]

Alexander traveled to Richmond and was appointed assistant provost marshal of Richmond. When Castle Thunder was opened as a prison in 1862, Alexander was placed in charge of it. His tenure as commandant of Castle Thunder was marked by widespread criticism from both the North and the South. Rumors circulated that many of his prisoners were removed to Shockoe Cemetery and hanged.[7] More than a century later, questions remain unanswered about Alexander's treatment of prisoners.

As commandant of Castle Thunder, Alexander was accused of performing his duty with "great enthusiasm, dictorial tactics, and excessive zeal." At the same time, he was praised by his friends and superiors who believed his treatment of the prisoners was justly deserved, since most were Confederate deserters and civilians suspected of disloyalty. There were also Union soldiers, women, and slaves confined there. Some of the prisoners thought Alexander was too harsh; others thought him fair. It was rumored that there was a plot to assassinate Alexander and his officers because of their "inhumanity."[8]

Reports of the mistreatment of prisoners at Castle Thunder persisted, and in the spring of 1863, the House of Representatives of the Confederate Congress appointed a special committee to conduct an investigation. After hearing testimony from numerous witnesses, Alexander was acquitted of charges of cruelty and mistreatment of prisoners. Yet his enemies persisted and managed to have him arrested again and suspended from duty. Alexander demanded an inquiry, and again was acquitted. However, Alexander's days at Castle Thunder were over.

While some people viewed Alexander as being a harsh and cruel man, he was also "sensitive," and had a talent for musical composition.[9] Alexander wrote a play entitled *The Virginia Cavalier*, which was performed in Richmond numerous times.[10] The play was a success with the war-time audience who sought a respite from the realities of war.

After General Robert E. Lee surrendered at Appomattox on April 9, 1865, Alexander became a wanted man because he had been in charge at Castle Thunder and at Salisbury Prison. He made his way to the Mississippi River and reached safety in Canada, where he spent a number of years as a teacher of the French language to children. After the amnesty of 1872, he returned to edit the *Sunday Gazette*, a Democratic paper published in Washington, D. C. Later, he worked in Baltimore, Maryland, and he died in Laurel, Maryland, in 1895.[11]

Alexander was a man who encouraged controversy, and evoked both criticism and praise. Because he was unique, he was controversial — an enigma, whose life provided the fuel for scandals, rumors, and legends. He played all the parts, from hero to villain.

After a century and a half, from the existing documentation, we can cut through the layers of rumors and accusations to the heart of the matter and perhaps find the man who generated the "thunder" in Castle Thunder.

Chronology of Alexander's Military Career in the Confederacy

(Copied verbatim from Microfilm M331, #3, National Archives, Washington, D.C. Items in brackets are my additions.)

July 12, 1861— Prisoner of war confined in Fort McHenry, Md. Escaped Sept 7, 1861 (*O. R.*, Series 2, Vol. 2, p. 226).

October 2, 1861— Writes to Sec. of War from Richmond reporting his escape, and says when fit for duty will report in person (*O. R.*, Series 2, Vol. 3, p. 724) Signed as "1st Lieut, P.A.C.S."

[**January 31, 1862**— Alexander received letter to report to General J. H. Winder in Richmond to appear as a witness in a trial to be held there.]

June 1, 1862— Gen. Winder, Comdg. Dept of Henrico, recommends appointment of G. W. A. as an Asst. Adjut Gen. (W, 901, A & I G. O, 1862).

June 12, 1862— Appointed Capt. A. G. Dept. and ordered to report to Gen. Winder for special duty (Ref. Rough book Report A. O.).

Oct 27, 1862— Relieved from command of C. S. Prisons by Capt. T. P. Turner, G. O. #25, Dept. Of Henrico (*O.R.*, Series 2, Vol. 4, p. 928).

Nov 12, 1862— Signs an application for an appointment of a hospital steward as A. A. G. & A. P. M. Was in Richmond at this time (B-2424, A. & I. G. O, 1862).

February 15, 1864— By S. O. #37, Hdqrs. Dept. Of Henrico, dated Richmond, Feb. 16, 1864, signed by Brig. Gen. J. H. Winder, Capt. Geo. W. Alexander was ordered to proceed to Charlotte, N. C., and relieve Capt. Richardson of the duties assigned to him by S. O. #36. Hdqrs. Dept. Of Henrico. He signed vouchers for expenses incurred as A. A. G. (Personal papers).

[**April 1, 1864**— a pay voucher, dated April 1, 1864, indicates he was on duty at the military prison at Danville, Virginia at this time.]

May and June, 1864— Was Capt. & A. A. G. in command of post at Salisbury, N C. (Report A. O.).

June 4, 1864— Writes to the Sec. of War, from Salisbury, N. C., saying that he was ordered to the command of the Post, and upon arrival found many things requiring attention, etc. (A-631, A. & IGO, 1864).

June 8, 1864— Relieved from duty at Salisbury, N. C. (Order A. & IGO, 10, & 13.?).

June 22, 1864— Writes from Richmond, Va., asking assignment to duty (A. 653, A & IGO., 1864).

July 2, 1864— Writes from Richmond asking to be assigned to duty with Brig. Gen. Wm. Gardner. By endorsement Gen. G.

declines to ask for this assignment. No action noted. (A-696, A. & IG.O. 1864)

Nov. 28, 1864—Tenders resignation to take effect December 31, 1864. He signs as A. A. G. of Barton's Brigade and says he has been on duty for the last two months (Personal papers).

Dec. 31, 1864—Alexander's resignation accepted as A. A. G. by S. O. 285 (23) A & I. G. O., Dec. 1, 1864, to take effect on December 31.

Capt. Alexander was evidently placed in command of Castle Thunder when relieved form command of C. S. Prisons Oct. 27, 1862, and remained in command of that prison (except for a short period when absent at Charlotte, N.C. under order of Feb. 15, 1864) until sent to Salisbury, N.C. After he was relieved from the latter post and until he is found as A. A. G. with Barton's, his status cannot be determined. J. S. M.

1

Around the World with the United States Navy

"Where lies the land to which yon ship must go?"
—*William Wordsworth, "Where Lies the Land"*

An article which appeared at the time of his death stated that George Washington Alexander was born in Francisville, Pennsylvania, in 1831.[1] A birth date of 1829 is carved on his tombstone.[2] Nothing is known of his parents but that they were born in Scotland, according to information given by Alexander himself for the 1880 census.[3]

The village of Francisville can no longer be located on a highway map. It was absorbed into the greater town of Philadelphia in 1854, along with a number of outlying townships, villages, and settlements, and consolidated under one municipal government, the boundaries of which made up the old county of Philadelphia.[4]

Some sources report Wilkes County, Georgia, as the place of birth for George Washington Alexander,[5] but his Pennsylvania birthplace is further verified by his own hand on his acceptance form for his commission in the United States Navy.[6] Indeed, there were a number of famous Alexanders from Georgia, including Edward Porter Alexander.[7] The 1850 Federal Census, per search results provided by Ancestry.com, lists no fewer than 16 men named "George W. Alexander," in the states of Alabama, Connecticut, Indiana, Kentucky, Missouri, New Hampshire, New York, Ohio, Pennsylvania, Tennessee, and Wisconsin. Unfortunately, none of those is Captain George Washington Alexander, who was on the *USS Mississippi* at sea when the census was taken.[8]

Ancestry.com also lists 27 men named "G. W. Alexander" who served the Confederacy in one or more companies and regiments. Two of those listed are the one subject of this book—George Washington Alexander, who is listed first as a first lieutenant in Capt. Walters' Maryland company (Zarvona Zouaves), and second as a captain and a staff officer.[9] Needless to say, not all of the men are actually named *George Washington Alexander*, but the listing does show there were many Alexanders fighting for the South and that the name was common throughout the entire nation.

The given name George Washington was popular in many Alexander families. A search of Ancestry.com lists three other men with that same name who were about the same age as the subject of this work. The first was born in 1831, state not given; the second was born about 1832 in Tennessee; and the third was born about 1836 in Illinois.

Marriage to Miss Ashby

During some of the time that George Alexander was in the U.S. Navy, he was stationed at the Portsmouth navy yard. In or around Portsmouth, he met and married a lady of the city, Miss Susanna S. Ashby.[10] Mrs. Alexander was a remarkable woman, as will be seen in subsequent chapters.

Career in the United States Navy

George began his career in the United States Navy in 1848 as a Third Assistant Engineer. He rose slowly through the ranks, but was promoted to Second Assistant Engineer on February 16, 1852, and to First Assistant Engineer on June 27, 1855. He held that position until he resigned on April 5, 1861,[11] to offer his services to the Confederacy.

The Navy must have held a special fascination for men of the Alexander clan. Sixteen men with the surname Alexander were officers in the United States Navy and the Marine Corps from 1775 to 1900.[12] With that many who attained the rank of officer, the number who were ordinary sailors and marines must have been substantial.

Between the War of 1812 and the American Civil War, the United States Navy expanded greatly to protect American overseas commerce. In order to safeguard American interests, the Navy had to combat pirates and smugglers, perform limited diplomatic duties, and maintain a presence in various ports around the world. Whereas earlier the role of the Navy had been seen as limited to the Caribbean, the Mediterranean, and the Atlantic, by the 1850s, the territory and duty of the Navy was expanded to defend American lives and property, and trade overseas in the growing markets. The Mediterranean Squadron continued to be the most prestigious duty, but the America Navy was also evident in Latin American, the Pacific Ocean, and the East Indies. The United States Navy assumed a larger role in the diplomatic and commercial arenas that shaped the nation's overseas economic development.[13]

Toward that end, Commodore Matthew C. Perry played an important part in the change from sail to steam-powered ships. He envisioned a warship powered by steam. Congress authorized the construction of the *Fulton II* in 1834. Although there were problems with the vessel, Perry worked hard to demonstrate that an ocean-going steam warship was practical. For his efforts, Perry is deemed "the father of the steam navy."[14]

Matthew Perry came from a family of naval men. Fondly called "Old Bruin," Matthew had served on wooden sailing vessels and rose to command the African Squadron. During the Mexican War, he commanded the Gulf Squadron, and led the expedition against Tabasco and the capture of Vera Cruz. Perry was progressive and a strong advocate of technological advances. He had long been in favor of steam power.[15]

With the advent of steam ships, engineers were necessary. These were men who knew how to keep the steam engines in tip-top shape and how to repair them when the pipes or the boiler leaked, or when other problems developed.

The duties of an assistant engineer were:

> In the absence of the chief engineer—
> When there is no chief engineer on board, the duties assigned to him will devolve on the senior assistant engineer.
> To carry out orders—
> Assistant engineers are, at all times, faithfully and zealously to carry into prompt execution all orders they may receive from the engineer officer in charge on board, or others their superiors; and they are to be especially careful in the management of the engines, boilers, and their dependencies, to adhere strictly to the directions of the engineer in charge, and to notify him instantly on discovering anything going wrong about them.
> To prevent waste of coals, oil, tallow and other stores, and to record—
> They are to be particularly careful to prevent the waste of coal, oil, tallow, and all other stores in the engineer's department; and to record, at proper intervals, all the information required in relation to the working of the engines, etc.
> In the absence of the principal engineer—
> In the absence of the principal engineer officer belonging to the vessel, the one remaining on board highest in rank or seniority is to be held responsible for the good order of the engine-room, and for the proper discharge of all the duties connected therewith.
> He will note on the steam-log—
> The engineer of the watch will be careful to note hourly, on the steam-log, all the information which the columns in it require, and to place in the column of 'remarks' full information of the state of the weather and sea, and all accidents to, or defects in, the engines or their dependencies, the quality of the coal, or other circumstances which may be useful for determining the powers and qualities of the vessel and the engines, under the various circumstances to which they may be exposed."[16]

Alexander was "warranted" on October 4, 1848, as Third Assistant Engineer in the United States Navy.[17] The "warrant" portion of a warrant officer's title is derived from the old French word that meant "a protector, a defense and an authorization." The older word is also the source of the modern word *warranty*. Back in 1040 when the five Cinque ports began furnishing warships to King Edward the Confessor of England in exchange for certain trading privileges, they also furnished crews whose officers were the Master, Boatswain, Carpenter and Cook. Later, these officers were "warranted" by the British Admiralty. These officers maintained the ship and were standing officers of the navy. The warranted officers were permanent members of the ship's crew. They stayed with the ship while it was in port between voyages as caretakers, and they were the ones who supervised repairs and refurbishing. In the 14th century, the Purser was added to the list of warrant officers. In the following centuries, the position of Gunner, Surgeon, Chaplain, Master-at-Arms, Schoolmaster, and others were added.[18] As the ships themselves became larger and more complex, and their operation more complicated, additional warrant officers were added as needed.

In the United States Navy, warrant officers were a part of the crew from the beginning, as far back as the American Revolutionary War. When Congress created the navy in 1794, it listed warrant officers as: "the Sailing Masters, Purser, Boatswain, Gunner, Carpenter, Sailmaker and Midshipman."[19] The ships these men maintained were boats that were powered by wind and sails. Other positions, such as Chief Engineer, First Assistant Engineer, Second Assistant Engineer, and Third Assistant Engineer, were added when the navy began using side-wheelers, and ships powered by steam engines.

Table I: G. W. Alexander's Naval Service Record

Ship	Date on	Date off	Destination
USS Mississippi	11-21-1848		
USS Mississippi	5-15-1849	11-13-1851	sea service
USS Mississippi	2-1-1852	4-25-1855	Japan
USS Mississippi	4-26-1855	9-5-1855	New York
orders revoked			
USS Susquehanna	3-31-1856		Mediterranean
USS Fulton	5-15-1859	10-27-1859	Carribean to St. Lawrence R.
USS Seminole	3-1-1860	5-24-1860	
detached to await orders	6-16-1860		
resigned commission	4-5-1861		

In 1853, warrant officers began wearing stripes of blue and gold on their caps. A stripe of gold lace half an inch wide was separated by a stripe of blue cloth one-quarter of an inch wide.[20]

Alexander's acceptance of his appointment can be found in Record Group 45, Records Collection of the Office of Naval Records and Library, Acceptances of Appointments of Officers. Because it is in fragile condition, copies are not available.[21]

The next month, on November 21, 1848, Alexander was assigned to the USS Mississippi. He served from May 15, 1849, to November 13, 1851, on the Mississippi, then took a three-month leave. On November 22, 1851, he took an examination, passed, and was promoted on February 16, 1852, to Second Assistant Engineer. On February 20, 1852, he returned to the USS Mississippi.[22]

The Mississippi was one of the finest ships of her type, and she demonstrated her sea-worthiness on the three-year voyage to the waters of the East, which included two trips to Japan.[23]

1. *Around the World with the United States Navy* 11

U.S. steam frigate *Mississippi* near Madeira on historic voyage to Japan.

The *Mississippi* was a 229-foot-long, side-wheel steamer. It was built in the navy yard at Philadelphia 1839–1841, under the personal supervision of Commodore Matthew C. Perry. The *Mississippi* was commissioned December 22, 1841. In 1863, it sank at Port Hudson on the Mississippi River. The *Mississippi* and her sister ship, the *Missouri*, were the U.S. Navy's first side-wheeled steamers capable of ocean travel. Because the reliability of steam was still unknown, the ships also had masts and sails. A smokestack was aft of the paddle wheel. The ship carried 12 guns and a tonnage of 1,692.[24]

After the United States gained California from Spain and gold was discovered there in 1849, there was a need to improve trade routes across the United States. A transcontinental railroad was planned, and regular steamship routes across the Pacific to China were established. All the major nations were interested in developing trade with Asia and its vast market for trade goods. Japan lay between California and China. Trade with Japan was seen as a necessity, and an expedition under Commodore Matthew C. Perry was sent to Edo Bay in Japan. He prepared for the visit by reading everything he could about Japan and talking to anyone who had been there.[25] Perry's expedition was the fourth sent by the United States. None of the others were successful in negotiating a trade agreement with the Japanese.[26]

During the period that G. W. Alexander served on the *Mississippi*, the steamer cruised the Mediterranean (1840–1851). Then the ship returned to the United States to prepare for service as Commodore Perry's flagship on the historic voyage to Japan. The squadron was given a send-off by President Millard Fillmore, and the departure received widespread publicity, to alert the Japanese of the intended visit. On

November 8, Perry held a farewell party for the president. A large group boarded the *Mississippi*. President Fillmore was given a 21-gun salute, and the naval yards were filled with sailors in dress blues. A band played a lively tune. The President was accompanied by his daughter and William Sinclair, a friend of Perry's from the Navy Department.[27]

The roster of the United States Navy for 1853 lists Commodore Matthew C. Perry, Commander-in-Chief of the East India Squadron. The steam frigate *Mississippi* served as his flagship. Commander Henry A. Adams was Captain of the Fleet, and S. P. Lee was Commander. G. W. Alexander was listed as one of three of the Second Assistant Engineers. Other officers were the Surgeon, Assistant Surgeons, Chaplain, Acting Master, Marine Officer, Passed Midshipmen, Chief Engineer, First Assistant Engineer, Second Assistant Engineer, Third Assistant Engineers, Boatswain, Gunner, Carpenter, and Sailmaker.[28]

Commodore Perry described the performance of the *Mississippi* on the voyage. Upon leaving the Chesapeake Bay, the wind blew for 10 days from the south. It then changed to north-northeast, making a heavy "wallowing" sea, and then the wind changed to the west with such force that it made the ship "uncomfortable." The *Mississippi* "behaved admirably, and averaged more than seven knots during the voyage to Madeira."[29]

The squadron sailed out of Hampton Roads of the Chesapeake Bay on November 24, 1852, for Madeira.[30] The squadron arrived in Madeira on the coast of Africa 17 days later. The *Mississippi* anchored below an old Portuguese fort which stood on a hill above the harbor. Commodore Perry went ashore to obtain coal. The *Mississippi* consumed 26 tons of coal each day. Over the course of two days, the ship's crew loaded 440 tons of coal into the bunkers. They then took on 10,000 gallons of fresh water and 6 bullocks. The Commodore also loaded 15 quarter kegs of the best Madeira wine for his friends in New York. Once loaded, the *Mississippi* headed for the Canary Islands. In order to save on coal consumption, Commander Sidney S. Lee ordered the paddle boards removed from the stern wheel, the water was blown from the boilers, and sails were set to propel the ship toward the Cape of Good Hope.[31]

The *Mississippi,* under the power of the giant paddle wheels, cut easily and steadily through the waves. Extra copper lined her bottom and the coal bunkers had been enlarged to hold 600 tons, rather than the usual 450 tons. The ship thus drew three additional feet of water, and her bow dipped into the waves.[32] The ship sat "unusually deep in the water, but eight of her twelve furnaces were put in requisition," and the daily "consumption of Cumberland coal was about twenty-six tons."[33]

The squadron rounded the Cape of Good Hope, then reached Hong Kong and Shanghai. Commodore Perry's ships arrived at the Chinese port on May 4, 1853.[34]

Turning toward Japan, the squadron entered Edo Bay (near what is now Tokyo) on July 8, 1853, with four ships mounting 61 guns. The warships were six times larger than any of the Japanese ships, and because of their dark-colored hulls, they were called the "black ships."[35] The four ships of Perry's squadron carried 560 men of the United States Navy. The *Mississippi* and the *Susquehanna* were steam ships. The *Plymouth* and the *Saratoga* were three-masted sailing ships towed behind the stern. The Japanese called these four vessels "The Black Ships of the Evil Men."[36]

The *San Jacinto* and the *Susquehanna* were steam frigates authorized to be built by Congress in 1847. At the same time, side-wheel steam sloops *Saranac* and *Powhatan* were authorized.[37]

The arrival of the foreign ships terrified the Japanese. That night a meteor with a long, fiery tail streaked across the sky. Perry saw the meteor as a good omen, and he wrote in his journal "...we pray God that our present attempt to bring a singular and isolated people into the family of civilized nations may succeed without resort to bloodshed."[38]

All the temple bells were rung, and the priest told the worshipers that the barbarians were going to punish them for their sins. The Shogun had disregarded reports that the American were on their way. Japan, surrounded by the Pacific Ocean, existed in a feudal society similar to that of Europe in the Middle Ages. The Japanese had not been involved in a war since it invaded Korea in 1597, 256 years before.[39]

Perry was given a letter from President Millard Fillmore to deliver to the Shogun of Japan. Filmore proposed that the "United States and Japan should live in friendship and have commercial intercourse with each other." Filmore also asked that Japanese ports be opened so that American ships could obtain coal and other provisions. Also, men who had been shipwrecked on Japanese shores were asked to be treated with kindness. This point was included because many American whaling ships had been wrecked near Japan and the castaways had been "jailed and abused."[40]

Commodore Perry intended to deliver the letter and leave. He would spend the winter months in Hong Kong, because with four ships and only one month's supply of food, he could not wait long for the Shogun's reply.[41]

Perry carefully planned to gain the confidence of the Japanese in order to meet the prince. An invitation was issued to the prince to meet with him so that Perry could get the letter from President Filmore to the Emperor. The letter contained several requests, and Perry promised to leave and return later for the Emperor's answers.[42]

Perry and his squadron arrived on Friday, July 8, 1853. His flagship was the *Susquehanna*. Perry described the arrival:

> The steamer, in spite of the wind, moved on with all sails furled, at the rate of eight or nine knots, much to the astonishment of the crews of the Japanese fishing junks ... who stood up in their boats, and were evidently expressing the liveliest surprise at the sight of the first steamer ever beheld in Japanese waters.... As the ships neared the bay, signals were given by the commodore, and instantly the decks were cleared for action. When the squadron had approached within two miles of the land a fleet of large boats... pushed off with the seeming intention of visiting them. They were, however, not waited for, and were soon left behind, much puzzled, doubtless, by the rapid progress of the steamers against the wind.... At about five o'clock in the afternoon the squadron came to anchor off the city of Uraga, on the western side of the bay of Edo.[43]

On July 14, 1853, the *Susquehanna* and the *Mississippi* moved closer to land, anchored, and aimed their guns toward the shore. The men were told to prepare for battle, in case their landing party was attacked. All the crew members were eager to go ashore, but since the ships had to be guarded, the sailors drew lots to see who would go. Fifteen launches carried 100 marines, 100 sailors, and 40 musicians toward land. The American sailors and marines wore their blue and white uniforms. The officers were in full dress. All were heavily armed with guns and cutlasses. Commodore Perry wore his heavy uniform, buttoned all the way to his throat, despite the heat of the July day. He staged a show for the curious Japanese. He had the marines form two lines at the wharf. Then came the sailors, who marched to the lively music of the two bands. The ships' cannons roared a salute, and after Perry disembarked, the bands played "Hail, Columbia." Perry was flanked by two tall, black bodyguards. The Japanese had never seen black men before.[44]

The Japanese put on quite a show themselves. Thousands of Japanese soldiers lined the shore dressed in armor, and they carried deadly weapons — pikes, bows, and swords. Samurai warriors and cavalry stood behind foot soldiers. Flags displaying heraldic emblems flew above the soldiers to identify them. Some of the warriors wore frightening face masks; other warriors displayed a fierce look on their faces, as they had been trained.[45]

The Japanese people were amazed by the American visitors. They had never seen Western-style clothing, nor had they ever seen men with brown, blond or red hair. The Americans towered over the little Japanese, most of whom were only about five feet tall.[46]

On February 11, 1854, Perry returned to Japan with eight ships to negotiate a treaty with the Shogun's government. He met with five commissioners at Yokohama, but the Japanese wanted to delay the treaty. Perry wisely pointed out that if he went home without a treaty, his government would send an even larger squadron back. He also mentioned that a treaty had already been signed between Britain and China. Finally, on March 31, 1854, Perry and the commissioners signed the Treaty of Kanagawa, which assured American castaways good treatment, and allowed American ships to obtain supplies at two Japanese ports, Shimoda and Hakodate.[47]

After the treaty had been signed, the squadron sailed for the United States. The *Mississippi* arrived in New York harbor on April 23, 1855.[48] Two days later, on April 25, 1855, George W. Alexander was granted another three-month leave. He took another examination, passed it, and was promoted on June 27, 1855 to First Assistant Engineer. On September 5, 1855, he was detached from special duty at New York and assigned to the *USS San Jacinto* on September 20, 1855. Those orders were revoked, and he was told to await further orders. Thus, Alexander was never a member of the crew of the *San Jacinto*. On March 31, 1856, he was assigned to the *USS Susquehanna*.[49]

The beauty of the *USS Susquehanna* was depicted in an oil painting, probably by DeSimone, showing it and the *USS Congress* at Naples in 1857.[50]

The *Susquehanna* was side-wheeled steamer, built in Philadelphia. She carried a tonnage of 2,450, as well as 9 guns. She was 257 feet long, and was considered a very "ineffective ship," described as a "technological monstrosity."[51]

Before Alexander was assigned to sail on the steamer *Susquehanna,* the ship was part of a squadron that sailed to the Far East. The *Susquehanna* was launched April 5, 1850. The ship was assigned to the Far East and arrived in Hong Kong on February 5, 1852. The ship and the squadron were under the command of Commodore John Henry Aulick, who had orders to negotiate a treaty with Japan. However, he was relieved of his command and it was left to Commodore Perry to complete the treaty negotiations that opened the doors of Japan to world trade.[52] She served in the Mediterranean Squadron from 1856–1858, and again from 1860 to 1861. She then became part of the Atlantic Blockading Squadron in 1861.[53] While the ship was in Jamaica, the crew was disabled by yellow fever. Alexander was not on board the ship when the disease struck, because he had been detached on April 19 and ordered to the office of the Engineer in Chief in Washington on June 15, 1858. The Thirty-Fifth Congress of the United States passed a joint resolution to express its thanks to British Admiral Sir Howston Stewart and his officers for the hospitality they extended to the crew of the *Susquehanna* when it arrived in Fort Royal on Jamaica. Eighty-five of the stricken crew members were taken to the hospital and treated by the medical officers, nurses and attendants there, which kept the loss of lives to a minimum. The President ordered a gold medal to be struck which was to be presented to the Assistant Surgeon Frederick A. Rose of the British Navy, who volunteered to join the crew on its return voyage from Jamaica to New York so that he could care for the sick who remained on board.[54] The *Susquehanna* was decommissioned in 1883.[55]

On June 15, 1858, Alexander was sent to the Engineer in Chief's office in Washington, D. C. He attempted another promotional examination on March 12, 1859, but failed. On May 14, 1859, he was detached and assigned to the *USS Fulton.*[56] The *Fulton* was the first steam ship in the United States Navy. It was the second ship with that name, and was a side-wheel steamer. It was launched on May 18, 1837, by the New York Navy Yard, with Captain M. C. Perry in command. The *Fulton* cruised the Atlantic coast, while conducting ordinance experiments and training officers to man the guns. Decommissioned in 1842, the *Fulton* was rebuilt and her machinery completely replaced in 1851. The *Fulton* was recommissioned on January 15, 1852, and assigned to duty in the Home Squadron. It sailed from New York on February 22, 1852, and for the next six years patrolled the Atlantic from the Caribbean to the Gulf of St. Laurence in Canada.[57] During the period from May 7, 1859, until July 30, 1859, the time in which Alexander was assigned to duty on her, the *Fulton* cruised near Cuba in an attempt to suppress the slave trade. It was laid up at Pensacola, Florida, in mid-October of 1859, at which time First Assistant Engineer Alexander was detached from duty.

On October 27, 1859, Alexander was detached from duty on the *Fulton* and assigned to "special duty" in Warrington, Tennessee. On March 11, 1860, he was detached and assigned to the *USS Seminole.*[58]

On February 21, 1861, G. W. Alexander applied for permission for another examination. However, he probably never took it. He resigned his position in the United States Navy on April 5, 1861,[59] shortly before Fort Sumter was fired upon and captured by Confederate forces under P. G. T. Beauregard.

In mid April of 1861, after Alexander had resigned, the *Pawnee*, Commodore Perry's flagship, and about 600 men cast off from Fort Monroe. The *Pawnee* steamed up Hampton Roads toward Norfolk and entered Grosport harbor. The citizens of Portsmouth and Norfolk were filled with trepidatation. They thought that the *Pawnee*, in conjunction with the *Cumberland* and the *Pennsylvania*, would bombard the towns for having obstructed the channel. The *Pawnee* docked and Colonel Wardrop stationed men at the gates of the Navy Yard. The Commodore ordered the transfer of all books and papers from the *Cumberland* and the *Pennsylvania* to the *Pawnee*. Also transferred was also a large amount of gold from the custom house in Norfolk. Then the marines destroyed everything else on the two ships, including carbines, revolvers, Dahlgren guns, and other cannons, so that they would not fall into the hands of the Confederates.

The work was done during the night under a full moon. By morning, the *Pawnee* was headed out of the Gosport harbor, with the *Cumberland* in tow. As the Federal ships left, a rocket was sent up to start a fire in some of the ship houses. The vessels which caught fire were the *Pennsylvania, Merrimac, Germantown, Plymouth, Raitan, Columbia,* and *Dolphin*. The old ships, *Delaware* and *Columbia*, were sunk at the docks.[60]

2

Sailing for the Confederacy: The Capture of the *St. Nicholas*

"Let's vary piracee with a little burgalree."
—William S. Gilbert, *Pirates of Penzance*

After resigning his commission from the United States Navy on June 15, 1861, Alexander joined with a group of men from Maryland and they made their way to Richmond to offer their services on behalf of the Confederacy to Governor John Letcher.[1]

Alexander was asked to take command of an expedition backed by Baltimore merchants to recapture the island of Sombrero in the West Indies. The island had been captured by a group of New Yorkers, and although it is worthless today, at the time it had large deposits of guano, which were used as fertilizer.[2]

Alexander and his crew sailed out into the Atlantic but encountered a storm, and the ship wrecked off Point Lookout. The crew was given shelter by the Thomas family at their home, Mattaponi. Here, Alexander met Richard Thomas, a man who had served under Garibaldi in the Sicilian campaign.[3] They would join forces and embark on a mission that would change their lives.

Richard Thomas was born in Saint Mary's County, Maryland, on October 27, 1833. He attended school at Charlotte Hall and at Oxford on the Eastern Shore. He attended the United States Military Academy at West Point for a short time, but did not graduate. He was a non-conformist, an adventurer, and a wanderer. After leaving West Point, he is reported to have traveled to the Far East and was involved in war against Chinese pirates who were terrorizing the seas. He then visited Italy, and fought under Garibaldi during the war for Italian independence. It was in Italy that he assumed the name *Zarvona*.[4]

Thomas and Alexander became friends, and they decided to go to Baltimore to enlist others for Confederate service. They recruited a company of 62 men. The men were carried on two steamers of the Patauxent line to Millstone Landing in Maryland. Back at the Thomas plantation, the new recruits were organized and drilled as a company of Zouaves. Richard Thomas was chosen captain, and George Alexander first lieutenant. J. W. Torsch was elected second lieutenant and Frank Parsons third lieutenant.[5]

Although many Marylanders were pro–Confederate, Maryland was never allowed to join the Confederacy, and was quickly occupied by Federal troops. The Federal troops kept the area under close surveillance.

Early in July of 1861, the first company of Maryland Zouaves was formed. They met on July 4 in Richmond and elected William Walter of Baltimore as captain, and G. W. Alexander as first lieutenant. Other officers elected were John Forsche, first lieutenant; Charles Hemling, second sergeant; F. Daffin, third sergeant; J. L. Quinn, fourth sergeant; John D. Mitchell, first corporal; William Uncle, second corporal; John H. Rusick, third corporal, and William A. Ryan, fourth corporal. Alexander was also Adjutant of the Zouave Regiment.[6]

Thomas and Alexander knew they were not safe in Maryland. To reach safety in Virginia, they obtained a large boat that had been used to carry swine. The boat had to be hauled 16 miles to reach water. It must have been a large craft, because it took 10 yoke of oxen to pull the boat over land. In the process, the boat got stuck in the mud near a church where a service was in progress. Boldly, Alexander asked the preacher to halt his sermon so that the congregation could help move the boat. The preacher refused but Alexander, who not take "no" for an answer, soon had the entire congregation out of the church and marching to where the boat was stuck. After all had put their shoulders to the task, the boat was soon on its way. When it reached the river, sails were put up, and the boat got underway at about 11 P.M. A passing federal patrol boat sent Alexander and his men scuttling back to shore, to wait until after midnight to start out again. The group sailed up the Potomac River and landed at Machodoc Creek.[7]

Now safe in Virginia, Thomas, Alexander, and their company of Marylanders approached the governor of Virginia. They presented a plan to capture the warship *Pawnee*, which was lying at anchor in the Potomac River near Alexandria. Thomas wanted to seize a steamer as it made its way between Baltimore and Washington, and use it to board the *Pawnee*. The officers of the *Pawnee* would be distracted by the delivery of mail from the steamer.[8]

Governor Letcher thought it was a good plan, and he provided money for arms. Richard Thomas went to Philadelphia and got a supply of Sharps rifles and revolvers, which he had shipped to Baltimore.[9] The governor commissioned him a colonel, and he took the oath before Joseph Mayo, Mayor of the city of Richmond.[10] Governor Letcher also provided Colonel R. T. Zarvona, of the "Potomac Zouaves," a pass to travel freely over all the roads and rivers of the commonwealth of Virginia, together with his "men and baggage." The Governor directed all officers, both civil and military, to afford him all respect, and to "give him such facilities as he may require...."[11] (These documents would later be found on Zarvona when he was captured.)

Capture of the *St Nicholas*[12]

On June 28, 1861, Richard Thomas and eight men boarded the *St Nicholas*, a 1,200 ton side-wheeler,[13] in Baltimore. It was bound for Washington, D.C. At Point Lookout, Lieutenant George Alexander and eight armed men disguised as passengers boarded the *St. Nicholas*. The captain of the *St. Nicholas* was Captain Kerwin. Alexander found Thomas in a cabin in the disguise of a "French lady" who called himself "Madame LaForce." Thomas gave Alexander the keys to the trunks in which the guns were concealed. Thomas then returned to his stateroom and put on his Confederate uniform, and then slipped outside and signaled his men. Within only a few minutes, the ship's captain, pilot, and engineer surrendered when confronted with the guns of Confederate soldiers. The lights were extinguished on the ship and it was directed toward the Coan River on the Virginia shore for a rendezvous with Captain George N. Hollins of the Confederate States Navy. Hollins, being the senior naval officer, came aboard and directed the subsequent activities.[14] However, Zarvona was the "key man."[15]

In conjunction with the capture of the *St. Nicholas*, Colonel Bates of the First Tennessee was to come aboard and take part in the attack on the *Pawnee*. However, he did not arrive until noon the next day, and this delay resulted in a halt in plans. Since the captured *St. Nicholas* had already missed its regular trip, it would be under suspicion. A change in direction was ordered, and the *St. Nicholas* headed for the Chesapeake Bay where it captured three vessels. These ships were loaded with coffee, ice and coal valued at $400,000. The valuable cargo was taken up the Rappahannock to Fredericksburg, and the prisoners were sent to Richmond.[16]

One of the captured vessels contained some "excellent old whiskey." Another captured boat contained ice. According to one account, Virginia's governor Letcher took charge of both, and "furnished mint." Soon, there were few sober soldiers in the executive mansion.[17]

A Federal report from J. P. K. Mygatt, acting lieutenant on the USS *Reliance*, reported apprehending two men attempting to make their way down the Potomac River to the Virginia shore. The men told him of the capture of the *St. Nicholas* by "a party of men off Point Lookout, who went on board in women's clothes at the point and took possession of her after leaving the wharf." They also reported that the captured ship was taken up the Coan River and down the bay into the Rappahannock. The two men tried to explain their presence by saying they had been hired to take some men across to Baltimore. The men were searched and found to be holding $13 in Virginia paper money and 70 cents in silver. The lieutenant naturally took the two men in custody and turned them over to Lieutenant R. B. Lowry of the USS *Thomas Freeborn*.[18]

Charles Worthington wrote to Gideon Wells, the United States Secretary of the Navy, to provide additional details about the captured ship. The steamer *St. Nicholas* left from Baltimore on Friday at 4 P.M. loaded with a cargo intended for the citizens of St. Mary's and Charles County, Maryland. Other cargo was destined for Washington, Alexandria and Georgetown. There were a number of passengers on board the steamer who were to be put off at the regular stops along the Maryland shore of the Potomac River. Worthington passed on the report of the officers of the steamer *Diamond State* who claimed they saw the *St. Nicholas* traveling at great speed leaving Point Lookout and headed for the Virginia shore, probably to dock at Kinsale. The conclusion was the ship had been forcibly taken by parties who had boarded as passengers (which was indeed the case), or by a force from Virginia. Worthington reported that he and Captain Ward had agreed to a plan to prevent "the landing on the Maryland shore of any articles intended for transportation across the river into Virginia and at the same time avoiding any unnecessary detention to her." They had agreed to meet the ship every Saturday morning to present a pass allowing the ship to proceed.[19] The plan was of no use since the ship had been captured. However, it was hard to keep plans secret. Samuel Hinks reported that he had heard that the capture of the *St. Nicholas* was a "trap set to catch the *Pawnee*."[20]

The group of Confederate "pirates" did make several more conquests. Sailing with Captain George W. Hollis of the Confederate States Navy, the group of officers, seamen, and Maryland Zouaves captured the *Monticello*, *Mary Pierce*, and *Margaret* in the Chesapeake Bay on June 29, 1861. Those responsible for the capture were regular naval and army officers of the Confederacy.

The Role of Commander Hollis

A full report of the capture of the *St. Nicholas* was made by Commander George N. Hollis. The daring episode began when the *Mary Washington* left Baltimore on June 18, 1861. Hollis pulled in at a landing on the river and disembarked to go to a nearby plantation. There he met with others and suggested that the *St. Nicholas* be captured. The steamer regularly plied the waters between Baltimore and Washington. Once the *St. Nicholas* was captured the plan was to take the *Pawnee*, a Federal steamer commanded by Ward. The *Pawnee* had been a danger to Confederate ships entering and leaving the Potomac River. Someone in the group suggested the plan would fail because there were too many "Union men about," and that they would be discovered before the capture could be accomplished. Hollis gave up, and crossed the Potomac in a small boat pulled by four Negroes.[21]

After he reached the Virginia shore, Hollis went to the house of Dr. Howe, about 20 miles from Fredericksburg, Virginia. He was welcomed and entertained by Dr. Howe, and then taken to Fredericksburg, where Hollis stayed at a hotel. The next morning, Hollis went to Richmond on the train, and to the Navy Department. He was commissioned by the Secretary of the Confederate States Navy, Stephen Russell Mallory.[22]

Immediately after receiving his commission, Hollis went to the Bureau of Details and met some of his old friends who had also resigned from the United States Navy. In talking with his friends, Hollis suggested the capture of the *St. Nicholas*. Here again he met with opposition, and was informed that Secretary Mallory would not agree to it, but that probably Governor Letcher would. Hollis obtained permission from Mallory to set up a meeting with the governor of Virginia, and Letcher, "without a moment's hesitation," agreed to the plan. Letcher gave Hollis a bank draft for $1,000 to obtain arms for the men. He also introduced Hollis to Colonel Richard Thomas of Maryland, already using the alias *Zarvona*, and vouched for Thomas as a man who could be trusted to go North to get the arms and conduct other business.[23]

From his meeting with the Governor, Hollis went to Point Lookout, Maryland. Along the way, he met his two sons who were on their way to Richmond. That evening, the three crossed over the Potomac to St. Mary's County, Maryland, where they stayed with a friend. The next morning, Hollis, his two sons, and five other men started out in a wagon in the rain for Point Lookout. They knew the *St. Nicholas* would stop there on her way to Washington. The steamer arrived at the wharf about an hour after the men.[24]

The bank draft from Governor Letcher was endorsed and given to Colonel Thomas. He took it and went on the Patuxent boat to Baltimore, then to Philadelphia to buy guns for the men. He was instructed to return down the bay on the *St. Nicholas* with as many men as he could. Hollis promised to join him when the ship docked at Point Lookout. At 12 P.M., Hollis boarded the steamer with his small group of men. Colonel Thomas was already on board, disguised as a woman. The disguise was necessary because the guns and ammunition were concealed in a number of large trunks, "such as milliners use." Hollis ordered Thomas to stay hidden until the ship left the wharf. Shortly after the steamer got underway, Hollis gave the signal, the large trunks were opened, and the Confederates took out the guns. Hollis grabbed a Sharps rifle and a pair of pistols and ran up to the wheelhouse, where he informed the captain of the ship that he and his men had captured the steamer. Hollis ordered the captain of the *St. Nicholas* to steer the boat over to the Coan River, but the captain refused and said that he was "no pilot." Hollis then threatened him and declared he would burn the *St. Nicholas*. This got results as someone, not the captain, piloted the steamer to the desired location at Coan River Landing. Once safely across the Potomac, a group of Confederate soldiers and sailors, commanded by Captain Lewis, came to assist Hollis.[25]

Lieutenant George Washington Alexander described the incident: "In a few minutes we overpowered the passengers and crew, secured them below the hatches, and the boat was ours."[26]

By chance, Hollis picked up the morning newspaper and learned that Captain Ward, commander of the *Pawnee*, had been killed while attacking Mathias Point, and that all the Federal gunboats had gone up the Potomac River to Washington for his funeral. Thus, the plan to capture the *Pawnee* had to be abandoned. Since the captured steamer *St. Nicholas* was not armed, Hollis decided to go to Fredericksburg, so he headed out into the Chesapeake Bay. He soon saw a brig, the *Monticello*, from Rio, loaded with a cargo of coffee and headed for Baltimore. The *Monticello* was captured and the crew, except for the captain and his wife, put aboard the *St. Nicholas*. One of Hollis's men, Lieutenant Robert Minor, was put on the captured brig and ordered to take it to Fredericksburg.[27]

Their luck held, and in less than an hour, the Confederates had captured another ship, a schooner from Boston loaded with ice and headed for Washington. As before, Hollis placed an officer and a "prize crew" on board and sent the schooner to Fredericksburg. The ice came in handy for the wounded and sick in the hospitals who "were suffering from want of it"; and the Yankee captain of the schooner attended the sale. He promised to return to Boston and bring another load of ice down, and would let Hollis know where to meet him so that the Confederates could capture another vessel. The Yankee ship captain proposed a plan to sell the second vessel and to divide the profits.[28]

Hollis, Thomas, Alexander and the rest of the men on the expedition then captured a third vessel. This one was from Baltimore and loaded with coal bound for Boston. The capture provided coal for the ship, which was running low. With the third ship in tow, Hollis and his sailors and the Maryland Zouaves returned to Fredericksburg. The Government bought the *St. Nicholas* for "about $45,000 and turned her into a gunboat." The coffee was sold, and the Confederate Government paid 12 center per pound to "Messrs. Spence and Reid." It was then sold in Richmond for 25–30 cents per pound. The vessel was returned to its owners, because it was owned by an individual of Baltimore.[29]

Captain Hollis returned to Richmond and was ordered to command the fortifications on the James River. After some time there, he was ordered to take command of a station at New Orleans, and was promoted to commodore.[30]

The officers were: George N. Hollins, captain; Charles C. Simms and Robert D. Minor, lieutenants; Charles E. Thorburn, lieutenant, Virginia navy; Thomas Skinner, acting master; Algernon S. Garnett, assistant surgeon; Charles Schroeder, first assistant engineer; John W. Tynan, second assistant engineer; John M. Maury, captain, provisional army of Virginia; and ___ Harrow and ___ Yancey, Army officers.

Seamen were: John Curran, Peter Manning, John Colbert, Daniel W. Williams, Charles Summers, James M. Smith, Owen Corbatt, Hiram Whetmore, Louis Buissere, Antonio Frances, George Bennett, and Henry Cheny.

The "ordinary" seamen were: James P. Hunt, James Murray, Nicholas Brady, and Edward Cone. The lone "landsman" was James Thomas.

The sailors and seamen were assisted by the Maryland Zouaves: Colonel R. Thomas commanding, George H.[W.] Alexander and F. Gibson, lieutenants; Fred H. Hollins, George N. Hollins, Jr., William O'Keefe, William Powers, R. Fellon, Francis Duffin, Joseph Thompson, G. H. Frazier, John Daley, George Watts, John Brown, James Laughlin, Richard Fuller, and Samuel Tatem, privates.[31]

Zarvona Captured

In July of 1861, Colonel Richard Thomas and Lieutenant George W. Alexander, along with Lieutenant Blackiston, conducted a second expedition in which they captured the *Georgeanna*. The group had further plans to seize Federal ships. At Millstone Landing, Thomas, in disguise, boarded the *Mary Washington* in order to reach Baltimore to cash a bank draft from Governor Letcher. However, even in disguise, Colonel Richard Thomas was recognized by Captain Kerwin, the same captain from whom Alexander had taken the *St. Nicholas* the month before.[32]

No detailed report exists on the capture of Richard Thomas "Zarvona" although there were accounts on July 9, 1861, in two Baltimore newspapers. The story in the papers described how two members of the Baltimore police force, John Horner and Lieutenant Thomas H. Carmichael, were being sent to Fair Haven in Anne Arundel County to arrest Neale Green. Green, a Baltimore barber, had been involved in the attack on the Sixth Massachusetts Regiment which had recently passed through the city. They boarded the steamer *Mary Washington* bound for Baltimore. The boat had barely left the dock when Lieutenant Carmichael discovered that the elusive "French Lady" was on the boat in disguise, along with a number of her men. Zarvona's companions had tried to dissuade him from going to Baltimore so soon after the capture of the *St. Nicholas*, but the "daring Colonel" was set on carrying out his plans. So, rather than allow him to go alone into danger, his friends and comrades had accompanied him on the ill-fated voyage.[33]

Carmichael ordered the captain of the *Mary Washington* to set a course for Fort McHenry and let his passengers off there rather than at the regular dock. Thomas grew suspicious and approached Carmichael to inquire why the ship had been diverted. Carmichael told him that the change was due to police orders. One of the passengers recalled the action that followed. Zarvona called his men together, drew a pistol on Carmichael, and threatened to throw him and Horner overboard. A woman screamed and ran out of her cabin. The police officers pulled out their guns, and with the backing of a number of male passengers, forced Zarvona and his comrades to surrender.[34]

Once they reached Fort McHenry, the police officers reported to General Banks, and he sent a company of infantry to board the boat and bring the captives to the fort. They were all arrested, excepted Colonel Zarvona, who managed to escape and disappear. After an extensive search, he was found hiding in a large bureau in a ladies' cabin. A report made two years later to Secretary of War Stanton stated that at the time of his arrest, Zarvona was in female attire. However, Scharf, in his *History of the Confederate Navy*, denies that.[35]

Subsequently, Richard Thomas was held for piracy, but later he was indicted in the United States Court for the District of Maryland on treason only, and was held as a political prisoner.[36] He was registered as a prisoner at Fort McHenry on July 8, 1861, and he remained at Fort McHenry until December 2, 1861, when he was transferred to Fort Lafayette, New York.[37]

Zarvona was considered a important political prisoner, and a number of the members of his crew were also held as witnesses for a trial which never took place. Colonel Dix wrote to General McClellan that among the prisoners held in Fort Mc Henry was:

> ... the celebrated Thomas or Colonel Zarvona, commonly known as the French lady. He is of one of the first families in Maryland; is rich, intelligent and resolute. His nervous system is much broken by confinement and want of active occupation and he

Sally Port Guardhouse-Prison where Alexander was confined on July 12, 1861. (Library of Congress, Prints and Photographs Division, Washington, D.C., HABS, MD, 4-BALT, 5-25)

has made earnest appeals to me for the privilege of walking about the garrison within the walls on his parole of honor not to attempt to escape. There is no doubt it would be sacredly respected....[38]

Alexander Captured

After Alexander learned of Thomas' arrest, he attempted to lead the men from the Eastern Shore of Maryland to Virginia, but he was captured. According to a report Alexander filed with Secretary of War Benjamin, Alexander was captured by Governor Hicks and the Dorchester Guards at Cambridge, Maryland.[39] An article written several years after the event described Alexander's capture.

Once Lieutenant Alexander determined that the Federal authorities were looking for his ship, he decided that Annapolis would be the safest place. He made for the harbor and anchored the *Georgeanna* under the guns of Fort Severn. He remained there a day and the following night. The next day, Alexander sailed for the Chester River. The ship's pilot ran ashore between Eastern Neck Island and the mainland.

Alexander had heard nothing from Zarvona, so he boarded the *Arrow* at Kent Island expecting to find Zarvona there. He then learned from the newspapers that his friend had been captured. Immediately, he split his men into two squads and ordered one to remain under his command. The other was placed under the command of Lieutenant Blackiston. Blackiston then took a boat across the bay and escaped with his men. Alexander and his men tried to make the Eastern Shore. However, one of his men, Samuel H. Owens, was recognized by a relative who reported him. That night the place at which they had stopped was surrounded by a company of militia under the command of Lieutenant Colghan. Alexander and his men were taken to the county jail. The next day they were sent on a steamer to Fort McHenry and confined along with his friend and compatriot, Richard Thomas Zarvona.[40]

Records of Fort McHenry indicate that Alexander was admitted as a prisoner on July 12, 1861.[41] Initially, he was confined in room 1837 of the Sally Port Guardhouse-Prison at the entrance of the old star-shaped fort. (This prison room is now used as a storage facility).[42] Alexander was charged with treason by committing piracy, and also charged with being a spy.[43]

Under indictment for treason and piracy, Alexander and Thomas awaited trial while imprisoned in Fort McHenry.[44] If convicted, they would be executed. It would take George Alexander several weeks to formulate an escape plan, but escape he did.

3

Escape from Fort McHenry

"I'll come to thee by moonlight, though hell should bar the way."
—*Alfred Noyes, "The Highwayman"*

The daring escape made by First Lieutenant George Washington Alexander is perhaps the first documented escape by a Confederate officer from a Federal prison.[1] That he was successful in his escape was even more unusual.

Fort McHenry is one of a number of star-shaped forts constructed in the early part of the 19th century to guard the coast of the United States from invasion. Francis Scott Key wrote *The Star Spangled Banner* from Fort McHenry while the fort was under bombardment by the British in September of 1814.

Located at Whetstone Point, which had been used as a defensive position since 1776,[2] the fort was surrounded on three sides by water. Ships attempting to attack the city of Baltimore would have to pass by the fort. The fort was garrisoned by Federal soldiers early in the war, and their presence helped prevent Baltimore and the state of Maryland from joining the Confederacy.

Fort McHenry was designed by the Frenchman Jean Foncin. Construction began in 1799 and was completed in 1805. The exterior walls are 15 feet high and comprise 22,261 square feet. The length of the seawall is 12,500 feet. The fort has 30 rooms, two powder magazines, and the outer battery had four underground chambers. The fort was named for James McHenry, Secretary of War under President George Washington.[3]

The time spent awaiting trial in Fort McHenry did not sit well with Lieutenant Alexander, and he was not a docile prisoner.

The hot, humid weather made the small cells stifling and almost unbearable. To relieve some of the discomfort, the door to the cell in which both Alexander and Zarvona were kept was left open through the day until 9 o'clock at night. However, one of the guards, a lance corporal, attempted to close the door one evening at 8:30 P.M.

The prisoners asked by what right did he close the door early, and he replied, "Damn rebels have no rights," and he tried to close the door. Immediately both Alexander and Thomas fell upon him and "beat him like the devil." The other guards were hesitant to come to rescue the corporal because they knew he had been in the wrong. The guard had reportedly acted with unwarranted "impudence" toward Thomas and Alexander and, as a result, the two prisoners grabbed the guard and beat him.[4]

Alexander and Thomas were punished for their attack on the guard and placed in a dark, underground cell for six weeks. They were given only bread and water to sustain them.[5]

The prisoners were guarded by Company I and K of the Second Artillery of the U.S. Army. Someone approached each of the guards and offered them a bribe of $1,500 in gold, but none would accept it.[6]

During this time, indictments were drawn up against Thomas ("Zarvona"), Alexander and their men for piracy and treason. After six weeks, Alexander and Thomas were removed from the underground cell. Alexander decided to try to escape.[7] To do so successfully, he needed outside help.

Susie Ashby Alexander, the wife of George Alexander, traveled from Richmond to visit him in prison. She had obtained an order from Secretary of War Cameron to allow her to visit her husband daily. She was determined not to let bad weather deter her, and she crossed the Potomac River on a night when any sensible person would have stayed ashore.[8]

Together, George and his wife carefully planned his escape. On one of her visits, she brought her husband a life preserver in the form of a waistcoat and clothes line, which she had concealed under her hoop skirt. Standing in the corner, she cut the string that held the items under her hoop skirt and kicked them under the cot. She had also obtained some letterhead stationery which had a picture of Fort McHenry and the surrounding area. On this, she had marked in blue ink the positions of various sentinels about the fort.[9]

Everything was in place for Alexander's escape, but when his wife visited him on Saturday, she made him promise to wait until Monday so that she would have another chance to see him before he tried to escape. It was a dangerous plan, and he could be killed in the attempt. But that night, Alexander could wait no longer. About dark, Colonel Thomas left the cell and walked up and down with the guard in front of the door to Alexander's cell. While Thomas distracted the guard, Alexander arranged his bed to make it look like he was in it, and hiding behind the door, he put on the life preserver over a Federal uniform that his wife had smuggled into his cell. Then, he moved to the door, and as the guard's back was turned, he entered the corridor and walked away. When the guard turned around, Alexander saluted him and the guard saluted in return, not recognizing Alexander as his prisoner.[10]

Alexander moved quickly, and in passing by the mortar batteries that had been set up to fire on the city of Baltimore, he knocked down a crowbar. The loud noise that resulted startled Alexander and he hurried faster to reach the ramparts on the Patapsco side of the fort.[11]

An article written at the time of Alexander's death says that he was noticed by one of the guards who fired at him, and he "leaped over the wall into the river."[12] Here, the ramparts were high above the river, and Alexander had forgotten to bring the clothes line his wife had brought him to use to climb down.[13] There was no other way to escape except to jump. He did not hesitate to do so, but landed on the hard ground. When he attempted to rise, he found he had injured his right leg and shoulder. He managed to crawl to the river, and slipped into the safety of the water just as a guard was passing. The cold water helped ease the pain in his leg, but the sky was black and the wind was rising. He inflated his life preserver and began to swim. The prospects of ever seeing his lovely wife again seemed remote at the time.[14]

Alexander began to swim as fast as he could, and after two and a half hours, he managed to reach the shore near Riverside Park. He crawled out of the river toward a light which came from a cabin in which sat an old man. The old man asked him, "Are you drunk?" A cold and wet Alexander replied, "Not drunk but badly hurt."[15]

The old man and his daughters carried Alexander into the house. The girls had seen him at the fort and recognized him. The old man told Alexander that he must leave, because his property would be confiscated if it was learned he had harbored an escaped prisoner. The girls, however, begged their father to take Alexander away in their buggy. The old man agreed, and as he lay in the bottom of the buggy, the girls concealed him by covering him with their voluminous skirts. He was taken to the house of W. H. Norris, who then took Alexander in another carriage to Hoffman Street. There he was able to meet with his wife for a moment. He was then taken to the home of E. Law Rogers and was treated by a surgeon. Still later, Alexander was taken to the home of Charles Carroll in Carrollton, who gave him a warm welcome, and treated him with the utmost kindness.[16]

In a report of prisoners taken, released and still in custody at Fort McHenry since March 4, 1861, G. W. Alexander was listed as "Escaped Sept. 7, 1861."[17] Subsequently, the escape was noted in the Baltimore papers. Alexander's status was listed as a "political prisoner."

> *An Escape from Fort McHenry.*— Major Alexander, formerly of the United States revenue service, but late an officer in the Confederate army, and one of the political prisoners confined in Fort McHenry, made his escape from his cell at the fort, sometime between ten o'clock on Saturday night and yesterday morning, and succeeded in getting off, eluding the guards and outposts. It is thought his escape was effected by means of a disguise of some kind, but nothing positive is known. Major Alexander was arrested at Cambridge about the time of the St. Nicholas affair.[18]

Undoubtedly the fort officials soon learned the details of how Alexander made his escape — with the help of his wife. The fort commander, Major Morris, immediately took steps to prevent further escapes by the political prisoners confined in the fort. Morris revoked the passses which had been issued to the friends and family of the prisoners, and decreed that in the future, "no such passes will be granted to any person whomsoever."[19]

Naturally, the Federal authorities were angry over his escape. A reward of $10,000 was offered for his capture. But luck was with him, and as soon as Alexander was able to travel, Frank Key took him in a buggy to a place below Fort Washington, and then, accompanied by a Confederate officer, they crossed the Potomac into Virginia. A Federal gunboat passed by several times as they hid on the riverbank awaiting a chance to cross. Finally, the pair made the crossing and George W. Alexander traveled to Richmond.[20] He arrived in Richmond around October 2.[21]

Once safely in Richmond, Alexander sent a report to Judah P. Benjamin, the new Confederate Secretary of War.

> Having with Colonel R. Thomas Zarvona captured the Saint Nicholas, I accompanied him on a second expedition. I was captured by Governor Hicks and the Dorchester Guards at Cambridge, Maryland, and confined with Colonel Z. in Fort McHenry about seventy days, when I effected my escape. Springing from the ramparts I sprained my ankle.[22]

Soon after Alexander's arrival in Richmond, he chanced to meet General Johnston. Johnston smiled and said, "Well, Lieutenant, I see you have saved us as an exchange!" Alexander replied, "Yes, but lost you a soldier." Alexander would soon embark in a new direction when he became a provost marshal with the Eastern District of Virginia.[23]

Shortly after his escape from Fort McHenry, Alexander placed a notice in the Richmond *Dispatch* inviting people to come listen to him express the views of the imprisoned Colonel Richard Thomas. Thomas hoped to see a battalion formed from Maryland for the Confederacy. The new company was to be called the "Zarvona Zouaves." Alexander noted that they already had one company, fully armed and equipped, but needed three more immediately. The meeting was scheduled for 8 P.M. on 10th Street, between Main and Cary, "two doors below Snead's Locksmith establishment."[24]

The meeting was held and a large party met at Adam's building on 10th Street in Richmond. Those who attended expressed their sympathy for Colonel Richard Thomas, and pledged to organize a battalion to be named after him. The meeting was called to order by Captain Dugan. The object of the meeting was then explained by Adjutant G. W. Alexander, and Captain Lookerman was appointed secretary. A three-man committee was appointed to draw up resolutions, and then the men who wished to join were to be enrolled. Their departure was scheduled for Sunday. The article noted that Alexander, while still on crutches, was recovering from injuries to his leg incurred during his daring escape.[25]

A few days later, Alexander was at a camp at Tappahannock organizing the volunteers into guerillas. Others who wished to join were told to apply to Mr. William O'Keefe at the Confederate States Work-Shop on 7th Street, "opposite the Laboratory."[26]

After spending over a week at camp, Alexander returned to Richmond and made his headquarters briefly at the Powhatan Hotel. Those Marylanders wishing to join the Zouaves were urged to contact Adjutant Alexander at the Powhatan Hotel from 8 to 11 A.M. until next Wednesday. The ladies of Richmond came to the aid of the new battalion. One lady had made shirts, drawers, and socks for 24 of the Zouaves. However, 40 more still needed articles of clothing, which could not be obtained from their homes.[27]

Alexander and his men appreciated the efforts of the people of Richmond on their behalf. Alexander sent a letter to the editor of the Richmond *Dispatch* to express his thanks to those who had donated items. He did not even know the names of many of the donors, but he exclaimed with the optimism that was the norm in 1861: "The *'widow's mite'* was received. God bless you, Madam. I will try to merit your consideration. We will win this fight."[28]

In November of 1861, Alexander (who signed his name *G. Washington Alexander*) thanked four little girls for their contribution to the Zarvona Zouaves. He does not mention what their contribution was, perhaps some items of clothing needed by the Zouaves, as he had asked for in previous newspaper articles. He had learned the names of the contributors, and he wanted to publicly thank Farnie W. Parker, Sue J. Taliaferro, Sue B. Sutton, and Ida D. Evans.[29]

Some of the new recruits had marched at night for 10 miles during a storm to Fort Lowery. A few of those who had just arrived from Maryland had not even been mustered in. They had served as escorts for Mrs. Alexander to Westmoreland, where she was lodged safely. A newspaper article noted her role in her husband's escape from Fort McHenry, and that Colonel Thomas (Zarvona) was a heavily-guarded prisoner there still.[30]

The Zarvona Zouaves, under the command of Captain Waters, camped for some weeks on the Rappahannock, where they received their rations from the Confederate government. They were ordered to Acquia Creek to support the battery there. They were soon assigned as Company H, 47th Virginia. In October of 1861, the men of Company H were assigned to guard the new batteries at Evansport. Here, under the command of Captain Snowden Andrews, the company spent the winter of 1861–1862. During the reorganization of the army on the Peninsula, this Maryland company was left out of the 47th Virginia, and a Virginia company took its place. The company was assigned to the Second Arkansas, a battalion of Major Brenau, which consisted of three companies. They thus took part in the battle of Williamsburg, and the Second Arkansas became part of Pettigrew's Brigade of Smith's Division. This group of Marylanders also took part in the battle of Seven Pines. When their term of service was up in June of 1862, the company was disbanded. Some went to Richmond and others remained with the army. Most later joined the 2nd Maryland Battalion.[31]

Shortly after George W. Alexander escaped from Fort McHenry, prison authorities discovered that Richard Thomas Zarvona had set up an organization for the capture of the fort. This sort of activity could not be tolerated and Zarvona was placed in a cell devoid of light for nine months. The cell, as described by Captain Marks, had only a small source of light which came from a chink in the door barely wide enough for a knife blade. The prisoner spent countless hours at the door trying to peer out of the crack. Like a caged animal, he could be heard moving his head to and fro trying to see the light.[32]

It was only through the efforts of Governor Letcher that Zarvona was taken out of the dark cell. However, the months of solitary confinement in total darkness had damaged his mind. Governor Letcher did everything in his power to obtain Zarvona's release. He wrote to President Lincoln and he offered to exchange four Union colonels for him. Letcher even threatened to hang four Federal officers if the indictments against Zarvona and Alexander were not dropped. The indictments were eventually quashed.[33]

4

Assistant Provost Marshal Alexander

"But Who is to Guard the Guards Themselves?"
—*Juvenal,* Satires

When George Washington Alexander escaped from Fort McHenry, he had no idea that within the next two years he would become one of the most hated men in the country. As assistant provost marshal and commander of one of the most infamous prisons in the Confederate penal system, Alexander would evoke even the wrath of the Confederate Congress and be the subject of an intensive investigation. How did a former officer in the United States Navy descend from being a hero to becoming a man hated and despised for his treatment of prisoners in his custody at Castle Thunder? Was he truly the villain the Federals believed?

From November of 1862 until December of 1863, Assistant Provost Marshal George W. Alexander was in command of Castle Thunder. The new prison soon acquired a bad reputation for unnecessary brutality. It was reported that vengeance was practiced with regularity within the walls of Castle Thunder, and that the "thunder" came in the human form of George Washington Alexander. As the prison commandant, Alexander would come to be described as "harsh, inhuman, tyrannical, and dishonest in every possible way."[1]

Some believed that Alexander was the "right man in the right place," and that he was well qualified as superintendent of Castle Thunder. He performed his duties to the satisfaction of the "commander-in-chief." While he made many enemies, Alexander also had a great number of friends. When he accepted the job as prison commandant, the position was one that few envied. His charges were a class of ungovernable and desperate men. They were "the refuse of the southern army—men who would fight like tigers when the contest was on hand, but who would brook no control during the intervals of inaction in camp; men capable of committing any crime within the decalogue without the slightest compunctions of conscience."[2] Captain

Alexander's job was to confine and control prisoners who had no scruples to prevent them from stealing from each other, to strip a newcomer of his clothes, to knock out the eye of a fellow inmate, to assault guards in escape attempts, and even to kill to gain access to the outside.[3]

Although George Alexander had served 13 years in the United States Navy, and had been a prisoner-of-war himself, nothing in his experience had prepared him for the problems he encountered during his supervision of thousands of prisoners at Castle Thunder. Somewhat of an "invalid" from the injury to his leg when he escaped from Fort McHenry, Alexander ruled with "an iron hand." His administration of Castle Thunder was done with "vigor and determination," so much so that soon his methods came to the attention of the Confederate House of Representatives.[4]

In order to understand why this occurred, a brief history of the Confederate prison system and the evolution of the provost marshal's role is necessary.

The Need for a Military Prison System

The First Federal Prisoners

The first Union soldiers taken prisoner arrived in Richmond at the end of July 1861, after the first battle at Manassas, Virginia (First Bull Run). The Confederate government had decided that Richmond was to serve as a depot for all Federal captives until exchanged. By the end of 1861, over 1,000 prisoners were being held in Richmond, although several hundred had been transferred to Charleston, South Carolina, and New Orleans.[5] At the beginning of 1862, the Confederate government reworked its network of prisons. Taylor's and Mayo's factories were converted into hospitals. Major George C. Gibbs was promoted and transferred to Salisbury, North Carolina, to establish a new prison there. Gibbs worked quickly to turn a cotton factory into a prison, and shortly he was able to accept 700 Federal prisoners in transfer from Richmond. This facility was also ready to accept prisoners from New Orleans, Tuscaloosa, Alabama, and South Carolina.[6]

The principal places in the South for confining Federal prisoners of war, deserters from the Confederate army, civilians suspected of disloyalty, spies, and captured runaway slaves were:

Alabama— Cahaba, Mobile, Montgomery, Selma, Tuscaloosa.
Georgia— Americus, Andersonville (Camp Sumter), Atlanta, Augusta, Blackshear, Camp Lawton (Millen), Madison, Camp Oglethorpe (Macon), Marietta, Thomasville, Savannah.
Florida— Tallahassee.
Louisiana— Baton Rouge, Mansfield, New Orleans, Shreveport.
Mississippi— Jackson, Meredian, Morton, Tupelo, Vicksburg.
North Carolina— Charlotte, Goldsborough, Salisbury, Raleigh, Tarboro, Wilmington.
South Carolina— Charleston, Columbia, Florence.

Tennessee—Chattanooga, Knoxville, Memphis, Nashville.
Texas—Camp Ford (Tyler), Camp Groce (near Hempstead), Houston.
Virginia—Aiken's Landing, City Point, Danville, Lynchburg, Petersburg, Richmond, Staunton, Winchester.[7]

Eventually, there were 150 different compounds established by the Union and the Confederacy to hold their prisoners. Prisons were located all along the East Coast as far north as Boston and as far south as the Dry Tortugas Island, off the coast of Florida. There were prisons in the west as far as Fort Craig, New Mexico.[8] Prisoners were crammed into these facilities without regard for capacity, hygiene, nutrition, or sanitary needs. Within a very short time, neither government could cope with the problem of caring for prisoners.[9]

Over the course of the next four years of bitter fighting, an estimated 674,000 soldiers were taken prisoner. Of the total enlistments, approximately 16 percent were captured, more than in any other war, before or since.[10] Lonnie Speer, in writing about the prisons during the American Civil War, quoted estimates of Union enlistments at 2,893,304; Confederate, between 1,227,890 and 1,406,180. The combined number of men in arms for both sides would equal somewhere between 4,299,484 and 4,121,194. The estimate of over 211,000[11] captured Union soldiers is staggering, and they became the responsibility of the Confederate government to feed, confine, and guard—a definite drain on the resources of the South.

An accurate count of the number of men in either army and the numbers killed, wounded, or captured is impossible. It is clear, however, that over the course of four years, 1861–1865, at least 210,000 Union soldiers were captured and imprisoned. Some of these were released on parole immediately, but a large part of those captured were placed in the hands of the provost marshal.[12] In addition, with the imposition of martial law, and restrictions on the activities of civilians, the provost marshal could and did arrest civilians and hold them indefinitely with or without trial. The interference in civilian life did not endear the provost marshal to the citizens of the Confederacy.[13]

Suspension of the *Writ of Habeas Corpus*

With the North and the South at war, loyalty of citizens in each section became of prime importance. On either side of the Mason-Dixon line there were those who did not support the country in which they lived. One remedy utilized by both the North and the South was the suspension of the *writ of habeas corpus*, which means "you have the body." The writ had various uses in criminal and civil cases. It is a means of determining whether it is legal to detain an individual in custody. Thus, when the *writ of habeas corpus* was suspended, there was no recourse for those who had been arrested to protest their confinement.[14] In times of peace, a judge could issue an order for the release of a prisoner under the authority inherent in a *writ of habeas corpus*.

In the North, the suspension gave authorities the power to arrest and incarcerate individuals for a number of reasons: interference with troop transportation, enlistment, conscription, or aiding the enemy in any way, either through acts, speech, or writing.[15]

The South was hesitant to suspend the *writ of habeas corpus* because the Confederacy was more sensitive to states' rights and civil liberties for whites. President Jefferson Davis only suspended the writ after he was authorized to do so by the Confederate Congress. Once passed, the act gave Davis the power to suspend the writ in areas under martial law. The suspension was authorized for a limited time, and President Davis had to plea for further suspensions. These were granted mainly for persons who had committed crimes against the Confederacy.[16]

Alien Enemies Act of 1861

Not only were prisons needed to confine captured prisoners of war and Confederate soldiers convicted of desertion and other crimes, but space was needed for the growing number of civilians who were arrested and held for disloyalty.

On August 8, 1861, the Confederacy enacted laws defining "aliens." Only the citizens of Delaware, Maryland, Kentucky, Missouri, the District of Columbia, and the territories of Arizona, New Mexico, and the Indian Territory south of Kansas were exempt.[17] President Davis issued regulations to enforce the act, and issued a proclamation to that effect. The new law decreed that all males over age 14 who were citizens of the United States living in the Confederate states had 40 days to leave the Confederacy. If a man stayed, that was evidence that he planned to be come a citizen of a Confederate state, and when he swore an oath of loyalty, he was to be exempt. All persons who remained loyal to the United States and who did not leave the Confederacy within the prescribed 40 days were to be considered "alien enemies."

The regulations regarding alien enemies ordered the provost marshals of the Confederate States to apprehend all aliens against whom complaints were made under said law, and to hold them in strict custody until the final order of the court, taking special care that such aliens obtain no information that could possibly be made useful to the enemy.[18]

Under this law, Confederate provost marshals and military officers could arrest and hold in prison any person believed to be an alien enemy. The law was designed to make citizens choose sides. This became a problem in counties like Fayette in western Virginia, when control shifted frequently between the Union and the Confederacy and its citizens were arrested by both governments.[19]

While it was never the intent of either side to eliminate the enemy by starvation and harsh treatment in prisons, nevertheless, many prisoners died as a result of their incarceration. The Federal government did institute retaliatory measures against prisoners by reducing rations, but the Confederate government passed legislation early in the war that decreed prisoners should receive the same quantity and quality of rations as those fighting in the field. Unfortunately, food shortages made it difficult for the Confederate government to feed its soldiers, much less its prisoners.[20]

The Evolution of the Provost (Military Police) System

The Confederate military police system — the provost system — was originally established to ensure military discipline in the Confederate armies. Eventually, with the increasing number of arrests of suspected disloyal persons, spies, draft dodgers, escaped slaves and other criminals, the job of the provost marshal was extended to exert even greater control over civilian activities.[21]

The military police system grew out of a system established by the British in the United States during the American Revolution. When the South began preparations for war, the Confederate Congress' first act was to established a War Department, and the provost marshal was an integral part from the very beginning.[22] The provost was established under the Articles of War adopted on March 6, 1861. This provided for provost marshals and for military courts to try offenders of military law.[23]

The Provost Marshal's Department in Richmond

President Jefferson Davis proclaimed martial law in Richmond out of necessity. The city had been overrun with gamblers, adventurers and other unsavory characters. Richmond had also become the center of a Union spy ring. Brigadier General John H. Winder was appointed provost marshal, and he was given the authority to become the military commander of the city and the surrounding territory.[24] Winder was charged with the task of bringing peace and order to Richmond. The streets of the capital were filled with lawlessness. Theft, arson, and garroting were prevalent. To alleviate the problem, Winder and his detectives were employed to reinstate peace in the city.[25] After martial law was declared in Richmond, the provost marshal closed the distilleries and saloons, and arrested drunks.[26]

Winder's detectives and the city police also kept watch for persons suspected of being disloyal. Citizens sympathetic to the Union were arrested and confined to Castle Thunder. Hundreds of civilians were confined to what one writer described was "the living death chamber" for the "bold, fearless men, who advocated their country's unity and welfare."[27]

Political prisoners were confined to Castle Thunder along with pickpockets and deserters. Once order was restored, the citizens were relieved. However, there soon came complaints of tyrannical abuses, and sentiment increased against martial law so much that the Confederate Congress modified Winder's powers.[28]

Under martial law the number of prisoners, both military and civilian, greatly increased. By October of 1861, 2,685 captives had been brought to Richmond, and additional buildings were confiscated to meet the need for housing.[29]

In October of 1862, the powers were extended to allow each army corps its own military court, and gave the provost marshal the power to issue the orders of the court. Those orders could range from imprisonment, to lashing, to execution by hanging or before a firing squad. The type of offenses that could come before the military court were broad, and they included not only offenses covered in the Articles of War, but offenses against the laws of the Confederate government and each individual state government as well.[30]

The provost marshal did not have a separate corps, but officers and men were detailed to provost duty on a temporary basis. Some of those so detailed were those who were not quite up to the rigors of battle, often men still recovering from illnesses or wounds.

The provost marshal functioned as policeman, judge and jailer. The role as jailer often took precedence and many persons were imprisoned on the order of the provost marshal. Under the initial Articles of War, military courts were set up to try military personnel accused of violating military law. The operation of the military courts was modified on October 9, 1862, which provided that each army corps in the field have its own court.[31] Each court was permitted to appoint a provost marshal with the rank and pay of captain of cavalry, with the authority to execute the orders of the court. The jurisdiction of the provost was extended to included offenses against certain articles and customs of war, of the Confederate States of American, and the laws of each state in the Confederacy.[32]

The provost marshal was responsible for arresting those persons suspected of being traitors. They were constantly alert for suspicious characters, and this surveillance often led to arbitrary and unfounded arrests, which was possible under the suspension of the *writ of habeas corpus*.[33]

The primary duties of the provost marshal were to carry out the orders resulting from a court martial, to keep order within the military establishment, and to arrest civilians suspected of disloyalty or giving aid to the enemy.

The secondary duties of the provost marshal were just as varied. They were charged with security and the protection of people, materials, buildings, and public and private property. The provost marshal was responsible for protecting Negro slaves from capture by Union officials, and to see that they did not run away to Union-held territory. They were also responsible for the custody of captured runaway slaves, who were held in prison until they could be identified and returned to their masters.[34]

Once conscription laws were passed, many eligible men fled to avoid being drafted into the army. It was the duty of the provost marshal to capture those dodging the draft. The provost marshal was also in charge of capturing deserters, and if they were sentenced to imprisonment, they were in the custody of the provost marshal. Another area in which the provost marshal was involved was capturing deserters from the Union Army.

The provost marshal was also responsible for the apprehension of Northern spies who roamed the South, and the provost marshal was assigned to guard the hospitals.[35]

The duties of the provost marshal involved both civilian and military segments of society, and they were authorized to act as the guardian of strict moral behavior, in their role of suppression of gambling, drinking, and prostitution.

As the war continued, the number of provost marshals increased. The provost was eventually set up in departments and divided into districts and subdistricts. A complete list of the departments can be found in William Frayne Amann, ed., *Personnel of the Civil War: The Confederate Armies*.[36]

The Provost Marshal in the Department of Henrico

There was much danger in the city, and the presence of the patrolling provost guards was greatly needed. For example, a body servant owned by George W. Alexander was accidentally shot and killed by a stray bullet which had first entered and exited another person's foot.[37]

Initially, the provost marshals rounded up and arrested all those suspected of disloyalty. They took the "riffraff" off the streets and put them in McDaniel's Jail, commonly called the "Negro Jail" because it had previously been used for the detention of runaway slaves. Soon, the prison overflowed and a larger one was needed.[38]

Hairston Appointed

Major J. T. W. Hairston was appointed by Adjutant General Samuel Cooper to take charge of the Richmond prisons. At first he was second in command to Captain Gibbs, who was promoted to colonel. That left Hairston in charge of about 3,500 Federal prisoners of war. Hairston described his new position as "anything but congenial to a liberal and enlightened mind," but he did his best with what he had available to make the prisoners comfortable. The duties of a "prisonkeeper," declared Hairston, were "never pleasant to a man of humane inclinations," and he found the job "intensely disagreeable when the retaliatory policy of our government" forced him to put 14 high ranking government officials in irons and "confine them in a dungeon." Hairston found he could not continue as a prison warden, so he begged to be transferred to the field. He was promoted to the rank of major and assigned to the staff of General J. E. B. Stuart in the spring of 1862. He served as custodian of the Federal prisoners from October 1861 until March of 1862.[39]

Brigadier General John H. Winder

John H. Winder began as inspector general of all camps, including the prisons, in the Richmond, Virginia, area. He was later given command of the Department of Henrico, and made provost marshal general of Richmond. His first command had five departments: 1) The Provost Marshal's Department, commanded by Major Isaac H. Carrington. This department had a passport office and a police organization. 2) Prisons for Federal soldiers captured. 3) Prisons for Confederate offenders and deserters from the Confederate army. 4) A barracks for holding transient soldiers. 5) A staff department.[40]

From Maryland, Winder had served on the frontier before resigning in 1823. He returned to the Army four years later as a tactical officer at West Point. He fought in the Seminole and Mexican wars and resigned on April 27, 1861. He was appointed a brigadier general in the Confederate Army the next month. His appointment as brigadier general was to rank from June 21, 1861.[41] He was then named Provost Marshal and commander of the Federal prisons at Libby and Belle Isle.[42]

Department of Henrico

In December of 1861, Winder was given command of the Department of Henrico.[43] He was named provost marshal and commander of the Federal prisoners in Richmond. From May 1862 until February 1864, he commanded at Richmond, and was also in charge of prisoners at Danville.[44]

An 1863 directory of the location of public buildings and officers of the Confederate and Richmond city government listed the staff of the provost department under Brigadier General J. H. Winder, commander of the Department of Henrico. Winder's office was in a new building at the corner of Broad and 10th Streets, called the "Winder Building." The staff consisted of Aids — Lieutenant R. W. Brown and Lieutenant Warner Lewis; Adjutants — Major J. W. Pegram and Captain W. S. Winder; and Chief Quartermaster — Major J. H. Parkill. Parkhill's office was in Room 8 on the second floor of the building. Assistant Quartermaster Captain C. Morfit had an office in Room No. 5 on the ground floor of the building. Commissary of Prisons, Captain Jackson Warner, had his office in Room 10.[45]

The office of Provost Marshal Major E. Griswold was in Room No. 7. Lieutenant Kirk was in charge of the Passport Office. The Provost Marshal's Prison ("Castle Thunder") on Cary Street between 18th and 19th Streets was under the command of Capt. G. W. Alexander, assistant provost marshal. Libby Prison held "prisoners of war" under the command of Captain T. P. Turner. He was assisted by Lieutenant La Touche, quartermaster. Other staff members were Captain Jackson Warner, commissary, and E. W. Ross, chief clerk.[46]

The third unit in the Henrico prison system was Camp Lee. It was a military post commanded by Colonel J. C. Shields, assisted by Captain William H. Fry, post adjutant. This camp was located at the new fairgrounds about a mile west of Richmond on the road from Broad Street and the Fredericksburg railroad. A train car made the run from the depot to the camp every hour.[47]

The orders issued by General Winder or at his command for the period April 14, 1863, through October 29, 1863, are housed in the Museum of the Confederacy in Richmond, Virginia. Orders were issued to Captain Alexander and other prison officials regarding the release, arrest, and transfer of prisoners from various sites. Special Orders No. 135 (June 4, 1863), Special Orders No. 153 (June 26, 1863), Special Orders No. 171 (July 17, 1863), and Special Orders No. 199 (August 19, 1863) were issued specifically to Captain Alexander. The order book also contained short correspondence from General Winder or one of his subordinates to Captain G. W. Alexander dated June 4, June 15, September 1, September 2, September 5, October 7, October 9, October 21, and October 26, 1863.[48]

Winder appeared to keep close watch on his prison superintendents. On October 26, 1863, he wrote Captain G. W. Alexander that he had been informed on two different occasions the previous day, when Detective Cashmyer delievered a prisoner to Castle Thunder, that there was no officer present who was authorized to sign the receipt for the prisoner. General Winder, through his Assistant Adjutant General W. S. Winder, reminded Captain Alexander to be sure that a "commissioned officer" was always available, both day and night, and if "additional officers are required you [Alexander] will ask for them."[49]

In May of 1864, Winder was assigned to the 2nd District of North Carolina and Southern Virginia, with headquarters in Goldsboro, North Carolina. In June of 1864, Winder was assigned to the prison at Andersonville, Georgia, then was given charge of all prisoners east of the Mississippi. He was criticized by many as being cruel and too strict on his prisoners.[50]

When Brigadier General Winder was setting up his administrative staff to oversee the prisons in Richmond, he selected young men, generally in their twenties, who had no previous experience in military command. Ultimately, this paucity of experience resulted in harsh treatment for some of the inmates.[51]

Eventually, Winder had a large number of men on his staff to run the numerous prisons in his department. One of those on General Winder's staff was Lieutenant David H. Todd, the brother of Mary Todd Lincoln. Although some newspapers described Lieutenant Todd as "a gallant and meritorious gentlemen," he was universally hated by the prisoners he guarded. He was reported to have shot a prisoner for sticking his head out of a window, and having struck a prisoner with the back side of his sword simply for not moving fast enough during roll call. A number of prisoners described Todd as "drunk during nearly the entire period of his authority at the prison," and that he was "seething with malignity and bitterness," so that he made the life of Federal officers who were prisoners almost unbearable with "daily indignity and hardship."[52]

At first the military police system was simple, and the departments they covered small. As the war progressed, the departments became larger and the duties of the provost increased. Therefore, the number of provost marshals increased. There was a great need for someone to enforce discipline in the army, and that task was relegated to the office of the provost marshal. When the number of desertions increased, the provost marshal and all its resources were kept busy with arrests, trials, and imprisonment of those not only convicted of military offenses, but civilians as well. Eventually, the provost marshal came to wield a great deal of power and could make a prisoner's life as easy or as difficult as he chose.

The Prisons of Richmond

As the capital of the Confederacy, and the location of the many departments of the Confederate government and the Confederate States Congress, Richmond was the center of the Confederate government. It became a hub through which prisoners passed, and several prisons were needed to confine them: Belle Isle, Castle Thunder, Crew's, Grant's Factory, Libby, Pemberton's, Scott's and Smith's Factory.[53]

Castle Godwin

The Henrico County Jail on Main Street was too small to hold the increasing number of prisoners. McDaniel's Negro Jail on Franklin Street was taken over for a prison. It was used to hold both civilian and military prisoners.[54] The old "Negro jail" on Lumpkin Alley, bounded by Franklin and Union Streets, was the first building used as a Confederate prison It was renamed "Castle Godwin," named after Archibald C. Godwin, assistant provost marshal of Richmond. After martial law was declared, Castle Godwin held 28 men and 2 women, civilians accused of disloyalty. Within five months, the little jail held 250 prisoners.[55] John Minor Botts and John M. Higgins were two prominent citizens held in Castle Godwin. After his release, Higgins was hired as a clerk in the Confederate War Department, where his job included the examination of prisoner's mail. Soldiers who had violated their passes were also confined at Castle Godwin. However, after Castle Thunder was opened, Castle Godwin was seldom used.[56]

This snug little brick building consisted of 13 "clear and well ventilated rooms" which were furnished with "comfortable beds and other conveniences," which surpassed most of the cheap boarding houses in the city. It was presided over in the spring of 1862 by George W. Clackner of Baltimore, deputy provost marshal, who was assisted by Warden George A. Freeburger. An armed sentry guarded the main entrance. Meals for the prisoners were furnished by the nearby Bradford's Eating Saloon.[57]

Richmond City Jail

The Richmond City Jail at 15th and Marshall Streets and the Henrico County Jail were confiscated to house political prisoners, deserters, and Confederate soldiers charged with minor offenses. The city of Richmond was also home to the Virginia State Penitentiary, which housed those sentenced by the civil courts of the state.[58]

Prison Opposite Castle Thunder

Located across the street from Castle Thunder was a prison sometimes erroneously called "Castle Lightening." This building was located on the south side of Cary Street, between 18th and 19th Streets. It was also the former tobacco warehouse of Palmer & Allison. Sometimes it is referred to simply as "Palmer's building." It was used as a provost prison for deserters, drunks, etc. On March 2, 1864, a detective was killed at the "deserter's prison" opposite Castle Thunder.[59]

Castle Lightning

Very little is known about a prison facility called Castle Lightning. It is mentioned in the *Official Records of the War of the Rebellion*. Castle Lightning was also reported to have been a former tobacco warehouse. Citizens suspected of disloyalty were kept here at one time, but its primary function was to confine Confederate soldiers who had either already been convicted or were awaiting trial for a variety of offenses.[60] Castle Lightning, at 6th and Cary streets was also known as Castle Booker or Castle Griswold. Deserters were confined there until it was closed in 1863.[61]

Prisoners were also confined in Harwood's Tobacco Facory at Main and 26th streets. New arrivals were kept in the railroad depot on Main Street. When the 775 prisoners from the battle at Manassas arrived, the Confederate authorities commandeered several more factories and warehouses.[62]

In 1861 and 1862, prisoners were being held at Castle Godwin, the Franklin Street Guard House, and the Henrico County Jail. Probably the guards at the railroad depot and on patrol were used to arrest deserters and maintain order in the city.[63] By mid June of 1862, there were 128 prisoners in Castle Godwin alone. However, some of them were supposed to be sent to Salisbury Prison in North Carolina.[64]

Libby Prison Added

The Confederate government began looking for larger buildings in which to confine prisoners, and the tobacco factories and warehouses seemed to be the ideal solution. The first commercial building used was at 25th and Main. It became known as Ligon's Military Prison. A three-story brick building at Cary and 19th streets was added to the prison system to confine captured Federal officers. Together with the two adjacent buildings, this facility became famous as "Libby Prison."[65]

Alexander Joins the Provost Marshal's Team

After his escape from Fort McHenry, it was some months before Alexander recovered from his leg injury. As soon as he was able, he returned to duty.

In early February of 1862, Alexander was summonsed to report immediately to Brig. General John H. Winder in Richmond, Virginia, to testify as a witness in a trial. At the time, Alexander was a Lieutenant with Company H, 47th Regiment, Virginia Volunteers. He was to be reimbursed for his mileage.[66]

By March of 1862, Alexander was working with the provost marshal. He arrested 89 suspicious persons and confiscated a large quantity of contraband liquors on Hughes' Row and in other taverns on 17th Street between the Old Market and the dock.[67]

Before he became associated with Castle Thunder, Alexander was charged with taking Timothy Webster to his execution. He carried him to the fairgrounds early on the morning of April 29, 1862. Webster asked a clergyman, Rev. Woodbridge, to read the Psalm of David to invoke vengence on his enemies. The Reverend refused. The prisoner was "visibly affected by the preparations for his hanging and the sight of his coffin." A rope was placed around his neck, Rev. M. D. Hodge gave a prayer, then a black cap was pulled over his eyes. When the signal was given, the trap door fell, but because the rope was defective, the noose slipped, and Webster fell on his back to the ground. The stunned, half hung man was raised up and a new rope readied. He was subsequently hanged properly. Webster had plenty of gold and Confederate notes which he gave to his wife, who was confined in Castle Godwin.[68] Mrs. Timothy Webster and Miss Anna Scott were ordered to be released from Castle Godwin and returned to their homes in the North.[69]

By the first of May, 1862, G. W. Alexander, acting as assistant provost marshall, was concerned about the number of guards he had available at the various prison facilities. He wrote to Archibald Campbell Godwin, then provost marshall of Richmond, to report that his detail consisted of 24 at Castle Godwin; 24 at the Guard House on Franklin Street, 5 at the Henrico County Jail, 6 at the Virginia Central Rail Road depot; and 36 on patrol. The total was 90 men. Godwin had noted on the bottom of the letter from Alexander, "I consider the above detail absolutely necessary for Eastern District."

On June 1, 1862, General Winder recommended the appointment of G. W. Alexander to the post of Assistant Adjutant General.[70] By June 12, 1862, Alexander received his appointment and was ordered to report to General Winder for special duty.[71]

Alexander was commissioned captain in October, and a month later became commandant at Castle Thunder. He was also assistant provost marshal of Richmond, and assistant adjutant general to Brigadier General Winder.[72] Alexander's promotion to captain was confirmed by the Confederate Senate. Henry Wirz was appointed A.A.G. the same day.[73] After the war, Wirz would be executed for his treatment of prisoners at Andersonville.[74]

As assistant provost marshal and assistant adjutant general, and also commandant of Castle Thunder, the Eastern District Military Prison, George W. Alexander was under the immediate supervision of General John H. Winder and had to carry out his directives and those of the court. Alexander proved to be a stern disciplinarian who treated the prisoners roughly sometimes; at other times he could be very kind and considerate.[75]

As the war continued, the prison population in Richmond continued to increase. A raid on homes in the area on March 19, 1862, resulted in 89 persons being arrested for distributing contraband liquor. These were housed in Castle Godwin, and it was not long before the small structure was crowded beyond capacity. Those intolerable conditions led to two escapes from the facility. Public reaction was quick to demand safer prisons and extra security, so the search for more and better buildings began.[76]

Alexander had not forgotten his friend Colonel Richard Thomas, also known as Zarvona, who, by June of 1862, had been imprisoned for twelve months. Governor John Letcher of Virginia and George Alexander worked for Zarvona's release. When

Zarvona was threated by the Federals with hanging on a charge of piracy and treason, the Governor of Virginia threatened to hang two of his grade in retaliation. Alexander assured the Governor that the commandant at Fort McHenry was made aware of the content of the Governor's note. The Governor had also sent funds for the prisoner's benefit. All efforts on behalf of Zarvona by both the governor and the Confederate War Department failed to obtain an early release for the prisoner.[77]

By July, General Winder was tired of playing host to the "reprobates" and using Castle Godwin as a place of "temporary detention." However, many of the Confederate officers who had sent their delinquent soldiers for punishment had come to the conclusion that Castle Godwin was "nothing more nor less than a hospital for incurables." To solve the problem, the general decided to advertise their names, and if the prisoners were not called for, they would be released.[78] Once the list of names of the soldiers confined for various offenses at Castle Godwin was published, the prison population was greatly decreased. Some officers who had sent men there for weeks and months seemed to have forgotten them, and only discovered the "fact for the first time by the announcement in the papers."[79]

By August, Castle Godwin was full. The count was 172 persons, more than the little jail had ever held.[80]

That same month, 3,000 Federal prisoners held on Belle Island were transferred to "Varina," the farm of Albert Aiken. The farm was 12 miles from Richmond. Captain Alexander's detective force was sent to escort them under a flag of truce to be exchanged. They were to be met by officers of the United States Army. On the way, the Federal prisoners were "permitted to go by the C. S. Military Prison," and while there, they cheered their fellow soldiers, generals and other officers being held there. The prisoners were happy to be going home, but the day was so hot that after they had been traveling for some time, many broke down and had to be left by the wayside. Two or three died. There remained 1,700 Yankees to be exchanged.[81]

The military prison system continued to evolve, and the number of facilities increased, along with personnel to man them. The military district over which Brigadier General Winder presided was a ten-mile radius around Richmond. Winder's office was on the south side of Main Street, near the corner of 9th Street. There, he adjucated cases and issued orders concerning the disposition of prisoners. Under him was Major E. Griswold, the provost marshall. Griswold had two subordinates: George W. Alexander, assistant provost marshall, and Lieutenant R. M. Booker, who was in charge of "Castle Grizzly," at the corner of 6th and Cary Streets.[82]

Winder's office issued the passes necessary for anyone wishing to visit a prison. Winder also had control over who would be allowed to visit. In the spring of 1863, Winder decreed that "unless in special cases, persons are prohibited from visiting Castle Thunder save on Wednesday and Saturday."[83] On October 9, 1863, Winder ordered Alexander "not to allow lawyers to visit the prisoners confined in [Castle Thunder] except upon a pass from these [Head] Quarters."[84]

Captain Alexander had his office on Franklin Street. He was in charge of Castle Godwin and a group of special police. Both Alexander and Booker were deemed "energetic and vigilant, and had never yet suffered a prisoner to escape from their custody without being afterwards arrested, and both prison discipline and hygiene are without reproach...."[85]

To ease the situation of prison overcrowding, the tobacco factory of Mr. William Greanor on Cary Street, betwen 18th and 19th Streets, was to become a new prison. The prisoners now confined in the guard house on Franklin Street and in Castle Godwin were to be moved to the new facility. Captain Alexander was to move his office there as well.[86] Alexander moved to Castle Thunder on August 13, 1862. The new facility was christened "Castle Thunder," to remind offenders of the terror of "Olympian vengeance." Castle Godwin was to be discontinued as a prison.[87] The 250 prisoners confined at Castle Godwin were to be moved to Castle Thunder, which would hold approximately 1,000 prisoners.[88] The inmates of Castle Godwin were moved to Castle Thunder on August 18, 1862.[89]

On October 27, 1862, Winder issued an order that replaced Captain G. W. Alexander by Captain Thomas P. Turner. This enabled Alexander to assume a new position as commandant at Castle Thunder.[90]

Alexander reportedly had performed his duties previously assigned him in an "admirable manner," and was greatly admired for his role in the capture of the *St. Nicholas* and his subsequent escape from the Federal prison at Fort McHenry. He was described in the Richmond *Enquirer* as "not only one of the most gallant, but one of the handsomest men in the Confederate service."[91] Yet the days ahead would thrust Captain George Washington Alexander into national prominence and unleash a legacy of hatred and bitterness that would follow him the rest of his life.

5

New Prison Opened in Richmond

"And he who rules the thunder can put this rogue and whore asunder."
—*Jonathan Swift, "Marriage certificate"*

The Confederacy was fortunate to have a number of buildings in Richmond which could be used as hospitals, prisons, storehouses, or guard barracks. These were the large buildings used as warehouses and tobacco factories. Tobacco warehouses and factories made excellent prison facilities. Usually, they were of brick construction, several stories high, and the rooms were large. The Confederate government took possession of these buildings and put them to use. The prisons established at Seabrook, Libby, and Castle Thunder had all been busy, spacious tobacco warehouses. Other private buildings were confiscated for hospitals. The availability of these buildings saved the Confederacy much time and money, and once the war was over, they reverted to their original usages.[1]

In the summer of 1862, there were 4,000 prisoners in the city of Richmond. At Libby Prison, 1,468 well prisoners and 637 wounded were confined, and at Greanor and Palmer's factories (later called Castle Thunder) there were about 1,450 prisoners. Lieutenant Shin was in charge of the prisoners at Greanor and Palmer's Factories. Barrett's factory on Main Street held another 1,268. Yankee officers were being held in one building on 18th Street, between Main and Cary.[2]

Because of the notoriety of Libby Prison, Castle Thunder is seldom mentioned. It may have something to do with the fact that Libby Prison held only Federal prisoners-of-war, while the prison population at Castle Thunder was a mixed variety, and included more civilians and Confederate deserters than Yankees captured in battle.

Yet, over the period Castle Thunder was used as a prison by the Confederate

5. New Prison Opened in Richmond   47

Castle Thunder, Petersburg, Virginia, view of back side and enclosed yard. (Library of Congress, Washington, D.C., LC-USZ62-59871)

government, it probably housed more desperate and dangerous prisoners than any other prison in the South.[3] The name, *Castle Thunder,* was also given to another Confederate prison at Petersburg, but it is seldom mentioned in the literature. Only in *The Photographic History of the Civil War* is more space devoted to the Petersburg "Castle Thunder" than to Richmond's "Castle Thunder."[4]

Captain Thomas P. Turner, commandant at Libby Prison, said that the character of the prisoners held at Castle Thunder was "the worst in the land.... Some of the most desperate men in the Confederacy are there."[5] Those held at Castle Thunder were, indeed, some of the most dangerous of prisoners — spies, double agents, deserters, traitors, and those under sentence of execution — desperate characters all.

The new facility in Richmond was named Castle Thunder to instill fear and be a "terror to evil-doers." It became a place of terror to many who were incarcerated there. Soon, the name of the prison would be indicative of the treatment the inmates received.[6] Some of the "thunder" heard within the walls of Castle Thunder came in the form of one man — George Washington Alexander, the prison's first commandant. He was described as "harsh, inhuman, tyrannical, and dishonest in every possible way."[7]

In the types of prisoners it housed, Castle Thunder was similar to the Old Capitol Prison in Washington, D.C., where prisoners of state, persons suspected of disloyalty, persons charged with bounty frauds, counterfeiters, government swindlers, spies, and others who may have been arrested by detectives on "trumped-up charges" were held.[8]

Provost Marshal's Uniform

Captain Alexander presented a formidable appearance as he galloped through the streets of Richmond on his black horse with his long black beard flowing in the wind. At his heels was always the magnificent black dog, "Nero" (Hero).[9] Based on appearance alone, it was no wonder that both the citizens and the prisoners feared him. Indeed, Captain George W. Alexander, with his black beard, black hair, and black eyes completed the picture of terror. His normally fierce appearance was made more formidable by the standard uniform required of the provost marshal. Instead of the elegant gray of the official Confederate uniform, each provost marshal wore a tight-fitting black suit. The trousers were buckled at the knee, below which he wore black stockings. His loose black shirt had a white collar.[10]

Today's provost guard re-enactor wears a black cotton suit consisting of a long coat, trousers (held up by suspenders), and a sleeveless vest. The coat is buttoned by shiny brass buttons initialed with "CSA." A star with the inscription "Provost Guard" is pinned to his left shoulder. Underneath the vest, he wears a white cotton shirt and a black necktie. In the summer, he wears a black straw hat, and in the winter a black wool hat. Wool socks were worn inside leather brogans. Drawers of cotton are worn in the summer, and wool in the winter. In addition, during the winter months, he wears long-handle, flannel underwear of red wool.[11] A provost marshal usually carried two Colt. 44 black powder revolvers in black leather gun holsters, one on each side. Attached to his belt is a cartridge box and a cap box. A canteen and a haversack hung by a strap across his shoulder.[12]

The tools of his trade hung on his left side from his leather belt: a truncheon (short club); a pair of leg irons; and two sets of handcuffs, one for males and one for females, who had much smaller wrists. Some provost marshals also carried a sword held in a scabbard.[13]

Buildings and Grounds

Castle Thunder opened as a prison in August of 1862. The three-building complex was on the north side of Cary Street between 18th and 19th Streets. The central core was originally Greanor's Tobacco Warehouse. The former Greanor's Warehouse, which faced Cary Street, was three and a half stories high. It was the largest of the three buildings and could hold 650 prisoners. Attached to each side were Palmer's Factory and Whitlock's Warehouse. Palmer's could hold 400, and Whitlock's another 350, for a total inmate population of 1,400.[14]

Behind Palmer's and Whitlock's, a high fence connected the two buildings. Water was pumped from the James River. The buildings were heated by gas.[15]

5. New Prison Opened in Richmond

Castle Thunder, facing Cary Street, Richmond, Virginia. (Library of Congress, Washington, D.C., LC-B8171-3160)

Behind the three buildings was an enclosed yard where prisoners could exercise. The latrines were located here as well. The windows were barred. Gaslights and water were available with the guards' approval. However, the quality of air inside the buildings was poor, and the odor of many unwashed bodies was most foul. Prisoners slept on blankets or straw. The second floor had a number of cells that were about 15 feet square. These had boarded-up windows. A long hall led to a big room that had four barred windows. This was called the "prison parlor," where prisoners could "stroll without interference." The third floor was divided into two rooms, a larger one for prisoners of war, and a smaller room confined for Confederate soldiers who were awaiting a court martial.

The first floor had an inner room, in which the balls and chains were kept. Also on the first floor were two cells for condemned prisoners. There was a foul-smelling latrine in the center of that room, and the floor was covered with filth. A door at the back of this room led into the "execution yard."[16]

Efforts to Relieve Overcrowding

The prisoners were segregated by type. Greanor's held Confederate deserters and disloyal citizens. Whitlock's held blacks and women. Federal deserters were put in Palmer's Factory. However, as the war continued and the prison was packed beyond capacity, the segregation was not strictly enforced. By 1863, Castle Thunder held 1,500 prisoners.[17]

To relieve overcrowding, prisoners were constantly being moved from one facility to another. Space was always at a premium. The Confederacy was not prepared for the tremendous expenses and energy involved in guarding thousands of prisoners. Shortly after Castle Thunder opened, Captain Alexander was ordered to turn over to Captain Turner, commander of the C. S. Prison (Confederate States Prison), all the Negro prisoners in his custody and to give an accounting of all that had been delivered to him and to other prison wardens.[18]

On August 1, 1863, following the loss of Vicksburg and the defeat at Gettysburg, President Jefferson Davis issued a proclamation describing what would befall the South if the North won the war. He urged all those who were absent without leave to return to duty so as to erase the disparity in numbers between the two armies. He promised a general amnesty to all deserters who returned within 20 days, and he urged the families of the men "not to shelter the deserters." The terms were generous, but did little to refurbish the ranks of the Confederate army.[19] Soldiers continued to desert and they were hunted down, arrested, and confined to prison.

A group of deserters was sent to Castle Thunder in August of 1863. They were "not entitled to the benefit of the Presidential Proclamation as they were ... taken with arms in their hands and resisted arrest." Some of those listed were Robert Patterson of Company F, 57th Virginia; G. B. Trent, Company A, 58th Virginia; J. Denham, Company A, 58th Virginia; W. R. Glass, Company F, 52nd North Carolina; J. W. Meadows, Company A, 23rd North Carolina; and Lemuel Watson, Company K, 53rd North Carolina.[20]

Deserters were often forwarded to Alexander with instructions to send them on to their regiments. Sixteen prisoners were sent under guard from Lynchburg, Virginia, on October 16, 1863, to Captain Alexander. Eight deserters had been arrested by Lt. W. W. Davidson, Provost Marshal, Dublin, Virginia; four had been arrested as deserters in Amhurst County. One, Jacob Klyne, was a paroled Yankee arrested by Lt. Davidson. Alexander was instructed to forward the men to General Bragg's Army, Bucker's Division.[21] This procedure became more common as the war progressed, and the number of desertions increased.

Castle Thunder was used to punish those in the military who had broken military rules. Military tribunals sentenced offenders to incarceration at the Castle.[22] Military offenders from camps all over the Confederacy were sent to Castle Thunder to await sentencing. These soldiers were charged with such military crimes as impersonating an officer, falsifying place of residence, forging discharges or pay accounts, entering Richmond without a pass, and drunkenness. Whole companies were sometimes put under arrest. All the privates of Company D, 20th Virginia Battalion, were arrested on "mutinous conduct charges," because they had demonstrated against the "ill treatment of the battalion commander, Major Delagnel."[23]

Castle Thunder Detectives

A detective force was stationed at Castle Thunder. They were used to arrest deserters and suspicious persons, and to track down escapees. However, early in April of 1863, that force was divided, and Detectives Crow, Causey, and Schaeffer were ordered to report to the headquarters of the provost marshal in Richmond. Four detectives, Perdue, Folks, New, and Thomas, were to remain at Castle Thunder.[24]

Alexander kept Castle Thunder under strict security. Two of the guards who were known for their callousness and cruelty were the Frenchmen, Lieutenant Virginius Bossieux and his brother Cyrus. They were assigned to Castle Thunder shortly after it was opened. Virginius later earned a bad reputation among the prisoners while stationed at Libby and Belle Isle.[25]

While the capacity at Castle Thunder was 1,500, the daily number of prisoners averaged around a thousand. Over the course of its existence, approximately 40,000 prisoners were held there. The treatment the prisoners received was not always kind. However, those confined at Castle Thunder faired much better than those at Andersonville, or even Salisbury Prison, when it became overcrowded in the fall of 1864. Treatment at prisons in the North could also be cruel and inhumane.

In July of 1863, not long after the battle of Gettysburg, Surgeon Barton, in charge of Castle Thunder's Hospital No. 13, wrote Major William A. Carrington, Confederate medical director, that he was sending to Castle Thunder a number of citizens for examination. Undoubtedly, they were to be examined as to their physical capabilities for military service. Those named were: John Adams, L. Cunningham, Edward Coleman, P. H. Cavinaugh, James Corey, E. P. Davis (Baxter), S. M. Day, E. B. Hopkins, H. A. Joynes, James Jackson, Frank Mires, Mike Martin, E. J. Miller, Samuel Sprouse, Daniel Scully, William Tilly, James Williams, Jesse Wright, and J. H. Wooten. Another group were "unable to attend on account of severe sickness." They were L. Collier, J. S. Davis, William Fitzgerald, James Gillmore, Hugh Miller, Smith (a deaf mute), and H. D[unreadable].[26]

Strict Rules and Regulations

As the number of prisoners increased, so did the number of problems concerning them. Control within the prison system was tightened as breakouts, riots, and unrest increased. Lieutenant Major Thomas P. Turner, acting under Brigadier General John

H. Winder, commander of the Department of Henrico, issued a set of 15 "Rules and Regulations of the C. S. Military Prisons."[27] These rules applied to the prisoners and their guards.

> I. All orders affecting prisoners of war and the general discipline of the entire command, will be issued only by the officer commanding, and order proceeding from any other source will not be regarded by officers on duty at the prison.
>
> II. There will be a roll-call daily of the prisoners at 7 ½ A.M., and at 5 P.M., and the officer of the guard must be present at each.
>
> III. No prisoner, whatever his rank, will be allowed to leave the quarters to which he is assigned, under any pretext whatever, without special permission from the officer commanding; nor shall any prisoner be fired upon by a sentinel or other person, except in case of revolt or attempted escape.
>
> IV. No letters, packages or parcels of any kind, can be passed with persons outside of the prison, and no visitor will be allowed an interview with a prisoner without permission [from the Brigadier General commanding the department of Henrico.] From Hd. Qrs.
>
> V. Prisoners are not allowed to converse with the sentinels; nor must they congregate about the windows after dark.
>
> VI. The firing of one gun at night, or two during the day, will be the signal for immediate assembling of the guard.
>
> VII. Under no circumstances will the sentinel be allowed to sit down upon post, or to rest their guns on the ground.
>
> VIII. At 9 o'clock P.M., the lights throughout the prison, except in the hospital and officers' quarters, must be immediately extinguished; and it shall be the duty of the Officer of the Guard to inspect the prison at that hour, to see that the lights are put out, fire secured, and that everything is quiet.
>
> IX. No conversation, intercourse, or trading with the prisoners, in any manner whatever will be allowed.
>
> X. The Officer of the Guard must not be absent at any [one] time from his post [for a period exceeding one hour.]
>
> XI. The guard off post must remain constantly at the guard-house ready for instant service, and their guns must be kept on the rack.
>
> XII. Every guard room must be policed each morning by the old guard, and will not be received by the officer of the new guard unless in good order. Both the officers of the old and new guard will be held responsible for the execution of this order, and also for the safe keeping of all articles left in the guard house.
>
> XIII. These rules and regulations must be read to the new guard every morning before posting the first relief.
>
>> (Signed) Th. P. Turner
>> Lieut Major Comd'g.
>
> *Approved*
>> John H. Winder,
>> Brig. Gen. Comd'g Dept. Henrico.[28]

In addition to the rules and regulations from Winder's officer, Captain Alexander made rules of his own, which he strictly enforced. The prisoners complained that nearly every week Captain Alexander imposed some "new restriction." As time passed, and more and more prisoners were incarcerated, security was tightened. Yet, to the prisoners, it seemed that the guards watched for an excuse to shoot a prisoner if they even looked out the windows. Tensions mounted, and a guard shot and killed another guard who had looked out the window from one of the upper stories.[29] A shooting also occurred at Libby Prison, when a prisoner was shot in the arm while throwing water out of a window.[30]

Prison Guards

A large number of guards were required to enforce these rules and regulations and to keep prisoners from escaping. By the fall of 1864, General Kemper had been put in command of the reserve militia of Virginia, and two regiments, the First and the Nineteenth, were assigned to duty at Libby Prison, Castle Thunder, and other prisons. The First Regiment was described as composed of "old men and boys," over and under conscription age. The Nineteenth Regiment was composed of foreigners who were allowed to remain in Richmond because they were tradesmen — shoemakers, blacksmiths, etc.[31]

The First Battalion Second Class Militia (City Battalion), commonly known as the Second Virginia Reserve, served as guards for Castle Thunder during most of the war. These guards were mostly boys between 16 and 18 years of age and men between 45 and 55. According to the Richmond *Dispatch,* these young prison guards were inexperienced, "unconcerned with duty," and "lamentably deficient in the requisite knowledge" of how to perform the simplest tasks. The citizens of Richmond were not sure that the large number of prisoners held at Castle Thunder were being adequately guarded. They did not believe that the guards from the Reserve were qualified.[32]

Routine Paperwork

A mountain of paperwork was involved in maintaining records of prisoners and their location. Receipts were written when prisoners were received and when they were transferred. Daily accountings were made that listed the men confined in various parts of the building. Many of these have been preserved on three rolls of microfilm available from the Virginia Historical Society, Richmond, Virginia.

Also on the microfilm are hundreds of letters, many written by the prisoners. Most of the preserved material consists of letters from prisoners to General Winder and Captain Alexander, or to friends and family members as the prisoners sought help in getting released. A few letters are reproduced in the *Official Records of the War of the Rebellion.* Some of these letters from prisoners were never forwarded to their intended recipients but remained with the provost marshal's department. The quality of some letters and reports is excellent, the handwriting good, the spelling excellent. However, other letters, because of the blue-lined paper they were written on, are totally unreadable. Other letters can be deciphered by using a strong magnifying glass.

When writing official letters, Captain Alexander headed his with East District Military Prison, Richmond, Virginia, instead of "Castle Thunder." One such letter was directed to Major William A. Carrington, a doctor, and commissioner for the Examination of Prisoners:

> E. Dist. Mil Prison
> Richmond, Va. Oct 29, 1863
>
> Permit me respectfully to call your attention and ask you for advice in the case of Private Sam J. Peck of the Goochland artillery. Shall I assume [?] you advise me to send him to his company with the copy of the proceeding finding, & I think from the dates etc. he should be restored to duty.
> Respectfully,
> G. W. Alexander
> Capt Commandant of Post[33]

Department of Henrico, 1863

The Confederate Department of Henrico encompassed the county of Henrico, which included the city of Richmond. The department was extended on March 26, 1862, to include Petersburg and vicinity. Winder, who was commander of the department from December of 1861 to May of 1864, was responsible for the Federal prisoners held on Belle Isle and Libby Prison. Winder was, at the same time, provost marshal general of the Confederacy and provost marshal of the city of Richmond.[34]

From 1862–1863, the Department of Henrico and its prison system seemed to be working properly, but the public did not know what went on behind the thick walls and iron bars of Richmond's prisons, as the next chapters will reveal.

6

The Lighter Side: Alexander — Poet, Dramatist and Actor

"All the world's a stage, and all the men and women merely players."
—*William Shakespeare*, As You Like It

Although many dwell on the darker aspects of the personality of George W. Alexander, there was another side to him. Alexander was a product of the times. Trained in the harsh ways of military and naval discipline, Alexander was dedicated to his job as provost marshal in charge of Castle Thunder. Yet he appreciated the finer things in life — music, literature, and drama.

The citizens of Richmond sought solace and attempted to forget their troubles and the heart break and horror of war through the gaiety of entertainment provided in the theaters. There was a great outpouring of poetry, songs, and dramas about the South, its soldiers, and their loved ones. Sometimes, these were all combined into a play which was performed in the theaters of Richmond and elsewhere.

A calendar of the performances at the Richmond Theatre and the New Richmond Theatre was compiled from the files of Richmond newspapers from 1861 to 1865, including *The Daily Dispatch, The Daily Richmond Enquirer, The Daily Richmond Examiner, The Evening Courier, The Richmond Whig,* and the *Public Advertiser.* A total of 439 different plays and other forms of entertainment that were performed during the war years has been documented.[1]

The Richmond Theatre opened its doors for the fall season in 1861 on November 2. A variety of entertainment — tragedies, comedies, farces, operas, etc. — ran through January 1, 1862. The theater building caught fire and burned early in the morning of January 2, 1862. Since "the show must go on," the company reopened at the Richmond Varieties on January 6, and the troop continued to perform there until February 4, 1863. The New Richmond Theatre, on the corner of 7th and Broad

Streets, opened its doors on February 9, 1863, and continued until Richmond was evacuated on April 2, 1865.[2] The theater building was owned by Mrs. Elizabeth Magill. Richard D'Orsey replaced John Hill Hewitt as theater manager on June 24, 1862, and he continued in that position through September of 1864.[3]

Captain G. W. Alexander wrote several plays. He even appeared at each performance of one of them. *The Virginia Cavalier* was performed on March 16–26, April 2, May 7, 18, October 10, 17, November 25, December 19, 29, of 1863, and January 1, 2, February 8, 20, April 19, and June 22, of 1864.[4]

Although Alexander's play was a great favorite with the people of Richmond during the war, critics panned it as "an abominable play, with absolutely nothing to recommend it," yet it became the "greatest hit of the Confederate state." Captain Alexander was not a cavalier, and he was not even in the cavalry, but he was part of the hated military police. The theater critic writing for the *Southern Illustrated News* was not complimentary:

> The play contained nothing strikingly new or original—'twas the same old story of "virtue rewarded—villainy foiled"—interspersed with singing and dancing. As the plot began to unfold itself, some of the literary gentlemen groaned inadvertently, and despondingly moved towards the door....
>
> The plot of the "Cavalier" is similar to that of the "Guerrillas," which was produced some months ago at the Varieties, though we will do the author of the last named piece the justice to say, that so far as dramatic situations and beauty of composition are concerned he is head and shoulders above the unknown captain. We have never before seen a play put upon the stage in which there was not at least one good character. In the "Virginia Cavalier" not even one good character can be found—there is not a character in the entire *dramatis personae* of the play that might not have had its origin in the veriest dunce of the country school. The dialogue is stupid, the incident are stale, and the plot ridiculous. The best company ever put on the American stage, would fail in making a point or hit in such a place.[5]

One of the songs in the play was "The Southern Soldier Boy." The lyrics, by Capt. G. W. Alexander, were sung by Miss Sallie Partington during the performance of Alexander's play to the tune of "The Boy with the Auburn Hair."[6] The sentiments brought out in this song pleased the Confederate soldiers so much that, for more than a year, the play was performed frequently at the New Richmond Theatre, and it was greeted with wild hurrahs by the Blockade Rebels. Miss Sallie was hailed as the prima donna of the Confederacy.[7]

Southern Soldier Boy
Lyrics: Captain G. W. Alexander
Tune: "The Boy With the Auburn Hair"

Verse 1: Bob Roebuck is my sweetheart's name
He's off to the wars and gone;
He's fighting for his Nanny dear,
His sword is buckled on,
He's fighting for his own true love;
He is the darling of my heart,
My Southern soldier boy.

6. The Lighter Side: Alexander—Poet, Dramatist and Actor

Chorus: Yo! ho! yo! ho! yo! ho! ho! ho! ho! ho! ho! ho!
        He is my only joy,
        He is the darling of my heart
        My Southern soldier boy.

Verse 2: When Bob comes home from war's alarms,
        We'll start anew in life;
        I'll give myself right up to him,
        A dutiful, loving wife.
        I'll try my best to please my dear,
        For he is my only joy,
        He is the darling of my heart,
        My Southern soldier boy.

Chorus: Yo! ho! yo! ho! yo! ho! ho! ho! ho! ho! ho! ho!
        He is my only joy,
        He is the darling of my heart,
        My Southern Soldier Boy.

Verse 3: Oh! if in battle he were slain,
        I know that I would die,
        But I am sure he'll come again
        To cheer my weeping eye.
        But should he fall in this our glorious cause,
        He still would be my joy,
        For many a sweetheart mourns the loss
        Of her Southern soldier boy.

Chorus: Yo! ho! yo! ho! yo! ho! ho! ho! ho! ho! ho! ho!
        I'd grieve to lose my joy,
        But many a sweetheart mourns the loss
        Of a Southern Soldier Boy.

Verse 4: I hope for the best, and so do all
        Whose hopes are in the field;
        I know that we shall win the day
        For Southrons never yield;
        And when we think of those who are away,
        We look above for joy,
        And I'm mighty glad that my Bobby is
        A Southern soldier boy.[8]

The Library of Congress, Washington, D.C., holds another song written by Captain Alexander. Although undated, this one is entitled "Dedicated to the Baltimore Light Artillery, CSA."[9]

Verse 1. The Maryland Boys are coming,
        Dost hear their stirring drum?
        Our homes are now before us,
        Dear Mother, we will come.

Chorus: March away! March away!
        The old Line's bugle yet is sounding,
        March away! march away!
        Our hearts with hopes abounding.

Verse 2. Old North Point's brilliant story
        Still cheers us every man;
        Our banner led to glory,
        Waves proudly in the van.

Front page of sheet music, "The Southern Soldier Boy," words by G. W. Alexander, performed in his play *The Virginia Cavalier*. (Rare Book, Manuscript, and Special Collections Library, Perkins Library, Duke University, Durham, North Carolina)

> Verse 3. At Guilford and Long Island,
> The Old Line stood the shock;
> Our fathers struck for freedom,
> And stood firmly as a rock.
>
> Verse 4. Our mothers, sweethearts, sisters,
> The fond but absent wife;
> All look to us for succor,
> Then strike while there is life.

Verse 5. Let our motto be "DEAR MOTHER,"
They can kill but nothing more;
Our name will live in story,
Then strike for Baltimore!

The chorus was repeated after every verse.

Hero (Nero), the Guard Dog of Castle Thunder and Stage Performer

In one scene of his play, *Virginia Cavalier,* Captain Alexander, in his black provost marshal's uniform, mounted his black horse and galloped across the stage while his big black dog, Hero (Nero), followed, barking at the horse's heels.[10] Alexander's appearance was an exciting spectacle, and always generated loud and lengthy applause from the delighted theater patrons.

There is some disagreement about the name of the Bavarian boar hound who became a part of the security system at Castle Thunder. Some references call him "Hero," others "Nero." Perhaps the prisoners thought the dog reminded them of the cruel Roman emperor *Nero,* while the prison officials saw him as a hero for preventing escapes. The dog became famous, partly because of his role in Captain Alexander's play, and also because of his unusual appearance. When not on the stage, Hero (Nero) returned to his post as a sentinel at Castle Thunder, where he remained until Monday evening, April 3, 1865.[11]

All references to the dog agree that he was a huge, black dog, owned at one time by Captain George W. Alexander. However, the character of the dog is disputed. Some described him as vicious, others as gentle as a puppy.

The background and history of Hero/Nero, according to information obtained from Mayor Joseph Mayo and the Honorable James Lyons, is that of a Bavarian boar hound puppy which was brought to Richmond in 1859 or 1860 by the captain of a Bavarian ship which landed at Rockett's, a dock in the city. Bavarian boar hounds were used in the dense forests of Germany to hunt wild boars, very dangerous, vicious, and formidable animals. A wild boar has huge, sharp tusks, sometimes seven inches long.[12]

The captain gave the puppy to Mr. John Allen, of the firm of Ginter & Allen. Allen, in turn, passed him to Mr. James Lyons. Lyons then permitted Mayor Joseph Mayo to take the dog and keep him at the city jail, as a sort of guard dog, because he was far too large to be permitted to roam about the city. When grown, the black dog weighed 182 pounds or more. When Captain Alexander came to Richmond, he saw the dog at the city jail and was impressed by his size and beauty. Alexander obtained the consent of both Mayo and Lyon to take Nero to Castle Thunder, where he remained until the end of the war. The dog was permitted the run of Castle Thunder, and was generally good natured, playful, and docile, but when angered or provoked, he could be dangerous. Captain Alexander reportedly whipped him with a horsewhip while holding a cocked revolver in his other hand, which he would sometimes fire over his head. The dog would then appear subdued.[13]

Captain Alexander's dog may have been a Great Dane. The Great Dane is also known as "Duetsche Dogge, German Boarhound, Alano, Dogo Aleman." Colors can range from black to brindle, fawn to harlequin.[14] Currently Great Danes range in weight from 100 to 120 pounds and stand from 30 to 32 inches high. Traditionally, they are highly intelligent and easily trainable. They were originally developed to hunt boar during the Middle Ages, and the Germans developed the breed as we know it today. Some believe the Great Dane is a cross between the ancient Mastiff and the Irish Wolfhound.[15] It is generally agreed that the Mastiff group is one of the oldest and most significant of all dog groups. In temperament, the Great Dane is loving and kind toward people, especially children. He is not agressive, but he makes an excellent watchdog. He is generally a one-man dog, and for the person to whom he attaches himself, he will do almost anything.[16] This seems to be a good description of the dog which followed Alexander across the stage and was also a faithful guard at Castle Thunder prison.

According to a report written after the war's end, the dog was a cross between a Russian bloodhound and a bulldog, a combination of the faithfulness of the former and the viciousness of the latter. He was known to seize a small dog and shake it to cast it 20 feet away. He could bring the stoutest man to the ground by gripping his throat. It was difficult to get him off his prey once he had tasted or smelled blood.[17] George D. Putnam, first lieutenant and adjutant of the 176th Regiment, New York State Volunteers, was a Federal prisoner on parole in Richmond. He occasionally went to Castle Thunder, and he said that the hound "had been taught to go for anybody wearing blue cloth!"[18]

The dog undoubtedly loved Alexander, and frequently the pair could be seen galloping at full speed through the streets of Richmond. Alexander, in his black uniform of the provost marshal, his black beard flowing in the wind, rode astride his huge black horse, followed by the "magnificent black dog Nero at his heels."[19]

There was more than one dog at Castle Thunder. When a crane was shot, someone brought it to Castle Thunder and the prison surgeon amputated the crane's injured wing. Some of the dogs at the Castle attacked the giant bird, but he repulsed them. In defending himself, the bird put out the eye of one of the dogs.[20] There is no mention that Hero was blind in one eye, and this must refer to another dog.

In 1864, there was a roundup of stray dogs. City employees were led by police officers in a raid on the canines. Hundreds of dogs were caught and they were not allowed to "sleep the last sleep" as previously was the custom at "Horse Heaven" near Howard's Grove, but after they were killed, they were carried out to the Confederate States' nitrate beds. The mayor's big black dog, formerly kept by Captain Alexander, was captured while Alexander was away from Castle Thunder at Salisbury Prison. However, Alexander's dog was saved from an untimely demise.[21]

7

Life Within the Castle: The Dark Side

"Man's Inhumanity to man makes countless thousands mourn."
— *Robert Burns, "Man Was Made to Mourn"*

Federal soldiers had been confined in Richmond since the first prisoners of war were captured at the First Battle of Manassas (Bull Run), Virginia, on July 21, 1861. Those captured numbered about 1,000.[1] As the war continued and the numbers of prisoners became greater, Confederate officials were urged to find more facilities in which to house inmates. Overcrowding, sickness, and shortages of food, clothing, and other necessities made prison life miserable. Letters appeared in newspapers which described the plight of the prisoners in Confederate prisons. In a letter to the Washington, D.C. *Star* on December 11, 1861, Isaac Hart described the condition of prisoners in Richmond:

> ... this communication is to call the attention of your numerous readers to the condition of the Federal prisoners of war at this point, for every sympathetic emotion is called up when we behold from day to day their entire destitution and suffering. I have been frequently inquired of by the pale, sickly, half-clad heart-broken soldiers, away from home and in prison in an enemy's land: "When will our Government send us some clothing and blankets? ... If our parents knew how we suffered here they would send to our relief, but I supposed they think that the Government will see to it."[2]

Alfred Ely, a member of congress from Rochester, New York, wrote a letter to the Richmond *Enquirer* while held as a prisoner. Ely stated, "The Yankee prisoners of war in this city are beginning to feel the want of proper clothing." He offered to furnish money for their clothing himself, out of his ample funds.[3] Although at first prisoners were promptly exchanged, as the numbers increased, the process became slow and cumbersome, and the prisons overflowed before prisoners could be exchanged.

Those unfortunate enough to find themselves confined to Castle Thunder sometimes noted that they must have "invoked the thunder of the gods," to deserve being consigned to such a place.[4] Junius Henri Browne graphically described his own experiences in Castle Thunder, Libby and Salisbury prisons:

> Few persons can have any idea of a long imprisonment in the South. They usually regard it merely as an absence of freedom — as a deprivation of the pleasures and excitement of ordinary life. They do not take into consideration the scant and miserable rations that no one, unless he be half famished, can eat; the necessity of going cold and hungry in the wet and wintry season; the constant torture from vermin ... the total isolation, the supreme dreariness, the dreadful monotony, the perpetual turning inward of the mind upon itself, the self-devouring of the heart, week after week, month after month, year after year.[5]

A High-Risk Institution

For deserters from the Confederate services, Castle Thunder sometimes proved to be more life-threatening than the battlefront. Many prisoners were given 50 lashes across their bare backs by fellow Confederates employed as prison guards. Some were hustled back to their regiments while others were sent on to Camp Lee where they were executed by a firing squad. Castle Thunder, even in the best of times, was a "high risk" institution.[6]

Many deserters from the Confederate States Army were caught and imprisoned. After they had served their time in Castle Thunder, they were taken back to their regiments. There were 185 inmates at Castle Thunder sent from the prison to their respective regiments in Winchester, Virginia.[7]

Prisoners were separated to avoid collaboration and large-scale escape attempts. Occasionally, overcrowding interrupted the standard procedure, but normally the Gleanor factory building served to house deserters from the Confederate army and political enemies. Whitlock factory building held black men and white women. Federal deserters and prisoners of war were confined to Palmer's factory. Castle Lightening, across the street from Castle Thunder, was used to hold Federal deserters near the end of the war.[8]

Some of the rooms at Castle Thunder could hold up to 100 prisoners. Some prisoners were given individual rooms, and they were allowed to purchase furniture to make their quarters more comfortable. Stoves were placed in almost every room, but wood for heating and cooking was hard to obtain. Prison authorities were hesitant to supply furniture because the prisoners would break it up and use it to fuel the stoves.[9]

Some prisoners were transferred to Castle Thunder only until they could be exchanged or transferred to another facility. In 1863, Castle Thunder housed Union soldiers in transit. General Winder ordered a large number of Federal prisoners from the 148th Pennsylvania to Castle Thunder before they were transferred to Belle Isle.

In January of 1863, Winder transferred 100 prisoners from Libby Prison to Castle Thunder because of overcrowding at Libby.[10]

In the spring of 1863, Henry Dedrick, of the 52nd Virginia Infantry, talked to his friends William Offlighter and Hiram Coyner, both of whom had been brought before a military court and were confined to the brigade guardhouse while awaiting their sentence. Offlighter and Coyner described Castle Thunder as "the worst place that they ever seen," but said they "got plenty to eat."[11]

Some Federal soldiers of the First North Carolina Union Volunteers who had been captured near Elizabeth City, North Carolina, in March and April of 1863 were confined at Castle Thunder. According to Federal reports, three of those captured March 12 were put in an awful dungeon, and two died from that confinement. Twenty-eight men were kept in a "gloomy cell 15 by 20 feet." According to Captain E. C. Sanders of Company D, First North Carolina, these Federal prisoners, who were probably Negroes, were treated as "felons of the deepest dye instead of prisoners of war because they [were] North Carolina Union volunteers."[12]

I. M. Hatch, a Union spy masquerading as a deserter from the Federal forces, was confined in Castle Thunder for three weeks in the fall of 1864. He had to wait until a sufficient number of deserters were collected before being exchanged. He reported that when he arrived, 165 Union army deserters were sent away. Nine new deserters arrived that same day, of which seven were sailors from the *Commodore Morris*. He was told that 500 deserters had been sent through the blockade to "some foreign port," since nearly all of them were "foreigners by birth." Hatch said a number of "Negro soldiers" were forced to "do all sorts of menial duty about the streets of Richmond, work on the fortifications, etc."[13]

Alexander's Pets

Alexander, like all people in power, had a few "pets," prisoners who received greater consideration and preferential treatment.

Miss Charlotte Gilman, charged with counterfeiting, and Captain Henry Edenborough, an East India Royal Navy officer charged with not having the proper credentials, were both treated with kindness and courtesy. Miss Gilman was frequently allowed to leave the prison. Captain Edenborough was given good quarters, and his meals were delivered from nearby hotels. He was also at liberty to visit the hotels for his meals, if he chose to do so.[14]

One group Alexander favored was the reporters and news correspondents.[15] Although he was described as a "regular Bombastes Furiso," the commandant did have some "literary pretensions" and they were "purely pretensions."[16]

The reporters lived in comparative luxury. They played cards, talked among themselves, or read. Their meals were prepared for them, and between meals they could snack on coffee, sardines and jams, or smoke a good cigar — all items purchased from the prison sutler's store. The reporters became known as the "Bohemian Brigade," all of them having traveled extensively.[17]

Junius Henri Browne, special war correspondent for the New York *Tribune*, could testify first hand as to the conditions of Richmond's Prisons. He was captured at Vicksburg on May 3, 1863, and was subsequently imprisoned at Vicksburg, Jackson, Atlanta, Richmond and Salisbury, before he escaped.[18] He believed Castle Thunder was preferable to Libby Prison. Although the character of the inhabitants of the Castle was more "disagreeable," there was less "tyranny and contemptible malice there than at the other Richmond Prison." At Libby, Browne noted, the boredom was relieved by conversation with "intelligent and well-bred officers," but at Castle Thunder, prisoners were "forced to depend on their own society," and that was made up of "deserters, thieves, swindlers, and loyal but ignorant men...."[19]

Castle Thunder: The Southern Bastille

Browne called Castle Thunder the "Southern Bastille." He compared conditions there to French prisons during the French Revolution where once imprisoned, a person might perish from sheer neglect, and all "trace be lost of him."[20] He witnessed a great deal of suffering among the prisoners at Castle Thunder. Yet Browne and others shared several boxes of supplies from the North, and made themselves fairly comfortable. His quarters were the "least bad in the Prison," and during his "long incarceration," he acquired a number of articles "necessary to housekeeping." He was neither "hungry nor ragged," but others in the prison system were. Browne denied that any Union prisoners he saw were ever given a blanket or clothing. He described the attitude of his captors as uncaring. If a prisoner froze, that was one less Yankee to feed. The prison guards and officials, according to Browne, were "indifferent to the sufferings" of the inmates and were without sympathy or commiseration. Southern citizens who were imprisoned were treated even worse, "especially if they were poor and friendless."[21]

Some Ohio soldiers sent by General O. M. Mitchell to destroy a railroad were captured and eventually sent to Richmond. Taken at first to Libby Prison, the Ohio boys were told they would be exchanged. After only a short time they were marched, under guard, to Castle Thunder and "put in a little room upstairs, of which three sides were only weather boarded." They remained there during December and January, "without any fire, and with a very scanty supply of clothing, as they had taken all our blankets from us when we left Atlanta...." They had managed to hide two small blankets, which was all the covering that the six Ohio boys had during the worst winter months. These soldiers were listed on the prison log as "citizens," although their names were listed as soldiers together with names of company and regiments. Seven others of this group who were classified as soldiers had been tried and executed.[22]

Work Release

Early in the war, prisoners were released on parole. The Confederate War Department issued orders to General John H. Winder that a number of prisoners be released on parole to work at various jobs. Amos Hemmings, Frederick Cullen, James McLaughton, Francis T. Treanor, Peter Blair, Aaron Ankrum, William H. Maguire, Thomas Hankels, Felix Willet, John Green, and John Miller were to be offered the Oath of Allegiance, and if they swore, they were to work under the direction of Captain G. W. Alexander, assistant provost marshal for the city of Richmond.[23]

William Edwards and his daughter were also to be released on parole and assigned to work under Captain Alexander. Orders were issued for a William B. Taylor to be sent to the hospital and his brother, Jacob R. Taylor, was to be employed in that same hospital and paid, if his health would permit it. Others, suspected as spies, were to be retained as prisoners of war, at least until any information they might have would be worthless to the enemy.[24]

Care of the Prisoners

Political prisoners held at Castle Thunder and sick prisoners in the prison hospitals received boxes of medicine and hospital supplies sent to Southern officials.[25] Miss Elizabeth L. Van Lew, a woman with abolitionist sentiments, frequently visited the prisoners. Although she pretended she was crazy, in reality, she was a spy for the North. She kept a diary, and on June 21, 1862, she mentioned that Captain Alexander warned her that she had been reported "several times."[26] "Crazy Bet," as she was called, obtained permission from Confederate authorities to minister to the Union prisoners and bring food and medicine. She used those visits to gather information which she passed on to General Grant through a network of spies.[27]

Blankets and Clothing

In January of 1863, Federal Agent of Exchange Lieutenant Colonel Ludlow had written Robert Ould, his counterpart in the Confederacy, to complain that prisoners being held in Richmond and Salisbury were suffering from lack of clothing. Ould replied that the report was not true, and that he would report to Ludlow when clothing for the prisoners was received.[28] However, Ludlow's plea was successful and three weeks later Captain Alexander received four boxes of clothing for Castle Thunder prisoners, including 75 coats or jackets, 75 pairs of boots, 75 flannel shirts, 100 pairs of socks, and 75 pairs of trousers or pants. The boxes were sent by Thomas P. Turner, commander of the Confederate States Military Prison, at the request of General Winder. Winder instructed that the articles be carefully "counted and distributed as requested in Colonel Ludlow's letter to Hon. Robert Ould."[29]

In the fall of 1863, Robert Ould notified officials that supplies of blankets and clothing sent for prisoners held in Richmond would be issued according to the instructions accompanying them.[30] The Confederate government welcomed these gifts because prisoners were dying from the effects of insufficient clothing during cold weather, and hats, shoes, socks, blankets, shirts and other clothing simply were not available for the prisoners.

Sanitation

Castle Thunder was probably cleaner than most prisons. Alexander, having served on board ships in the United States Navy, would have been trained to keep everything in order and as clean as possible. He ran his prison as a captain would run a ship. Thus, the floors of Castle Thunder were washed every morning by the prisoners. Once a week the whole prison, inside and out, was whitewashed. The appearance of the facility was always neat and clean, and this attention to cleanliness helped promote the health and comfort of the prisoners.[31] The Richmond *Daily Dispatch* described Castle Thunder as "one of the neatest prisons" in the Confederacy. The floors were clean, the furniture in good order, and "everything betokens attention to small as well as grave matters."[32] A detective noted that "the prison is kept very clean — as clean as it well can be. The printed rules require this."[33]

An investigation by the Special Committee revealed that roll call was conducted every morning, and that the sick were admitted to the prison hospital. Floors were swept at least once daily, sometimes twice, and were white-washed every Saturday. Yet inmates testified that there was not enough wood in the winter, that vermin and rats were prevalent, and that they could not even go to the windows, because of the rules and restrictions, to obtain a breath of fresh air and a respite from the foul bodily odors of a large number of men confined in a closed space.[34]

Food

While prison fare was never great or overly abundant, during the latter part of October, 1863, meat was very scarce. Prison commanders reported to General Winder that no meat had been issued to them for the prisoners. Winder, in turn, informed Confederate Secretary Seddon that this was the fourth time there had been no meat for the prisoners. Winder was wary that the prisoners would revolt, saying, "No force under my command can prove adequate to the control of 13,000 hungry prisoners." Eventually an agreement was worked out under Seddon to settle the dispute between the commissary general and the quartermaster general, and the commissary general agreed to furnish rations to the prisoners.[35] It was at this point the decision was made to give the prisoners the same rations as the soldiers in the field. Furthermore, should it become impossible to feed both groups, the soldiers should have preference. During the temporary meat shortage, General Winder was told to buy beef for his prisoners which was being shipped to Richmond.[36]

George Alexander wrote Captain W. S. Winder, Assistant Adjutant General, on October 28, 1863:

> Sir: Permit me respectfully to inform you that no beef has been furnished for the use of this prison this day, and I understand from Captain Warner, assistant quartermaster, that the prospect of getting any is bad. It is almost impossible to conjecture the evils that will arise if the prisoners are not furnished in proper time. A prompt supply, even if the ration should be short, will ensure discipline and, I think, prevent violence.[37]

Several other prison commanders also complained, and were told that no meat could be supplied that day, and probably not the next day.[38]

At times when meat was available, the prisoners complained that it was "nothing but horse meat and mule meat. [It's] always after a cavalry fight of any magnitude that our rations are more liberal!" The prisoners claimed that several attempts had been made to smuggle out the bones left from their meals to Federal authorities. As one prisoner was being released, he put some of the horse bones in his carpetbag, but they were discovered by Captain Alexander, who sent the man back to his cell and charged him with attempting to "carry contraband information to the enemy."[39]

At the Congressional hearings in 1863, Caleb Herbert raised questions about the amount of food prisoners were given. Dennis Callahan, former adjutant, testified that "as far as I know, they [the prisoners] get more to eat than our [Confederate] soldiers."[40]

T. P. Sayre of Company B, 21st Illinois Volunteers, and about one-third of his company, were captured and confined at Castle Thunder from Atlanta. When they arrived, they were searched for loose change. Some of his buddies hid coins in the hem of their pants. Sayre wrote that his daily ration was a "small piece of light bread" and a piece of "mule" bread. One of his group sold his watch, valued at $10, for 15 loaves of bread. Those with whom he shared the bread promised if they lived to be released, they would repay the soldier for the watch. Years later, while living in Kansas, he and his wife were able to repay the fellow prisoner the $10.[41]

Sayre was one of the lucky ones. Weak from lack of food, he was sent to a hospital where he and 250 others were shortly exchanged. When he arrived in Camp Parole, Annapolis, he weighed on some scales and found that his weight had dropped from 195 pounds down to 125, after only three months in prison.[42]

By 1864, inflation made the price of food exorbitant. This reflected on the food available for the prisoners, citizens, and soldiers all. Federal authorities reported that flour was scarce, and if available, sold for $325 per barrel. The stalls for the sale of meat in the city market at Richmond had been reduced to two or three in number. Pork was unavailable, and the fresh meat that was obtained was bought by the Confederate Government and sold to the poorer classes at a fixed price. The meat sent to General Early and the Confederate troops was of very poor quality.[43]

During the winter of 1864–1865, the rations issued the prisoners were reduced until inmates received only "one pound of corn bread, one-third of a pound of bacon, and eight quarts of peas or ten pounds of rice to the hundred rations made into a palatable and nutritious soup." Sometimes meat was only issued five or six days during an entire month.[44]

Sutler's Store

Initially, there had been a sutler's store at the Castle where prisoners could buy food and other articles not included in their daily rations. This was abolished in July of 1864, and thereafter no supplies were "to be furnished the prisoners on private account except upon an order through the commandant of the post." This order had to be endorsed by Major Carrington, the provost marshal.[45] The prisoners had it bad under Captain Alexander, but conditions worsened after he left his post.

Religion

The Reverend J. L. Burrows, minister of the Broad Street Baptist Church, came to the prison to preach. His audience was very attentive. The sermon was from the text, "Turn ye, turn ye, for why will you die." The prisoners sang hymns. A number of visitors were also present.[46]

Mail and Boxes from Home

Mail from home was always welcome by the prisoners, and they also sent letters. One civilian, James B. Hamilton, was supposed to have been transferred from Castle Thunder to Salisbury and three letters from his wife were forwarded there. However, in December of 1863, he was returned to Richmond, but his letters which had been forwarded to Salisbury had not reached him. He urged his wife to write again and to put on the outside of the letter "Per Flag of Truce via Fortress Monroe," in care of Captain Alexander. He was sure, if she put a three-cent stamp on it, it would be delivered to him.[47]

A. D. Richardson believed he fared better in Castle Thunder than in Libby Prison. At the Castle, the officers "did not cast any of those gratuitous indignities upon prisoners, to which they were subjected at the latter place." He also received several boxes of clothing, provisions, and books from home. However, when he was moved to Salisbury, "one box was broken into and stolen with the most systematic regularity."[48]

All mail had to pass through the office of Brigadier General John Winder. Many letters were not forwarded, as can be seen in those that have been microfilmed from the files of the Department of Henrico.

Daily Routine

The daily routine of the prisoners at Castle Thunder and other prisons in the Confederacy, as well as those in the North, was repetitive and monotonous. There was roll call early in the morning, and then guards opened the doors and announced breakfast. Inmates were permitted to wash and dress before going to the mess hall for breakfast. Sick call was at 9 A.M. After lunch, prisoners were allowed 30 minutes for exercise in the yard. This was a time prisoners looked forward to where they could breathe fresh air and talk with other prisoners. Supper was also served in the mess room. At night, just before dark, the guards called the roll again. Taps was played to signal lights out. Between these standard events, prisoners were on their own and had to find means to occupy their time to relieve boredom.[49]

Entertainment

In the summer of 1864, after Captain Alexander was no longer commandant at Castle Thunder, a pugilistic match was held. The two combatants were best friends, but one wore his hair cropped short and the other had "long matty locks." The long hair put that fighter at a disadvantage, and after his opponent had pulled out great hunks of his hair by the roots, the long-haired fighter called quits until he could get his hair cut short. The onlookers wagered bits of their rations or pieces of tobacco on the outcome of this and other contests.[50]

Prisoners played chess, cards, dice and other games such as whist or backgammon.[51] They wrote letters to loved ones at home, and to General Winder for release, or at least a hearing, or for a transfer to the Navy. Michael C. Burns wanted to join the navy, so he wrote asking General Winder for a recommendation to the Secretary of the Navy.[52]

Prisoners read newspapers, the *Bible*, and other books. They debated current issues and held mock trials. They sang songs. They smoked, told stories, and played games of chance.[53]

Legal Representation

In 1863, John Hussey reported that there were half a dozen sutlers and sutler's clerks confined at Castle Thunder. This group hired Attorney Humphrey Marshal to obtain their release. He was successful, except for getting the consent of Mr. Ould. Ould proposed to let the sutlers go in exchange for citizens being held by the Federals.[54]

Visitors from the North

The commandant of the Old Capitol Prison in Washington, D.C., a Mr. Wood, visited Castle Thunder accompanied by Captain Cashmeyer of the provost guard. Captain Alexander received the visitors and provided a tour of the prison himself. Wood was pleased by the "evidences of cleanliness, comfort, and discipline" at Castle Thunder. Wood attempted to negotiate an exchange of all State prisoners. During the tour, one of the Irish prisoners asked Wood if he "would not like to have Capt. Alexander." Wood replied, with a laugh, that "they had had the Captain once, but could not keep him."[55]

Inmates Hold Their Own Court

There was danger inside the prison from the prisoners themselves. D. J. Bule, of Company H, 3rd North Carolina, was incarcerated for being "drunk and disorderly." His fellow prisoners relieved him of his "hat, pistol, and thirty dollars." He managed to save sixty dollars, because he had fastened it to the pocket of an inside shirt. He wisely handed that sixty dollars over to the commandant to keep until he would be released when he was sober.[56]

After Alexander left, the prisoners established their own court to try those caught stealing. It was not a mock court, but a regular proceeding conducted as a court outside the prison would be. If a prisoner was convicted of stealing, he had to undergo punishment by being whipped on his bare back. As in a civil court, where fines are sometimes substituted for imprisonment, those who were financially able could avoid the law by "treating the court and the jury."[57]

Right to A Speedy Trial

By the end of 1862, Castle Thunder was famous as the "headquarters of the offenders throughout the Confederacy." Although many who were inmates undoubtedly deserved sympathy, the majority of the prisoners are "doubtless justly detained." The Richmond *Whig* cited the case of the poor man who was carrying a keg of brandy to a friend for a Christmas gift when he had been arrested and sent to Castle Thunder. The newspaper thought that such persons should have an opportunity to state their case and obtain their liberty as soon as possible. In other areas, the paper reported that the hospital at Castle Thunder, under Dr. Coggins, was in "excellent order," and that the sick were well attended to.[58]

False Claims

A prisoner named Andrew Johnson complained that he had been subject to "terrible treatment." There was a great deal of correspondence between Confederate and Federal officials concerning this prisoner, and a letter from Brigadier General S. A. Meredith, Commissioner for Exchange at Fort Monroe, was forwarded to Captain Alexander. Alexander replied that the "only complaint Johnson makes is that his diet is not as good as he desires." Robert Ould, Agent of Exchange also investigated and reported that, after a diligent inquiry, he could find no basis for the charge that Johnson's treatment had been horrible, or that he had been treated any differently from the other prisoners.[59]

In early summer of 1863, Castle Thunder housed about 600 prisoners. Renovations were undertaken which improved the comfort as well as the "commodious appearance."[60]

One of the improvements was the large plaza in which the prisoners could exercise and get a breath of fresh air. The plaza had already been conducive to "good health and discipline."[61]

Libby Prison Newspaper Describes Castle Thunder

Libby Prison had its own newspaper, *The Libby Chronicle*. Editor-in-chief Louis N. Beaudry was chaplain of the Fifty New York Volunteer Cavalry. The *Chronicle* described life in Libby, and also had news from Castle Thunder. In Volume I, No. 2, someone wrote a lengthy poem about Castle Thunder. It describes the place and its prisoners:

CASTLE THUNDER

PART I

On Cary street, in Richmond, there is a ongrel den
Of thieves, sneaks and cowards mixed up with gentlemen.
Oh what a living shame to huddle in together
Men and beasts, wild and tame, like birds of every feather!
The Reb authorities scared up this greatest wonder,
Made it a prison, and named it Castle Thunder.
Here they tumble in characters of every hue,
Reprobates steeped in sin with the Christian and the Jew.

Conscripts by the dozen, at daylight and after dark,
Come pouring in the Castle, like animals in the ark;
Some are small, some are great, some show pluck, some white liver,
Some from Mississippi State and "Goobers" from Tar river.
Substitutes and deserters come in sorry plight,
And sub-gents also are here quartered for the night.
Blockade runners are here shut up, they say, for a warning,
But seldom leave as promised, early the next morning
While on Potomac's banks both parties try to nab 'em,
If they escape the Yanks, Old Jeff is sure to grab 'em.

So-called spies are castled here, who think it real hard luck,
They are all from Yankeedom, excepting one Kennuck
Disloyalists are here, and one for being a guide
They boys called "Doodlebug," for he piloted Burnside.
Here's an oyster man, who the officers discover,
Is Union on the York, but Secesh on James River.
Part first tells you where the Castle is, and who are there,
And part second will disclose the manner of our fare.

PART II

We've a dozen rooms or more, and in some two or three,
The "boys" wear handcuffs, balls and chains, Confederate jewelry;
Some rest on cots, on boards, with blankets, some without them,
And when they get asleep the big bugs often rout them;
They never sleep in peace, though ever so much drowsy,
The vermin are so big the lice themselves are lousy.

We have eighteen kinds of food, though 'twill stagger your belief,
Because we have bread, beef and soup, then bread, soup and beef;
They we sep'rate around with 'bout twenty in a group,
And thus we get beef, soup and bread, and beef, bread and soup;
For dessert we obtain, though it costs us nary red,
Soup, bread and beef (count it well) and beef, soup and bread.

The bread we daily get is of a very good sort.
True, it's the staff of life, but our staff is rather short.
Our beef's so lean and dry, that, swallowing, it will bound back,
Unless are recollect afore to grease the hollow track.

It is too tough and strong for our noses or our knives,
The cattle were so poor and thin, were killed to save their lives.
The hides are made up into shoes, the sinews into strings,
The marrow into soup and the bones in pretty rings.
Our soup is much too weak to please a very high liver,
'Tis made of beans, bugs and rice with extract of James River.

Now, I've told you what we eat, whether we're well or sick,
What we drink is never strong, though sometimes rather thick.
We rarely drink river water, except to save from death,
And then for want of whiskey we smell Reb, officer's breath.
Meat and drink are now so scarce as to raise a serious doubt,
Whether the Confederacy is not about played out.
Part one and two you have heard, and now in division third,
I will say a word about the way we are officered.

PART III

Military officers of the very meanest stuff,
For every local post, are considered good enough
In officering Richmond they varied not this general rule,
So we've a drunkard, a tyrant, a coward or a fool.
It is plainly to be noticed that in a little while,
When Satan scoops his jewels up, Richmond will give a pile.

At the head of Richmond post they've placed a Marylander,
Lo! Like the devil in regions lost, there's General Winder.
He snaps and snarls, he rips and swears, whether sober or tight,
The old villain's heart is as black as his head is white.
All through this vicinity they hate him as hard as they can,
Nor ever slander him with epithet of decent man.
However mean, he's a patriot, let that be understood,
For when he left the Yankee land, 'twas for that country's good.

We come to Major Griswold, who is our Provost Marshal,
He's a little prejudiced which makes him rather partial.
But when compared to Winder, he seems no virtue to lack,
As green or blue is almost white by the side of jet black.

And there's judge Baster who also is a queer old case,
He has so large a centre he can hardly change his base.
He says whiskey's a dangerous thing to have about the town,
So with all his might and main he's for putting whiskey down.
Whiskey is fifty cents a drink, and of the meanest sort,
The Judge to get his money's worth swallows it by the quart.
I will slyly tell you, boys, (if your money you begrudge),
Just how to get your whiskey, cheap, step up and tap the Judge.

In the door of the Castle like a stopple in a jug,
To shut the prison's mouth they've stuck a "Baltimore plug;"
It's Captain Alexander who is so cross and spunky,
He's certainly not fit to command an oyster pungy.
The Captain is such a case, boys, as may be often seen,
Who thinks he's very smart, but is invisible green;
He is a thundering blower, but would not dare to fight,
As dogs that bark the loudest are seldom known to bite.
Yet he has streaks of good as well as mean, mixed for relief,
The first are scarce and thin like fat in Confederate beef.

7. Life Within the Castle: The Dark Side

He also came from Maryland, mean as Nick can make him,
The reason we keep him is because the devil won't take him.

Allen is a smooth old rat, this is truthfully said,
He shines with black from boots to hat, his face shines with red;
He pours down whiskey double-quick, there is no doubt of that,
Sometimes he thinks he's sick, but it's a brick in his hat.
Old Allen is a villain of the very darkest stripe;
He'll go home to purgat'ry even before he's ripe;
If he does not blow off steam and soon shut down the brakes,
In a dream delirious he'll find his boots are full of snakes.
He has an oily tongue and face full of deceit and evil,
Should Old Nick miss that scape-grace, there's no need of a devil.

Private.

8

Spies, Traitors, and Hostages

"As out of place as a Presbyterian in Hell."
— *Mark Twain, from* Albert Bigelow Paine

Castle Thunder served as a place of confinement for a variety of prisoners — civilian men and women, both black and white, held on suspicion of treason, espionage, or for a variety of crimes; Confederate deserters; Confederate soldiers convicted of any breach of military law; and sometimes Union deserters, and Union soldiers and officers captured in battle. When Libby Prison was full, Yankee prisoners of war were sent to Castle Thunder and housed in some of the lower rooms.[1]

In June of 1863, after the battle of Chancellorsville, there were 600 prisoners being held at Castle Thunder. Two hundred were described as "desperate characters, two hundred disloyal men from various parts of the State, including North Carolina 'buffaloes' and runaway negroes; one hundred and thirty Confederate soldiers under sentence of court martial; and the rest deserters, stragglers, etc."[2]

Spies

Brigadier General William Jackson Palmer of the 15th Pennsylvania Cavalry (the Anderson Cavalry) was later famous for his work in establishing the Denver and Rio Grande Railroad. When the Maryland Campaign began, the authorities in Pennsylvania feared an invasion. Governor Andrew Curtain telegraphed the War Department and asked that the Anderson Cavalry be sent to patrol the Pennsylvania-Maryland border. A detachment of 250 men were sent to the area and were engaged in several skirmishes with Confederate forces shortly before the battles in Maryland at South Mountain and Sharpsburg (Antietam) in mid–September of 1862. After the battle of Sharpsburg, Palmer, then a captain, volunteered to cross the river to gain information about troop movement.[3]

On an information-gathering mission for General McClellan, Palmer was captured within Confederate lines in civilian clothes. An officer caught in civilian clothes behind enemy lines would be treated as a spy and executed. In order to survive, Palmer gave his name as "W. J. Peters," and claimed to be a mine owner on an inspection trip. He was arrested, however, and taken to Castle Thunder and placed in a large room with 200–300 other prisoners. The tobacco presses still remained in the room. Palmer remembered that there were "twenty professional Union spies" in the same room with him. Some were Northern men, others were foreigners. The spies had been captured in Virginia, Tennessee, and Texas. Those engaged in espionage did so for a variety of reasons: some purely for patriotism, others for adventure, and some for monetary gain.[4]

While Palmer was confined at Castle Thunder, new prisoners often recognized him. He lived in fear that someone would report him, and he would be executed as a spy. However, after a few months, Palmer/Peters was exchanged for a man named "White," also a civilian political prisoner being held in a northern prison. Soon, Palmer had rejoined his regiment and returned to the task of rehabilitating the unit and honing its military efficiency. This was accomplished through strict drill and discipline, and instruction. A few officers were unhappy with the new routine, and Palmer accepted their resignations.[5]

An elaborate account of Palmer's capture and his confinement in Castle Thunder appeared in 1867 in *Harper's New Monthly Magazine*. The article does not mention Palmer's name, and uses fictional names for the other characters. However, it is believed to be basically an accurate account, gleaned from Palmer himself after the war was over.[6]

Alfonzo C. Webster

Christened Charles W. Brown at his birth in Maine, this 23-year-old man enlisted as a first lieutenant in the 9th Pennsylvania Cavalry on October 3, 1861. He tried to get a number of his fellow soldiers to go with him to Boston to raise a new company. For his efforts, he was court martialed and resigned. However, he followed his regiment when they moved to Louisville, and on board the ship attempted to get some of the soldiers to join him. When the boat docked at Louisville, Webster (Brown) was arrested and charged with "inciting soldiers to desert." He escaped, and became a private in the Confederacy's 8th Virginia Infantry. In March of 1862, Webster disappeared. He resurfaced soon and was joined by a young Confederate, Charles Cooper. The pair ran mail across the lines. Webster's activities were noted by the Alan Pinkerton Detective Agency, and his name put on their list of spies.[7]

While in Waterford, Virginia, Webster was recruited by Captain Samuel C. Means for Means' Loudon Rangers, a Union cavalry unit. Webster was described as rather tall, 5 feet, 10 inches, and he weighed 180 pounds. He was very proficient with a saber, pistol and carbine, the result of military training. He was made drillmaster for the unit, and charged with training new recruits during July of 1862.[8]

Webster and two of his company were sent to capture Confederate Captain James Richard Simpson at his home. Simpson, of the 8th Virginia Cavalry, was in Loudon County on a recruiting mission. When Webster called Simpson to come out of his house, the Confederate ran out the back door. Webster tracked him down and killed him, probably in an attempt to prevent him from telling of Webster's former service for the Confederacy.[9]

In August, Mean's Rangers were engaged in a battle with the 35th Virginia Cavalry and some of them, including Webster, were trapped in the Waterford Baptist Church. Webster surrendered to Confederates. He and several other Federal officers were released on parole, after surrendering their weapons and horses.[10]

While Means was on sick leave, Webster took charge, held elections, and had himself elected first lieutenant. When Means returned, he declared the election invalid, and to get rid of Webster, signed an order for him to recruit his own company. Governor Francis Pierpont of West Virginia signed an order to establish the Loudon Rangers, 3rd Cavalry Regiment of Virginia Volunteers, with Webster as captain. During this time, Webster met and then married Alice Downey, daughter of the former speaker of the Virginia House of Delegates. The announcement of their wedding on October 20, 1862, listed the groom as "Lt. Alphonso E. Webster, 2nd Massachusetts Volunteers."[11]

Events then took a turn for the worse. Early in December, Webster was arrested in Georgetown for stealing horses and was put in the Old Capitol Prison in Washington. He was released on a technicality. Because the horses had been taken in Virginia, the Washington judge had no jurisdiction there. He left Washington determined to find Means and punish him, because he believed Means was behind his arrest. Still wearing a blue Federal uniform, Webster teamed up with his friend Charles Cooper and they, with several other Confederates, went to the camp of Major Elijah V. White and his 35th Virginia Cavalry. Webster had a plan to use White's men to raid the camp of the Federal Captain Means. However, when Major White appeared, he went into a rage and ordered Webster bound and gagged. White believed Webster was there to kill him.[12]

Webster was sent to Richmond as a "dangerous criminal," and put in Castle Thunder. Confederate officials could not determine whether to charge Webster with being a deserter or of being a spy, or for the murder of Captain Simpson. On February 25, Secretary of War Seddon ruled that Webster should be tried by a military court. Confederate Captain James Wampler of the 8th Virginia who had known Webster, wrote: "I can provide evidence in the persons of Major White and my wife that said Webster is a spy and has operated on both sides — the federal and confederate from Mississippi to Virginia. He is a villain and too dangerous a character to let go."[13]

As soon as Webster had been put in Castle Thunder, he began planning to escape. On Christmas Eve he led a group in an aborted escape attempt. He tried again the next night, but found that armed guards were positioned to shoot any escapees. After that he was put in irons, but on March 9, 1863, he unlocked his irons with a key carved from bone. This attempt failed. Again on March 27, while handcuffed and under special guard, he jumped from his bed to a window and was about to exit. A guard took aim but his gun misfired, and Webster fled out the window to the shed roof. He jumped 15 feet to the ground below, and the impact broke both his ankles. He hobbled away, despite being shot at by the guards.[14]

The court martial began March 11, 1863, and by March 26, Webster was found guilty of the murder of Captain Simpson and of John Jones of Hillsborough, of parole violation, and of horse stealing. He was sentenced to hang on April 3. In a last effort to save himself, Webster appealed to President Davis. Davis granted the condemned man a few days more, and rescheduled the hanging for April 10. He had to be taken to the hanging strapped in a chair because his ankles had not healed properly for him to stand.[15]

Dressed in his Federal uniform, he met his death with composure. An unusual man, the comments from those who knew Webster were as diverse and contradictory as his life. Captain Alexander, Castle Thunder's commandant, declared that Webster was "a master fiend." Fellow ranger Briscoe Goodhart knew Webster as an "efficient drillmaster" and "brave and meritorious officer." Goodhart said that "nothing was too risky for him." Even Captain Means, when he wrote to Webster's father, admitted that the condemned man was "as brave a soldier as ever faced an enemy." Another who knew him called him the "daring Webster," and declared that he doubted if "in the annals of rascality a more finished character than Webster ever had a place."

The man was mysterious then and now. While two Confederate regimental histories have much to say about Webster, he never appeared on the official rolls of the Loudon Rangers. There are at least 25 documents about Webster in the Confederate records, but the Federal records are blank — "There is no record of the service of this soldier."[16]

Prisoners from the Andrews Railroad Raid (The Great Locomotive Chase)[17]

Six of the original 22 Union soldiers involved in the "Great Locomotive Chase" were held in Castle Thunder. On April 22, 1862, the group of Federal soldiers, led by Mr. James G. Andrews, a citizen of Kentucky, penetrated deep into Confederate territory in an attempt to cut the rail line between Marietta, Georgia, and Chattanooga, Tennessee. All the men had been selected for their "courage and discretion."[18] At Kenesaw, Georgia, the Union soldiers stole the engine of a train, the *General,* and headed north. Along they way, they stopped frequently to cut telegraph lines and pile cross ties on the track. They continued to Chattanooga while Confederates pursued them in the *Texas.* After nearly 90 miles, the stolen engine ran out of fuel, and the raiders were captured. Andrews, the leader, and seven others were executed in Atlanta.[19]

After an escape attempt by the remaining 14, six were recaptured and taken to Castle Thunder. They were Corporal William Pittenger, Private Jacob Parrot, Private Robert Buffum, Corporal William H. Reddick, Private William Bensinger, and Elihu

Mason.[20] The six were eventually paroled. They became the first to receive the Congressional Medal of Honor.[21]

Alien Enemies

James B. Hamilton (1830–1864) was born in Nicholas County, Virginia, but moved with his family to Hawk's Nest on the New River in Fayette County, Virginia. His father, Thomas B. Hamilton, was a lawyer. Educated at Virginia Military Institute, Hamilton was better suited for an academic career, and he built his own school house. He acquired wealth by operating a general store, through real estate, and by his marriage into a prominent family. When the war began, Hamilton volunteered to help train the Mt. Cove Guards. Eventually, the recruits he drilled became part of the First Kanawaha. After the passage of the "alien enemies" act in 1862, the citizens of Fayette County were in danger of arrest from both sides. Confederates had arrested 25 Fayette County civilians, and the Union had arrested 15. Forced to swear loyalty to one side or the other, Hamilton chose the Union. He was arrested in July of 1863 by scouts from General Echols' brigade, one week after the Confederate defeat at Gettysburg. After a hearing before a military commissioner, Hamilton was ordered to be "confined as a conscript refusing to serve and as a traitorous citizen." As an "alien enemy" and a disloyal citizen, all efforts to obtain Hamilton's release failed. Virginia Governor Smith ruled on September 3, 1864, that Hamilton should not be released, and 20 days later, James Hamilton died in Salisbury Prison.[22]

His arrest was the result of a "complaint of a refugee, through malice, on false charges," charges which Hamilton was given no opportunity to disprove.[23] He fared very well in Castle Thunder, but died of typhoid in September of 1864 after being sent to Salisbury Prison.[24]

Union Soldiers and Officers

Major Thomas Jefferson Jordan, of the 9th Pennsylvania Cavalry, was transferred from Libby Prison to Castle Thunder. The citizens of Sparta, Tennessee, charged that Jordan had allowed his men to commit atrocities and outrages. Jordan denied the charges and stated that he was only in the area once, and that was when he was chasing Confederate John Hunt Morgan about eight miles beyond Sparta. Jordan declared he was very strict in his discipline of his men, and no other reports of any cruelty or outrages had been reported. That was supported by Major G. B. Brown of the 9th Pennsylvania Calvary, who wrote on Jordan's behalf.[25]

When General John Hunt Morgan's men attacked the Federals near Tompkinsville, Kentucky, on July 9, 1862, Jordan, his horse wounded, was captured. Jordan refused a parole from Morgan, and declared that the Confederate general was not an officer, but only a marauder. Thus, Jordan gained an enemy.[26]

Jordan was promoted to Colonel on January 13, 1863, and Brevette Brigadier General on February 25, 1865. He survived the war and died in 1895.[27]

Female Prisoners

Hundreds of women were held at Castle Thunder on suspicion or conviction of treason, disloyalty, contributing to the demoralization of the soldiers, and a number of other offenses. Several women were arrested and charged with being spies because they were caught wearing men's clothing. The courts occasionally convicted women of disloyal or treasonable activity and ordered them confined to Castle Thunder for long periods.[28]

During one of the times when the town of Winchester, Virginia, fell into Confederate hands, Confederate officers arrested many women and children as Union sympathizers. In the latter days of June 1863, 38 women and children were sent to Castle Thunder from Winchester for being connected to the Union army in some capacity, or because they were the wives and children of Union officers.[29]

None of the women held at Castle Thunder ever escaped, and no woman was executed.[30] While Alexander was in charge there, the female prisoners were turned over to him. He was, reportedly, fond of "loose women." Whether he was or not, one male prisoner used that to accuse the Captain in a letter which was published in the New York *Herald*.

> [Alexander's] whole night is spent in drinking, gambling, etc., in which women are allowed to participate. After each of these bacchanalian revels, if the Captain has been successful, he is all smiles and liberality; if he has on the other hand, been unfortunate — which it is usually his luck to be — he is as profane and brutal as a pirate, and orders half a dozen niggers flogged, and twice as many prisoners tied up by the thumbs, or bucked and gagged, and managed in the course of a few hours to outrage every inmate of the Castle.[31]

Mary and Molly Bell, according to the diary of Edmund Ruffin, were sisters from southwestern Virginia who had served for two years in the Confederate Army dressed in male attire. One reached the rank of corporal and the other that of sergeant. When their true sex was discovered, the girls were confined to Castle Thunder until they could be returned to their relatives.[32]

Millie Bean was another female soldier who had served in the 47th North Carolina for over two years before she was discovered[33]

Laura J. Johnson arrived somewhat dazed in the city of Richmond. When she was stopped by guards at the Mayo Bridge, she told them an almost unbelievable story of how she had followed her fiancé from Raleigh, North Carolina. Along the way, she had been attacked. Laura did not have a pass and did not convince the guards, so they took her to Castle Thunder. When her situation became known, she was offered bed and board by officials, who also gave her clothing and enough money for her return trip home.[34]

Elizabeth Needham of Lynchburg was another female held in Castle Thunder as a suspicious person.[35] She was placed in Castle Thunder on September 4, 1862.[36]

Loreta Janeta Velazquez (alias Lt. Harry T. Buford/alias Mrs. Alice Williams) was a Cuban widow of a Confederate soldier. She reportedly donned a Confederate uniform and, in the guise of Lieutenant Harry T. Buford, organized a Confederate infantry unit called the Arkansas Grays. While in Richmond, General Winder became suspicious of her, and she was called to give an account of herself. She was arrested "on the charge of being a woman in disguise, and supposedly a Federal spy, and was conducted to Castle Thunder to reflect upon the mutabilities of fortune" until she could come up with a plausible explanation.[37] Mrs. Velazquez liked Captain Alexander, and described him as a gentleman "who, ever since [making] his acquaintance" by being placed in his custody, she had been "proud to number [him] among [her] best and most highly-esteemed friends."[38]

In her autobiography, Loreta stated that both "Major" Alexander and his "lovely wife" showed "the greatest interest in me, and they treated me with such kindness and consideration that I was induced to tell them exactly who I was, what my purposes were in assuming the male garb, what adventures I had passed through, and what my aspirations were for the future." The Alexanders believed her story. However, both Alexander and his wife were "shocked" at the "idea of a woman dressing herself" as a man and "attempting to play the part of a soldier."[39] Alexander not only arranged for her to be released, but also highly recommended her to General Winder, so much so that Winder offered her a job in the Confederate Secret Service. His only requirement was that she dress as a woman. She agreed, although reluctantly, and embarked on a new career as a Confederate spy known as "Mrs. Alice Williams."[40] Her memoirs, published in *The Woman in Battle* in 1876, were discounted by scholars, who claim the work is entirely fiction. Modern historian Richard Hill, in *Patriots in Disguise: Women Warriors of the Civil War*, published in 1993, analyzed whether her claims were accurate history or fictionalized.[41]

Captain Alexander was quoted as saying that Mrs. Velazquez "was particularly distinguished for her devotion to the cause, for which she made many sacrifices. She also was brave, noble and generous in disposition, ready at times to do anything in her power for the Confederacy."[42] A Richmond paper noted on July 16, 1863, that "Lt. Buford, otherwise Mrs. Alice Williams," who had been masquerading as a female lieutenant, had been released from Castle Thunder and was going South to Atlanta, Georgia. She was described as a "brave but eccentric woman," who was expected to take part in the fighting in Jackson, Mississippi. She was reported to have already taken part in battles in Kentucky and Mississippi, and was wounded at Shiloh.[43]

Charlotte Gilman was incarcerated in Castle Thunder on a charge of counterfeiting. Charlotte had been confined in both Castle Godwin and Castle Thunder for a period of 12 months. She spoke highly of Captain Alexander at the Confederate Congressional hearings, and said, "All the ladies there spoke of Captain Alexander in the highest terms. All like him." Charlotte had received special consideration from Alexander, and he testified that he had gone to General Winder and obtained an order for her "washing." Charlotte agreed with that, and stated that he had also let her "go out very often."[44]

Mary Lee was confined in Castle Thunder for disloyalty. While there, she gave birth to a baby girl, who she named Castellina Thunder Lee.[45]

Anna Scott, a milliner, was arrested at Leesburg by the order of Brigadier General Hill in March of 1862.[46] She was accused of being a spy. She was held for several months in Castle Godwin before being sent north into Union territory.[47]

Margaret Underwood of Washington, D.C., had a sweetheart in the Confederate army. She could not bear to be separated from him, so she enlisted as a "substitute" in her beau's regiment. Disguised as a Confederate soldier, she served for some time. However, when she was finally discovered, because she was from the North, she was charged with espionage, and her loyalty and character were questioned. She spent six months in Castle Thunder before being released.[48]

Dr. Mary Edwards Walker[49] was one of the most unusual female prisoners every confined at Castle Thunder. Dr. Walker was awarded the Congressional Medal of Honor on the recommendation of General William T. Sherman and George H. Thomas. In April of 1864, Walker, who was also a doctor and assistant surgeon for the 52nd Ohio Infantry, encountered a group of Confederate soldiers at Tunnel Hill in Georgia led by General Daniel Harvey Hill. She was taken prisoner and conveyed, in full military uniform, to Richmond.[50] Dr. Walker was sent to the female ward at Castle Thunder, since Libby Prison had no facilities to accommodate females.[51]

Dressed in full male costume with the addition of a gypsy hat, her appearance on the streets of Richmond on April 21, 1864, created quite a stir. Her outfit consisted of black pants and a black or dark "talma or paletot." A Richmond paper also described her as "ugly and skinny," and "above thirty years of age."[52]

Her uniform consisted of wearing trousers under her skirt and a man's uniform jacket. Dr. Walker was ridiculed in the Richmond papers because of her unconventional form of dress and her occupation.

> Miss Doctress, Miscegenation, Philosophical Walker, who has so long ensconced herself very quietly in Castle Thunder, has loomed into activity again. Recently [Walker] got mad, pitched into several of her room-mates in long clothes, and tore out handfuls of auburn hair from the head of one of them. Then she proclaimed secession, and went into another apartment, where she is now lady and lioness of all she surveys. Sometimes she exhibits herself in costume on the balcony of the Castle, or walks in the garden below by permission of the urbane commandant of the post, Captain Richardson. Her miscegenation suit is getting rusty, and she thinks it hard, very hard, that she is not allowed to go home. She is very fond of listening to the thunder thuds of Papa Grant's pop-guns below, and when they sound, her favorite song is "The Camels are coming, hie, oh, hie oh," &. It is said she has a Yankee Major lover among the prisoners at the Libby Prison, which is one square below the castle, and within easy signal range.[53]

By June 10, 1864, the newspapers reported that Walker was "very tired of her captivity in Castle Thunder. She wants to go home...."[54] She was allowed a private room and given extra privileges, which included being allowed to stroll outside on the streets of Richmond. She seemed to enjoy the attention she generated by her unwomanly mode of dress.[55] In 1982 the United States Post Office issued a commemorative stamp with her likeness.[56]

Mrs. Timothy Webster (Hattie H. Lawton) was a clever female spy. Her supposed "husband" Timothy Webster was a detective for the Pinkerton Agency, who had been caught in Richmond and charged with spying. He was hung on April 29, 1862.[57] Mrs. Webster was still in Castle Thunder in October of that year when she wrote President Jefferson Davis pleading to be released.[58] Mrs. Webster was not Webster's wife, but in reality she was Hattie H. Lawton, alias Hattie Lewis Lawton, a member of Pinkerton's Female Detective Bureau.[59] Mrs. Webster's plea to Davis was successful and she was finally exchanged for a Union soldier. Afterwards, she disappeared without a trace,[60] and probably assumed another identity.

Elizabeth Van Lew visited Mrs. Webster after Timothy Webster was hung. She noted that he had been convicted on the testimony of Scully and Pryce. Elizabeth "Crazy Bet" went to the prison to stay with the woman who was believed to be Webster's wife. While Elizabeth Van Lew was at the prison, the body of Timothy Webster was brought back, and Captain Alexander invited them to see it. She described the woman who was really another spy as a "poor agonized creature" who "never forgot the heartless murder."[61]

Eleven unidentified Yankee women were captured in the summer of 1863 at Winchester, Virginia. According to the Richmond *Dispatch* of June 26, 1863, they were taken to Richmond and imprisoned in Castle Thunder. Secretary of War Edwin M. Stanton was concerned about them and began immediately to attempt to gain their release. He contacted Colonel William H. Ludlow at Fortress Monroe and asked him to ascertain the validity of the report.[62] Ludlow replied that it would take several days to obtain a reply from Richmond by a flag-of-truce boat.[63] Stanton suggested to Major Turner at Annapolis that it might "become necessary to take hostages for their safe return."[64] Several days later, Stanton learned from Colonel Ludlow that a total of 47 Union women and children had been captured and taken to Richmond.[65] These female prisoners were fortunate and were soon removed to Washington, where they were lodged in the United States Hotel.[66]

Sometimes, the women who followed the armies, or "camp followers," were placed in Castle Thunder, where a whole section was devoted

> to the detention of a number of depraved and abandoned women, to prevent their following the army and contributing by their pestilential presence to the destruction of the morale of the soldiers. Several of them are yet good looking and may at one time have been beautiful. It has been found necessary to keep them in constant confinement, as once at liberty they follow and hover in the tract of an army like carrion crows that snuff a field of slaughter.[67]

By the end of the war, over 100 women had been confined at some point in Castle Thunder.

Slaves Held in Castle Thunder

In the summer of 1863, there were 70 slaves confined at Castle Thunder. Sixty-five had been captured by Stewart on the Pennsylvania border.[68] A list of their names and the names of their masters was published in the Richmond *Sentinel*. The slave population included both males and females, young and old.[69] As a result of the list of names being published, several Southern gentlemen came forward and recovered their "property." Those who were released into the custody of their masters at Castle Thunder were: Samuel Chinn, slave of C. Brown; Richard Poindexter, slave of Robert Goodman; Jas. Sigal, slave of Benj. Temple; Walter Wiley, slave of Dr. Harding. Some of the slaves claimed to be free, but were recognized and reclaimed by their masters. They were John Anderson, John Phoenix, James Ashton, John Jones, Jim Bailey, Thos. Lemkens, and W. H. Washington.[70]

9

General Hospital No. 13, "The Lunatic Hospital"

"The place where optimism most flourishes is the lunatic asylum."
— *Havelock Ellis,* Impressions and Comments, series 3

Alexander Establishes Hospital

Because the prison population was more susceptible to the same diseases that affected the general population, Captain Alexander established a hospital at the prison, and his wife Susan was placed in charge of the patients. Diarrhea, dysentery, typhoid, pneumonia, and smallpox all swept like wildfire through the prisons of Richmond. It is believed that Alexander paid for the establishment of the hospital but was never reimbursed for his expenses.[1]

The Alexander Hospital was established prior to June of 1862. On June 26, 1862, Mr. Ogden, the manager of the entertainment theater known as the "Varieties," gave Captain Alexander the sum of fifty dollars to be used for the benefit of the sick and wounded patients in the Alexander Hospital.[2] The hospital was located somewhere on Main Street, and was a prison hospital. The 25 patients at the Alexander Hospital were transferred to Castle Godwin on August 8, 1862.[3] This was before Castle Thunder was opened, while Alexander was in charge at Castle Godwin. After he was placed in charge of Castle Thunder, Alexander maintained a hospital there as well.

Captain Alexander did not want to give up his hospital, because it was too much trouble to cart patients back and forth to the Libby Prison hospital. After the report by Major Carrington, the hospital was "revived," and Dr. W. W. Coggin put in charge. The area used for the hospital was the upper story of the building, and it was to have full ventilation. The area was also isolated from the noise of the prisoners below. Cots for 50 patients were prepared, as were separate apartments for convalescing patients, a kitchen and a druggist.[4]

General Hospital No. 13

General Hospital No. 13 was also known as Castle Thunder Hospital, Prison Hospital, or the Lunatic Hospital. The former tobacco factory of Christian and Lea was taken over in the spring of 1862 for this hospital. Located on the east side of 20th Street, between Main and Franklin Streets, the present address is 21–23 North 20th Street. The factory was a four-story, brick structure, with a flat roof.[5] There were many windows in this building, as can be seen in a photograph taken from Church Hill in Richmond.[6]

It served adequately as a hospital for sick prisoners from Castle Thunder and those with mental disorders. At first, the mental patients were kept at Castle Thunder, which could house 50 patients. Later, they were moved to General Hospital No. 13 with the other patients.[7]

General Hospital No. 13 could hold 150 patients. Thirty persons were employed to care for them, with Dr. W. W. Coggin as the surgeon-in-charge.[8] At some point during its operation, William D. Hoyt was the surgeon-in-charge, assisted by E. L. Carter, and R. C. Carroll.[9]

Early in the war the Confederate Congress established a "hospital ration" in order to give soldiers nourishing food. The surgeon-in-charge was authorized to buy rations outside of Richmond at a lower price, and have them delivered by train. This not only saved money but saved the resources of Richmond from depletion. As inflation soared, Congress increased money for the hospital ration in proportion.[10]

Generally, inmates at Castle Thunder's hospital never suffered for want of food, but frequently medical supplies were depleted. The hospital had adequate funds to buy needed flour, meal, rice, sugar, and salt. Seldom was beef unavailable. When it was in short supply, salt pork was used as a substitute.[11]

An inspection was made of the hospitals in Richmond on October 3, 1862, by Surgeon William A. Carrington. At Castle Thunder the doctor found there were 70 patients housed in a garret room, more than double the optimal capacity of 32 patients. The room was 40 by 80 feet, with a low ceiling, and "very imperfect ventilation." There was no bathroom, linen room or hospital clothing for the patients. The beds and bedding "were filthy & the clothing & persons of the patients in the same condition." The patient population consisted mostly of "stragglers" and privates with "irregular furloughs" who had been arrested for desertion. The food served the sick was the same as that served to the other patients. Carrington reported that there was no medical officer, but he was told that Dr. Hammond was under contract to visit daily. The hospital steward was also an officer of the prison who had been detailed by Captain G. W. Alexander. Carrington instructed that these patients be removed to the Libby Prison Hospital, which was now "being whitewashed" in preparation for their arrival. He recommended that the patients be removed to General Hospital No.

10

Escape Attempts

"So every bondsman in his own hand bears the power to cancel his captivity."
—*William Shakespeare,* Julius Caesar

Both civilians and soldiers, men and women, were arrested and held for extended periods in Castle Thunder. Some inmates faced long-term incarceration or even execution. Other prisoners were awaiting trial, and some were never allowed a trial. All those confined in Castle Thunder were desperate to get out, but it was far easier to get into the Confederate prison than to get out of it.

1862–1863 Escapes

There were many escape attempts at Castle Thunder. Prisoners complained that punishment, especially under Captain Alexander, was brutal; that the guards were careless and inexperienced; and as the war progressed, that the quality and quantity of food diminished.[1]

Breakouts began almost as soon as Castle Thunder opened as a prison. With nothing else to do, the prisoners spent their time devising methods of escape. The Richmond papers recorded many successful and unsuccessful attempts by prisoners to put Castle Thunder behind them.

The First Attempt

On August 24, 1862, during the first week that Castle Thunder was used as a prison, John Farmer was seen at the rear of the building and was shot by a guard as he attempted to escape. He sustained a flesh wound in the arm and was taken to the hospital for the wound to be treated.[2]

The easiest method of escape was to obtain civilian clothes and simply walk off the premises, unnoticed by the guard and mistaken for a visitor.[3] George Gerbert, alias Moore, attempted to gain his freedom by dressing in a nice suit of clothes and passing the guards unnoticed. He was captured a short distance from Castle Thunder, still on Cary Street, by Detective Folks.[4]

Private John R. Jones had deserted from Company C, 18th Battalion, Virginia Heavy Artillery, but a detective officer arrested him in Petersburg on or about the January 14, 1863, and brought him to Castle Thunder in Richmond. At his court martial, a statement that Jones had made about his escape was written into the record. Jones had said that some eighty men were sent to Jackson's Army from Castle Thunder and that he came out of the prison in the crowd, and when the train went off, he hid and escaped without notice.[5]

Some of the more popular means, though not always successful, were climbing down a rope from a window or digging a tunnel.

Out A Window

The tools needed to carry out an escape were contrived from every available source. It is estimated that at least one third of all the blankets distributed at Castle Thunder were cut up and used to facilitate an escape. Blankets were turned into ropes and were "zealously guarded by the prisoners."[6]

It was very common for prisoners to bribe their guards. Officers might bribe a guard or even an enlisted man to exchange identities, if the enlisted man was soon to be eligible for exchange. In November of 1862 there was an ingenious escape. A group of desperate prisoners decided there was no chance to bribe the sentinels, because they had no money with which to buy their aid, so they came up with a plan to fool the sentinels into thinking that they had a large purse of money. If the guard should have his back turned while they were escaping from a window, the money would be his. They selected a window in the northeast corner of the second story. The window overlooked the platform on which the sentinels walked, and there was a stairway which descended to the street, and a second sentinel was on guard there. At the appointed time, the sentinel who had been chosen to be enticed was called to the window and the prisoners propositioned him. "If you will help us get out to night, we four will give you fifty dollars a piece — that'll be two hundred dollars!" The sentinel replied, "I'll see," which meant he had to check with his partner below. During the rest of the day, the sentinels met and discussed the proposition. When they returned to their posts, the prisoners were told that the guards were in agreement, and preparations were begun for a "grand exit." A window was opened, and the leader stepped out. "Where's the money?" whispered the sentinel. The leader lied and said, "The last man has got it," and he left. Then came the second, third, fourth, fifth, sixth, and seventh man, and more would have escaped, but the sentinel began to get suspicious. He ran to the window to put a stop to the escaping prisoners, and gave the alarm. Meanwhile, the sentinel on the ground let the prisoners pass before the alarm was spread, and they got away.[7]

On Saturday, Captain Alexander and a force of detectives set out in search of the escapees. After much searching, they arrested two. He learned from those two the details of the escape, and which two sentinels had helped. The two sentinels were members of a corps who were usually on duty at a prison opposite Libby Prison and had been detached to duty at Castle Thunder. They were arrested and placed in irons to await trial for their offense, "the penalty of which is death."[8]

On October 9, 1862, James Jennings, a substitute soldier arrested for desertion, escaped from Castle Thunder by jumping out a window on the western side. He had been gone for several days when Detective New saw him in a cigar store on Main Street in Richmond. The detective arrested him and returned him to Castle Thunder. The prisoner did not resist, although he could have probably escaped, because the detective had two other prisoners in tow at the same time.[9]

Another conspiracy to escape Castle Thunder was discovered. The hopeful prisoners had made a long rope from cotton sheets, and a condemned prisoner scheduled to be shot on Saturday helped them out through the window. After their discovery, the escapees were put in the dungeon. The increasing efforts to escape could only be stopped by increased vigilance and the shooting of those seen escaping.[10]

August Wile, a Yankee, escaped in November of 1863 by climbing down to an out building and sliding to the ground.[11]

Holes in the Wall

On January 5, 1863, about 70 prisoners plotted to escape through holes in the walls. Each prisoner had managed to obtain either a knife or a revolver. Thus armed, they would kill any guard who attempted to prevent their escape. However, informers told prison officials of the plan, and the ringleaders were questioned and punished.[12]

J. Wrenn and M. J. Lemmon escaped by digging through the rear wall. They were recaptured after a short period of freedom as they attempted to board a train leaving Richmond, and were returned to Castle Thunder.[13]

A Richmond newspaper reported just before the hearings were opened into the treatment of prisoners at Castle Thunder: "This military rendezvous [Castle Thunder] was like an unpatronized hotel yesterday—few arrivals and fewer departures. A daily attempt or two on the part of the inmates to escape enliven the dull routine of the guard."[14] Two days later, another paper reported that "a number of prisoners" had attempted to escape by cutting through a wall. They had been discovered by the guards and "driven back to their quarters."[15]

Prisoner Killed

More information on the escapes appeared in print on April 7. Instead of all the prisoners being driven back, Charles Carroll, alias John Byas (or Byzas), was shot and killed trying to escape. He and several fellow prisoners had cut a hole through the wall of the room in which they were held. They managed to get to another room and were actually out on the balcony when discovered. One of the prisoners stepped back inside, but Carroll remained, and was shot "through the heart" and died instantly. Another report said he was shot "between the eyes."[16] He was a deserter from the 54th (or 53rd) Virginia Regiment.[17]

The two prisoners were being held in the condemned cell, but they succeeded in cutting their way through a partition wall, and they were able to reach a window which faced Cary Street. As the men were about to jump, a guard called out a warning. The prisoners did not answer, so the sentinel fired. Carroll died instantly. His companion, William Campbell, then ran down the main gangway and, because of the confusion, was able to get past a guard and onto the street. Detective George W. Thomas ran after him and fired two pistol shots. The detective captured Campbell at the corner of 18th and Main. Campbell's fourth escape attempt was again unsuccessful.[18]

William Campbell tried again to escape. This time he remained at large for some time before detectives Thomas, Folks and Perdue found him in bed at a house of ill repute in Lombard alley. He was hauled out of bed and returned to the Castle. The papers reported that this was his fourth attempt, but it may have been his fifth. He swore that Castle Thunder could not hold him.[19]

Tunnel

Fifteen prisoners tried to dig out of the Palmer's Factory Building, which had been converted to a hospital temporarily. Their plan became known and as the first one crawled out of the tunnel, Captain Alexander was waiting there with a gun. Alexander ordered the man to proceed, and then he captured the rest of them as they exited the tunnel.[20]

One prisoner did not even make it outside. James Howell was discovered digging in an old excavation tunnel which had been filled in. He was put in irons to prevent another escape attempt.[21] In the fall of 1863, some prisoners decided to dig a tunnel as a means to escape. The site of digging under the walls of the stable was discovered. The diggers had masked their dig with a pile of rocks, which hid the dig from view.[22]

On Saturday, November 14, 1863, thirty-five Yankee deserters escaped from Castle Thunder. They had been confined in a room on the second floor at the rear of the building. They cut a hole in the floor and descended to the room below, which had been a storeroom. From this room, they cut a hole through the fireplace and dug a length of 15 feet under an alley large enough for a man's body. The tunnel ended in Mr. Sinton's lot beyond the alley, about a foot beyond the fence that connected the buildings that made up Castle Thunder. The prisoners made their escape undetected. A reporter who viewed the escape tunnel declared that the men who had constructed it must have been miners. By 12 o'clock that same day, two of the escapees had been recaptured attempting to make their way to the peninsula.[23] A week later, twenty-nine prisoners had been recaptured; only six got away.[24]

Another group tried tunneling out, but were betrayed by a traitor in their midst. They were taken before the Commandant who told them:

> There is no use, men, of trying to get out of here; it is absolutely impossible! You can make no movement; you can not breathe; you can not have a thought that is unknown to me. You might as well attempt to scale Heaven as escape from the Castle; so you had better behave yourselves, and become resigned to your situation.[25]

The Captain's talk had little effect on the determination of the prisoners, and the next night the first ten plus another twelve escaped and "were never afterward heard of by the Rebels."[26]

Guards Bribed

Often the prisoners were assisted by the guards in their escape. William E. Meade, a guard, had helped some prisoners to escape, but his part had been detected. To avoid imprisonment himself, he took advantage of the confusion and made his own escape from Castle Thunder. He was sought just as vigorously as were the escapees.

The prisoners simply would not give up trying to escape. Another attempt was made on Monday night, May 18, 1863, to escape by sawing off bars. Even with the aid of a rope and a bribed guard, the attempt failed.[27]

Only two days later, Patrick Garrack was caught trying to escape. He had tried to bribe one of the sentinels during the night, and the guard, while pretending to go along with the prisoner, notified the commandant. Garrack was seized the moment he descended down a rope. If he had succeeded, 15 more planned to follow him.[28]

Forged Release Order

Every means possible to escape was tried. One prisoner, Fleming Brazer, tried to get released on the basis of a forged special order. The document was presented as being a release order from General Winder by Lieut. W. L. Soles, from a Florida Regiment. When it was discovered that the order was forged, both the prisoner and the forger were soon captured and returned to Castle Thunder.[29]

Sentinel Killed

A successful escape was managed by E. D. Boone, Edward Carney, Thomas Cole, and John A. Chipman, "all desperate characters," who were housed in Castle Thunder on serious charges. They had already tried to escape once, and thus had been placed in the condemned cell, with a guard on duty at all times. The men managed to obtain some tools and cut through the floor into the Commissary's room which was directly beneath the condemned cell. There they grabbed some firearms and rushed into the reception room. They overthrew the sentinel inside the door, and when they encountered a sentinel outside, one of them put the muzzle of a gun to his head and fired it. The sentinel was a young man named Sutton Byrd, a private in Company C, 53rd North Carolina Regiment.[30]

A crowd of soldiers gathered around the body of their fallen comrade. Captain Alexander's dog, Hero (Nero) placed himself beside the body, and would let no one approach until the proper officer relieved him of his duty, then he followed the corpse as it was carried into the building. Everyone was moved by this display of "canine affection."[31]

By October 26, 1863, Boone, "the Castle Thunder Murderer," had made his way to safety within Yankee lines at Williamsburg. The group of prisoners had separated just outside Richmond, and each took a different route.[32]

Each successful escape attempt spawned more escape efforts by prisoners. The week of April 15, 1863, five prisoners escaped from Castle Thunder. This was only a day or two after Tim O'Brien escaped from the county jail, where he had been held for forging a check.[33]

Out on Oath of Allegiance

Yankee prisoners at Castle Thunder, Alfred Turner, Edward Hill, Henry Page, William Fisher, J. Wilson and Eugene Delaney, took the oath of allegiance to the Confederacy and were released "to earn, if possible, an honest living."[34]

By Flag of Truce

Thirty-one Yankee deserters who had been confined in Castle Thunder made known their desire to return North. Their wish was granted. They were first sent to Libby Prison where they were to be sent North under the first "flag of truce."[35]

Escape Through Winder's Legion

One means of getting out of Castle Thunder was to volunteer for "Winder's Legion," to aid in the defense of Richmond. The Winder Guards was an organization formed among the Confederate prisoners held in Castle Thunder. Two companies, comprised of about 150 men each, were on duty in May under the command of Major Vowels. A Richmond newspaper commented that only two "hard cases" had deserted, and the command was better off without them.[36]

After the battle at Gettysburg, Pennsylvania, in which the Army of Northern Virginia under General Robert E. Lee suffered heavy casualties, a group of the prisoners asked for and received permission from Captain Alexander to form a battalion in case of an emergency. Captain Alexander was appointed Major of the unit, and he helped the men prepare in their efforts to expel "from Southern soil its ruthless invaders." The first company was armed and ready, having been drilled by Lieutenant Callahan, adjutant of the post. These 300 men were already veterans, and it was expected they would do their duty when faced with the enemy.[37]

The efforts of the former prisoners did not go unnoticed. The group of 300 prisoners who had volunteered to man the batteries were ordered to be "discharged and returned to their respective regiments without trial," just as soon as there was no longer a need for their "present organization." The Richmond *Examiner* noted that some of the prisoners had been confined on "very grave charges," but Jefferson Davis' order covered all "who have behaved themselves," and they had, except for one or two.[38]

On May 27, 1864, the Winder Legion returned to Richmond and was reviewed before General Winder's headquarters. The group had asked President Davis to "authorize the permanency of their present organization." The group, now about 250 men, was quartered in the Soldier's Home.[39]

Death Opens a Door

James Hancock, held in Castle Thunder during the winter of 1864–1865 on suspicion of being a spy was a "jolly, rollicking fellow having wonderful facial expression and great powers of mimicry." One evening, he suddenly staggered and fell to the floor. Some of the men inspected his body and said he was dead. The guards were notified and the surgeon called to determine if the man had fainted or if it was a true case of sudden death. The surgeon declared, he was "dead as a door nail!" In less than 20 minutes, the body had been loaded on a wagon and headed for the hospital, to be put in a cheap coffin and taken to a cemetery. However, when the driver reached the end of his journey, the body was gone. The driver thought the body had fallen out of the wagon, and he retraced his route looking for the lost corpse.

Hancock's "sudden death" was a part of his plan to escape. On the way to the hospital, he had simply gotten out of the wagon and started walking along the street. When the wagoneer returned to Castle Thunder, an alarm was spread all over Richmond. Hancock had some money in the lining of his vest, and he went to the best hotel in town and registered as being from Georgia. There he spent a restful night, and the next morning he got new clothes and walked around Richmond. However, shortly after dinner he was arrested on Main Street by the provost guards. But, no sooner had they taken him in custody, than he crossed his eyes and pulled his mouth so it appeared drawn to one side. The confused guards let him go. Four days later, he was arrested again in the post office. This time, he drew his mouth to the right, squinted his left eye, and pretended to be deaf. He was taken to Castle Thunder, where neither the guards nor his fellow prisoners recognized him. He was locked up until he could be investigated. Finally, he got tired of holding his eyes in a squint, and then he was recognized. Had the war lasted 10 more days, he would have been shot as a spy.[40]

Escapes in 1864

In 1864, after Alexander had been replaced by Richardson, only 57 prisoners escaped from Castle Thunder. However, of those 57, only 18 were successful.[41]

Escapes from Castle Godwin

A prisoner in Castle Godwin made a hole in the wall and attempted to escape. As he exited the prison, he fell into the arms of a guard who had been watching the prisoner's efforts for some time. The prisoner was kept in irons on his legs and arms thereafter.[42] Another prisoner, William Lacy, escaped from Castle Godwin, but was soon arrested by the detectives of Assistant Provost Marshall Alexander. Lacy was returned to Godwin and charged with "almost every crime in the catalogue."[43]

An escape from Castle Godwin was attempted by John Keyer, alias William Shulta. This deserter from Captain Marmaduke Johnston's Battery blacked his face with soot, and with an old basket, "hobbled out, in negro fashion, and succeeded in passing the guards." The guards became suspicious of his "color" and gave chase. He was captured and brought back. He was ordered to be punished severely by "bucking."[44]

The Great Libby Prison Escape

As far as escapes go, probably the greatest escape from a Richmond prison was that of 109 Yankee officers who tunneled out of Libby Prison. When morning came and roll call turned up a number of missing prisoners, a search was undertaken. In the basement, at the base of the east wall and about 20 feet from the front of the building on Cary Street, they discovered a tunnel. The entrance was hidden by a large rock which fit the hole exactly. Once removed, a small Negro boy was sent into the hole to explore. The tunnel had been dug directly beneath the place where three sentinels daily marched back and forth. The tunnel ended in the rear of Carr's warehouse, where the escapees emerged, one by one, at least 60 feet from any of the sentinels on duty. To reach the tunnel, the prisoners cut through the hospital room and a closed stairway which led to the basement. The authorities surmised the work must have been done at night, and the debris cleared away before daylight. The completion of the tunnel must have required several months of digging, since it was three feet in diameter, and at least 60 feet in length. Four of the prisoners were recaptured shortly, two about 20 miles below Richmond, and two near Hanover Court House.[45]

Zarvona Tries to Escape

While Captain Alexander was trying to keep prisoners in Castle Thunder, his friend Richard Thomas Zarvona was trying to escape from Fort Lafayette in New York harbor. Zarvona had made repeated appeals for release on parole.[46] Then he was placed in strict confinement for allegedly sending coded messages to friends outside the prison.[47]

On a stormy night in April of 1862, after being in prison almost a year, Zarvona attempted to escape. By getting the guard to let him go to the "water closet," although heavily guarded, he managed to gain the top of the sea wall, and plunged into the waters of the harbor in the midst of a raging storm. He headed for the shore of Long

Island. However, his freedom was cut short when the prison officials sent guards in a boat. They soon reached him and returned the prisoner "dripping but undaunted to his cell."[48]

The amazing thing about the whole escape attempt was that Zarvona could not even swim. He managed to fashion a life preserver by "corking up a number of tin cans and suspending them around his waist" with a cord.[49] He did not drown, but as a result of his failed attempt to escape, he was put in greater confinement, and allowed no visitors. His solitary confinement resulted in a breakdown of both his mental and physical health.[50] Secretary of War Stanton even revoked his mother's pass, so that she could not visit her son.[51]

11

Cruel and Unusual Punishment vs. Standard Fare

"Let the punishment match the offense."
—*Marcus Tullius Cicero,* De Legebus

The inherent nature of prisons, and the type of prisoners confined therein, dictate the kind and severity of discipline required to maintained order. Captain George Alexander had served 13 years in the United States Navy where, due to the close confinement aboard ship, discipline is more strict than on land. As an officer in the Navy, George W. Alexander experienced first hand the necessity of obedience to orders and the need for strict discipline, and the punishment inflicted on board ship for disobedience was often harsh.

As prison commandant, Alexander ruled with an iron hand. He expected his orders to be carried out to the letter. He had his prisoners watched closely, and monitored their activities. He was quick to punish those who disobeyed his rules or attempted to escape.[1]

Accustomed to Navy discipline as he was, it was only natural that when Alexander assumed the management of Castle Thunder, he would instigate certain rules and regulations for the prisoners and the guards. Failure to obey these rules and regulations resulted in the offender being subject to immediate punishment. Those who disobeyed Alexander's rules knew what punishment to expect. They knew that, according to Alexander's rules, they would be whipped, put in irons, tied up by their thumbs, confined to a sweat house, bucked, tied around a post so that they could not sit or lie down, put in barrel shirts or jackets,[2] or put outside in the cold without adequate clothing and shelter. In some cases, the punishment was carried out before the entire prison population.[3]

Some Common Forms of Punishment

Alexander sometimes used stern measures in dealing with offenders, and strong and abusive language, such as "put them in there, God damn them."[4] However, Alexander's forms of punishment were neither excessive for this time period, nor unique in any way.

Barrel shirts were more uncomfortable than harmful. The prisoner was forced to wear a large flour barrel from which both the top and bottom had been knocked out. Armholes were cut in the sides, and it was held up by straps attached over the shoulders. Sometimes, the nature of the prisoner's crime was painted on the sides of the barrel in large letters. The prisoner was then paraded through the compound, under guard, followed by a drummer, to call attention to the man, his crime, and his punishment.[5] Another name was "wooden overcoat," which was a barrel shirt without the armholes cut into the sides.[6]

Bucking was very common form of punishment used in prisons. The prisoner was put in a sitting position on the ground, his hands tied together over his knees, and a stick passed over his arms and under his legs. Thus tied, he could not move, and the position caused pain and suffering, especially if he was also gagged. A gag was made by using either a rag or a stick put in the mouth and tied with a cord around the back of the head.[7]

The chain gang: a group of 6–18 men were fastened together with a heavy chain attached to their ankles, passing from one to another. Heavy iron balls were attached to the chain, making movement difficult. Sometimes, a chain was also attached to the necks of the prisoners.[8]

Spread eagle was a punishment often used by Indians. The victim was spread on the ground on his back with his arms and legs spread apart as far as possible and tied to wooden stakes.[9] (Indians tied the limbs with wet rawhide that shrank as it dried in the sun, and usually placed the victim over an ant hill. Few ever survived the Indian form of torture.)

Stick carry involved having a prisoner stand for long periods of time with a heavy tree limb or log across his shoulders behind his head. His arms were extended straight out from his sides and lashed to the log.[10]

Stocks were another common form of punishment in both New England and on the Southern plantation. These were wooden frames in which men were fastened by the neck and hands, or ankles, and forced to remain, usually outside, for a number of hours. They were given no food, water, or shelter, sometimes for several days.[11] The stocks and pillory were usually standard forms of punishment and one or both could be found near the jail of most counties.

The sweat box was a coffin-sized box, about 18 inches deep and six feet tall. The prisoner was forced to stand for long periods of time inside this box, which was often covered with a lid, and, if placed in the sun, was almost like an oven.[12]

Thumb hanging (trysting) was a common practice, both in the United States Navy and various military prisons, including Castle Thunder.[13] The hands of the victim were tied behind his back and a strong, slender rope was tied around his thumbs. The person to undergo the punishment was then drawn up by the rope placed over a beam and hung suspended from the ground. The pain and agony were terrible if this went on for any length of time. Sometimes a victim of this punishment fainted after only a few minutes. He was revived and his torture begun again.[14] Some drawings depict a prisoner suspended by the thumbs with his hands tied behind his back. If this was done, the shoulders would have been dislocated almost immediately from the weight of the prisoner's body upon the joints.[15]

The wooden horse was another cruel form of punishment that, while not exactly permanently disabling, could cause death if the person forced to ride the "horse" were left exposed to the elements. On Belle Isle, the wooden horse was a high trestle which the victim was forced to straddle. A gag was placed in his mouth and his hands were tied behind him. His legs were drawn apart and attached at his ankles to stakes in the ground. Sometimes the prisoners were kept riding the horse until they nearly froze to death, especially during the winter months.[16]

Other common forms of punishment were whipping, solitary confinement, restrictions of the daily amount of food and water, handcuffs, and leg irons with the attachment of a heavy iron ball of either 12 or 24 pounds.

Court Ordered Punishments

Some punishments were meted out because of conditions attached to sentences ordered by the military court. As commandant of Castle Thunder, Alexander was responsible for carrying out any and all sentences imposed on Confederate soldiers by a court martial. Those sentences and conditions could range from imprisonment for various terms, whipping, wearing a ball and chain for a specified time, and even death. (See Appendix 2 for transcript of a court martial.) Private John R. Jones was found guilty of being absent without leave. At his court martial, Jones, of Company C, 18th Battalion, Virginia Heavy Artillery, was sentenced to forfeiture of pay for the period of two months and to six months hard labor with a ball and chain.[17]

General Orders No. 19, issued at Petersburg, March 5, 1863, listed a number of court martials, the charges against the prisoners, and the sentence imposed.[18]

James Brown, Company D, 47th Regiment, Alabama Volunteers, was found guilty of "conduct prejudicial to good order and military discipline," and was sentenced to "hard labor upon one of the fortifications of the Confederate states." He was to wear a "ball weighing twenty-four pounds attached to his left ankle, by a chain three feet long, for a term of six months, and to forfeit six months' pay."[19]

Private Henry G. Reynolds, Company Battalion, Georgia Volunteers, was charged with violating Article 6 and Article 9 of the Articles of War and "threatening to take the life of his Commanding Officer." Found guilty on all charges, he was sentenced to hard labor at a Confederate fortification, to wear a 24-pound ball attached by a 3-foot chain for six months, and to forfeit six months' pay.[20]

At a court martial held in Kinston, North Carolina, 48 soldiers were tried on a variety of charges, mostly for either desertion or being absent without leave. The majority of the prisoners were sentenced to work on some fortification with a 12-pound ball and a 3-foot chain attached to their left ankle. Usually, the prisoner was to forfeit four months pay as well. Only one prisoner, Private Thomas R. Quime of Company D, 38th Virginia Regiment was sentenced to be executed. He was charged not only with desertion but with "persuading and inducing others to desert." He was sentenced to be "shot to death with musketry."[21]

The sentences of the men tried at Kinston did not specify where they were to be confined. However, one of this group of prisoners, Private Israel Laprad, Company F, 53rd Virginia Regiment was known to have done time at Castle Thunder. In addition, Laprad was also to be branded with the letter "D" for "deserter" on his left hip, with a branding iron that left a scar one and a half inches in diameter.[22]

Other sentences were not quite so harsh and did not involve corporal punishment. Captain William L. Jones, Company D, 10th Battalion, Georgia Volunteers, was "cashiered, and dismissed" from the Confederate States service. He was found guilty of appropriating public property for private use and at "conduct unbecoming an officer and a gentleman."[23] To be "cashiered" was to be discharged from the military service and to be given a final paycheck or money due by the officer in charge of payments (the cashier).

Alexander's Authority

In areas other than corporal punishment or mental and verbal abuse, Alexander could prohibit a prisoner from having counsel for defense simply because he could and because, as he put it, "we have our rights and you have your rights."[24]

It was also Alexander's responsibility to prevent prisoners from committing crimes against each other, as well as to prevent their escape from prison. Prisoners often attacked new arrivals and robbed them. Once, prisoners knocked out the eye of an old prisoner, without any provocation.[25] Attacks on prisoners by other prisoners was so common that the term *mugger* came into use, and its meaning was the same as it is today. New prisoners, called *fresh fish*, were relieved of their blankets, clothing, and other valuables before they even got settled in.[26]

At Castle Thunder, discipline for infraction of Alexander's rules was immediate and expected. Punishment could be minor, more humiliating than painful, or severe, according to the nature of the offense. Alexander's personality came into play in how he treated the prisoners. Although he usually remained calm and it took much to provoke him, Alexander sometimes "spoke to and treated the prisoners harshly when there was no occasion for it," according to Detective Robert B. Crow.[27]

When a prisoner was found guilty of having committed an offense against the prison rules, the guilty prisoner was taken to one of the larger rooms and "stripped to the waist, and then his hands were tied around a post." He was surrounded by guards, and all of the other prisoners were ordered to watch the punishment about to be inflicted. Captain Alexander would then address the prisoners and advise them of the crimes committed. Afterwards, he gave the order for a detective to administer 39 lashes to the offender's bare back.[28]

The whipping seemed to be effective. Guard John Caphart testified at the Congressional investigation that after Alexander began whipping the "ringleaders" the "conduct of the prisoners [has] improved since."[29]

Alexander employed other means of punishment as well, some of which were practiced in the United States Navy, such as tying a prisoner to a cross beam so that his feet would not touch the ground, putting the offender on a diet of bread and water for a week or more, or putting the offender in a solitary cell. These methods were designed not only to punish those who broke the rules or tried to escape, but to prevent other prisoners from committing the same offenses.[30]

Often a prisoner was sent to Captain Alexander with instructions that he be kept until sent for, and to be fed on bread and water. This was the fate of R. C. Campbell (landsman) for leaving his ship without permission.[31]

Then there was the "sweat room," a small, dark square room, in which a prisoner survived on a diet of bread and water. A pail was furnished to hold bodily waste, and there was no respite from the heat of the summer or the cold of the winter.[32]

For calling the guard names from a window, a prisoner was fired upon. The shot struck the window casement, causing the wood to fragment and send splinters flying that cut the prisoner's face, causing the blood to flow freely.[33] Some guards watched for opportunities to shoot prisoners, and the word *sporting* became synonymous with *hunting*.[34]

Castle Thunder was not unique in this respect. At the Old Capitol Prison in Washington, when some of Mosby's guerrillas threw bricks from an old fireplace in their room at the sentinels, Colonel N. T. Colby ordered the guards to fire on anyone who showed his face at the window.[35]

Standard Treatment or the Exception

John Adams, a deserter, was confined in Castle Thunder for seven months for going A.W.O.L. He claimed he was severely punished on charges which were never proved. "There was an attempt to bribe the sentinel, and I was taken and handcuffed, and ironed around a post, and tied up by my thumbs with a rope, my toes just touching the floor." He testified that his thumbs were painful as a result. When Adams was handcuffed around a post, he was kept in that position for over an hour until Captain Bossieux released him. Then he was put in the "sweat house" for two days and nights. The floor of this small room was covered with mud and water. There was no dry spot on the floor, and the room was not tall enough for him to stand up. Adams also bore scars on his wrists from being handcuffed. After being tried before a court martial, Adams was sentenced to wear a ball and chain for six months, and then to be sent back to his company.[36] (Since he stated this occurred in March of 1862, it would have been before Castle Thunder opened, and before Captain Alexander had been put in charge.)

At the Congressional inquiry into conditions at Castle Thunder, Attorney Ward tried to get Adams to admit that instead of being tied up by his thumbs, the "rope was around your wrist, and thumbs, and over the nail, and not around your thumbs."

The treatment of these prisoners, no matter how harsh, was believed justified by both Alexander and his guards. They saw the inmates of Castle Thunder as the worst kind of prisoners, and Detective John Caphart believed it was "unsafe for any Confederate official to walk in their midst."[37] Of the prisoners confined at Castle Thunder, some of the most difficult to handle were the "plug-uglies" from Baltimore, Maryland, and the "wharf-rats" from New Orleans.[38] These views perhaps motivated Caphart to curse and threaten prisoners with little or no provocation, according to his fellow detectives.[39]

Treatment of Alien Enemies

Not all prisoners were treated the same. The arrest of civilians came under the authority granted under the "Alien Enemies Act" approved by President Davis on August 8, 1861.[40] Under this act, anyone even suspected of being disloyal could be arrested and held, and many were (see Appendix 1 for some of their names and the reasons they were arrested).

The disloyal Confederate citizens lodged in Castle Thunder received the most verbal and mental abuse.[41] These people were seen as traitors to the cause, and the indirect vehicle for the suffering of loyal Confederates and their brave soldiers. The attitude of Captain Alexander toward the prisoners was reflected in their treatment by his officers and guards. Alexander seemed to "possess a sense of ultimate power and superiority over all captives," which sometimes resulted in overzealous punishment.

The Georgia Train Engine Thieves

A group of prisoners were brought to Castle Thunder from Atlanta in October of 1862. These Federal soldiers had been caught conducting a raid to cut railroad and telegraph communications between Chattanooga, Tennessee, and Marietta, Georgia, April 7–12, 1862. The 22 raiders were put in the Negro jail at Chattanooga, where they occupied a single room. There was not even enough space for them to sleep lying down. The only entrance was through a trap door in the ceiling, through which meals were lowered twice a day in a bucket. The prisoners were handcuffed, and with "trace-chains" secured by padlocks around their necks, they were fastened to each other in twos and threes.[42]

At the time of their capture, the raiders had been healthy, but after three weeks they were scarcely able to walk. Finally, 12 of them, including five who had agreed to testify, were transferred to a prison in Knoxville, Tennessee. There, seven were tried before a court martial and charged with being spies. Counsel for the defense argued that their being in civilian clothes was no less than that authorized by the Confederate

Government for guerrillas. Their counselor cited instances when Confederate John Hunt Morgan had dressed his men in the uniform of Union soldiers, and had succeeded in reaching a railroad in the north and destroying it. The defense pleaded that the prisoners having been in civilian clothing should not deter from the protection offered prisoners of war. He also stated that those involved did not know the purpose of the mission, but had been told their object was a "purely military one, for the destruction of communications, and as such, lawful, according to the rules of war." The prisoners were then removed to Atlanta, and the seven who had been tried in Knoxville were hung.[43] Andrews, the leader of the expedition, was tried and executed in Atlanta on June 7 as a spy.[44]

Fourteen of the "engine-thieves" remained confined in prison in Atlanta. As members of Sill's Brigade, Buell's Division, the 14 petitioned Major-General Braxton Bragg, Commander of Department Number 2, that they be treated as prisoners of war and exchanged. The 14 who signed the petition were W. W. Brown, William Knight, Elihu Mason, John R. Porter, William Bensinger, Robert Buffum, Mark Wood, and Alfred Wilson, all of the 21st Ohio Regiment; William Pittenger of the 2nd Ohio Regiment; William H. Reddick, John Wollam, D. A. Dorsey, M. J. Hawkins, and Jacob Parrott of the 33rd Ohio Regiment.[45]

The surviving members of the Andrews' raiding party were confined in the jail at Atlanta until October, when the prisoners were overheard talking about their jailers' plan to hang them as they had others of their group. The prisoners became desperate and attempted to escape. They seized the jailer when he entered their cell to take away their supper bucket. They seized the guards and escaped. Six were recaptured and taken to Castle Thunder, where they were treated harshly.[46]

According to J. Holt, Judge Advocate-General, these six prisoners were "shut up in a room in Castle Thunder, where they shivered through the winter, without fire, thinly clad, and with but two small blankets, which they had saved with their clothes, to cover the whole party." These prisoners had been confined for 11 months in prisons in the South, where they endured "pitiless persecutions" and suffered "indignities."

Whether their treatment was any worse than the rest of the prisoners confined at that time is not known. Certainly, the survivors of Andrew's raid did not suffer in Castle Thunder as much as they had in the Negro jail in Chattanooga.

Execution

The ultimate punishment was execution. Spies often met that fate. One man convicted for desertion and spying was Spencer Kellogg. He was taken from Castle Thunder to Camp Lee for the execution. A large crowd was present, both military personnel and civilians. He remained calm, cool, and collected to the last minute, and he was the one to give the signal for the drop to be released. When he reached the platform where the noose swung, he tested it to see if it was strong enough, and before he was hung, he carried on a conversation with Captain Alexander and others.[47]

Captain Alexander was simply carrying out the orders of the court; he did not execute prisoners without orders from the court.

An example was made of Spencer Deaton. Originally in a Confederate regiment, Deaton deserted and joined the 6th Tennessee, a Federal regiment. He was captured and a military court sentenced him to be hung in the courtyard at Castle Thunder in full view of the other inmates. A Richmond paper stated, "It is to be hoped that the fate of this man will have a tendency to make all who contemplated violating [laws], respect the laws of the county in which they reside."[48]

Inexperienced Prison Guards

Many of the prisoners' complaints centered on the guards. These inexperienced young men were quick to shoot when other actions would have been more advisable. There was a standing rule that guards were not to fire on prisoners before giving a warning, but this was often ignored. The guards also had standing orders not to fire on prisoners who were attempting to escape if they could be recaptured without injury. In the excitement created by an escape attempt, the guards often disregarded the rules.[49]

Richard Morris, a guard from the City Battalion, was shot and killed during an argument with Newson, another guard. Newson believed that he was doing his duty by ordering Morris away from the building because he believed Norris was attempting to talk to a prisoner. Captain Alexander explained that his sentinels had orders to "prevent persons from talking with or making signs to the prisoners."[50] Thus Newson was not punished for the killing of another guard.

Sometimes, prison guards found themselves in prison for even minor offenses. Two guards, both members of the City Battalion, were arrested for "sleeping at their posts." On orders of Captain Alexander, both J. C. Johnson and George H. Snider were confined inside Castle Thunder.[51]

A Kind-Hearted General

Kind-hearted General Edward Porter Alexander was a well-liked and intelligent man from Wilkes County, Georgia. A graduate from the United States Military Academy in 1857, third in a class of 38, Porter Alexander taught at West Point. When Georgia seceded, he resigned and became a Captain of Engineers for the Confederate States Army. He saw action at Second Bull Run and Antietam in 1862. He commanded an artillery battalion on Marye's Heights at Fredericksburg in December of 1862, and was with Jackson at Chancellorsville and Longstreet at Gettysburg. He later published several books on railroading. His book, *Military Memoirs of a Confederate*, a classic, was published in 1907.[52]

A court martial was ordered to be convened in his camp, and he was appointed to preside over the proceedings. The court session lasted for nearly a month and many prisoners were tried from various commands. Two men from Woolfolk's Battery were tried for capital offenses. Howard had deserted, gone home, and was caught by a conscript guard. Wilson, a substitute, had joined only a week before deserting. He was presumed to be a "bounty-jumper." He was to have been paid a thousand dollars, but General Alexander was told to hold back part of the money. Alexander had warned Wilson against deserting, but the soldier did not heed the warning, and deserted in less than a week's time. Woolfolk's men were watching Wilson closely, and he had been gone only a few hours when he was recaptured and put in irons.[53]

When the cases came before the court, both men were clearly guilty of desertion and were sentenced to death, but their sentences had not been made public. General Alexander knew that he would be breaking camp and going into battle, and that his men had no muskets with which to guard prisoners, only swords. Alexander felt sorry for Howard, and did not believe he had intended to desert, but only to go home for a while to see his family, and maybe a sweetheart. He was caught before he could return. Wilson, on the other hand, was a professional "bounty-jumper." Alexander decided to make an example of him. He sent both men down to Richmond to Castle Thunder with a letter stating that they had been tried "for the gravest crime, and were awaiting results," and he asked that special care be taken of them until General E. P. Alexander sent for them.[54]

On the retreat from Gettysburg in July of 1863, General Porter Alexander learned that the court proceedings against the two men had been "acted upon, and approved," and an order had been issued for General Alexander to execute his two deserters. While camped in an old field that evening, one of the two, Howard, walked up and "reported himself for duty." He told the general that he had been turned loose from Castle Thunder, along with many others, and had been told to come and meet his battalion. He had obeyed orders, and walked most of the way. Alexander knew that orders had already been signed to shoot him. General Alexander believed if he went to General Lee and begged that he would commute Howard's sentence. Yet, if General Lee refused, there would be nothing else that could be done. General Alexander then decided to allow Howard to escape, and he told Howard that he could not return to duty, but that he must be kept under guard until his sentence was published. General Alexander confided in Captain Woolfolk that he hoped Howard would be allowed to escape, and the next morning the prisoner was gone. The next day, the execution orders arrived, and General Alexander sent to Castle Thunder for Wilson, but there was no record of Wilson having been admitted or discharged. Both deserters were saved from a firing squad.[55]

Alexander Is Investigated

Captain George W. Alexander was known for instituting a system of strict rules and regulations which decreed severe punishment for those who broke the rules and ignored the regulations. The kind of prisoners in his care necessitated having strict rules and swift retribution for infractions. The way in which Alexander handled these prisoners was common knowledge outside the prison. His methods became cause for concern among the citizens. Eventually, the people of Richmond complained enough about the treatment of the prisoners in Castle Thunder that the Confederate Congress appointed a special committee to investigate. The hearings were conducted over 19 days in April of 1863. A variety of witnesses were called to testify as to Alexander's operation of the prison and his treatment of the prisoners.[56]

A popular ballad among prisoners contained a stanza about Castle Thunder, which did not improve either the image of Castle Thunder or its warden:

> I'd rather be on the Grandfather Mountain
> A-taking the snow and rain
> Than to be in Castle Thunder
> A-wearin' the ball and chain.[57]

The testimony of the witnesses during investigation was printed in the *Official Records of the War of the Rebellion*. The opinions of the Congressional investigative committee were published in the Majority Report and two Minority Reports. (See Chapters 12 and 13.)

12

The Congressional Investigation

"The abuse of greatness is when it disjoins remorse from power."
—*William Shakespeare,* Julius Caesar

The stories circulating about Castle Thunder were numerous, and none of them good. The facility gained an evil reputation for the cruel punishment inflicted on the prisoners held there. The people of Richmond heard stories about the brick wall at the rear of the prison that was "scarred as a result of numerous executions by firing squads"; they heard tales of the torture room in the center of the prison which had fifty pairs of balls and chains, leg irons and cuffs. Stories circulated of severe punishment being meted out for hurling insults at prison guards, trying to bribe guards, fighting among themselves, stealing, and for attempting to escape. Cruel forms of punishment were practiced on the prisoners, such as hanging prisoners by their thumbs, or handcuffing them to a post and leaving them for long periods. Flogging, bucking, and gagging, chaining prisoners to the walls or the floors and even branding was practiced.[1]

One rumor accused Alexander of selling the prisoners' food. A rhyme about him was widely circulated:

> He used to take the rations,
> And sell them for cash,
> So that he with the ladies,
> might cut quite a dash![2]

Alexander was accused of using medieval torture methods at Castle Thunder.[3] It was common knowledge that Captain Alexander was an eccentric and a strict disciplinarian, but after the Richmond *Sentinel* reported the latest escape attempt and stories circulated of "barbarous cruelties inflicted upon the inmates of the prison"[4]; complaints increased and only a Congressional investigation could pacify the public.[5]

The stories grew more terrifying as more and more prisoners were ordered to be confined in Castle Thunder. The accusations of cruel and inhumane treatment of prisoners were finally investigated by the Confederate Congress.[6] Thus, in the spring of 1863, Captain Alexander and his method of discipline at Castle Thunder became the focus of an investigation by the Confederate Congress.[7]

The standard practices of hanging up prisoners by their thumbs, whipping, and bucking may have helped deter insubordination in the army and navy, but these same methods of punishment were deemed cruel when used by Captain Alexander and his guards, especially when coupled with stories of the wanton shooting of prisoners. The public demanded and was granted a Congressional investigation.[8]

The Scope of the Investigation

On April 4, 1863, the Confederate House of Representatives passed a resolution to appoint a special five-man committee to inquire about and report back to the House as soon as possible. The committee was to investigate:

1. What punishment if any in violation of law has been inflicted upon prisoners confined in Castle Thunder; the kind and character of the punishment inflicted by the officers of the prison.
2. How many have been killed, by whom and the circumstances under which they were killed.
3. That the committee have power to send for persons and papers.[9]

On Monday, April 6, 1863, the Chairman of the House of Representatives of the Confederate Congress announced the names of those who had been appointed to the committee to investigate the conditions at Castle Thunder. They were: Messrs. Herbert of Texas, Smith of Alabama, De Jarnette of Virginia, Clark of Georgia, and Simpson of South Carolina.[10] The Committee called a variety of witnesses to testify: prison guards, officers, prisoners, hospital attendants, and even Alexander himself.

The hearings began on Saturday, April 11, 1863, and continued until April 29, 1863, when the testimony ended. However, subsequently a number of depositions and sworn statements from those unable to attend the hearings were included in the record.[11] Captain Alexander was represented by Attorney Ward.

Witnesses for the Prosecution

Witnesses for the prosecution were: William Causey, J. F. Schaffer, Robert B. Crow, George W. Thomas (detectives); T. G. Bland (former steward of the prison hospital); Stephen B. Childrey (commissary of prison); Baldwin T. Allen and Marion C. Riggs (prison wardens); Dr. Lunday; John Adams, J. T. Kirby, John Shehan, Charlotte Gilman, William Campbell, Dennis O'Connor, Henry Edenborough (prison inmates); Attorney V. T. Crawford; Cyrus Bossieux, John Caphart, Frederick F. Wiley (prison guards); and Judge Robert Ould (judge-advocate of the court martial).[12]

Witnesses for the Defense

Witnesses who testified for the defense were: Dr. Farrar, Captain Jackson Warner, William F. Watson (Confederate States Commissioner), Dr. John DeButts, Colonel Robert Mayo, Captain Thomas P. Turner (commandant at Libby Prison), Lieutenant Dennis Callahan, J. B. Evans, James Jennings, John Doyle, James McClasher, George W. Waymack (prisoners); Mr. Wynne (doorkeeper of the House of Representatives); Judge Baxter, Captain W. N. Starke (investigator for General Winder), and Lewis J. Blankenship (wardmaster of the hospital).

In addition there were statements read from Greenlee Davidson and General John H. Winder.

The testimony revolved around the treatment of the prisoners and the attitudes of both Captain Alexander and his guards. Most of the witnesses for the prosecution described in detail events they had witnesses. Others told of rumors and gave hearsay evidence. The main concern was the type and severity of the punishment, and whether it had been court ordered or meted out on orders issued by Captain Alexander or others.

Witnesses were questioned by Captain Alexander, his attorney, and Committee members.

Alexander Requests Witnesses be Kept Apart

During the hearings, Captain Alexander suggested that the witnesses who were to testify should not be in the room hearing the witness on the stand giving testimony. The Chairman of the committee stated that he believed the "witnesses present were all honorable men," who would not be influenced by the statements of others. However, he yielded, and ordered all the witnesses except the one being questioned to leave the committee room.[13] This was probably a wise move on Alexander's part.

The Issues Under Examination

1. PUNISHMENT— to determine if any punishment in violation of law has been inflicted upon prisoners confined in Castle Thunder, and the kind and character

A wide variety of punishments were used in prisons during the 19th century. The most common were "trysting," bucking and gagging,[14] whipping, shooting, wearing barrel shirts, being handcuffed around a post or pillar, shackled with handcuffs and a large ball and chain (reserved for the worst offenders), solitary confinement, and being confined in the "dungeon."

Although some of the punishments were more humiliating than painful, "trysting" could cause the blood to stagnate in the thumbs, and turn them black. Sometimes prisoners' hands were bloody after being tied up by their thumbs.[15]

The character of the prisoners had a great bearing on their treatment. Detective George W. Thomas described the treatment of prisoners as generally good. There were two classes of "desperados" who were confined at Castle Thunder, one from far down South, and the other from Baltimore; the "wharf rats" of New Orleans, and the plugs from Baltimore. The majority of the prisoners fell in a third class, and were mostly "inoffensive soldiers."[16]

"Trysting" Up by the Thumbs J. F. Schaffer testified that he had seen prisoners being tied up by their thumbs. It is an old "sailor's punishment."[17] The prisoner was suspended by a rope tied to his thumbs so that his feet did not touch the floor. If prolonged, it could cause permanent damage from loss of circulation.

William Causey testified that he had seen prisoners severely punished, and tied up by their thumbs as punishment for disagreements among the prisoners themselves. He saw a man handcuffed around a post, raised up, and cut down when his "blood had stagnated."[18]

Warden Baldwin T. Allen testified that he saw Martin Darby, a Confederate soldier, tied up by his thumbs for several hours.[19] T. J. Kirby testified that he saw men tied up by their thumbs with a "small sized whip cord." They were left tied up from morning until night. One prisoner's thumbs were black and blue, but he did not complain of the pain.[20]

Whipping Detective J. F. Schaffer said that the prisoners were treated "according to their behavior. Some of them ... have been cruelly treated. They were punished for fighting, sometimes stealing." He said he had seen men whipped and given anywhere from 15 to 35 lashes. Two men, he said, had been whipped by "order of the court martial."[21]

Prison guard John Caphart described how two prisoners "whom nobody could manage" were whipped. "They were not tied up by their thumbs, but the whipping was all done with a leather thong or strap, about two feet long." He testified that he had seen men whipped by order of General Winder and by order of Captain Alexander as well. Whippings were administered on the order of Captain Alexander with the permission of General Winder for stealing from other prisoners or for "mal-treatment" of other prisoners.[22]

Detective Robert R. Crow testified that had heard reports that Captain Alexander had ordered one prisoner whipped for "garroting or robbing another prisoner." He did not witness this whipping.[23] Crow testified later in the hearings that he witnessed the whipping of a man who had knocked out the eye of a fellow prisoner. Crow stated that, rather than a court ordered whipping, he believed that same punishment was directed by Captain Alexander alone.[24]

Mr. T. G. Bland, who had formerly worked in the prison hospital, testified that he had been a prisoner in Fort Delaware, and he believed the prisoners received better treatment in the Federal prison than they did in Castle Thunder. He stated that the prisoners at Castle Thunder were treated "most barbarously and inhumanely." He remembered that on one occasion, 10–15 prisoners were brought out to a large hall because two of them had been accused of stealing. The prisoners were stripped and whipped, each getting 10 to 12 lashes, at Captain Alexander's order. Bland testified that Captain Alexander had said "Lay it on!" Some of those whipped had undoubtedly stolen money, but the others did not have a chance to vindicate themselves. Bland stated that, while some of the officers treated the prisoners "very good," others treated them like they were "dogs instead of soldiers."[25]

Captain Alexander had once intervened in a court sentence that decreed an old man was to be whipped. He took an interest in the old man and got the sentence remitted.[26]

Warden Allen stated that he had seen a prisoner given as many as 50 lashes, but only by order of a court martial. Generally, the men received six, eight, or ten lashes.[27] However, Allen stated that while whipping of the prisoners was "rare," it had a "beneficial effect wherever it has been done."[28]

Captain Henry Edenborough testified that in the East India Royal Navy, whipping was considered "an ordinary punishment. It was not considered a great indignity in the English service to be whipped with a cat-o-nine tail."[29]

Barrel Shirt Bland also saw a prisoners having to wear a barrel shirt as punishment for fighting. The barrel shirt is made by taking a wooden flour barrel and cutting it in half. Then arm holes are cut in the sides, and an opening in the top of the barrel for the prisoner's head.[30] John Caphart stated that he saw one man in a barrel shirt, but that was by order of a court martial.[31] Detective George Thomas said he saw two forced to wear barrel shirts, but this was by order of a court martial.[32]

Bucking and Gagging Detective Schaffer saw men bucked for one or two hours for attempting to escape and for "insulting the officers of the prison."[33] T. G. Bland stated that he saw 15 to 20 prisoners bucked and gagged at the same time.[34] Stephen B. Childrey, the prison commissary, stated that the prisoners who were bucked were "desperate character."[35]

Warden Allen stated that men were bucked for a variety of offenses.[36] Prisoner T. J. Kirby said that he saw men bucked for "two days."[37] However, he seemed to exaggerate all his statements. More likely, prisoners were bucked for up to four hours, and usually for rioting inside the prison.[38]

Prison warden Marion Riggs stated that bucking was "severe and degrading punishment. It is done by passing a split across the elbows and tying them beneath the thighs," like taking a "calf to market."[39]

Out in the Cold The Committee heard how a group of prisoners was punished in an unusually harsh way by being kept outside over several days and nights in winter weather. The prisoners had put gunpowder in a stove and it exploded. Although interrogated by both General Winder and Captain Alexander, none of the prisoners would confess. So Alexander put all of those who were suspected of the deed outdoors for several days. It was November of 1862, and cold, heavy rains fell. The prisoners, although unharmed, suffered from the lack of shelter and blankets, and several died of pneumonia as a result.[40] The back yard of Castle Thunder in Richmond where the event occurred probably looked similar to the back of Castle Thunder at Petersburg (see photograph in Chapter 6).

Because none of the prisoners would tell who had set off the explosion, they were put outside without any blankets, but some blankets were lowered from the windows afterwards. Captain Alexander never did learn the names of the guilty parties.[41]

More details of the same story were related by witness William Causey. A group of prisoners filled a canteen with gunpowder put it in a stove where it exploded. For that, Captain Alexander put the men in a pen outside where they remained for two or three days. They had no covering and it was raining.[42] This was corroborated by Detective Schaffer, who added that the men were punished because they "would not tell who did it." He did not know for certain, but he believed Captain Alexander gave the order for the men to be put outside.[43] Detective Crow added that when the prisoners were put outside it was "quite cold weather, and rainy, and they had nothing to cover them but the clothing they had on, and no roof covering to shelter them."[44] T. G. Bland, who worked in the prison hospital, testified that later some of the men got sick with pneumonia, and that he heard Dr. Coggin, the surgeon, say that the exposure out in the yard made them ill. Several later died in the hospital of pneumonia.[45]

Dennis O'Connor, one of those put outside in the yard, said it snowed the first night and rained the second. The ground became muddy after "our feet cut it up." He stated that there had not really been any danger of blowing up the building, but that the explosion had been set off to "frighten some North Carolina soldiers who were lying by the wall asleep."[46]

T. J. Kirby, a Canadian held as a spy, stated that all the occupants of Room No. 2, about a hundred, had been put outside in the cold in November or December. They had been left out there for four or five days.[47]

Detective George Thomas thought that the prisoners were generally treated kindly, except on the occasion of when the prisoners were "put in the back yard as punishment for outrages." Thomas reported the condition of the prisoners, and Alexander had them brought in immediately. Some of the prisoners had been warmly clad, others not. The more desperate had stolen blankets from others. Thomas believed, however, that this punishment had been ordered by General Winder.[48]

Prisoner John Shehan stated that a large number of prisoners were put outside in November. Some had bed covering. Some were already in bad health, and some became sick immediately afterwards. He remembered hearing that one had died in the hospital.[49]

Warden Baldwin Allen testified that prisoners were punished by putting them out in the yard more than once. Several prisoners were put out in the cold without fire or shelter for "robbing and stealing, breaking windows, and gross violation of the rules." That was done again in either October of November, without covering or shelter, except their "blankets and clothing."[50]

William Campbell, a deserter from a Louisiana regiment, who admitted that he had escaped three or four times, was one of those put out in the cold yard in November of 1862. He said he had also been "bucked."[51]

"The Dungeon" and Solitary Confinement with Restricted Diet   After being overheard making the remark, "I have no more respect for Captain Alexander than I have for my *royal Bengal stern,*" suspected spy T. J. Kirby was confined to Cell No. 3, a room about 15 feet square with one boarded-up window. Whereas he had been eating with a group of men in a mess, Warden Allen denied him the food sent from the mess, and sent it back. Kirby was not allowed to purchase anything from the commissary, and when he asked for rations, they were denied. He had nothing to eat from Friday morning to midday on Saturday.[52]

Prisoner John Shehan testified that he had been put into a solitary-confinement cell called the "sweat house" for going outside as a "corporal of the prison, and getting drunk." The room was only eight feet square. There was no window, and no relief from the heat or the cold. He was placed in irons, as well.[53] This may be the same room Bland called the "dungeon."

Those men who were caught attempting to escape were put in the sweat house and given only bread and water, according to the testimony of one of the guards, Marion Riggs.[54]

Guards Not Exempt from Imprisonment   Bland also testified that he had been imprisoned for disobeying an order from Captain Alexander. The order was to prescribe medicine for a patient, but T. G. Bland refused because he was "not a graduated physician, and it was against the orders of the surgeon in charge." For disobedience, Bland claimed he was put in a cell about six feet square, which was not tall enough for him to stand. He was give no chance to vindicate himself. Although he sent for Captain Alexander, he did not come. Bland was kept in the "dungeon" overnight, but he knew of others who had been kept there for three or four days.[55]

John Caphart, a guard, testified that the reason Mr. Bland was imprisoned was because he would not "render service to a sick child." Bland absolutely refused to obey Captain Alexander, and when asked again, he refused again. Captain Alexander then ordered Caphart to put Bland in the cell. Caphart said that "Bland was intoxicated on that occasion."[56]

The Deranged Prisoner—George Wright   The former hospital steward, T. G. Bland, testified that he had found George Wright, a deranged prisoner, lying on the floor behind a door in the prison room. Wright was lying in his own filth, with no clothing except a "short swallow-tailed coat." His body was covered with scabs and vermin. Some of the prisoners stated that Wright had been lying there for a week. He was taken to the hospital and treated medically.[57]

Stephen Childrey contradicted Bland's statement, saying that Wright was given clothing but that he "would tear the clothes off his person." He moved about the been placed in the dungeon for refusing to obey orders. Bland testified that another time, Captain Alexander had sent a boy to the steward's room for a bottle of whiskey. Bland said he had orders not to give out anything, and so informed Alexander. Alexander then wrote an order for the whiskey, and summonsed Bland to his quarters. When Bland arrived, there was "a little dinner party going on." Alexander again asked Bland to "furnish whiskey for the party," and Bland again refused. Then Captain Alexander said, "Suppose a man was suffering from a broken leg, and I was to order you to furnish whiskey for his relief, and you refuse, I would put you in the cell." That was what happened later when Bland refused to "prescribe for a patient."[77]

When Captain Alexander asked Detective Thomas if he thought he was a cruel man, the detective replied, "No, sir, I do not."[78]

In the Captain's favor was the testimony that after some of the battles around Richmond, Alexander sent out men to gather clothing and blankets from the battlefield to supply clothes for some of his prisoners who were badly in need.[79]

Prison Warden Baldwin T. Allen spoke up for Captain Alexander. He said that the character of the prisoners had much bearing on their treatment. Captain Alexander, Allen said, had found it "necessary to enforce very rigid rules. If they had been less rigid, he would have been unable to keep one of them [prisoners] there."[80]

Prisoner T. J. Kirby testified that Captain Alexander was at times kind, and other times "extremely rough and uncouth; then kind again, and then rough, as the fit takes him."[81] In other words, Alexander was quite unpredictable.

Yet John Shehan, a prisoner who had once been put in solitary confinement in the sweat house, admitted that Captain Alexander had treated him well. He did not find fault with the harshness of Alexander's rules, but declared that it was "impossible to keep so many men in perfect order."[82]

A female prisoner, Charlotte Gilman, who was being held to testify in a counterfeiting case, stated that she had been well treated. She said that all the ladies liked Captain Alexander and "spoke of Captain Alexander in the highest terms."[83]

Marion C. Riggs stated that he thought Captain Alexander's punishment was "more severe than the cases demanded." In addition, Alexander showed favoritism, and there was always "some friend whom he shielded." While he testified that he thought Captain Alexander was "by nature, a cruel man," he also testified that the Captain was kind to him and the other officers.[84]

Attitude and Actions of Guards

Several witnesses testified as to the character, attitude, and treatment of the prisoners by John Caphart. One of the detectives said Caphart did not treat them kindly, but he had heard Caphart say, "Damn them, I'd take a knife and cut them in pieces." Caphart was described as being "generally rough; it is natural with him." The witness had seen Caphart "shove and push prisoners about as though they were Negroes."[85]

Detective Thomas knew Caphart had filled the office of jailor to prisons for too many years, and was accustomed to "dealing with bad fellows." As a result Caphart had grown callous and unfeeling. However, Caphart did not exult over the punishment. He viewed it in the light of a "moral corrective." The prisoners hated Caphart and threw bones at him.[86]

The spy, T. J. Kirby, swore that Baldwin Allen, a guard, was "generally intoxicated," and he seldom spoke kindly to the prisoner. He also viewed John Caphart as a "vile, low, inhuman person." Only Marion Riggs was considered to have treated the prisoners with kindness and respect, and for that, he was looked down on by the other officers.[87]

Riggs testified that Caphart seemed to take pleasure when he was ordered to tie up and buck prisoners. "He would tie them up as tight as possible, and I myself have let them down.... I have never heard him express any regrets for them." He reported that another guard, Baldwin Allen, did not use physical force, but he had heard him "curse the prisoners." At the time of the hearing, Riggs was no longer employed at the prison as a guard. He had been relieved at the first of the month (April 1863) to "reduce force and expenses."[88]

Cross-Examination of Witnesses

When John Caphart was cross-examined by Captain Alexander, he testified that in his 31 years working inside prisons, he had seen many far worse than Castle Thunder. In most prisons, said Caphart, prisoners were put in irons and chained to "ringbolts" in the floor. When asked if he separated prisoners when they came according to their offenses, Caphart agreed that it was true. When questioned about a plot to assassinate Captain Alexander and other officers, to "set the board yard on fire, and liberate the prisoners," Caphart stated that it was "a well established fact, and A. C. Webster, who was hanged, was the ringleader of the plot." Even after Webster was condemned to death, and had been injured in an escape attempt, Caphart testified that Captain Alexander was kind to the prisoner; that he had "cut and fixed his food, and set up with him after he received his injuries," in a thwarted escape attempt.[89]

Handcuffed Around a Pillar

Another action which resulted in punishment was attempting to bribe the guards. Mr. Bland said he had seen a man "handcuffed around a large pillow [pillar]" for attempting to bribe a guard. The prisoner had been placed in handcuffs with his arms around the pillar sometime between 5 and 6 o'clock in the afternoon, and he was still in that position at 11 o'clock that night.[90] One prisoner testified that he had seen men "tied up around a post so tightly that they couldn't lie down or sit down." One such punishment was done at the order of Captain Alexander, who decreed that the prisoner should remain there overnight. However, some of the officers let them down so that they could sit or lie down at night.[91]

Affidavits from Supporters

Greenlee Davidson, a member of Walker's Artillery Battalion, was summonsed to appear before the committee on April 23, but the summons did not reach him until the 25th. He wrote to Captain Alexander to assure him that "it would afford me pleasure to bear testimony to the systematic and able command in which you have managed the provost prison under your charge and to the humanity and kindness with which you have treated the prisoners in your custody." Davidson believed that Alexander had "the greatest talent for controlling and managing desperate characters," and he did not believe there was "another man in the Southern Confederacy who [could] fill your present position."[92] This same letter was appended to the testimony before the committee, along with the letter from Brigadier General Winder.[93]

Once all the testimony was taken and the evidence in, the Special Committee had to make its decision as to the questions put before it. The committee did not reach a unanimous decision, but issued a Majority Report and two Minority Reports.

13

The Verdict

"One wise man's verdict outweighs all the fools'."
— Robert Browning, "Bishop Blougram's Apology"

Alexander's Statement

The testimony of the witnesses before the Congressional Committee was conflicting. It was the testimony of Captain George Washington Alexander on his own behalf that shifted the decision in his favor.

Alexander began his defense with a quote from Napoleon Bonaparte: "the first requisite in an officer was health, the second temper; without the first the second is seldom found and without the second a good officer, mingling the gentleman with the commander, cannot exist." Alexander firmly believed that to be respected, an officer should not forget that he was a gentleman, and a man who could not "command his tongue is the worst man to intrust with any command."

Captain Alexander reminded the committee that he was among the first to resign from the "old Navy and take up arms." He enrolled in the Army as a private, and followed his "unfortunate leader" within enemy lines. He reminded his inquisitors that he had been captured, but had escaped from Fort McHenry. "We fell. I suffered; but … escaped from the tyranny of the 'usurper of rights'".... However, the injuries he sustained in his escape were the reason he came to be in command "of this post."[1] Later on in his speech, Alexander told the Committee that while he was a prisoner, he saw only one man treated "well," and that man was a "psychopath" who "courted their favor." Alexander, while at Fort McHenry, was kept for three weeks in an underground cell only 7 by 4 feet, with no window.[2]

The commandant of Castle Thunder emphasized the character of the men and women in his care—"the murderer, the robber, the deserter, the substitute deserter, the pickpocket, and the skulker," a soldier who habitually avoided being engaged in combat. Castle Thunder held desperate criminals — spies, reconstructionists, and disloyal persons. Castle Thunder was the Confederate Penitentiary.[3]

Alexander defended his treatment and punishment of the prisoners by saying that the rules and regulations were regularly distributed, and the inmates were repeatedly told what would happen to them if they disobeyed the rules. He declared that if the place had "acquired a bad name," it was because of the "fiends who inhabited it." He used punishment only when it was absolutely necessary and it "had become unsafe for a man to enter the wards."[4]

Alexander reminded the Committee members that while their Confederate soldiers were subsisting in the field on corn, the prisoners were "being fed on full rations," and that they refused to rejoin their "suffering comrades." They could only be forced to rejoin their units "at the point of a bayonet."[5]

Alexander did not try to deny that he had whipped some of the prisoners, but stated that they had been whipped by order from a court martial or from a State representative. He did deny, however, that he had tied up men by the thumbs and gagged them.[6]

He did not try to deny that two men had been shot in an escape attempt, and he explained the shootings:

> That two men have been shot here is also true; one an Irishman who substituted for a gentleman from Halifax, and the same night deserted while in sight of the enemy, afterwards captured, locked up here and persisted in an attempt to escape was killed. Another, a Yankee, who rushing past the sentry attempted to fly by the back entrance — killed; they say he was crazy. The sentry did not know it nor I; or I might for I believe one-half of them are crazy.[7]

As to the charges of bucking, he asked: "Are not soldiers in camp when guilty of little peccadilloes bucked and made to ride a cannon or a wooden horse?" His prisoners were only bucked. He claimed to have been very lenient on the prisoners, and to have done "many acts of kindness and charity," which greatly outnumbered his "alleged cruelties." He defended his actions: "Have I not proven my vigilance and strict adherence to right and my energy in carrying out all orders of my superiors?" He claimed to have been economical and by his personal supervision had prevented "extravagance or waste of all Government stores" under his supervision. He stated that he had clothed many "prisoners who were being sent to the field." He explained his actions in putting the men who had tried to blow up the prison outside during cold weather. He reminded the Committee that the comrades of the prisoners, whom they had deserted, were "fighting our battles and sleeping on the cold ground without tent or other cover than the canopy of heaven."[8] He truly believed that prisoners of war should be treated better than the men he held who were "murderers, deserters, spies, etc."[9]

His best defense was the unfairness of taking evidence from those now in prison, such as Witness No. 2, T. J. Kirby, a spy. Kirby, Alexander testified, had been put in the "best room in the Castle, has a fire, a good bed and is allowed to purchase anything from the outside that he may require." Alexander did not think that the witness who would not tell where he was from should be believed, or should the testimony of Adams and Shehan, both habitual deserters, be taken at face value.[10]

Alexander tried to shift the focus to the good deeds he had done, such as establishing the little hospital known as the "Angel of Mercy," where 30 beds were kept and the patients cared for by his own wife. He pointed out that the records did not show the loss of a single patient, and that it had been supported entirely by his own money, and not funds from the Confederate government.[11]

Alexander closed his statement confident that any action the Committee took would be justified. He was not afraid to stand before the people or the press, and invited "the strictest investigation."[12]

Altercation with Representative Herbert

During the committee hearings, which were held in the Senate chamber of the Capitol, some of the members of the committee almost came to blows with Captain Alexander. After one of the witnesses had testified, the Honorable Caleb Claiborne Herbert of Texas exclaimed as he looked directly at Captain Alexander, "By God, if a man was to whip one of my sons I would kill him on sight!" Captain Alexander replied that if his son, or anybody else's son, had been in the prison, and had acted as his prisoners had, he would have inflicted the same punishment. That reply did not suit Mr. Herbert, and he arose and walked toward the captain and demanded, "Captain Alexander, you must take that back." Unafraid and undaunted, Captain Alexander calmly said, while placing his hand under his coat to grasp the handle of his pistol, "Sir, I have only stated what I should have done, and I will not take it back." Mr. De Jarnette saw a dangerous situation was developing and spoke up to remind the members of the Committee that the hearing room was not the place for an altercation. De Jarnette asked the men to take their seats, and they did. Afterwards, Mr. Herbert apologized and expressed his regrets that he had allowed his "indignation to overcome his judgment," and thus a conflict was avoided.[13]

Brigadier General John Winder supported Captain Alexander's actions and his methods of punishment:

> ... in consequence of the violent proceedings of the prisoners in blowing up the building, garroting and using sling-shots upon the newly-arrived prisoners, robbing and endangering their lives, I gave you [Alexander] orders to punish these ruffians severely and if necessary to resort to corporeal punishment.[14]

On May 1, 1863, by a suspension of the rules, Mr. Smith of Alabama reported on the results of the investigation of the special committee into the treatment of prisoners confined at Castle Thunder. The report was "laid on the table and ordered to be printed." Mr. Simpson gave the minority report, which was also placed on the table, and it, too, was ordered printed.[15]

Results of the Hearing

The Majority Report

After a month of hearings, the Majority Report found Alexander's actions justified.[16]

The Majority Report, based on the opinions of three of the five committee members, concluded that the discipline meted out by Captain Alexander was justified, "considering the nature of military prisons," and in view of "the desperate and abandoned character" of many of the inmates of Castle Thunder. Among them, according to witnesses, were "murderers, thieves, deserters, substitutes, forgers," and all kinds of "villains."[17]

The Majority Report exonerated Alexander of any wrongful acts and stated that he had "exhibited such traits of character as in our opinion eminently fit him for such a position."[18]

The majority of the committee members commended Captain Alexander for his management and the excellent discipline he maintained. The use of the whip as a means of punishment was condemned, but it was believed that it served a purpose when used prudently. As for the other alleged atrocities, the majority decided that they had been committed before the Congress outlawed the whip, and there was no valid reason to censure any of the Castle Thunder officials or guards.[19]

The First Minority Report

The Minority Report took an opposing view and condemned Alexander's methods. Since the minority believed that Alexander acted out of a sense of duty, no formal punishment for him was recommended.[20]

Two minority reports were issued. One of these only mildly censured Captain Alexander, but the other "condemned his administration."[21]

One minority report concluded that shooting prisoners simply for putting their heads out of the window was "not justifiable, although alleged to have been only as intimidation." The minority report also faulted Captain Alexander for whipping ten prisoners on his own orders. Although two had been whipped for fighting and insubordination, these offenses might have been "adequately punished without ... such humiliating infliction." Although Captain Alexander acted in some cases on the instructions of General Winder, the minority report thought that Winder's instructions should have been "tempered with discretion" to prevent such "extraordinary punishment except in cases where other punishments ... would have been inadequate."[22]

The minority report, signed by W. D. Simpson, stated that prisoners had been exposed out in the yard on three different occasions: two persons for fighting; 15–20 for fighting and insubordination; and 80 to 100 for igniting a flask of gunpowder and causing an explosion in an attempt to blow up part of the building and escape.[23] The report stated emphatically that "this mode of punishment (long exposure to weather in winter) is improper, because it cannot be measured and assigned with that definiteness which should characterize all punishment."[24]

However, the first minority report did conclude that there had been adequate testimony on everything from sanitary conditions to the general comfort of the prisoners. However, some had been conflicting. It did appear that Captain Alexander was kind to the majority of the prisoners, and "indulgent as could be expected or desired." In view of the lawless and desperate character of the prisoners, despite the fact that the use of certain modes of punishment was regrettable, the first report did not recommend the dismissal of Captain Alexander. The report did state that it believed Captain Alexander's use of corporeal punishment was both "illegal and improper," and that exposing prisoners to the weather was both "improper and unwarranted." The order to shoot prisoners at the windows was deemed unjustifiable, but had been declared necessary by Alexander to maintain "proper discipline" from his conception of his role as the "keeper" of the prison.[25]

The Second Minority Report

A second minority report was submitted unsigned but was indorsed by Caleb C. Herbert of Texas. In answering the first question as to "what punishment if any in violation of the law has been inflicted upon prisoners ..., " the report condemned the whipping of 10 or 12 prisoners charged with violating prison rules against fighting and stealing. The charges had been preferred by other inmates, and those punished were chosen by a vote among all the prisoners. Thus, those who made the charges also acted both as witnesses, judge and jury. This report condemned the "novel and original method of enforcing the discipline instituted by Captain Alexander," and declared it deserved the "severest censure at the hands of Congress."[26]

Committee member Caleb C. Herbert criticized both Brigadier General Winder and Captain Alexander for exhibiting a lack "of judgment and humanity in the management of that prison deserving not only the censure of Congress but prompt removal from the position they have abused."[27]

The report concluded that the punishment inflicted on prisoners at Castle Thunder had been "not only degrading and cruel but barbarous and inhuman." The report said even though Castle Thunder was a military prison and its inmates were "frequently of desperate character," that was no excuse for the way they were treated. The object of establishing and maintaining such a prison was to provide "protection of society by the confinement of persons dangerous to its peace." That end did not make it necessary to whip men or expose them to severe weather.[28]

As to the second question under investigation, the killing of prisoners, the second minority report found that the shooting of a deranged prisoner and another trying to escape were not justified. The report also noted that the guards who had done the shooting in these two cases had not been punished.[29]

The second minority report expressed the opinion that both Brigadier General Winder and Captain Alexander had "shown a want of judgment and humanity in the management" of the prison, and that they should be censured by Congress and removed from the positions they "have abused." The report stated that the charges of "cruelty and injustice" brought against Alexander were supported by the evidence heard by the committee, and that he had shown partiality to other prisoners. Those subordinates under him had followed Alexander's example in their treatment of the prisoners, with the exception of Riggs, who "is entitled to praise instead of censure for the course pursued by him, a course the more commendable as it is so remarkable an exception to the cruelty practiced by his superiors."[30]

Overall, the hearings conducted by the Confederate House of Representatives left the impression that it was right to let the punishment fit the crime, and that the degree of discipline administered should match the "refractoriness of the villains."[31]

The hearings were the talk of the town for a while, but the treatment of the prisoners inside Castle Thunder soon took a back seat to the news from the battle front, the heavy fighting just outside of Richmond at Chancellorsville, Fredericksburg, Spotsylvania, and other bitterly-fought battles. News of the terrible battle casualties shocked the city, and the care of the wounded soldiers took precedence over the plight of the prisoners in Castle Thunder.[32]

14

The Washington Adventure: Alexander Plays at Spying

> "And one man in his time plays many parts."
> —*William Shakespeare,* As You Like It

After the conclusion of the investigation by the House of Representatives, Alexander was cleared of all charges and he resumed his post. But he was not free to return his attention to a multitude of problems concerning prisoners in his custody.

The following letter shows just one of the myriad of problems that had to be faced each day. On May 8, 1863, Alexander reported to Captain William S. Winder, A.A.G., about the case of Nat Flannagan, alias Martin Hines:

> On the 27th day of April a man was received here who was committed and interred upon our Books as Nat Flannagan Co. B, 5th Texas Regiment. He had in his possession a descriptive list of Nat Flannagan of that Regiment and he was reported to head it under the name of Nat Flannagan. Some days afterwards two Gentlemen, Capt. John Sands and Capt. Coke, came down here and identified the said Nat Flannagan to be a man named Martin Hines who was a substitute in Co. C, 32nd Va. Regiment, consequently Flannagan & Hines are one and the same individual and we marked the alias opposite to the name of Flannagan on our Books and when Special Order No. 109, dated May 2, came down ordering the release of Martin Hines of Co. C, 32nd Va. Regiment, Flannagan alias Hines — the same person — was released and sent to his company.
> Respectfully
> G. W. Alexander[1]

Alexander's tenure as commandant continued to generate controversy. He was an adventurer at heart, and on June 6, 1863, he and several others slipped into Washington, D.C., with plans to go to the various army fortifications in the area. Just what he was about is unknown. Perhaps his only task was to scout out the fortification for possible future military attack by the Confederate army.[2] Union Secretary of War Stanton was aware of the breach by Alexander and four others. He telegraphed several officers to be on the lookout for the "rebel spies who have been in Washington within the last few days," because he suspected they would attempt to return to Virginia.[3] Stanton advised Colonel Fish, provost marshall at Baltimore, of the group and that they would probably try to return to Richmond or Culpepper, by way of Point of Rocks, Berlin or Harper's Ferry. He warned the provost marshal that one of the group of Confederate spies would be disguised and wearing a uniform of a United States officer or private. Captain Alexander was reported to be carrying a large amount of Confederate money, the plans for all the forts around Washington, and other valuable documents.[4]

Stanton was most concerned and wanted them arrested "at all hazards." He wanted every person leaving a train at the "Relay House, Harper's Ferry or any other point arrested, examined and held unless known to be loyal." He suggested sending soldiers to any point where Union lines might be crossed. Stanton truly believed that the greatest service a Union soldier could render was the "arrest of Alexander and his gang of spies."[5]

Alexander was so well known on both sides of the Mason-Dixon line that even Secretary of War Stanton could give an accurate description of him to warn the sentries when Alexander and several others were on a spying mission to Washington, D.C. Stanton sent a detailed telegram to Colonel Fish in which Captain G. W. Alexander was said to be about "five feet eight inches high, erect and well made, with keen black eyes and black hair." He reportedly wore a "heavy black beard," but could have shaved it off. Others with Alexander were Captain Summers, who had also been involved in the capture of the *St. Nicholas*; Leon Ellinger; and Fritz (or Fitzpatrick, the keeper of the Bull Run Hotel in Richmond). Summers reportedly was traveling in the uniform of a United States officer. The mode of travel of the spies was unknown, whether by rail, by buggy or on horseback.[6]

Alexander's foray into enemy territory came shortly before Lee's invasion of Pennsylvania, and the subsequent disastrous defeat at Gettysburg. Who tipped off the Federal government that a "ring of spies was operating within Washington City," is not known. However, Alexander and most of his fellow spies escaped.[7]

All the efforts expended by Stanton and the Federal forces were not enough to capture the wily Captain Alexander who, most assuredly, enjoyed his little adventure. However, one of Alexander's men, Simon Rosenfelt, was arrested in New York City. When questioned, Rosenfelt refused to divulge the whereabouts of Captain Alexander.[8]

Winder Makes Changes

To improve the prison system and its public image, General Winder made some personnel changes. In October 1863, he dismissed all but one of his detectives for "malfeasance, corruption, bribery, and incompetence."[9] Yet even with these dismissals, some citizens were not satisfied. One Richmond clerk thought that both General Winder and his provost marshal should resign.[10]

Alexander's enemies were determined to punish him, and they increased their efforts to blacken his name and have him charged with criminal activity while he was in charge of the prisoners at Castle Thunder. They would use any means, both fair and foul, to get Alexander removed from his position.

15

Under Fire Again

"People are not always what they seem."
— *Gotthold Ephraim Lessing,* Nathan der Weise

During its investigation, the Committee of the House of Representatives of the Confederate Congress did not find Alexander's methods of punishment cruel in some circumstances, although some of his practices were considered unusual. After many days of hearing testimony from a broad spectrum of witnesses, the Congressional Committee concluded that Alexander's actions had been necessary to preserve order in the prison.

The Congressional hearings had stimulated changes in the prison system. Later in the summer, both Captain Alexander and the commandant of Libby Prison, Captain Thomas Turner, took a fifteen-day leave of absence. By September 1, they had both been ordered back to resume their posts by the Commanding General.[1] Shortly thereafter, one inmate wrote the Richmond *Sentinel* to report that Castle Thunder was not such a bad place to be. He also complimented the officers in charge.[2]

In October of 1863, Brigadier General John Winder asked the City Council if he could put the prisoners that were then in Castle Thunder in the City Alms House. He did not have the authority to make the move without the council's approval. Winder said that there was a large number being held in Richmond at present and more were on the way. Mr. Burr, one of the council members, opposed the use of the Alms House for prisoners on the "grounds of inhumanity." The request was unanimously rejected.[3]

Once the Congressional hearings were over, Alexander assumed his troubles had ended and he could settle down to his normal routine. He was mistaken. His problems had only just begun, and there were moves to discredit him and get him dismissed from his position.

While Alexander had done many good deeds, many people, both inside the prison and outside, did not like him. He gave the milk rations for Castle Thunder to the needy of Richmond, and he reportedly established, with his own money, the Angel of Mercy Hospital in Richmond. He put his wife, Susan Ashby Alexander, in charge of the hospital.[4] Yet, despite his good deeds and good intentions, he had made many enemies. Those enemies would not rest until he was removed as head of Castle Thunder, and they continued in their efforts.

Counterfeit Money

Some counterfeit money was sent to the Federal prisoners at Castle Thunder. Brigadier General S. A. Meredith, U.S. Agent of Exchange, sent $500 in Confederate money to be distributed to the most needy Federal prisoners. However, $200 of that amount was counterfeit. Robert Ould returned 40 counterfeit $5 bills to Meredith, and sent the rest to Captain Alexander ($300.00), for which Ould wanted a receipt. Another batch of $500 in Confederate currency sent from W. P. Wood, superintendent of Old Capitol Prison, to Brigadier General Neal Dow, was also returned as counterfeit.[5] Captain Alexander handled these funds appropriately.

Alexander Charged with Contempt

In the fall of 1863, Captain George Alexander was charged with "contempt of the authority" of the court. On November 10, 1863, the case of Captain George W. Alexander was tried before the Confederate States District Court. Alexander was charged with "alleged defiant contempt of the authority of the above Court." The case was scheduled for Saturday, November 7, but was continued until Tuesday, November 10. The Richmond *Sentinel* reported that "there must have been some misunderstanding or misconception in this matter."[6]

The case came before Judge James D. Halyburton presiding over the Confederate States Court for the Eastern District of Virginia. James Lyons, Esquire, was counsel for Alexander, and P. H. Aylett, Confederate States' Attorney, was counsel for the Confederate government. During his defense, Captain Alexander had more to say than did his counsel. However, what he said was directly to the heart of the matter and, after a full hearing, Alexander was "honorably discharged from the accusation made against him.[7] The papers did not go into the details of the accusations.

Alexander Indicted Again

In December of 1863, Alexander was charged with "malpractice in office," and confined to his quarters. He was accused of "extensive trade in greenbacks and accepting heavy bribes from prisoners."[8] Through the use of an agent named Bendix, Alexander was accused of trading in greenbacks and accepting bribes from the prisoners to ensure their release.[9]

The matter was to be brought before a court martial, and the nature of the charges would not be made public until then. He obtained his release from arrest, and asked that an investigation of his official conduct come before a Court of Inquiry. This request was granted.[10] Alexander was suspended from his duties, but he would not let the allegations go unchallenged and he demanded an inquiry.[11]

There was an unwritten rule that prisoners could keep their own money to buy items from the prison commissary or the sutlers who visited the prison. Since prisoners at Castle Thunder were allowed to have their own money, it was easy to assume that some may have used their funds to bribe Captain Alexander.

The Richmond *Sentinel* reported that Captain Alexander had been "confined to his quarters, charged with malpractice in office." The charges would not be made public until after the trial. A footnote to the article stated that Alexander had been released from arrest, and he had "invited an investigation of his official conduct before a Court of Inquiry." That request was approved and the court was to convene at "an early day."[12] General Winder relieved Alexander of his command on December 19, 1863. Both men demanded an official investigation.[13]

George W. Alexander was determined to clear his name of any wrong doing, and he had pushed for an inquiry. A court of inquiry was authorized with Colonel Wyatt M. Elliottt presiding. Elliott was a graduate of V.M.I, and a former Richmond journalist.[14] After a lengthy investigation by the Court of Inquiry, the court adjourned with a not-guilty verdict.[15]

On February 15, 1864, the court decreed that there was no evidence to sustain or support the charges against Captain Alexander.[16] However, the court suggested that since Captain Alexander had made so many enemies and had become so unpopular with the people of Richmond that his commanding general, Brigadier General Winder, should assign him elsewhere. Therefore, Winder sent Alexander away from Richmond and assigned him to other positions. In the spring of 1864, Alexander would be sent to North Carolina, and would be in command of the Confederate prison at Salisbury, North Carolina.[17]

Thus, Alexander's days at Castle Thunder came to a close. He had been kind to many of the prisoners, and some had no complaint about him. However, those who disobeyed felt the full force of his wrath and punishment was swift.[18]

The new commandant at Castle Thunder was Lucien W. Richardson. He took up the task on December 19, 1863.[19] Richardson was a former member of both the First Battalion Virginia Light Artillery and the James City Artillery. Military training had helped him develop a sense of responsibility and administrative skills.[20] He was a quiet man and an efficient administrator, the direct opposite of the flamboyant and dashing Captain Alexander. Richardson had begun his military service in the Confederate artillery, and was put in charge of a battery of the 1st Battalion Virginia Light Artillery. Shortly thereafter, he was placed in command of the James City Artillery. During 1862 and 1863, Richardson's artillery helped to defend central Virginia.[21] No doubt Richardson was chosen because of his personality, to end the criticisms of the administration of Castle Thunder, and to improve public opinion of the facility.[22] Richardson did just that and kept the prison out of the limelight, while he worked behind the scenes to improve the prison.[23]

Richardson was meticulous in his record keeping. An inspection conducted in June of 1864 by Inspector C. McRae Selph described Richardson's books as neat and orderly, and they presented a complete and comprehensive record of each prisoner received.[24] The books in which the records of prisoners were kept were divided as to the type of prisoner: 1) register of Negroes; 2) hospital; 3) court-martial, listing sentence, etc.; 4) morning reports of commitments; 5) index of commitments, 6) register of Yankee deserters; and 7) a register of all other prisoners.[25]

Richardson changed the rules about prisoners having money, and emphatically stated that "no monies are to be received [by prison officials from prisoners] except in cases where the charge relates to money, then to be taken out and sent to the Provost Marshal." The rule about money was added to the official guidelines and posted on a broadside at various locations in the prison.[26]

The new commandant kept a tight reign on the guards, and saw that all the prison rules were enforced. He was praised in the inspection report for his efforts to promote the comfort of the prisoners in his care.[27] Richardson, like Alexander, also held the post of Assistant Provost Marshal and Assistant Adjutant General.[28]

Junius Henri Browne, a newspaper correspondent, was a prisoner under both Alexander and his successor, Lucien Richardson. He thought Richardson was even worse than Alexander, although Alexander had been accused of all manner of "debaucheries and cruelties." Lucien Richardson would not allow the prisoners to purchase "a particle of food, or even a copy of a newspaper." The inmates of Castle Thunder suffered greatly from the premeditated cruelty of the new commandant.[29]

Others believed Richardson had fewer difficulties with inmates than did Alexander. Richardson tried very hard to keep himself and the prison out of the limelight. He seems to have succeeded, and at a prison inspection on June 6, 1864, the inspectors noted the commandant's "laudable desire to promote the comfort for the prisoners under his charge."[30]

16

1864: Charlotte, Danville, and Salisbury

"When one door closes, fortune will usually open another."
— *Fernando de Rojas,* La Celestina

Charlotte, North Carolina

On February 15, 1864, Special Order No. 37 was issued from Brigadier General J. H. Winder, of the Department of Henrico, which directed Captain George W. Alexander to proceed to Charlotte, North Carolina. He was to relieve Captain Richardson of his duties there. Alexander signed vouchers for expenses incurred as A. A. G.[1] He stayed in Charlotte only a couple of months, and this assignment is seldom mentioned.

Danville, Virginia

A pay voucher issued April 1, 1864, indicates that Alexander was on duty at the military prison in Danville, Virginia. If he was stationed in Danville, he did not remain there long.[2] At Danville prisoners were housed in six separate tobacco warehouses.[3]

One writer described the conditions in Danville as "truly horrible."[4] Patricia Mitchell quotes prisoner Samuel S. Boggs: "In all my eighteen months' prison experience, the Rebels never furnished us one item in the way of cups, cooking vessels or clothing [except water pails at Danville, Va.]."[5]

Major Abner Small of Company D, 16th Main Volunteers, described conditions in Danville Prison No. 3 as "so crowded that none of us had more space to himself than he actually occupied, usually a strip of the bare hard floor, about six feet by two. We lay in long rows, two rows of men with their heads to the side walls and two with their heads together along the center of the room, leaving narrow aisles between the rows of feet."[6]

Major Small was grateful to be housed on the top floor, just below the roof, where it was warmer in the winter. The prisoners were permitted to exercise outside in the daylight hours, and were permitted to use the backyard for cooking. A wooden trough was provided for washing. Water was plentiful, because the prison was near the Dan River, and details of prisoners were sent under guard to the river for buckets of water. Occasionally, a few prisoners were allowed to bathe in the river.[7]

Salisbury Prison, Salisbury, North Carolina

Captain Alexander was then assigned as commandant of Salisbury Prison during May and June of 1864. His appointment dates from May 1, 1864.[8] He replaced Captain Archibald Godwin, later a brigadier general, who had been appointed provost marshal of the eastern district of Richmond on March 1, 1862, when martial law was imposed on the city.[9]

Brigadier General John Winder frequently shifted prisoners of war from Castle Thunder to other prisons, such as Libby, Belle Isle, and Andersonville. Disloyal persons were generally sent to Salisbury, North Carolina, especially those convicted of crimes against the Confederacy. More and more prisoners were transferred to Salisbury to relieve overcrowding at other facilities.[10]

In the spring of 1864, a large number of Castle Thunder prisoners were sent to Salisbury Prison. Fifty-eight were sent in mid–April.[11] In May, 78 prisoners under sentence of court martial were transported to Salisbury.[12] Thus, when Captain Alexander arrived at Salisbury Prison he was greeted by some "old friends."

The same was true of some of the prisoners. Junius Henri Browne, who was in Salisbury Prison from February 1864 until January 1865, wrote, "On the afternoon of the second day we reached Salisbury, and entering the inclosure [sic] of the Penitentiary, we were warmly greeted by prisoners we had known at the Castle [Castle Thunder in Richmond]...." He described the class of prisoners as "Rebel convicts, Northern deserters, hostages, Southern Union men," and anyone the Confederacy wanted to hold. In late winter, there were 600–700 prisoners at Salisbury Prison. Browne preferred Salisbury over Libby or Castle Thunder because he could be outside and had the opportunity daily to "breathe the external atmosphere, and behold the overarching sky."[13]

The Cotton Factory

Salisbury Prison evolved around a former cotton factory building. Chaplain A. W. Mangum, a Methodist minister and a professor of English Literature at the

University of North Carolina, described the evolution of the small cotton factory into one of the most notorious prisons in the South. The story began on February 19, 1839, when a group of Salisbury citizens decided to build a steam cotton factory. A company was organized and 16 acres of land, located in a "beautiful oak grove that bordered the town on the south" was purchased. Soon, the grove was alive with activity, after the factory was built and operated by local men and women, and "the cheerful song and laughter of the busy factory boys and girls," filled the air. "Those were the halcyon days of peace," and a scene of "beauty and pleasure...."[14]

After a few years, the factory closed, and the property was acquired by the trustees of Davidson College. In a deed dated November 2, 1861, the old cotton factory property was conveyed to the Confederate States of America, and it would become a prison for Confederates under sentence of court martial, citizens arrested for disloyalty, deserters from the Federal army, and prisoners of war captured in battle.[15]

A local newspaper reported: "The Government has bought the old Salisbury Factory, and is now preparing to fit it up for a prison to accommodate some thousands or more of Yankees who are encumbering the tobacco factories of Richmond. Our citizens don't much like the idea of such an accession to their population, nevertheless they have assented to their part of the hardships and disagreeables of war...." From December 1861 through April 1864, the Salisbury Prison contained fewer than 1,500 prisoners. This low number assured that living conditions were relatively comfortable. That all changed, however, when the exchange of prisoners was stopped.[16]

The prison at Salisbury housed Confederate convicts, deserters, conscientious objectors, disloyal Southern civilians and ex-slaves, as well as Union soldiers. Until the fall of 1864, conditions were comparatively good.[17] The main building, a former cotton factory, was a four-story, brick building, about 40 feet wide, and 100 feet long. Nearby were four or five tenement houses.[18]

Chaplain Mangum vividly described life inside Salisbury Prison as he saw it.[19] He noted that Dr. J. W. Hall of Salisbury was appointed surgeon for the prison. Mangum reported in March of 1862 on the condition and the treatment of the prisoners. He noted the "fidelity of the officers, the care and attention of the Surgeons and the management of the hospitals." At that time, there were 1,427 prisoners, of which 251 had received medical treatment, and only one had died. In his quarterly report, which covered the period from December 1861 through March of 1862, Dr. Hall noted there had been 509 cases of sickness and only three deaths. There had also been much sickness among the guards.[20]

Mangum described the activites during the summer of 1862, when ladies and gentlemen from the town were allowed to visit inside the stockade. Both visitors and prisoners were entertained with a dress parade by the garrison troops, which was held near the southwest corner. Afterwards, some of the officers and men joined in a game of ball, a sight which was enjoyed by all — prisoners, officials, and visitors from outside, both male and female.[21]

During the spring and summer of the early months of the war, when Salisbury

16. *1864: Charlotte, Danville and Salisbury* 135

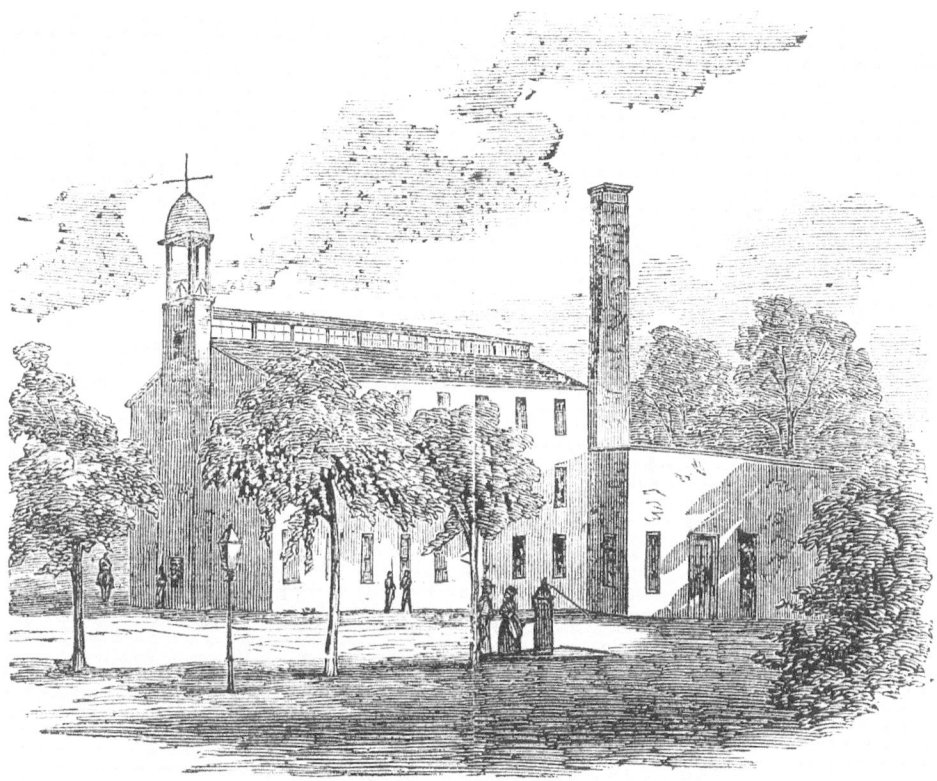

The Confederate Military Prison at Salisbury, North Carolina, reproduced from *Harper's Weekly*, June 14, 1862, p. 357. (Southern Historical Collection of the University of North Carolina at Chapel Hill, North Carolina)

prison was not overcrowded, the prisoners were allowed to pass the time playing baseball. The prisoners played New York–style baseball, and Salisbury Prison soon became known for its leisurely baseball games.[22] The United States Sanitary Commission recommended the game as a means to preserve the health of the soldiers, "amusements, sports, and gymnastic exercises should be favored amongst the men." Baseball was one of the activities that was approved, and officers encouraged the men to participate to relieve the boredom of prison life.[23] Beginning in the early part of 1862, baseball was played almost every day, weather permitting, at the prison at Salisbury. W. C. Bates wrote in *Stars and Stripes*, "... we have no official report of the match-game of baseball played in Salisbury between the New Orleans and Tuscaloosa boys, resulting in the triumph of the latter; the cells of the Parish Prison were unfavorable to the development of the skill of the 'New Orleans nine.'" Gray, a prisoner at Salisbury, noted that the baseball games played there were the first baseball games ever played in the South.[24]

Chaplain Mangum recalled prison conditions before the great influx of prisoners in the fall of 1864. In the first years at the prison, citizens of Salisbury remembered hearing the prisoners singing in the quiet hours of a summer's night. They sang hymns and songs of home, and they called up memories of a "better land, where peace is never broken and freedom has no foe or fear."[25]

Prison Commandants

Salisbury Prison had nine commandants during its existence from December 9, 1861, until February 22, 1865.[26] The commandants were: Braxton Craven, Major George Gibbs, Captain Archibald Godwin; Captain Henry McCoy, Captain Swift Galloway; Captain G. W. Alexander; Colonel J. A. Gilmer, Major John Henry Gee, and General Bradley T. Johnson.[27] Louis Brown, who did extensive research on Salisbury Prison, he believed that the commandants who served between McCoy and Major Gee were of "little consequence to the prison."[28]

Chaplain Mangum praised the prison commandants who preceeded Captain Alexander. Colonel Gibbs left the post when his regiment, the 42nd North Carolina, was complete. He was followed by Colonel A. C. Godwin, who, like Colonel Gibbs, was "a gentleman and a soldier." Godwin had previously managed a prison in Richmond, and because of his kind treatment of prisoners there, when he was captured on the Rappahannock and sent to a Northern prison, "he was sought out and signally favored in grateful return by either the individuals he had kindly served in their captivity, or by their relatives and friends."[29] While Godwin was commandant, he ordered a flag pole erected near the main entrance to the compound, and a number of the Salisbury citizens attended the flag-raising ceremony. Colonel Godwin left his post with a regiment, the 57th North Carolina, built around a nucleus of prison guards. He was followed by Captain Henry McCoy, a relative of General John H. Winder, who held the office for some months. McCoy was also Quartermaster.[30]

The Stockade and "Dead Line"

However, Chaplain Mangum failed to even mention the brief tenure of Captain G. W. Alexander, but stated in his account that Captain Swift Galloway was succeeded by Colonel John A. Gilmer. Gilmer, of the 27th Regiment, North Carolina Troops, had been severely injured and was unable to perform the duties of active service.[31]

During the early part of 1864, the facility at Salisbury was converted to a military prison by building a stockade around it and enlarging the area to about sixteen acres. The stockade was made by putting 15-foot pine logs in the ground to a depth of about three feet. These were boarded up and down to form a solid wall. Along the outside of this enclosure, about three feet from the top, a platform or walk was added on which sentinels were stationed about 10 paces apart. The sentinels paced back and forth, day and night.[32] At the northwest and northeast corners of the stockade, loaded howitzers were kept ready to fire inside at the prisoners in case they attempted to escape.[33]

Officers and enlisted men were kept separated by a "dead line" vigorously guarded by Confederate sentries. The guards had standing orders to shoot everyone who dared cross the dead line, or gave any sign of provocation, or made any move to escape. The dead line was a ditch dug along the east, west and north sides of the stockade, three feet wide and two feet deep. Any prisoner crossing this line, accidentally or on purpose, was shot without further warning.[34]

Living Quarters

Initially, the buildings provided ample shelter, and the well provided clean, refreshing water. A number of huge oak trees provided cool shade inside the compound. Another escaped prisoner was complimentary of the "genial courtesy and generosity of Captain Swift Galloway, who was the commanding officer at that time immediately preceeding Captain Alexander. The prisoners had clean mattresses for the sick, and a hospital which could accomodate 40 patients.[35]

Except for the prisoners' loss of freedom and confinement, in the early days of the war Salisbury Prison was not a bad place in which to be confined. Yet even then two or three officers were held in close confinement in retaliation for a like number of Confederate officers whom the Federal government threatened to execute in retaliation for the death of some criminals ordered executed by Confederate authorities. The situation of these officers was "severe, but alleviated by the magnanimous treatment of the commandant."[36]

One Yankee officer imprisoned at Salisbury described the quarters he was confined in as "very undesirable, being about ninety by forty feet, with barred windows, dirty floors, partially occupied by rude bunks, and two broken stoves that gave out no heat," but only smoke from the green pine used as fuel. The men were not allowed any sort of light at night, but sat there each night in the "thick darkness, inhaling the foul vapors and the acrid smoke," while longing for morning.[37]

The main building, the former cotton factory, had an elevator at one end. Some of the prisoners found that they could go to the room above by climbing up the rope inside the elevator shaft. Those housed on the upper floors found that they could come down the rope, visit a while, and return. William H. Jeffrey, a former Federal prisoner confined at Salisbury, found that the "love of fun in some Yankees was greater than his love of Confederate bacon," and someone "spared enough from his ration to grease the rope." The next day, when some of the prisoners in the upper floor decided to visit, their cellmates had great fun watching the boys "as they shot down through the other stories to the ground floor." Try as they would, they could not get back up, so they had to get permission from the guards. Understandably, the rope was removed.[38]

Major Abner R. Small of the 16th Maine kept a diary of his time in Salisbury Prison, and also wrote up the regimental history, submitted articles to newspapers, and penned a short memoir. He described the horrors of his first night at Salisbury in the summer of 1864.

> We were forced up the factory stairway, step by step over nameless filth, to the monitor room under the roof. The fiendish "Muggers" crept in and robbed several of our number before an alarm was given. Two officers, then stationed at the door

with billets of wood, will never be held accountable for the skull-crushing blows that beat back a "Mugger" as he attempted to force his way in. He fell backwards with a wild scream, and I heard him bound from stair to stair down, down, into what I hope was the Bottomless Pit.[39]

After Small and others in the factory building complained, they were transferred to quarters in one of the small outbuildings and were allowed the use of the grounds within the stockade. These huts were "close quarters for us, and were filled with vermin; yet they were preferable to the factory.[40]

The enlisted men had no shelter at all, and not enough food. In summer and fall of 1864, those prisoners were "thinly clad; many had no shoes, few had overcoats, and hundreds had only ragged trousers and shirt to cover their nakedness.[41]

Additional Buildings Constructed

In the early months of 1864, another frame building was constructed. It was about 20 by 70 feet, and it was used as a hospital. This two-story building was poorly ventilated, and uncomfortable both summer and winter. The main building, the hospital building, and a small building used as an office, together with about six Bell tents and six or seven log huts, comprised all the shelter available at Salisbury prison.[42]

Available Water

William H. Jeffrey wrote that their water came from two wells, one with very good water, the other with "sulphur water." The water in the good well soon gave out, and they were left with the sulphur water. The water level in that well became so low that when the bucket was lowered, it returned with only a "partially-filled bucket of muddy stuff."[43] Major Abner Small wrote that when the number of prisoners increased, the two wells were insufficient. The prisoners were given "two worn shovels" and told to dig. They dug down for about 15 feet until they came to water. They were given an old wooden bucket, a rope, and a windlaw was made from green firewood. Mud and water were scooped up, and the water held "in dippers till the mud had partly settled," and then the water could be drunk. Small remembered how he was often so thirsty that his "ears rang" and his "tongue swelled in [his] mouth." They were forbidden from digging another well because the authorities feared the prisoners were digging an escape tunnel.[44]

There was no stream running through the stockade to carry away bodily waste and other filth. Major Small described the ground as "reeking and the air was sour and heavy with the stench of offal." It was on that filthy soil that the prisoners "lived, slept, and died." [45]

A. D. Richardson, who had been a prisoner at Vicksburg, Jackson, Libby Prison, and Castle Thunder, at first thought his removal to Salisbury Prison was as a punishment. Yet at Salisbury, he found he could "exercise freely in the blessed open air," which he had not been able to do for the previous nine months.[46]

The prisoners soon became "overrun with vermin and reduced to mere skeletons." A "Committee of Public Safety" would take them in hand and wash them, shave their heads, and then "show them off on a sort of race course, for the amusement of the public."[47]

Food

A prisoner who escaped from Salisbury was a newspaper reporter. He wrote that the "rations were tolerable both in quality and quantity." At this time, the prisoners were allowed to buy a variety of articles from civilians outside the prison. The news correspondent recalled that once his "mess had seventy-five dozen eggs." During the spring, summer, and fall, Salisbury citizens sent quantities of provisions to the prisoners.[48]

When the prisoners were stricken with scurvy, a peck of Irish potatoes was given the prison. There were enough so that each person could have one or maybe two. They ate the potatoes raw. Once a woman visited the prison with sweet potatoes, and those that had money bought them.[49] Prisoner A. D. Richardson recalled that he could purchase supplies of food from outside the prison.[50]

The food supply dwindled as the war continued, and during the summer of 1864, the guards themselves committed "henroost robberies," a form of thievery prevalent when food was scarce.[51]

Prison Guards

William H. Jeffrey described the guards as "not very formidable fellows," and many were "unfit for field duty." The guards at Salisbury Prison consisted of young boys, old men and "cripples." One of the young boys performed his guard duty with a bayonet on the end of a broomstick. Once, some Yankee prisoners stole the bayonet from the gun of a sentinel while he was on duty. Even though a thorough search was made, the stolen bayonet was never found.[52]

Even the guards fell victim to depression and low morale. Perhaps this contributed to the fact that prisoners were sometimes successful in bribing guards to help them escape. The morale of the guards was not helped by fact that they had no new uniforms, but wore homespun clothing. The guards were described as a "motley crew."[53]

It was difficult to keep guards at Salisbury, and some deserted their duty. Beginning in the fall of 1862, notices appeared in the Salisbury *Watchman* offering $15 for the capture of guards who had deserted their posts, and $30 for their return to the prison. This was the same reward offered for escaped prisoners of war. While Alexander was commandant, he added the names of the absent guards to the notices.[54]

By the summer of 1864, the attitude of the soldiers toward guard duty changed from what it had been early in the war. After the horrendous casualties at Gettysburg and other major battles, guard duty came to be the preferred form of service. An inspection report done in June of 1864 listed 200 guards organized into three companies. One of the companies was from Alabama, and the other two were local recruits.[55]

Alexander and Staff, May–June 1864

While Alexander was in command of the Confederate States Military Prison at Salisbury, the officers and guards were listed in the Salisbury newspaper:

>Capt. G. W. Alexander, Commandant of Post
>Capt. J. A. Fuque, Ass't.
>Lieut. F. D. Stockton, Adjutant
>J. M. Abernathy, Assistant Surgeon
>G. B. Paulson, Hospital Steward
>James Martin, Sergeant Major
>J. L. Lyerly, Prison Clerk
>B. James Best, Commandant's Clerk
>
>*Prison Guard*
>
>Capt. C. D. Freeman, Co. A, 110 men
>1st Lieutenant J. L. Shirley,   "
>2nd Lieut. J. A. Moore,   "
>Jr. 2nd. Lieut. M. C. Davis,   "
>Capt. H. P. Allen, Co. B, 108 men
>1st Lieut. G. A. Latham,   "
>2nd Lieut. C. H. Snead,   "
>Jr. 2d Lieut. G. T. Allen,   "
>Capt. E. D. Snead, Co. C, 112 men
>1st Lieut. R. H. Watlington,   "
>2nd Lieut. W. R. Snead,   "
>Jr. 2nd. Lieut. A. M. Whitsett,   "[56]

During Alexander's tenure at Salisbury, approximately 350 guards were available, in addition to his staff of seven officers.

The number of prisoners confined as of May 24, 1864, under the command of Captain Alexander were: "Confederates serving out sentences of court martial—310; Yankee deserters—95; Political prisoners—164; Prisoners of war—0"; for a total of 569.[57] This was about half the number of prisoners Captain Alexander usually had under his control in Castle Thunder.

While at Salisbury, Alexander sent a letter to Colonel John Withers, Assistant Adjutant General of the Confederate States Army, with suggestions questioning the loyalty of some Yankee prisoners. He noted that in 1863, several "Yankee deserters desired to take the oath of neutrality." They were given the oath, released, and "allowed to go to work," near the Salisbury prison. So far, their conduct had been "unexceptional." However, the enrolling officer had recently "conscripted" the Yankees. The Yankees protested, their claim based on the "oath of neutrality" they had sworn to, and that they had given their pledge to remain neutral. Alexander agreed with the former Yankee prisoners, and did not think they should be forced to break their oath.[58]

Alexander also informed Withers that a number of Yankee deserters being held at Salisbury Prison, "the worst prisoners we have in the whole place," had requested to be transferred to Andersonville, and treated as prisoners of war. This met with Alexander's approval, and he sought permission from Withers to ship the men out.[59]

The men would probably have fared better to have remained at Salisbury. In the fall of 1864, overcrowding there made conditions harsh, but nothing like the conditions at Andersonville.

Captain Alexander was reported to have brought to the prison the "discipline and order" that the citizens wanted for their own protection. His tenure, however, was short, and he was soon replaced by Colonel J. A. Gilmer, on Saturday, June 18, 1864.[60]

> Capt. G. W. Alexander, who during his brief occupancy of the position of Commandant of the C. S. Prison in this place, gave evidence of a disposition to enforce that discipline and order deemed by the citizens necessary for their protection, having been relieved from duty here, Col. J. A. Gilmore [*sic*] of the 27th N.C. Troops, assumed command on Saturday. Col. Gilmore [*sic*] is a native of Guilford county, and has born himself very handsomely in the field service of his County since the commencement of the war. He [Gilmer] is now a sufferer from a wound received in battle. We have heard him very highly spoken of as a gallant soldier and gentleman, and doubt not his qualifications for any post he would accept.[61]

When Colonel Gilmer assumed command of Salisbury Prison, the inmates were classified as follows: 310 Confederates under sentence of a court martial; 96 Federal deserters; and 164 political prisoners, for a total of 570.[62] This number could be accommodated easily within the space of the prison compound.

On August 24, 1864, Major John H. Gee took over the command.[63]

Conditions Worsen in 1864

Alexander had no idea just how fortunate he was not to have been in charge of Salisbury Prison during the fall of 1864. A huge influx of new prisoners made conditions at Salisbury Prison unbearable for all concerned. Early in October of 1864, the first of 10,000 prisoners arrived. Among the new arrivals was Robert Moffat Livingstone, son of the famous African explorer, Dr. David Livingstone. As a volunteer of Company H, 3rd Regiment New Hampshire, he was captured October 7, 1864, in the battle at New Market Road.[64]

Conditions at Salisbury were far, far worse than they had ever been at Castle Thunder. One prisoner described the prison as it was in the fall of 1864:

... nine or ten thousand scantily clad, emaciated, woe-begone soldiers — unnamed heroes ... in an enclosure of five or six acres, half of them without other shelter than holes they had dug in the earth, or under the small buildings employed as hospitals. The weather is cold; perhaps a chilly rain is falling, or the ground is covered with snow. There are the soldiers — hundreds of them with naked feet, and only light blouses or shirts, hungry, feeble, despairing of the present and hopeless of the future — huddling over a small and smoky fire of green wood, in a crowded tent, whose very atmosphere is poisonous; or standing shivering against the outside chimney of the squalid hospitals, hoping to warm their blood a little from the partially heated bricks; or drawn up in their narrow caves....[65]

Escapes: Successful and Unsuccessful

Even in the best of conditions, prisoners tried to escape. Twelve officers who were confined to the upper floor of the cotton factory building devised a plan to escape. They tied their blankets together and hung them out the window. A deserter, who was to be their guide, was the first to slide down the blanket rope. It tore under his weight and he fell to the ground. The sentinels discovered him, and the escape was thwarted.[66]

Tunnels were always being dug, and some were not discovered until after the prisoners had escaped. One tunnel ran from the commissary building to the stockade, but the guards discovered this one and foiled an escape.[67]

One successful escape was carried out on burial detail. One of the prisoners helping carry the dead outside the stockade for burial was a ventriloquist. He used his talent to throw his voice so that it seemed to come from within the coffin. The sound so frightened the guards that they ran and the prisoner escaped.[68]

Another ploy was to get sent to the hospital because it was outside the stockade. The "smallpox ruse" was used by a number of prisoners. They heated needles over a fire and burned small holes in their faces and bodies so as to appear to have smallpox. They then went to the prison surgeon who ordered them sent to the hospital. Once outside the stockade, after a short time, the crafty prisoners soon managed to escape.[69]

The Escape Plot of October of 1864 Fortunately, Captain Alexander was not in charge of Salisbury Prison when a mass escape was planned. The Federal prisoners planned to escape on October 18, 1864. They organized a corps of two divisions, each led by a capable officer, under the direction of General Joseph Hayes. Codes for signals were adopted and quickly learned, orders were written and wrapped around stones. After dark, these orders were tossed over the heads of the sentries guarding the dead line inside the stockade. The plot called for an attack on the guard, the main gate, the batteries outside the stockade, the commissary, the railroad station, and the town. Everything was in place, but the day before the attack was to be launched, Lieutenant Gardner of the 13th Connecticut threw his message-carrying stone to fast, and the message came off the stone and fell to the ground at the feet of a sentry. The prisoners waited as if paralyzed on both sides of the dead line. Before they could act, a Confederate officer shouted, "Turn out the guard! Man the guns!"

A search was begun for Lieutenant Gardner, but no one knew what he looked like. When he could not be located, the prisoners were ordered to form in rank, and the roll was called. Each officer, upon answering to the call of his name, was passed out through a gate in the stockade. Lieutenant Gardner disguised himself with dirt on his face, and changed his uniform for a ragged one. He then answered to the name of an officer who had jumped from the train on the way to the prison. The Federal soldiers were marched out and herded onto a train. At 5 P.M. on Wednesday, October 19, the prisoners were moved on a train to Danville and another prison.[70]

Salisbury Compared to Andersonville

Although former prisoner Benjamin F. Booth stated in his memoirs that he believed more Federal soldiers at Salisbury "were killed, died from starvation, and from numerous loathsome diseases and conditions, than in any other prison in the Southern Confederacy," Steve Meyer, a modern writer, makes it clear in his work that more Federal prisoners died at Andersonville. He also notes that the "South was not alone in indecent treatment of its prisoners during the war," but that an "equal amount of suffering was inflicted upon Confederate prisoners by the Union."[71]

Major John H. Gee

Major Gee was commandant at Salisbury Prison from 1864 until 1865, the time when the prison was grossly overcrowded and conditions were at their worst. After the war he returned to his home in Quincy, Florida, and was arrested there in October of 1865. He was imprisoned in the Old Capitol Prison in Washington on charges of cruelty and murder. Eventually, his trial was moved to Raleigh, North Carolina, and before a United States military commission he was unanimously acquitted of all charges.[72] A complete transcript of the trial of Major Gee was included in *The Captive*, a book by Annette Gee Ford, the great-granddaughter of Major Gee's brother.

17

The Final Months of the War, 1864–1865

"True it is that we have seen better days."
—*William Shakespeare,* As You Like It

After Captain George W. Alexander was relieved of his duties at Castle Thunder, Captain Lucian W. Richardson was installed as commandant. The Richmond *Examiner* had high praise for the new commandant, "an officer of most rigid discipline, and he takes nothing upon himself but the responsibility of keeping the prisoners in his charge securely, and at the same time in subjection. In this he succeeded wonderfully, and the castle was never in a better condition of order and discipline than at present."[1]

When Richardson took over command at Castle Thunder, according to a report by Colonel Archer Anderson, Assistant Adjutant-General, the provost marshal's post at Richmond encompassed the provost marshal's department, which included a passport office and a police organization; Federal prisons; prisons for Confederate offenders and deserters from the enemy; forwarding barracks for soldiers traveling through Richmond; and staff departments.[2] The Federal prisons were under the command of Major Turner, who was assisted by three lieutenants. All of the facilities were in the lower part of the city. The staff consisted of two clerks (one a soldier, the other a conscript), three policemen (disabled soldiers), one warden (a conscript), one commissary-sergeant, two soldiers detailed by the Secretary of War, one Yankee deserter, and cooks. On the day of inspection during the week ending May 31, 1864, there were a total of 2,239 prisoners being held in the Confederate prisons of Richmond.[3]

Winder Reassigned

Brigadier General John H. Winder, provost marshal general, had been assigned in May of 1864 to the 2nd District of North Carolina and Virginia, and his headquarters were moved to Goldsboro, North Carolina. During the summer of 1864, the prison facilities at Richmond were under the command of Major I. H. Carrington. In June of 1864, Winder was placed in charge of Andersonville Prison in Georgia, and the next month was assigned all the prisoners in Alabama and Georgia. In November, all prisoners east of the Mississippi River were under Winder's authority.[4]

Conditions in May of 1864

An inspection of the hospitals and prisons was conducted the last week of May 1864 by Colonel Archer Anderson, a member of General Braxton Bragg's staff. The inspector "expressed great gratification at the cleanliness and order," and the discipline in place at both Libby Prison and Castle Thunder. A Richmond paper reported that Castle Thunder held 700 prisoners, with 108 in the regular hospital and 14 in the smallpox hospital.[5]

Anderson's report noted that for 20 days during the month of May the prisoners were "without meat, but this was during the time that our communications southward were interrupted." The general fare was two pounds of bread and as many peas as they could eat. The food was served at 10 A.M. and 3 P.M. The prisoners were divided into "messes" of 50 persons each and put under the charge of one of their own sergeants. The prisoners were marched, under guard, to the kitchen to receive their food in buckets, and they took it back to the wards for distribution.[6]

Changes were made in the way that the monies and valuables of the prisoners were handled. Under the new commander, all monies and valuables were turned over to Major Morfitt, the quartermaster, who gave the commandant a receipt for the same.[7] When a prisoner arrived his or her name was registered, and a record was made of the amount of money they had, which was deposited with the quartermaster and was to be returned to the prisoners upon their release. There were a few complaints by the prisoners that their money was not returned to them. A Frenchman released by General Winder complained that $150 had been taken from him when he entered the prison, but when released he received only $50. The report recommended that a commissioned officer of character should be present when the money was confiscated, and that he should continue to "closely supervise the business in each case."[8]

It was noted that each prison had a hospital attached. The hospital staff consisted of "two surgeons, three assistant surgeons, four contract physicians, three hospital stewards, and ten disabled soldiers (nurses)" on duty. Food was prepared for the patients by captured Negroes.[9]

Over the past 17 months, which would have covered the period when Captain Alexander was in charge of Castle Thunder, 50,418 prisoners were incarcerated in the Richmond prisons. Of those, 9,904 were treated in the hospital and 2,885 of those died. Nearly two thousand men were treated in the hospital because of wounds, and of those, 148 died, their deaths attributed to their wounds.[10]

The report noted that Castle Thunder was the facility for confining Confederate offenders and Yankee deserters. This prison received "deserters from the enemy, deserters from our Army, disloyal citizens, soldiers under sentence, Negroes recaptured." On the day of inspection, Castle Thunder held 700 prisoners. Captain Richardson, now in command, was assisted by three lieutenants. However, Captain Richardson had applied for retirement. Castle Thunder employed six detectives whose job was to carry prisoners to and fro, and to watch what was happening inside the prison. They were to prevent prohibited items from being smuggled into or out of the prison. They could make arrests. There were three clerks and three wardens. Records of the prisoners were kept in several books—register of Negroes; hospital books; court-martial books, which listed names and sentences; morning report of commitments; index of commitments; a register of all Yankee deserters; and a register of all other prisoners. This inspection commended that the wards were as clean as could be expected and apparently free from vermin. The prison was guarded by militia and there were 26 sentry posts.[11]

In June of 1864, another inspection of Castle Thunder was conducted by C. McRae Selph, Assistant Adjutant and Inspector General. Selph sent a detailed report to Colonel R. H. Chilton, Assistant Adjutant.

> *Prison buildings.*—There are three buildings used as prisons, viz, Castle Thunder, with a capacity for 650 prisoners, containing at present 442; Whittock's building, used for negro quarters and prison for women, with a capacity for 350 prisoners, containing at present 100, and Palmer's factory, used for Yankee deserters, with a capacity for 400 prisoners, containing at present 100.
>
> The prisons are clean and healthy and the sinks free from noisome smells and filth.
>
> There is, however, one room in the wing end of the Castle the roof of which leaks, and I deem it necessary for the health of the prisoners and the protection and preservation of the building that it be repaired at once.
>
> *Prisoners.*—There are 711 prisoners confined in the different buildings. They are hearty and well cared for, receiving kind treatment from both officers and employees.
>
> *Rations.*—The rations furnished the prisoners are the same furnished to the prisoners of war in the Libby and other prisons in Richmond, being one pound of corn bread, one-third of a pound of bacon, and eight quarts of peas or ten pounds of rice to the hundred rations made into a palatable and nutritional soup.
>
> *Books of records, etc.*—The commandant, Captain Richardson, keeps a most excellent system of records and registry. His office books are neatly and accurately kept, and exhibit a complete and comprehensive record of each prisoner received.
>
> *Cells.*—The cells are not properly ventilated and are not sufficient in number. There are four besides the condemned cell. I would respectfully recommend that four additional cells be constructed, and that the old ones be reconstructed so as to allow sufficient fresh air for the health of those confined in them.
>
> *Guards.*—The guard is kept under strict discipline and a rigid compliance with the prison rules enforced. The commandant evinces a laudable desire to promote the comfort of the prisoners under his charge, and permits them to cultivate a small garden within the walls of the prison, the produce of which will greatly add to their comfort and health.[12]

Back in Richmond — July 1864

By July 4, 1864, Alexander had returned to Richmond. Seeking a new assignment, he wrote to ask to be assigned to duty with Brigadier General William Montgomery Gardner. However, the endorsement for the assignment was declined by General Gardner, and no further action was taken.[13]

Gardner had previously fought in the Mexican War and as an Indian scout before resigning and accepting a commission as lieutenant colonel in Bartow's 8th Georgia Regiment. He was seriously wounded at First Manassas, but recovered. He was, however, unable to resume field duties, and was promoted to brigadier general on November 14, 1861. He was given command of the District of Middle Florida. On July 26, 1864, he was named commander of all military prisons in the states east of the Mississippi, excluding Georgia and Alabama. In November of 1864, he was given command of the Confederate prison at Salisbury.[14] However, he was quickly replaced by General Bradly T. Johnson, who took up duties there on December 18, 1864.[15] Gardner then returned to Richmond where he commanded from January–April 1865.[16]

Conditions at Castle Thunder, July 1864

Life went on inside Castle Thunder without Captain Alexander. On July 11, 1864, Lieutenant General R. S. Ewell reported that there were "several hundred Confederate prisoners" being held in Castle Thunder, "to great inconvenience both as regards rations and guards." Ewell, a military commander who was always in need of men, said that many of the prisoners were from the Army of Northern Virginia, and that some were being held "without charges, some having been confined for months." Some were being confined "at the insistance of regimental officers who still have the necessary paper." He noted that a complete list had been sent to Major Bridgford, the provost marshal of the Army of Northern Virginia. Ewell believed that the best course of action would be to send those men who should not be pardoned to Salisbury, North Carolina. He also wished that the same rule could be applied to the Federal prisoners. The move to Salisbury would lessen the number of men needed to guard the prisoners, and give Ewell "more troops for the defense of the city."[17]

In mid–July of 1864, a large number of prisoners were to be sent from Castle Thunder to Salisbury, North Carolina, just as soon as they could be properly classified. The removal of several hundred prisoners from Richmond would help relieve the demand on food consumption and leave more for the citizens and the defenders of that city.[18]

Alexander Resigns

After his return to Richmond and the failure of his request to be assigned to Brigade General William Gardner's staff, Alexander spent several months with Barton's Brigade.

Seth Maxwell Barton was appointed to brigadier general on March 11, 1862. He led a brigade under Kirby Smith in Tennessee until he moved to Vicksburg, where he was captured, paroled and exchanged. In January of 1864, Barton commanded a brigade at New Bern, North Carolina, and fought under Ransom at the Wilderness. He was criticized for his lack of cooperation. Barton asked for a Court of Inquiry, but none was ever granted. However, his regimental commanders sent a petition to Richmond attesting to their confidence in him. As a result, he was given a brigade in the fall of 1864 and charged with the defense of Richmond.[19] Alexander served with Barton's Brigade for a couple of months prior to his resignation.

From the headquarters of Barton's Bride near Fort Gilmer, Virginia, Alexander wrote a letter of resignation to General S. Cooper, Adjutant and Inspector General, Confederate States Army:

> Hdqrs. Barton's Brigade
> In the barraks near Fort Gilmer [Virginia]
> Nov. 28, 1864
>
> As you have decided that I cannot be assigned to duty where I am now and I have been serving for the last two months to the satisfaction of my Brigade, Division and Corps Commanders, I must respectfully tender my resignation to take effect from the 31st day of December, 1864.
>
> There are several members of the Battalion I recently commanded, to be tried by Court Martial. I am a witness. The Battalion (Castle Thunder Batty) having been disbanded it is necessary to inform the different commands to which the men properly belong of the disposition made of the men, this will take me some time as I think there are over one hundred and two different commands to write to and already some officers are enquiring of me the whereabouts of their men so that they can properly arrange their rolls.
>
> General in taking leave of your Department I do so with grief. I have tried to be all a soldier should be — many are trying to get out of the field I am begging to be kept in it.
>
> But, Sir, I am respectfully
> Your obt. Servt.
> G. W. Alexander
> Capt. & A. A. G.[20]

Alexander's resignation was accepted,[21] and there is no further mention of him in the official records until after the war ended and he was on the list of prison officials who were wanted by the Federal Government.

Winder Dies

Brigadier General Winder died of fatigue and strain on February 7, 1865. Many criticized Winder for his strict methods and even cruelty to prisoners, but others, such as President Davis, Cooper, and Seddon, and many of his former prisoners, defended his actions. Other prisoners and even some Southerners called him a "brute and a monster." Some even believed that if Winder had lived, he, rather than Wirz, would have hanged for the treatment of prisoners at Andersonville.[22] A Philadelphia paper commented on General Winder's death: "His harshness and brutality to Union officers and soldiers under his charge has covered his name with an infamy that will not soon be forgotten."[23]

Shifting of Prisoners

By March of 1865, a move was afoot to exchange civilian prisoners. The Union General Grant had been pushing for the release of "political and citizen prisoners."[24] Robert Ould, Agent for Exchange, was given instructions to "liberate all the citizen prisoners held by the Confederate States as soon as the exchange of the military prisoners to be delivered near Richmond was complete." He then ordered the release of citizen prisoners at Salisbury and other prisons to be brought to Richmond, and others to be delivered to Wilmington, North Carolina. Ould had compiled a list of all the prisoners held at Castle Thunder, in order to determine just which of them were actually "prisoners of war," and those would be sent to Libby Prison. Ould determined that there are "not more than forty civilian prisoners (all told) within our custody."[25]

Major General E. O. C. Ord reported on March 9, 1865, that a "Refugee from Richmond, lately released from Castle Thunder and deserted from Camp Lee, left Richmond last night," and had reported to Federal army officers that detachments of Confederate troops had moved through the city of Richmond a few days before. Rumors also told of Generals Sherman and Schofield combining, and that the cavalry was moving westward.[26]

The Last Count

Probably the last tally of prisoners in Richmond was the Morning Report of Prisoners of the C. S. Military Prisons, Richmond, Virginia, dated Saturday, April 1, 1865, submitted by Captain Massey and approved by Major Thomas P. Turner that showed there were 729 prisoners of war and 22 Negroes for a total of 741. Two hundred new prisoners were added on that day, and four officers, for a grand total of 954 prisoners. The report noted that 175 North Carolina and 25 from Virginia were added to the eight already on hand. Four "Swamp Dragons" were ordered transferred by Major Isaach H. Carrington to Castle Thunder.[27]

J. G. Conner, who had been held as a spy in Castle Thunder for eight months, found himself free in the excitement of the evacuation of Richmond. "Displaying his true colors again," he immediately set about helping the invading Union officials in making some arrests, "which no other man could have brought about."[28]

Richmond Evacuated

When the decision was made to evacuate Richmond, the scene was one of pandemonium. Edward A. Pollard, an editorial writer for the Richmond *Examiner,* was an eye-witness. He described the scene:

> Wagons on the street were being hastily loaded at the [government] departments with boxes, trunks, etc., and driven to the Danville depot. Those who had determined to evacuate with the fugitive government looked on with amazement; then, convinced of the fact, rushed to follow the government's example. Vehicles suddenly rose to a premium value that was astounding; and ten, fifteen, and even a hundred dollars, in gold or Federal currency, was offered for a conveyance. Suddenly, as if by magic, the streets became filled with men, walking as though for a wager, and behind them excited negroes with trunks, bundles, and luggage of every description. All over the city it was the same — wagons, trunks, bandboxes, and their owners, a mass of hurrying fugitives, filling the streets. The banks were all open, and depositors were as busy as bees removing their specie deposits; and the directors were equally active in getting off their bulllion. Hundreds of thousands of dollars of paper money was destroyed, both State and Confederate. Night came; and with it came confusion worse confounded. There was no sleep for human eyes in Richmond that night.[29]

Confederate General Ewell issued orders to set fire to the tobacco warehouses, the flour mills, and other buildings. By morning, the roar of the "immense conflagration" could be heard. Flames leapt from street to street, as through the black smoke looters and plunderers moved, taking away everything they could carry.[30]

By April 2, 1865, Castle Thunder held a large number of Federal prisoners, but the number of guards had not been increased. As the evacuation began and General Richard Ewell set fire to the warehouses, the order was given to move the prisoners from Castle Thunder and Libby to the south. However, in the panic and confusion that resulted, many prison guards deserted and left the prisoners unprotected and unsecured.[31]

Remarkably, some buildings survived, and once the city was placed under military rule of the Federal troops, they began putting out the fires. The heart of the city was destroyed, including many of the great warehouses, the post office, and many private homes; almost a third of the city. However, Libby Prison, Castle Thunder, and the Tredgar Iron Works were unharmed.[32]

The Richmond Theatre, where Captain Alexander's play was performed many times, was spared and it was scheduled to reopen on the night of April 5.[33]

George Alfred Townsend, a reporter for the *New York World*, described Richmond as of April 3, 1865: "There is a stillness in the midst of which Richmond with her ruins, her spectral roof afar, and her unchanging spires, rests beneath a ghastly, fitful glare — the night stain which a great conflagration leaves behind it for weeks." Townsend graphically described the prisons of Richmond: "Struggling silently with colossal shadows along the foreground, two hideous walls alone arise in front, shutting these gleams. They are the Libby Prison and Castle Thunder."[34]

Changing of the Guard at Castle Thunder

That same day, Federal officials began confining Confederate soldiers and citizens in Castle Thunder.[35]

When the Federal troops entered Richmond, the soldiers began putting out the fires set by the retreating Confederates. The people of the city were suffering and the poor were "destitute of food." Of the 20,000 inhabitants, half were of African descent. The Union troops under General Weitzel took 1,000 prisoners. Another 5,000 were in nine hospitals. The Tredgar Iron Works survived the flames, as did Libby Prison and Castle Thunder. These facilities were now employed to house the prisoners captured by the Federal troops.[36]

The Federal forces used Castle Thunder to house citizen prisoners.[37] It was not long before both Castle Thunder and Libby Prison were again filled to overflowing with prisoners, although this time the Federal soldiers were the jailers. A thousand prisoners were held in the Castle, and over a hundred in Libby. Reports printed in a New York paper stated that the prisoners were awaiting parole. It was reported that several hundred Confederate officers and privates were roving about the city of Richmond. Out on parole, these enlisted men had taken the Oath of Allegiance, and "did it very cheerfully."[38]

The fate of Hero/Nero, Captain Alexander's dog, was also of interest to the people of Richmond. The dog had kept watch over the prisoners at Castle Thunder during the tenure of several commandants. The dog had not been seen since the evacuation, and it was believed that the dog had been evacuated with the rest of the Castle Thunder officials, and that he had probably joined President Jefferson Davis and was on the Trans-Mississippi trail.[39]

When President Abraham Lincoln arrived in Richmond he went to the Jefferson Davis home, where General Weitzel had made his headquarters. Then Lincoln, accompanied by General Weitzel and Thomas T. Graves, a member of Weitzel's staff, went to Castle Thunder and Libby Prison. When Weitzel asked the President what they should do about the conquered people, Lincoln replied, "If I were in your place I'd let 'em up easy, let 'em up easy."[40]

The Last Commandant of Castle Thunder

The last commandant at Castle Thunder, Captain Callahan, Edward Folks, detective, and a Mr. Timberlake, clerk at Castle Thunder, returned to Richmond on April 17 and gave themselves up. Together with some other minor officials, the three were consigned to Libby Prison.[41] The next day, the papers reported that Captain D. Callahan had not been confined in Libby Prison, but had been "released upon his parole of honor." Callahan denied a previous report that he was "foot-sore, weary and dispirited." He admitted to being foot sore and weary, but denied he was dispirited and declared he had only done what his "Commander-in-Chief had done — surrendered to an inevitable necessity."[42]

Alexander's whereabouts from December 31, 1864, until the end of the war in April of 1865 are unknown. He is reported to have surrendered at Appomattox with General Lee, but this has not been verified. *The Appomattox Roster*, a list of the paroles issued to the men and officers of the Army of Northern Virginia at Appomattox Court House, published in 1887, does not list George Washington Alexander as one of those who were paroled.[43]

According to the official records, 27, 805[44] members of Lee's Army of Northern Virginia surrendered after Generals Grant and Lee met in the Wilmer McLean house on April 9, 1865. Over 28,000 paroled prisoners' passes were printed at the Clover Hill Tavern in duplicate and issued to the officers and men. The printing began on the afternoon of April 10 and continued, day and night, through the 15th of April.[45]

18

After the Surrender

"He has departed, withdrawn, gone away, broken out."
— *Marcus Tuillius Cicero, In Verrem*

Visitors poured into Richmond immediately after the war ended and as soon as the city was secure under the control of the Federal army. Some profited from their tour, such as John J. Trowbridge, 19th century novelist, poet, editor, and wartime journalist. Trowbridge published an account of his tour of the South shortly after the end of the war. In Richmond he noted that Libby Prison and Castle Thunder were still standing. Castle Thunder, with its iron-barred windows on the lower story and wooden-barred upper story windows, was still being used as a prison. The only difference was that now the soldiers were Confederates and the civilians were imprisoned by United States military authorities.[1]

Under the direction of Captain O'Brien of the 24th Massachusetts, Castle Thunder became a prison for political prisoners, although a number of criminals were confined there. These criminals had committed offenses against local civil law, and a few were deserters from the Union army. Under Federal control, the "horror of these prisons are all of the past, thank God!"[2] By May 31, both Libby Prison and Castle Thunder were emptied of all prisoners, except those held on specific charges, and they were few in number.[3]

Captain Alexander's Dog

Hero (Nero), Captain Alexander's big black dog, was abandoned when the Confederates fled Richmond.[4] The dog had been wrongly stigmatized by the Federal soldiers as a "monstrous savage Russian bloodhound." Reverend J. L. Burrows, who had petted the dog many times, described him as "one of the best-natured hounds whose head I ever patted, and one of the most cowardly. If a fise [feist] or a black-and-tan terrier barked at him ... he would tuck his tail between his legs and skulk ... and he was quite a playfellow with the prisoners when permitted to walk among them." Burrows knew that the dog had been taken to New York and the New England states where he was exhibited for profit as "a specimen of the cruel devices of Southern officials to worry and torture prisoners."[5]

Hero was last known to be in possession of Sidney Munn in New York City.[6] As reported in a Richmond paper, the dog that once guarded Castle Thunder had been taken to Washington by Union soldiers. "He has taken a fancy to his captors, and is trying to be a good, loyal, Union dog."[7] George D. Putnam, who had seen the dog when he was a prisoner in Richmond, reported that when Weitzel's troops entered Richmond, the dog was caught and taken to New York. There, he was sold at auction on the steps of the Astor House. Putnam hoped the purchaser of the dog would be careful enough not to allow any of his family to wear army blue, because "there must certainly have been trouble." The dog had been trained to attack anyone wearing blue.[8]

The big Russian bloodhound, along with Jack, the bloodhound kept at Andersonville Prison, were in Boston on exhibition in September of 1865.[9] Hero and Jack were reportedly shipped to the Chicago Sanitary Fair where the two dogs raised $2,100 for the Soldiers Fund.[10]

The Key to the Castle

Huge signs with letters a foot long were created to proclaim "Libby Prison," and "Castle Thunder" to visitors. The old signboard of Libby was sent North, as was a key to Castle Thunder.[11]

The key to the front door of Castle Thunder was taken to New York and auctioned off to help raise funds for orphaned children of Union soldiers.[12] Reportedly, it was carried North by a former prisoner of Castle Thunder. Undoubtedly it was only a ward or cell key and of little importance, because the prison was still being used, and a key is a necessary part.[13]

The key passed to the heirs of Colonel Mattison, and in August of 2000, the Northeast Auctions put it up for sale to the highest bidder.[14]

Retribution

Major Isaac H. Carrington, the provost marshal of Richmond and of Henrico County, was arrested and brought from Danville to Castle Thunder. Carrington had fled the city along with President Davis, but had remained in the Danville area instead of going farther south. It was not known what charges were preferred against him, nor by whose order.[15]

When all the prisoners held in the south had been released, and the Federal authorities saw the condition of some of the prisoners that were held in places like Andersonville, tempers ran high. The stories of the atrocities in the South (as well as those in the North) were confirmed. Those responsible were to be apprehended, tried and punished for their crimes. The leaders of the rebellions, according to the victors, had to be punished. Vengeance began with the search for, arrest and trial of the conspirators who assassinated President Abraham Lincoln.

With the arrest of Captain Wirz, there was a demand that those responsible for the cruel treatment of the Federal prisoners be punished. It was believed that Wirz committed wholesale murder as part of some malicious design on the part of the Confederate government. Those persons in charge of the prisons were seen as "men whose natural disposition especially qualified them for a brutal and base business."[16]

One New York newspaper recommended that the Confederate prison authorities be tried by a civil court rather than by court martial. This paper condemned the sensational articles that appeared in print even before the former prison wardens were tried. Everyone seemed to agree that the prisoners under Wirz had been treated inhumanely and barbarously, and that he should be punished. However, it was not "the duty of the newspapers to try him."[17]

Henry Wirz, commandant at Andersonville, was a native of Switzerland and had practiced medicine in Louisiana. Early in the war he was a clerk at Libby Prison. Later, he was wounded at Seven Pines, and after he recovered, he was sent to Europe. During 1863 he served as a courier. After his return to the South, he was placed in command at Andersonville in January 1864 and continued until the end of the war, when all prisons were horribly overcrowded and the means of caring for them greatly diminished.[18]

The trial of Wirz began August 21, 1865. There was some dispute over the charges and the court was adjourned after the first day to be reorganized. It reconvened on August 23 under the direction of General Lew Wallace with Colonel N. P. Chipman serving as judge advocate.[19] Basically, Wirz was indicted on two main charges — conspiracy with "Richard B. Winder, Isiah H. White, W. S. Winder, R. R. Stevens and others unknown to subject prisoners to torture and suffering by putting them in unhealthy unwholesome quarters, exposing them to the weather, compelling them to use impure water, and furnishing them with insufficient food." Wirz was charged with "willful and malicious neglect" in the care and treatment of the prisoners at Andersonville. The second charge was of several murders, deaths of prisoners which occurred after Wirz shot four with his pistol. Four others were killed by guards on Wirz's orders. Two died from being in the stocks, and one died on the "chain gang." The prison bloodhounds had been sent after one escaping prisoner and he died. The names of none of these men were in the specifications, and were not given by the witnesses.[20] One hundred sixty witnesses testified in the trial of Wirz, which continued until October 16. The testimony was overwhelming and all of it condemned Wirz. Wirz testified on his own behalf and noted that 145 of the witnesses had not seen him kill a prisoner, nor was there any evidence of a conspiracy. Colonel Chipman then summarized the evidence.[21] The prison commandant was convicted on the charge of conspiracy, and the names of President Jefferson Davis, James A. Seddon, Howell Cobb, Brigadier General John H. Winder and five others were added as co-conspirators. Wirz was also convicted for 10 of the 13 murders he was charged with. The total number of deaths from various causes was omitted. Wirz was condemned to death by hanging, which took place on November 10, 1865.[22]

A few other prison officials were held, but none executed except Wirz. Richard Turner was held in Libby Prison until June of 1866, and finally released from lack of evidence to convict him. Captain R. B. Winder was arrested in August and held as long as the Wirz trial continued, and although Captain Winder was named as one of the conspirators with Wirz, General Grant ordered his release in December. However, by March of 1866, Winder was still in prison awaiting preparation of charges by Ambrose Spencer.[23]

A report was made on October 12, 1865, which listed the Confederate prisons, the conditions that existed in each, and the names of those responsible for them. On the list of prisons in Richmond, Virginia, were Libby Prison, Belle Isle, Castle Godwin, and Castle Thunder. The report noted that G. W. Alexander, the assistant provost marshal and commandant of Castle Thunder, had held that post for two years. According to P. Cashmyer, Captain Alexander was an officer:

> ... whose only virtue was that of being a severe disciplinarian. He prostituted his authority to the arrest of all persons, Union or otherwise, whom he or his underlings could entrap into any expression of sentiment against those in authority or evasion of military law. This he made the process of a system of robbery, confiscation, and blackmail that would at this day require strong evidence to believe could have been practiced with such impunity. As a prison commandant he was harsh, inhuman, tyrannical and dishonest in every possible way he could practice these vices.[24]

Cashmyer's report made no mention of Alexander's time at Salisbury Prison, but from lack of information, cited only Colonel Godwin's term there and his treatment of prisoners as "unkind and severe."[25]

By November, a list had been prepared of those who were being sought for trial. Captain Alexander was listed twice, once for Castle Thunder in 1862, and again at Salisbury Prison. At the time the list was made, only R. B. Winder, J. W. Duncan (Andersonville), and Doctor Nesbit (Salisbury) were in custody. Major John H. Gee was being sought in North Carolina, and Lieutenant Colonel Iverson, of the 47th Georgia Volunteers, and Lieutenant Barrett, were being sought in Columbus and/or Augusta, Georgia, for their role in the treatment of prisoners at Florence, South Carolina.[26]

Colonel Gibbs, who had commanded Andersonville before the arrival of Wirz, was arrested, but released soon thereafter.[27] Major John H. Gee, commander at Salisbury, North Carolina, was tried before a military tribunal on charges of failure to provide wood, water, shelter, and bedding to his prisoners, and also on a charge of murder. However, he was found not guilty on all charges.[28] James W. Duncan, who had been at Andersonville, was arrested, tried and convicted of manslaughter. He was sentenced on June 8, 1866, to 15 years of hard labor at Fort Pulaski, but he escaped after only 11 months.[29]

Although there were no more trials of prison officials, the treatment prisoners received was not forgotten. Many former prisoners wrote their memoirs. In the years between 1862 and 1866, there were 54 books and articles published by Federal prisoners of their experiences in Southern prisons.[30] During the next five years, many more books were published, a trend that continued until the turn of the century.[31]

Amnesty

President Andrew Johnson first issued a "Proclamation of Amnesty and Pardon for the Confederate States" on May 29, 1865. However, a large class of Confederates was exempt from this amnesty. Those so excluded by the May 1865 amnesty were:

> First, all who are or shall have been pretended civil or diplomatic officers or otherwise domestic or foreign agents of the pretended Confederate Government.
> Second, all who left judicial stations under the United States to aid the rebellion.
> Third, all who shall have been military or naval officers of said pretended Confederate government above the rank of colonel in the army or lieutenant in the navy.
> Fourth, all who left seats in the Congress of the United States to aid in the rebellion.
> Fifth, all who resigned or tendered resignations of their commissions in the Army or Navy of the United States to evade duty in resisting the rebellion.
> Sixth, all who have engaged in any way in treating otherwise than lawfully as prisoners of war persons found in the United States service as officer, soldiers, seamen, or in other capacities.
> Seventh, all persons who have been or are absentees from the United States for the purpose of aiding the rebellion.
> Eighth, all military and naval officers in the Rebel service who were educated by the government in the Military Academy at West Point or the United States Naval Academy.
> Ninth, all persons who held the pretended offices of governors of states in insurrection against the United States.
> Tenth, all persons who left their homes within the jurisdiction and protection of the United States and passed beyond the Federal military lines into the pretended Confederate States for the purpose of aiding the rebellion.
> Eleventh, all persons who have been engaged in the destruction of the commerce of the United States upon the high seas and all persons who have made raids into the United States from Canada or been engaged in destroying the commerce of the United States upon the lakes and rivers that separate the British Provinces from the United States.
> Twelfth, all persons who, at the time when they seek to obtain the benefits hereof by taking the oath herein prescribed, are in military, naval, or civil confinement or custody, or under bonds of the civil, military, or naval authorities, or agents of the United States as prisoners of war, or persons detained for offenses of any kind, either before or after conviction.
> Thirteenth, all persons who have voluntarily participated in said rebellion and the estimated value of whose taxable property is over $20,000.
> Fourteenth, all persons who have taken the oath of amnesty as prescribed in the President's proclamation of December 8, A.D., 1863, or an other of allegiance to the government of the United States since the date of said proclamation and who have not thenceforward kept and maintained the same inviolate.[32]

George W. Alexander would have been denied amnesty under several of the 14 classes, especially the fifth and sixth, and probably the eleventh.

While this act granted amnesty to a large number of former Confederates, it effectively excluded all who had been civil officials and military officials, especially any who had resigned from duty in the United States Army or Navy.[33] There was also a clause that allowed the President to pardon any person who was in the 14 excepted classes, and the authority to extend clemency on an individual basis.[34]

Even those who did come under the shelter of Johnson's 1865 amnesty proclamation were required to take an oath to "support, protect and defend the Constitution of the United States...."

Thousands of those exempt from Johnson's amnesty of May 1865 petitioned President Johnson for pardons in 1866 and 1867.[35] Although President Andrew Johnson had extended the amnesty on December 25, 1868, still a number of high-ranking military and civil officials were exempted and barred from holding office. Congress declared the action unconstitutional. In 1872, a limited amnesty was passed by Congress and signed by President Grant, but it was not until 1898 that a general amnesty was extended to all those previously excluded.[36]

During the evacuation of Richmond, Major Thomas P. Turner, commandant at Libby Prison, fled and made his way out of the country to the safety of Cuba. On January 8, 1866, from the Hotel Cabanas in Havana, Turner wrote his friend S. Robert Shinn. Turner's letter described how he had left Richmond on the very day the Yankees entered the city. He was near General Lee's headquarters at the time of the surrender. Turner started for General Johnston's army, but was cut off by Stoneman's men. He made a "wide circumbendibus" and reached Augusta, Georgia. Then, he started toward Florida to join General Gardner and exit the country. He did not succeed in that route, but had to back track. General Gardner became ill, and Turner left him to travel onward to the Mississippi River alone. He used an assumed name, avoided towns and public roads, and slept in the woods. Turner finally reached the Yazoo Valley, left his horse, and using a dug out canoe he made his way through swamps. He was bitten by mosquitoes, buffalo gnats, and other creatures. He abandoned his canoe and walked 25 miles to the Mississippi in mud up to his knees. He finally reached the Mississippi and crossed over to Arkansas. With an Arkansas soldier as a companion, Turner made his way to Waco, Texas, and the Rio Grande. By then it was summer, and Turner decided to rest for a while with a Texas family. Confederate General Jubal A. Early reached the neighborhood, and they decided to continue their travels together, "to share weal or woe" in the pursuit of freedom from "Yankee thraldom."[37]

By mid–October, Early and Turner started for Galveston, where they boarded a ship destined for Liverpool. They reached the Bahamas and landed on the Bermine Islands. They secured passage on a schooner and arrived in Nassau on December 1. He arrived in Havana on December 10, 1865.[38] A picture of Turner and Early together in Havana was reproduced in Early's autobiograph, *Lieutenant General Jubal Anderson Early, C.S.A.: Autobiographical Sketch and Narrative of the War Between the States*.[39]

Turner was convinced that none of those connected with Confederate prisons were safe. He knew of the fate of Mrs. Surratt and the others who had conspired to kill President Lincoln, and he knew of the trial and execution of Captain Wirz.[40]

As had other wanted Confederate military and government officials, Captain G. W. Alexander fled the country. His journey was probably as fraught with hardships as that of Major Turner. After the surrender at Appomattox, he made his way by sea to New Orleans, then he traveled up the Mississippi to Canada. For several years Alexander resided in Canada, where he taught French to French children.[41]

Had Alexander not sought refuge in Canada, he might have found himself in prison for a number of months. If he had been in custody shortly after the war ended, he might have been tried and executed. Certainly, with the climate in the United States after the end of the war, the attitude of the Radical Republicans, and the hysteria generated by the Lincoln assassination and the trial of Henry Wirz, Alexander could have met a tragic fate. Fortunately, that was not the case, and he was able to remain out of the country until the political climate cooled. Once it did, and there was a new regime in Washington, Alexander returned to the United States to begin a new career.

19

1870–1890

"O Captain! My Captain! Our fearful trip is done
The ship has weathered every rack, the prize we sought is won,"

—*Walt Whitman, "O Captain! My Captain!"*

The Debate Over Treatment of Prisoners Continues

In 1869, the United States House of Representatives did a study on the treatment of prisoners. Naturally biased toward the North, the report concluded:

> In striking contrast with the uniform kindness of Union soldiers toward their captives taken in battle, was the treatment experienced by our officers and men immediately upon falling into the hands of the enemy. The harsh and brutal conduct of the rebels toward their unfortunate prisoners furnishes a constant and leading theme of the survivors.[1]

That report influenced opinions about treatment received by prisoners in southern prisons, and provided a blanket for the harsh treatment Confederates received in Northern prisons, such as Fort McHenry, Johnson's Island, and others in which Southerners were badly mistreated. There were some men in charge of prisons north of the Mason-Dixon line who were cruel to their prisoners. One such man, Captain McKee, who had been the provost marshal at Mt. Sterling, Kentucky, was captured, and put in Libby Prison. McKee was known to have treated Confederate prisoners with "great brutality."[2]

The debate over the treatment of prisoners during the war continued far into the 1870s. A number of articles were published in the *Southern Historical Society Papers* describing the treatment of Northern and Southern prisoners. One article, based on the figures of Secretary of War Edwin Stanton, pointed out the fact that more Confederates died in Northern prisons than did Federal prisoners in Southern prisons.[3] The gauntlet was taken up by *The Nation* and the New York *Tribune*. *The Nation* refuted the earlier article and emphatically stated:

> The evidence of abuses at the largest Southern prisons — Libby, Bell Isle, and especially Andersonville — is so extensive and so excellent (including the statements of both the investigating officers sent by the Confederate Government) that general denials by the author, or persons like General Lee, who do not appear to have had any personal knowledge of the matter, will hardly receive the attention the Secretary seems to expect, particularly as it appears plainly enough from the report that there is only too much foundation for the charges.[4]

As late as April 5, 1877, *The Nation* and others in the North continued to blame ex–President Jefferson Davis, and charged that "Mr. Davis was the author, knowingly, deliberately, quality and wilfully, of the gigantic murder and crime at Andersonville."

Cancellation of the Cartel Blamed

The Southern Historical Society refuted the statements which had appeared in *The Nation,* and issued its own counter-claim:

> ... suffering of prisoners on both sides could have been avoided by simply carrying out the terms of the cartel, and that for the failure to do this the Federal authorities alone were responsible; that the Confederate government originally proposed the cartel, and were always ready to carry it out in both letter and spirit; that the Federal authorities observed its terms only so long as it was to their interest to do so, and then repudiated their plighted faith and proposed other terms, which were greatly to the disadvantage of the Confederates; that when the Government at Richmond agreed to accept the hard terms of exchange offered them, these were at once repudiated by the Federal authorities; that when Judge Ould agreed upon a new cartel with General Butler, Lieutenant-General Grant refused to approve it, and Mr. Stanton repudiated it; and that the policy of the Federal Government was to refuse all exchange, while they "fired the Northern heart" by placing the whole blame upon the "Rebels," and by circulating the most heartrending stories of "Rebel barbarity" to prisoners.[5]

The cancellation of the cartel had little effect on the prisoners within Castle Thunder because most of them were Confederate deserters, spies, and civilian alien enemies. However, it did affect the Federal soldiers held as prisoner under Alexander's care at Danville and Salisbury, and those Federal soldiers held temporarily at Castle Thunder.

Alexander Returns

By the early 1870s, sentiment had shifted to favor forgiveness for and reconciliation with former Confederates. Such men as Carl Schurz and Horace Greeley did much toward influencing public opinion in that direction. The issue of amnesty for Confederates became a primary issue in the 1872 presidential election. Liberal Republicans abandoned Ulysses S. Grant and backed Greeley, who had been nominated by the Democrats. To counteract them, the regular Republicans in Congress pushed through the Amnesty Act of 1872.[6]

The Amnesty Act, signed into law by President U. S. Grant on May 22, 1872, removed the restrictions evoked under the Fourteenth Amendment for all but a few hundred Confederate leaders.[7] This bill was known as H. R. 2761.[8] With the political climate more favorable, and with Democrats back in Congress, George W. Alexander could return to the United States.

Alexander as Editor

Upon his return to the States, George Alexander became editor of *The Sunday Gazette*, a weekly paper published in Washington, D.C.[9] He edited the paper from about 1873 until 1880. However, a bibliography entitled *Bibliography of the District of Columbia,* published in 1900, only about 25 years after Alexander's newspaper days, made no mention of him or his publication. T. B. Florence was listed as the editor of the *Sunday Gazette*, a paper published weekly from 1868–1888. In addition, there were three additional listings for the *Washington Gazette* in the *Bibliography of the District of Columbia,* but those listed had all ceased publication before the 1870s.[10]

Some of the old newspapers in the collection of the Library of Congress recently have been transferred to the American Antiquarian Society, Worcester, Massachusetts. The Library of Congress index notes that publication of *The Gazette* began sometime between September 21, 1873, and October 11, 1874, with the latter issue described as being Volume 12, No. 21. The paper continued to be published as the *Sunday Morning Gazette*, and then simply the *Sunday Gazette*.[11]

After the death of John C. Proctor, editor of the *Critic,* a meeting of the members of the press of the Washington area was held. C. M. Barton, of the *Chronicle,* presided and John B. McCarthy of the Baltimore *Sun* was elected secretary. Several of those in attendance gave brief addresses as to the life and character of the late Mr. Proctor, and resolutions were adopted to pay tribute to his memory as well as to express sympathy to his family. The group resolved to attend the funeral, which was to be held at 4 o'clock P.M. on July 14, 1876. G. W. Alexander of the *Sunday Gazette* was named to a committee appointed to represent the press at Proctor's funeral.[12]

It was during the period Alexander was editor of the *Gazette* that his character was assaulted and he became the primary subject of a pamphlet entitled *The military-prison keepers of the late Southern Confederacy in the van of the Democratic Party*. The title page carried a notation that Alexander, a former Confederate military-prison keeper, was the present publisher of a Democratic weekly paper in Washington, D.C.[13] Actually, the pamphlet was a political ploy by the Republicans to discredit claims by the Democrats that Jefferson Davis did not personally know any of those in charge of the Confederate Prisons. The pamphlet alluded several times to a letter written by ex–President Jefferson Davis to George W. Alexander. The pamphlet alleged that Alexander used his recommendation from Davis to get contributions and monetary support from Democrats in Washington which enabled him to buy and operate his newspaper.[14] (See Appendix 5 for full text of this article.)

Alexander gave up the paper, and he and his wife settled in Baltimore, Maryland. There, he put his "scientific education and executive" abilities to use as a "sanitary engineer."[15] The 1880 Census listed George Alexander and wife, Susan S. Alexander, as living in Baltimore, Maryland. His age was listed as 50, place of birth as Maryland. He gave his occupation as engineer. Susan was listed as 46 years of age, born in Virginia, as were both her parents.[16] There were no children listed, nor any other persons living in the household, such as a housekeeper, maid, or cook. If they had such household employees, they did not reside in the home with the Alexanders.

George Alexander visited Richmond to attend the unveiling ceremony for a monument to General Robert E. Lee.[17] This fine equestrian monument to the most cherished man in the Confederacy was unveiled on May 29, 1890, at the intersection of Monument Avenue and Allen Street. The statue, which depicts Lee holding the reigns of a bowing horse, faces south and rises high about the street. Today, Monument Avenue is the only street in the United States that is also a National Historic Landmark. It runs though the historic Fan District of Richmond which, over the years, has become a much coveted residential neighborhood. Large, graceful homes, apartments, and churches in every style from English Tudor to Italianate Colonial to Spanish grace both sides of the five-mile, two-lane avenue. Other magnificent statues to Confederate heroes adorn the way: J. E. B. Stuart, Jefferson Davis, and Thomas "Stonewall" Jackson, as well as monuments to such nationally-known figures as Matthew Fontain Maury, "The Pathfinder of the Seas," and Arthur Robert Ashe, Jr., noted athlete, professional tennis player, scholar, and humanitarian.[18]

The last years of George Alexander's life were not happy ones. He suffered a series of strokes which resulted in paralysis. While each stroke diminished his physical capacities, his "spirit was untouched," and he bore his suffering with cheerfulness. After he became unable to work, he and his wife moved to Laurel, Maryland,[19] where they lived in a house on Montgomery Street, between 7th and Church Street.[20]

Laurel was a little town in Prince George's County, Maryland. In 1878, it had a population of less than 2,000 people. The 500-square mile county is bounded by the Patuxent River on the east, the Potomac River on the west, and the counties of Montgomery and Howard on the north, with Charles County on the South. Prince George's County makes the border of the District of Columbia on the eastern and northeastern edges. It is situated on the Washington Branch of the Baltimore & Ohio Railroad, 22 miles South of Baltimore. The Baltimore & Potomac Railroad and the Southern Maryland & Point Lookout Railroad also cross the county, making access easy for the residents to travel to Baltimore, Washington, or Alexandria. A fertile farming area, the town is near the Big Patuxent River. The surrounding land is a mixture of sand and clay loam and produces an abundance of tobacco, wheat, potatoes, corn and hay. After the war and the abolition of slavery, land prices dropped drastically, and farms could be purchased at $15 to $50 per acre, half the antebellum value. The once dense forests have been cleared, but towering hardwood trees — oaks, hickory, chestnut, gum, beech, and maple — still provide a variety of colorful leaves in the fall.[21]

George and his wife, Susie, were content to live out their lives in this quiet little town. He had only a few years to live. Always an active man, full of vigor and energy, George Alexander would come to welcome death as a means to escape the prison of his weak and paralyzed body.

Epilogue

"The wheel is come full circle."
—*William Shakespeare, King Lear*

Richmond Recovers

The South and its recovery was of continued interest in Northern publications. An article entitled "Richmond Since the War" was published in 1877. The city of Richmond is an example of the "wonderful recuperative power of its people."

> Hundreds of the most successful business men in Richmond to-day found themselves, on the morning of the 3d of April, 1865, stripped of their last dollar's worth of property. Many of them were gentlemen of the oldest Virginia families, owning large ancestral estates before the war, and strangers to want. But not a few of them possessed great resources of mind and body, and philosophy enough to dismiss their regret for the past, and to grapple resolutely with the exigencies of the occasion. The first thing to be done was to clear away the foundations and rebuild.[1]

After the war ended, the city of Richmond struggled to rebuild and regain some of its former glory.[2] Because of the fires at the end of the war, many of the buildings were destroyed, but by the 1890s new ones had been constructed, and the city again flourished.

Only a few of the old landmarks survived the evacuation fires of April 3, 1865. The capitol building was spared, as was the statue of George Washington by Crawford on the capitol grounds.[3] Libby Prison survived the war but was dismantled and taken to Chicago to be exhibited. That site now hosts an ice factory. The custom house building, used by President Davis and other Confederate officials, was remodeled and enlarged. The residence of President Davis remained unchanged, and soon was surrounded by new houses. The Spotswood Hotel survived the evacuation fire, but was destroyed in a fire on December 25, 1870. These and other changes in the city of Richmond were noted in a newspaper article written at the time of a Confederate reunion in 1894.[4]

Instrumental to the city's recovery was the Tredgar Iron Works, which had survived the fire. The works began a new process of iron manufacture, and other metal works were soon reopened. Work in the coal mines and granite quarries near Richmond was resumed, and soon hundreds of workers were employed. Other factories were opened for making steam and fire engines, steam saw-mills, paper, household utensils, cotton mils, tanneries, tobacco manufacturing and flour milling.[5]

Castle Thunder was returned to the private sector. The *Combination Atlas of Richmond, 1876,* shows the building being used as Turpin & Brother's tobacco factory.[6] It was demolished in 1879, and over one hundred years later was the site in 1990 of a paved parking lot for the employees of Phillip Morris.[7]

Death of Major Thomas P. Turner

Thomas P. Turner, famous as the superintendent of Libby Prison, returned to the United States after fleeing to Cuba when the war ended. Turner established a large dentistry practice in Memphis, Tennessee. He died in the Odd Fellows' Home in Clarkesville, Tennessee, on December 26, 1901, and was buried at the Odd Fellows' Cemetery.[8] His picture appeared in several books published after 1900.

The Fate of Colonel Zarvona

The treatment of Richard Thomas Zarvona is an example of Yankee brutality. Zarvona was kept in solitary confinement, in a dark, windowless cell until his health was ruined. Following efforts by many people on his behalf, Richard Thomas Zarvona was finally released in April 1863, after nearly two years of confinement.[9]

Once he gained his freedom, Richard Thomas Zarvona went to Europe and lived in Paris for a number of years. He was in France during the Franco-Prussian War, and he may have been involved in that conflict. By the early 1870s, he had returned to Maryland.[10] He died at "Woodberry," the home of his brother George Thomas, in March of 1875. Richard Thomas Zarvona is buried in the old Thomas family cemetery at the Thomas ancestral home, Deep Falls.[11]

Death of Captain George Washington Alexander

George Washington Alexander was a man who experienced the heights of glory and the depths of depravity. He was a unique and complicated man of many skills and talents. Yet his good name was forever stained by his association with the prisons of the Confederacy. Despite his other good works and accomplishments, his reputation never recovered from the accusations leveled at him, the Congressional investigation, and later indictment on charges of malfeasance in office.

A letter signed by several prisoners of war thanking Captain Alexander for his "kindness" to them was reportedly presented when Alexander resigned his post at Castle Thunder. This letter, dated December 15, 1863, disappeared on April 29, 1986, from the archives of the Maryland Historical Society.[12] It is unfortunate that this letter and others like it could not have been made public during his lifetime.

George Washington Alexander died on February 20, 1895, at his home in Laurel, Maryland. He was 66 years of age. The funeral was held at St. Phillip's Protestant Episcopal Church in Laurel, Maryland. His widow, Susanna S. Ashby Alexander, survived him.[13] He was interred at Ivy Hill Cemetery on Old Sandy Springs Road, near the intersection of Nichols Drive. A simple headstone is engraved with only the dates of his birth and death—1829 and 1895, respectively. A Confederate States Army marker has been placed at his gravesite.[14] The grave of Alexander is included in a list of burial sites in Prince George's County, Maryland, of Maryland Confederates.[15]

Before he became ill, Alexander had the foresight to make his will. On August 18, 1885, ten years before his death, he made out his last will and testament. He mentions no property, either real or personal, specifically, but left all of his estate of "every kind, sort and description" that he might own at the time of his death to his wife, Susanna S. Alexander. In addition, he appointed his "dear wife Susanna" as sole executrix of the will. The will was filed for probate on March 19, 1895, in Prince George's County.[16]

Mrs. Alexander lived on at least until after 1900. The Census of 1900 for Baltimore, Maryland, lists her as a matron in a Confederate Home in Baltimore. She gave her birth as January of 1837, and her present age as 63.[17]

Her date of death has not been found, and there is no marker for Susanna S. Ashby Alexander, the devoted wife of Captain George Alexander. Her place of burial is unknown, but more than likely she is buried in Laurel, Maryland, beside her husband, although there is no marker for her grave. Certainly she deserved to lie beside her husband, whom she helped save from execution at Fort McHenry in 1861 by her courageous efforts in helping him escape. She stood by him through the years, and helped him in any way she could.

When Alexander died, the incident of his arrest and subsequent escape from Fort McHenry was reprinted from the Baltimore *Sun* in the New York *Times*. The *Times* article stated that Alexander had risen from First Lieutenant to Captain, then was promoted to Colonel in the Army of Northern Virginia.[18]

So ended the life of a courageous man, a man who witnesses both victory and defeat, a man who was honored and despised. Alexander was a very complex man—an adventurer, a sailor, a pirate, a spy, a provost marshal and a prisoner, as well as an actor, playwright, songwriter, teacher, and newspaper editor. George Washington Alexander gave his all for the causes he believed in. Yet he is remembered by very few, the exception being on Confederate Memorial Day, when the local chapter of the Sons of Confederate Veterans decorates his grave.[19]

Perhaps this work will provide a more accurate description of the man and his unique life during the turbulent years of the 19th century, and maybe it will provide an understanding the people and the events that shaped our future and that of the world.

Appendix 1: Partial List of Inmates at Castle Thunder

This is a partial list of prisoners confined at Castle Thunder, Richmond, Virginia, while Captain George W. Alexander was in command (1862–1863) and under the command of Captain Lucian W. Richardson (1864–1865). This list includes Confederate deserters, Federal soldiers, spies, women, slaves, and civilians held on suspicion of treason or disloyalty to the Confederacy.

This list, although compiled from a variety of sources, is incomplete. Some of the names of prisoners I found, such as some prisoners' letters on microfilm, were of such poor quality that they could not be deciphered; other names were excluded because the handwriting was illegible.

For those names I could decipher, a brief notation about each prisoner provides a measure of insight into the type of inmates confined at Castle Thunder and their offenses. There are hundreds of letters written from prisoners to General John H. Winder, which all had to pass through Captain Alexander. There are also letters from various military authorities advising Captain Alexander of prisoners to be forwarded to his care.

Many of the prisoners' letters are preserved on microfilm, a copy of which can be borrowed from the Virginia Historical Society, Richmond, Virginia, although some of the letters are too dark to read. Undoubtedly because these letters were still part of the Department of Henrico files, they were never sent to those to whom they were addressed.

In addition to these letters, I have added many names to the list of those incarcerated at Castle Thunder from numerous sources, including the Confederate Congressional investigation of Captain Alexander and Castle Thunder.

The handwriting is excellent in many of the letters, as is the spelling and grammar. Some of the letters are three or four pages long, others only half a page, but all are pleas for release from Castle Thunder. When all else failed, many attempted to escape.

The following list of names is not included in the index at the end of this book, because they are already alphabetical.

Confederate States Army, Department of Henrico Papers, 1861–1864, Mss3, 67604a, on three rolls of microfilm, property of the Virginia Historical Society, Richmond, Virginia, has been abbreviated to DHP in the footnotes.

The multi-volume set compiled by Louis H. Manarin and Weymouth T. Jordan of North Carolina soldiers, *North Carolina Troops, 1861–1865: A Roster*, has been referred to as Manarin and Jordan, *North Carolina Troops*.

Appendix 1

Prisoners Held in Castle Thunder

Adams, John—along with McAlister and Shehan, made a rope out of a blanket and were going to escape. They were discovered and attacked the guard, Frederick F. Wiley, with a shovel, a razor, and a ball and chain.[1]

Adams, W. H.—from Laurel Grove, Virginia, was one of three citizens wounded in a train accident on the Danville Railroad. Charged with "offences against the Confederacy," Adams and two other citizens, Griffin D. Bailey and A. J. Dodson, were taken to Castle Thunder's Hospital No. 13 on 20th Street in Richmond. Three soldiers *en route* under guard to a military prison for army requisition violations were also wounded and taken to the prison hospital.[2]

Addcock, Reeves—a 55-year old man, in poor health, confined to the 2nd floor of Castle Thunder, wrote Major Carrington to request a hearing.[3]

Alexander, a slave belonging to William B. Randolph, of Henrico County, Virginia, was sent by General Longstreet to be confined at Castle Thunder. He was charged with helping Confederate soldiers desert to the enemy.[4]

Allen, William—In June of 1862, he was sent from Richmond to the Poplar Lawn Hospital in Petersburg, where he remained until August 4, 1864, with typhoid fever. During the time he was hospitalized, his captain brought charges against him for "absenting myself from my Co. and regt. without proper authority." The second "instance" occurred after his company had moved into Maryland and returned to Virginia by way of Williamsport and Harper's Ferry, and he was subsequently engaged in the battle of Sharpsburg. During this period of marching, Allen claimed he was without shoes. The second charge came about because on a night march, his feet became very sore, and he was compelled to stop and rest. He fell behind and did not rejoin his company for two days after the Battle at Sharpsburg. Still barefooted, he was detained as a rear guard and then proceeded to Winchester. There he was detained on Provost Guard where he remained until the army left the valley for Fredericksburg. Then, his captain had him arrested a second time for being "absent without proper authority." He was tried and found "not guilty." However, in the Hospital Charge he had no witnesses and could do nothing.[5]

Allred (Alread), Henry H.—a private in Company M, 16th North Carolina, was arrested for desertion and taken to Camp Holmes, where he arrived October 15, 1863. He was then transported to Castle Thunder along with 19 other North Carolina soldiers and one from the 5th Virginia Cavalry. All had been arrested for desertion or being absent without leave.[6] Allred was a resident of McDowell County, North Carolina, before he enlisted at age 23 in Gaston County on May 11, 1861. He was wounded at Mechanicsville on June 26, 1862. He returned to duty before March 1, 1863, and was present until he deserted while "on the march" on July 24, 1863. He rejoined his company on November 1, 1863. He was court martialed, and returned to duty January-February of 1864. He was captured near the North Anna River about May 24, 1864, and confined at Point Lookout, Maryland, until paroled and sent to Boulware's Wharf on the James River on March 16, 1865.[7]

Anderson, J. G.—sent from North Carolina by General Loring, charged with disloyalty in September of 1862. Assistant Secretary of War J. A. Campbell ordered Anderson to be discharged from arrest and confinement on December 16, 1862.[8]

Anderson, John—a slave recently committed to Castle Thunder (July or August 1863), was one of several who claimed to be free.[9]

Armstrong, Thomas D.—citizen of Doddridge County, western Virginia, was one of 56 citizens taken in a raid on the Baltimore and Ohio Railroad in May of 1863. He and several others were housed in Castle Thunder and held as hostages.[10]

Ashton, James—a slave committed to Castle Thunder (July or August 1863), was one of several who claimed to be free.[11]

Ashworth, J. H., Col.—originally housed at Libby Prison as a member of the First Regiment United States Georgia Volunteers, he was transferred to Castle Thunder. Ashworth was recognized as having been a captain in the Confederate States service.[12]

Atkinson, John—claimed his papers had been taken from him by the Yankees on the Fredericksburg Road, and because he did not have any "detail papers," he was arrested and put in Castle Thunder.[13]

Aughinbaugh, William L.—from Ohio, enlisted in Company E, 5th Ohio Infantry. While fighting under Hooker, he was captured at Chancellorsville in May of 1863, and taken to Castle Thunder. He stayed there only a few days before being returned north on parole. His diary describes the Battle of Chancellorsville and his capture.[14]

Avery, Henry — wrote to Major Carrington to ask that he and two others (John W. Login and Joseph Day) be released to serve in the Confederate service. He had experience in the artillery and in infantry.[15]

Bailey, Jim — a slave committed to Castle Thunder (July or August 1863), was one of several who claimed to be free.[16]

Bailey, Griffin D. — of Whiteville, Virginia, one of three citizens wounded in a train accident on the Danville Railroad. Charged with "offences against the Confederacy," Bailey and two other citizens were taken to Castle Thunder's Hospital No. 13 on 20th Street in Richmond.[17]

Baker, E. S. — Lt. W. S. Pilcher named Baker and 20 others, and notated that Baker's papers were with General Winder. All the men on the list swore they were "not members of any company" and did not know what they were charged with.[18]

Ballard, J. P. — Company F, 54th (?) North Carolina, arrested in Buncomb County, North Carolina, on October 1, for desertion. Sent to Camp Holmes, he arrived there on October 10, 1863, then was transported to Castle Thunder, where he arrived October 12, 1863.[19]

Barham, O. L.(?) — deserted from the General Hospital, but returned voluntarily. He had been accused of certain offences. Howard T. Barton sent him to Captain Alexander to hold, and noted that he had "proof in my possession," but that it was not "sufficient as yet to bring charges." Barton wanted an investigation conducted before a trial was ordered.[20]

Barker, J. J. — Company E, 2nd Tennessee, captured at Tazewell, Tennessee, May 3, 1862, for bridge burning, was sent from Atlanta to Castle Thunder.[21] He was paroled at City Point, Virginia, on March 17, 1863, and returned to his regiment.[22]

Barlow, G. W. — a citizen of East Tennessee, arrested March 1, 1862, and transferred from Atlanta to Castle Thunder, December 1862.[23]

Barnes, Charles T. — had been detained in Castle Thunder for four months and was sentenced to be shot in October of 1863, but he was reprieved until orders from the President were given. If allowed to rejoin his regiment, Barnes promised to be a "good & faithful soldier."[24]

Barrett, William — imprisoned for acting as a substitute agent.[25] Barrett applied to Captain Alexander to find out what he had been charged with. He claimed he was a private in Company I, 6th Louisiana Regiment, and had been arrested in the hospital at Mobile, Alabama, and brought to Richmond. A letter from John J. Revena, Captain commanding the 6th Louisiana, stated that he is "almost 2 years a deserter. Every effort made to apprehend him had been ineffective up to his recent arrest."[26]

Barry, Richard — a member of Company A, 10th Virginia Cavalry, had been under arrest since July 15, 1862, for shooting a member of his company. Barry wrote Captain Stark for help because his case had never been investigated. Barry claimed that he could prove that the shooting was accidental, because one of his lieutenants was in Richmond on the sick list.[27]

Barton, Alonzo J. — born in Poland, Chautauqua County, New York, on February 23, 1836, Alonzo enlisted in Company E, 9th New York Volunteer Cavalry. He served with this unit until captured and taken prisoner. He made a daring escape from Libby Prison by putting on a Confederate coat and simply walking out. However, Barton was recaptured only 30 miles from Richmond. He was returned to the city and placed in Castle Thunder where he spent 38 days in a "cold, damp, dark dungeon...." He was paroled in May of 1864, rejoined his regiment, and was mustered out of service in November of 1864 with the rank of Sergeant Major. He died in Baron County, Wisconsin, on October 14, 1888, at age 52, from "asthma" which he acquired while in Castle Thunder.[28]

Bayne, Lewis H. — of Company A, 15th Virginia Cavalry, arrested and sent under guard to Major Griswold to be confined in Castle Thunder for desertion and escape.[29]

Bean, Mary — from southwestern Virginia, Mary dressed as a man and, along with her cousin Molly, joined a Virginia cavalry unit. Later, the two women served in the 27th Virginia. Their identity was discovered after the battle of Cedar Creek, and they were sent to Castle Thunder as spies. However, after a review of their records, the girls were only held long enough to for arrangements to be made for "their welfare."[30]

Bean, Millie — Served in the 47th North Carolina for over two years before being discovered.[31]

Bean, Mollie—from southwestern Virginia. See Bean, Mary.

Beasley, Milton—a deserter from the Virginia Light Battery, was recaptured after six months. He was sent to Captain Richardson. Captain Thomas R. Thornton stated he wished to prefer charges against Beasley, and asked Richardson to keep him confined until the charges could be forwarded.[32]

Beaton, George E.—was arrested December 18, 1863, charged with desertion and confined in Castle Thunder in February 1864.[33]

Bechtol, Aaron—a citizen of Morgan and a member of the Union League of Western Virginia, was captured along with S. M. Shrives, Joseph S. Wheat, and Robert Finn. All were sent to Castle Thunder.[34]

Beckman, Henry—ordered confined in June of 1864 to Castle Thunder by Captain Charters of the Reserve Forces for "shirking" military duty and pretending to have a "game" leg.[35]

Bell, Mary and Bell, Molly—Both girls had served in the Confederate army dressed as men, according to a notation in the diary of Edmund Ruffin. See Chapter 8 for more information.

Bennett, Levi—a citizen who had resided in Norfolk, Virginia, who had been a former master of a steamboat confiscated by the Confederate government. After a stay with relatives in North Carolina, he returned to Norfolk, where he was offered a position of pilot by the Yankees. He was captured May 15, 1863, and confined in prison. He claimed he was a resident of "Fairfield, Hyde County, North Carolina, where he had a wife and three children, the oldest about five years old." To facilitate his release, he gave references of several officials and military personnel.[36]

Bensinger, William, Pvt.—Company G, 21st Regiment Ohio Volunteers, member of the Andrew's Raid to cut communications in Georgia. Captured on April 13, 1862, for theft of a train engine, he was held in Atlanta, then transferred in December to Castle Thunder.[37]

Bentley, Benjamin (Esquire)—a farmer from Alexander County, North Carolina, who enlisted in the 56th North Carolina Regiment on September 3, 1863, at about age 38. He deserted but was apprehended and court martialed. He was sentenced to be shot, and confined at Castle Thunder. He committed suicide at Castle Thunder on March 15, 1864, the day before his scheduled execution.[38] Bentley's wife was Frances (Fanny) Davis, according to queries posted on the Ancestry Message Boards.[39]

Bevill, James—of the City Battalion, and a guard at Libby Prison, was sent by Libby Prison authorities to Castle Thunder after a large-scale escape attempt.[40]

Bird, L. C.—see **Byrd, Lydolph C.**

Boone, E. D.—In October of 1863, he succeeded in his second prison escape along with three other prisoners, Edward Carney, Thomas Cole, and John A. Chipman. They overpowered guards, and shot one sentinel, Sutton Byrd, of Co. C, 53rd North Carolina Regiment.[41] Boone was described in another newspaper as "a noted ruffian, having made several escapes from different places," and was being closely confined for a previous escape attempt.[42]

Bowen, _____—along with White, another soldier, were charged with shooting two men in Richmond on Main Street between 6th and 7th. The soldiers were sent to Castle Thunder to await court martial.[43]

Bowler, John J.—private, along with Private W. J. Walker, was ordered by Major Bossiux to be confined at Castle Thunder to await charges being filed. They may have been members of Company G, 25th Virginia Battalion.[44]

Bowman, John J.—Company D, 12th Virginia Regiment, died in hospital September 8, 1862, buried in Oakwood Cemetery.[45]

Bowman, N.—48th Georgia, Company D, arrested in Catawba County, North Carolina, on October 11, 1863, for desertion. Sent to Camp Holmes, he arrived there on October 10, 1863, then was transported to Castle Thunder, where he arrived October 12, 1863.[46]

Bowman, Peter—a resident of Chesterfield County, was supposed to be a spy, but was also a "crazy man." He was sent to Castle Thunder by Colonel Miner, in charge of post at Farmville. Bowman changed his name, and answered to any other name which was called, except his own.[47]

Boyd, Henry—a private in Company D, First North Carolina Union Volunteers, captured April 6, 1863. He and six others were sent to get a load of wood. They went ashore at night at Little Fatty Creek and were captured by partisan rangers.[48]

Boyle, William, Pvt.—of the New York Mounted Rifles, was under a sentence of death for the murder of Lieutenant Disosway. He was allowed to escape by Private Abraham of the 139th New York. According to a report by Brigadier General I. J. Wistar, it was believed that Boyle had reached Richmond, and had been arrested and placed in Castle Thunder.[49]

Brazer, Fleming—a deserter who tried to get out of Castle Thunder with a forged special order. The forger, Lieutenant W. L. Soles, of Company K, 2nd Florida Regiment, presented a document supposed to be from General Winder for Brazer's release. The forgery was discovered, and both Brazer and Soles were captured by detectives and imprisoned.[50]

Brengle, Alfred F.—of Frederick, Maryland, a civilian employee of the Sanitary Commission when arrested, was confined in Castle Thunder. Major General Benjamin F. Butler requested that he be exchanged for a Mr. Thatcher, also a noncombatant.[51]

Brick, Patrick—arrived at Castle Thunder on December 15, 1862, from Gordonsville, courtesy of Major Boyle, provost marshal, charged with disloyalty to Confederate states.[52]

Bridman, Arthur P.—transferred from 8th South Carolina Regiment sometime during 1862 to Company I, 1st Infantry Regiment (Hagood's). Promoted to 3rd Corporal, then reduced in rank on May 1, 1864. Reported under arrest in Castle Thunder on June 30, 1864, but he was back with regiment by August 31, 1864.[53]

Brooks, Hiram—Enlisted at age 18 on April 16, 1861, at Martin's Ferry, Ohio, in Company B, 15th Ohio. He was captured December 31, 1862, at Stones River, and discharged at end of the war, after being confined. to Libby Prison and Castle Thunder.[54]

Broseus, Simon—a resident of Glenford, Perry County, Ohio, he enlisted on August 23, 1862, in Company K, 126th Ohio Volunteer Infantry. While in the infantry, he was taken prisoner and held at Libby Prison and Castle Thunder, and was confined for a total of 102 days. He died in Allen County, Ohio, in 1909.[55]

Brown, A. T.—of Company H, 47th Virginia Regiment, was sentenced to labor for five months for desertion.[56]

Brown, Andrew B.—a private in Company E, 4th North Carolina, was arrested for desertion October 3, 1863, in Alexander County, North Carolina, arrived at Camp Holmes near Raleigh on October 10, 1863, then transported to Castle Thunder, where he arrived October 12, 1863.[57] Brown, a resident of Alexander County, North Carolina, enlisted in Wake County at age 27 on April 23, 1863. He deserted shortly thereafter, prior to May 1, 1863. He was reported "in arrest" before January 1, 1864, and was on a list of prisoners facing court martial dated January 8, 1864. He died in a Richmond, Virginia, hospital on February 2, 1864, of "febris typhoides."[58]

Brown, Charles W.—see under Webster, Alphonzo C.

Brown, John F.—Company B, 55th North Carolina, reported in himself, taken to Camp Holmes on October 15, 1863, but arrested for desertion and sent to Castle Thunder in Richmond, Virginia.[59]

Brown, John L.—Private, Company B, 2nd Tennessee Infantry, died in captivity March 7, 1864, of smallpox at Howard Grove Hospital in Richmond. Confined as a political prisoner, he was apparently enrolled but never mustered. A farmer/distiller from Cumberland County, Tennessee, he was arrested November 5, 1861, and confined first at Salisbury, then Castle Thunder, then Libby.[60]

Brown, Joshua—a physician, he enlisted September 1, 1862, age 32, at Martinsburg, Virginia, in Company A, 116th Ohio Regiment. He was promoted to surgeon. Captured, he was confined to Castle Thunder, Belle Island, and Libby Prison, and was released at the end of the war.[61]

Brown, P.—a gas fitter, arrested for refusing to take up arms, by order of Capt. William A. Charters, Provost of the Reserve Forces.[62]

Brown, William—citizen of Preston County, in western Virginia, was one of 56 citizens taken in a raid on the Baltimore and Ohio Railroad in May of 1863. He and several others were housed in Castle Thunder and held as hostages.[63]

Browne, Junius Henri—A newspaper correspondent for the New York *Tribune* captured at Vicksburg on May 3, 1863, he was confined at various prisons, including Vicksburg, Jackson, Atlanta, Richmond's Libby Prison and Castle Thunder, and Salisbury. He published a book about his experiences.[64] Browne and Richardson, another reporter, remained in Castle Thunder until February of 1864, when they were transferred to Salisbury, North Carolina. From there, the two escaped and made their way to Federal lines in Tennessee.[65]

Buckley (Bulkley), Solomon T.—one of several reporters for the New York *Herald,* confined in relative luxury at Castle Thunder.[66]

Buffum, Robert, Pvt.—Company H, 21st Regiment Ohio Volunteers, member of the Andrew's Raid to cut communications in Georgia. Captured April 13, 1862 for engine theft, and held in Atlanta, then transferred in December of 1862 to Castle Thunder.[67]

Buie, D. J.—a private in Company H, 3rd

North Carolina Regiment, put in Castle Thunder for being drunk and disorderly on November 10, 1862. While in prison, he was robbed of his money, hat and pistol.[68] Buie was a resident of Bladen County, North Carolina, until he enlisted at age 24 on May 10, 1861. He was wounded at Malvern Hill, Virginia, on July 1, 1862. He deserted from camp near Skinker's Neck, Virginia, on April 4, 1863, and took the oath of allegiance in Washington, D.C., on December 26, 1863.[69]

Burke, George W.—from Wilson, North Carolina, the self-proclaimed "innocent, deaf mute," George wrote to General Winder as well as Vice President Stephens to gain his release. He was confined in late 1862 or early in January 1863.[70]

Burke, James—his name was on a list with 20 others made by Lt. W. S. Pilcher, with the notation that he had deserted from the 26th North Carolina. All the men on the list stated they were "not members of any company" and did not know what they were charged with. His papers were with General Winder.[71] Burke is listed as a Private in Company B, 26th North Carolina Regiment, in the North Carolina records. He resided in Catawba County and enlisted at Camp Mangum on September 28, 1862, but deserted October 13, 1862. He returned to duty the next spring on May 6, 1863. He was present or accounted for until he died in a Richmond, Virginia, hospital for a gunshot wound of the hip. The date and place of the wound is not given.[72]

Burnet, Patrick—his name was on list with 20 others made by Lt. W. S. Pilcher, with the notation that he was charged with desertion. The 21 men swore they were "not members of any company" and did not know what they were charged with.[73]

Burns, E. P.—Company K, 11th North Carolina, reported back himself, but was arrested for desertion and taken from Camp Holmes to Castle Thunder. Burns was a resident of Buncombe County where he enlisted at age 20 on March 1, 1862. He was present until he deserted on August 20, 1863. After his arrest, he returned to duty on November 10, 1863. He was later hospitalized in Charlottesville, Virginia, on December 25, 1863, with acute diarrhea and typhoid fever, and he died there on January 20, 1864, of pneumonia.[74]

Burns, James—along with James Gurphy, was sent to Castle Thunder by S. Van de Graaff, 2nd Lieutenant, Marine Guard at the C. S. Navy Yard.[75]

Burns, Michael C.—deserted from 18th Virginia Battalion, taken to Castle Thunder.[76] Originally a member of the 7th North Carolina, he was court martialed at Fredericksburg "for joining another regiment without permission," and sentenced to 30 days in the guard house. He wished to join the navy and wrote asking General Winder to recommend him to the Secretary of the Navy.[77]

Burton, James Henry—enlisted May 23, 1863, in Montgomery County, Virginia, as a private in Company G, 17th Virginia Infantry. He deserted in June of 1863. Confined to Castle Thunder that same month, he returned to duty in August of 1863. He was paroled at Appomattox Courthouse on April 9, 1865.[78]

Byas/Byzer, John—see Carroll, Charles.

Byrd, Lydolph C.—also listed as Bird, L. C., of Company E, 54th North Carolina, arrested for desertion on October 2, 1863, taken to Camp Holmes where he arrived on October 15, 1863, then sent to Castle Thunder in Richmond, Virginia, where he arrived the next day.[79] Byrd was a Wilkes County, North Carolina, farmer, when he enlisted at age 20 on March 21, 1862. He enlisted as a corporal, and was present on the company rolls through April of 1863. He deserted on August 5, 1863, and was reduced in rank. He was reported sick in a hospital in December of 1863. On March 4, 1864, he was listed as a deserter, but he returned to duty prior to June 1, 1864, when he sustained a fracture to his left leg at Cold Harbor, Virginia. He was hospitalized in Richmond on June 8, 1864, and granted a 60-day furlough on July 23, 1864. He was reported absent-wounded through October 1864, and he is known to have survived the war.[80]

Cagle, Riley—a private in Company D, 16th North Carolina, confined at Castle Thunder in June of 1864 for murder.[81] Cagle was a resident of Montgomery County, North Carolina, and enlisted in Wake County at age 28 on March 8, 1863. He was wounded at Chancellorsville, Virginia, on May 3, 1863. No particulars are given, but he is listed as having been confined at Castle Thunder on June 16, 1864 "charged with murder." He was confined there through August of 1864, but there is no further information in the North Carolina records.[82]

Campbell, William F.—deserted from 7th (or 14th) Louisiana Regiment, taken to Castle Thunder in March of 1863.[83] Campbell and

Charles Carroll attempted to escape. Carroll was killed, and Campbell was shot at, but not hit, and recaptured. The attempt in April was Campbell's fourth escape attempt.[84] Campbell testified at Alexander's trial, and said that he was one of those who had been put outside in the yard. He had also been bucked.[85]

Carden, A. J.—originally housed in Libby Prison as a Private of Company K, 2nd New York Independent Rifles, Carden was recognized as being Lieutenant-Colonel Carden, a member of the 18th Tennessee Regiment, CSA. He was removed to Castle Thunder to await a court martial.[86]

Carney, Edward—arrested and sent to Captain Alexander on October 2, 1863, by the adjutant of a Virginia Battalion, to be tried for desertion.[87] Later that month, he succeeded in his second prison escape along with three other prisoners, E. D. Boone, Thomas Cole, and John A. Chipman. They overpowered guards, and shot one sentinel, Sutton Byrd, of Co. C, 53rd North Carolina Regiment.[88]

Carper, John A.—left his company to visit his family when he was "encamped within ten or twelve miles of my home," because he had received word that his wife was ill. He intended to return to his company, but was "arrested and confined in Castle Thunder."[89]

Carroll, Charles (alias John Byas or Byzer)—An Irishman by birth, was shot and killed by a guard in escape attempt. He was a deserter from the 54th (or 53rd) Virginia Regiment.[90]

Carroll, Emma—a "very bright mulatto," who had recently had a baby, whom she christened "Georgianna Washington Alexandria," in honor of the former commandant of Castle Thunder (Captain George Washington Alexander), was transferred on August 3, 1864, with a group of 27 Yankee deserters, two Confederate soldiers, and 24 Negroes to Salisbury Prison. The baby went along with the mother to share confinement at Salisbury.[91]

Carroll, Nicholas—A deserter from Col. Danforth's militia regiment, he was placed in the Castle in May 1864.[92] He and 9 Italians, formerly confined in Castle Thunder for desertion, were released by the Governor's order to return to their regiment in the Virginia Reserves.[93]

Cassidy, James—Company A, 5th New York Heavy Artillery, was captured with several others by Colonel Mosby's command at Kabletown, near Snicker's Gap, during United States General Hunter's retreat from Lynchburg, Virginia.[94]

Castleman, John A.—a chaplain from Tennessee, serving in General Jackson's Corps of cavalry in Mississippi, he claimed to have been committed to Castle Thunder without "charges or specifications." He stated he had two sons in the C. S. A., and that he had been discharged from the army "on account of old age."[95]

Chifton, R. B.—Company E, Cutts' Artillery Battalion, incarcerated in Castle Thunder on June 16, 1864, for stabbing a fellow soldier.[96]

Childress, John O.—of Company F, 25th Virginia, a guard at Libby Prison, was arrested along with fellow guards S. Griffin and A. B. Mountcastle, and sent to Castle Thunder for trading with Yankee prisoners, in violation of a prison department regulation.[97]

Chinn, Samuel—A slave of C. Bronn, was reclaimed after a list of slaves being held in Castle Thunder was published in August of 1863.[98]

Chipman, John A.—In October of 1863, he succeeded in his second prison escape along with three other prisoners. They overpowered guards, and shot guard Sutton Byrd, of Co. C, 53rd North Carolina Regiment.[99]

Christy, H. F.—enlisted on April 21, 1861, in the Dixon Guards, later known as Company C, 11th Regiment Pennsylvania Reserves. He was captured at Gaines Mill on June 27, 1862, and sent to Castle Thunder, thence to Belle Isle. He was exchanged about August 4, 1862 with 3,000 others, and rejoined his regiment. Captured at Fredericksburg and confined to Libby Prison for 6 weeks until paroled, he was discharged June 13, 1864. Christy was admitted to the bar as an attorney in 1874, and in 1879 moved to Kansas.[100]

Church, _____—a Lieutenant charged with recruiting for the Union army within Confederate lines, was housed in Castle Thunder. He escaped in the final days of the war.[101]

Clayton, S.—of the 31st Georgia Regiment, was sent to Castle Thunder for forging a furlough.[102]

Coggins, Joshua C.—a corporal in Company B, 18th Tennessee Infantry, CSA, wounded at Marietta, Georgia, June 22, 1864, was sent to hospital at Castle Thunder. He enlisted in Company B, 17th Cavalry Battalion, which became part of the 9th Mississippi Cavalry.[103]

Cole, Thomas—in October of 1863, he succeeded in his second prison escape along with E. D. Boone, Edward Carney, and John Chipman. They overpowered guards, and shot the sentinel, Sutton Byrd.[104]

Coleman, Campbell—a Private in Company

E, 54th North Carolina, he was arrested for desertion and sent to Camp Holmes, and then to Castle Thunder. Coleman was born in Wilkes County, North Carolina, where he enlisted at age 30 on April 5, 1862. He deserted his company from their camp near Rapidan Station, Virginia, on August 5, 1863. He was arrested on October 2, 1863, and died in a Richmond, Virginia, hospital on October 22, 1863, of pneumonia.[105]

Coleman, John— of Richie County, western Virginia, was one of 56 citizens taken in a raid on the Baltimore and Ohio Railroad in May of 1863, and housed in Castle Thunder as hostages.[106]

Conley, Luke— complained to Major Carrington that, although he had been examined, both Major Carrington and Captain Alexander had failed to return him to his regiment as promised.[107]

Connely, Patrick— His name was on a list with 20 others made by Lt. W. S. Pilcher, with the notation that he had been sent from Staunton. The men on the list all denied that they were "members of any company" and did not know what they were charged with.[108]

Conner, J. G.— a citizen of Baltimore, Maryland, was held in Castle Thunder for eight months as a spy for the Union. After his release during the evacuation of Richmond, he returned to his profession as a spy, and helped bring about the arrest of several men.[109]

Conner, Michael— of Company D, 14th Virginia, was received as a prisoner by Captain Alexander on May 11, 1863.[110]

Cooper, James W.— Company G, 2nd Ohio Volunteer Infantry, served in battles at Perryville, Stone River and Chickamauga, where he was captured September 19, 1863. He was held prisoner at Belle Isle, Libby Prison, Danville Prison No. 5, and Castle Thunder from March 1 to March 11, 1864. He was released at Annapolis on March 14, 1864, due to the help of Miss Emily V. Mason of Richmond. Cooper was blind, and Miss Mason believed it was a "disgrace to keep a blind person in prison." Cooper had been sent to the smallpox hospital in Danville, where he suffered from "variola" which caused him to lose the sight in both eyes. He married Harriet Carlisle after the war, and had several children. He owned a cigar store in Steubenville, Ohio.[111]

Copley, Josiah, Jr.— a member of a Pennsylvania regiment, he was taken prisoner at Chickamauga in 1863, was held for 17 months in various prisons: Libby, Castle Thunder, Danville, and Andersonville. He was the son of Josiah Copley and Mrs. Margaret Chadwick Haas, the widow of a Philadelphia physician.[112]

Cotton, Charles— from near Fairfax Court House, he claimed he had been "forceably carried away by the enemy in July of 1861 to Washington, and put in prison there." He subsequently enlisted in the 2nd Maine Cavalry, and was attempting to escape while on picket duty at the Rappidan. While in Castle Thunder, he had volunteered to join "Letcher's Light Artillery," but had not done so because of sickness.[113]

Cowdery, H. H.— a citizen prisoner. General Benjamin F. Butler asked that Cowdery be exchanged for four citizens he held in February of 1864.[114] Cowdery wrote Major Carrington that he had been a prisoner for about 11 months, four of which had been spent in Castle Thunder. He had never had a hearing and did not know what the charges were against him. He pleaded with Major Carrington to investigate his case so that he might be discharged because he was "an old man in feeble health. He had a farm in Alabama where he had lived for the past 16 years.[115]

Cox, J. J.— a Confederate lieutenant arrested for having forged passes and a commission from the Federal government to arrest Confederate deserters and recruit them into the Union army.[116]

Craddock, D. F.— of Company B, 3rd South Carolina, had a misunderstanding with an invalid inmate of the Stuart Hospital. Craddock drew a knife and ripped the bowels of the other man, placing his life in danger. Craddock was arrested and confined at Castle Thunder.[117]

Craigle, Riley—see Cagle, Riley.

Cremarg, Antone— a German who refused to do military duty, was arrested by Detective Jones, and placed in Castle Thunder in May of 1864. The man's family assaulted the officer, but he still managed to bring the prisoner in.[118]

Crone, J. H.— a citizen of Ritchie County, western Virginia, was one of 56 citizens taken in a raid on the Baltimore and Ohio Railroad in May of 1863. He was confined to Castle Thunder and held as a hostage.[119]

Croughan, Patrick— a citizen of Ritchie County, western Virginia, was one of 56 citizens taken in a raid on the Baltimore and Ohio Railroad in May of 1863. He and several others were housed in Castle Thunder and held as hostages.[120]

Crump, Thornton—1st Sergeant of the 4th Virginia Cavalry, Hart's Legion, was sent to Captain Alexander to await a court martial.[121]

Cunbee, George M. — his name was on a list with 20 others made by Lt. W. S. Pilcher, with the notation that he was charged with desertion. All swore they were "not members of any company" and did not know what they were charged with.[122]

Cunningham, Jim — of the 15th Georgia, along with his friend John Willis, were arrested for attempting to sell a "furlough."[123]

Daniels, William — Captain Theodore T. Barham asked General Winder to release Daniels from Castle Thunder and give him a passport to Weldon, North Carolina.[124]

Darby, Martin — a prisoner who was punished by being hung up by his thumbs.[125]

Darden, Josiah — born in Wilson, North Carolina, where he lived and worked as a farmer before enlisting as a private in Company C, 43rd North Carolina Regiment at age 38 on February 8, 1862. He was present until he deserted March-April 1863. He returned to duty on August 15, 1863, but was reported under arrest from September 1863-February 1864. He was hospitalized at Richmond, Virginia, on May 26, 1864, with catarrhus, and sent to Castle Thunder Prison on May 28, 1864. Again, from January-February 1865, he was listed as a deserter. He was paroled at Goldsboro on May 5, 1865.[126]

Davis, L. — a prisoner at Castle Thunder, died of small pox at the hospital on Saturday, May 9, 1863.[127]

Davis, M. T. — of Company G, 17th Virginia, was arrested after being absent from his company for two years.[128]

Day, Joseph — a prisoner in Castle Thunder, when fellow prisoner Henry Avery wrote to Major Carrington to ask that he and two others (John W. Login and Joseph Day) be released to serve in the Confederate service.[129]

Daymond, William — from Wilmington, North Carolina, was committed on May 12, 1863, as a suspected spy. He wrote to Lt. C. W. Murdaugh stating that he had been one of the crew of the *Sabine*, and had been on his way to join Murdaugh's command when he was arrested in Richmond. Murdaugh wrote Captain Alexander that he was severely wounded and could not walk, but was willing for Daymond to enlist in his company, Company J, 61st Regiment Virginia Volunteers, Mahone's Brigade. He asked Capt. Alexander to forward the prisoner to him near Fredericksburg.[130]

Deaton, Spencer — a deserter from a Confederate regiment who had joined the 6th Tennessee, a Union regiment, was court martialed and sentenced to death. The court made an example of Deaton, and the execution was to be carried out by hanging in the prison yard in February of 1864.[131]

Delaney, Eugene — a Yankee being held at Castle Thunder, was released in November of 1863, after taking the oath of allegiance to the Confederacy.[132]

Dempster, John E. — born January 3, 1838, in Morgan County, Ohio, the son of Thomas Dempster of Maryland. John grew up on a farm near Taylorsville, Ohio. He taught school in Hickory Grove, Allen's Grove, and Winfield Townships for several years. He married Esther E. Burch on March 5, 1868, and they had three children. During the war, he was taken prisoner at Winchester, Virginia, and confined at Libby, Belle Island, and Castle Thunder prisons in Richmond. John died in Crawfordsville, Iowa, in March of 1878.[133]

Denham, J. — of Company A, 58th Virginia, one of a group of deserters, was sent to Castle Thunder in August of 1863. He was not entitled to the benefit of the Presidential Proclamation because he was arrested with arms and resisted arrest.[134]

Derby, Junius N. — a private, Company D, 3rd Virginia Infantry, had been confined at Castle Thunder since late in 1863 for assault on James S. Legon, Jr., a clerk at Castle Thunder. Legon explained that he had been assaulted and had shot Derby. Later Legon learned that Derby had been told that Legon was a "Yankee deserter and had no right to arrest his friend." Derby had used foul language and struck the clerk in the face. Since no charges had as yet been preferred, the clerk asked Major Carrington to release the prisoner.[135]

Dillard, Charles — a member of Co. I, 9th Virginia Cavalry, he was listed as being in a Richmond hospital from October 26, 1864, to November 24, 1864, and then was sent to Castle Thunder.[136]

Dishman, James M. — a private in Company E, 54th North Carolina, was arrested for desertion on October 3, 1863, in Iredell County, North Carolina, arrived at Camp Holmes near Raleigh on October 10, 1863, then transported to Castle Thunder, where he arrived October 12, 1863.[137] Born in Iredell County, North Carolina, he enlisted at age 23 on April 11, 1862, but was reported A.W.O.L. during May and June of 1862. He was hospitalized at Richmond, Virginia, November 9, 1862, with diarrhea. Given a 40 day furlough on January 17, 1863, he did not return, but was reported A.W.O.L. during March and April of 1863, and was listed as a deserter May-August 1863. After his arrest for desertion, he returned to duty on November 8, 1863. On August 1, 1864, he was hospitalized at Winchester, Virginia, for diarrhea and fever, but was able to return to duty on August 5, 1864. He was wounded at Winchester on September 19, 1864, but survived the war.[138]

Dishman, Silas—a Private in Company E, 54th North Carolina, was arrested for desertion on October 3, 1863, in Iredell County, North Carolina, arrived at Camp Holmes near Raleigh on October 10, 1863, then transported to Castle Thunder, where he arrived October 12, 1863.[139] Born in Iredell County, North Carolina, he was a farmer before he enlisted in Wilkes County at age 21 on April 20, 1862. However, he was reported A.W.O.L. May-June. He was hospitalized in Richmond on November 9, 1862, with rheumatism. He was granted a 40-day furlough on January 17, 1863, but did not return and was reported absent without leave March-April of 1863, and listed as a deserter August 31, 1863. He returned to duty, and was wounded in September 19–22, 1864, probably at Winchester or Fisher's Hill. He was reported absent wounded through October of 1864. He survived the war and applied for a pension which mentioned that he had been wounded twice, the first time in the right wrist on July 1, 1862(?) near Richmond, Virginia.[140]

Dodson, A. J.—of Laurel Grove, Virginaia, one of three citizens wounded in a train accident on the Danville Railroad. Charged with "offences against the Confederacy," Dodson and two other citizens were taken to Castle Thunder's Hospital No. 13 on 20th Street in Richmond.[141]

Dole, Mike—a citizen confined for "cursing the corporal of the guard."[142]

Dollar, W. G.—a North Carolinian, wrote his brother from Room No. 9 in Castle Thunder on January 15, 1864. He had been arrested in Cincinnati on October 8, 1863, for being a "southern man," and was inducted into the Federal army. He served from October 9 until November 28, and he left on the first opportunity. He was confined at Castle Thunder on December 5, and asked that his friends and county officials back home write letters attesting to his character.[143]

Doobar, A.—a Yankee, of the 1st Maryland Cavalry, placed in Castle Thunder.[144]

Doran, Frank B.—a civilian who arrived in Richmond on March 16, 1863, "unfortunately ... in the company with some Confederate deserters." The guard was told to put the deserters in Castle Thunder, and Doran in Libby Prison. However, instead, Doran was put in Castle Thunder and told he would be released by the "first boat." Captain Alexander informed him he would go by the next boat, but after several weeks he was still in the Castle. Eventually, although he wrote General Winder, he was sent to Salisbury Prison, from which he wrote the Secretary of War on August 18, 1864. Although Doran claimed that orders had not been issued for his arrest, Robert Ould recommended that this "flippant Yankee is where he ought to be."[145]

Douglas, Elam L.—private, Company D, 6th North Carolina, reported for duty after deserting, and was arrested and sent to Camp Holmes on October 15, 1863, then on to Castle Thunder. After his release, Douglas was captured at Winchester, Virginia, on July 20, 19864, and confined at Camp Chase, Ohio, until exchanged on March 2, 1865.[146]

Dowdy, C.—private, Company B, 2nd Virginia, was sent to Capt. Alexander "for retention until called for." No charge was specified.[147]

Dromey (Dromez?), P.—a private in Company B, 9th Alabama, along with Private J. D. White, Company E, 13th Alabama, and Private W. W. Smith, Company D, 44th Alabama, were sent to Castle Thunder for "exciting a mutiny in the Division." The case was under investigation for possible charges and court martial.[148]

Drum, Martin V.—Company F, 32nd North Carolina, returned on his own, but was arrested for being absent without leave, and sent to Camp Holmes on October 15, 1863. Drum enlisted at age 26 on October 22, 1862. He reported sick most of that time, and was listed as under arrest on November 9, 1863. He was court martialed on January 19, 1864. He returned to duty, and was captured near Spotsylvania Court House about May 10, 1864. Confined to the Federal prison at Point Lookout, Maryland, Drum was sent to the prison in Elmira, New York on August 3, 1864. He was paroled on October 11, 1864, and transferred to Fort Monroe, Virgina, where he died on November 6, 1864. Cause of death not reported.[149]

Dry, Adam—a resident of Stanley County, North Carolina, who enlisted as a private in

Company A, 27th North Carolina Regiment, at age 25 on March 12, 1863. Dry was arrested for desertion and confined at Castle Thunder on September 18, 1863. He was present or accounted for until wounded near the wilderness in May of 1864. He returned to duty before November 1, 1864, then deserted to the enemy on March 18, 1864. He was confined at Washington, D.C., on March 24, 1865, and released after taking the Oath of Allegiance. [150]

Duckworth, J. W.—a member of the 16th North Carolina, Company A, he was arrested for desertion on October 3, 1863, in Burke County, North Carolina He arrived at Camp Holmes near Raleigh on October 10, 1863, then was transported to Castle Thunder, where he arrived October 12, 1863.[151]

Duffey, John—Commandant Sidney Smith Lee wrote to Brig. Gen. Winder to obtain the release of Summers, McArthur, and Duffey, who were seamen anxious to join the naval service.[152] Duffey's name was on list with 20 others made by Lt. W. S. Pilcher, which carried a notation that he was was charged with desertion. All stated that they were "not members of any company" and did not know what they were charged with.[153]

Duffield, Peter—see Osborne, William P.

Duncan, James A.—born in Guilford County, North Carolina, where he resided when he enlisted at age 20 on February 22, 1862, as a private. He was wounded at Sharpesburg, Maryland, on September 17, 1862. He was detailed for hospital duty at Richmond on April 18, 1863. He transferred to Lynchburg, Virginia, for assignment as a hospital guard on July 1, 1863. Absent on detail through August of 1863, he was promoted to Corporal on October 31, 1863, and was present or accounted for until wounded and captured at Winchester, Virginia, on September 19, 1864. He was confined at Point Lookout, Maryland until paroled and transferred for exchange at Venus Point, Savannah River, Georgia on October 31, 1864. He was exchanged on November 15, 1864. On February 25, 1865, Duncan was admitted to a Richmond, Virginia, hospital with a gunshot wound of his left arm and right hip. He retired to the Invalid Corps on March 16, 1865, and assigned to light duty at Jackson Hospital on March 31, 1865, where he was captured on April 3, 1865. He was confined at Newport News, Virginia, until released on June 30, 1865, after taking the Oath of Allegiance. The lengthy service description in Volume III of *North Carolina Troops* does not mention his arrest for desertion, but the name "J. A. Duncan, Company E, 2nd North Carolina," appeared on the morning list at Castle Thunder for September 18, 1863.[154]

Dunham, Charles—suspected of "trying to go beyond the Confederate lines without a passport." He was carrying letters addressed to persons living in the North.[155]

Dunlap, William J.—enlisted in Company F, 63rd Pennsylvania Regiment, assigned to Second Brigade, Second Corps of the Army of the Potomac. He fought in many battles, including Yorktown, Williamsburg, Fair Oaks, and Savage Stations, where he was captured and confined in Castle Thunder for two months. He was later wounded in the head at Chancellorsville. Recovered, he re-enlisted on December 31, 1863, and was in the battles at the Wilderness and Spotsylvania. He transferred to Company H, 105th P.V.I. Wounded at Petersburg, he lost his right eye. He was honorably discharged July 28, 1865, and returned to Pennsylvania. He died in Clarion, Clarion County, Pennsylvania, on August 10, 1915.[156]

Dutertre, Arthur—wrote from the hospital to ask for a hearing, and hoped to be granted on before he was returned to Castle Thunder.[157]

Dutton, James—his name was on list with 20 others made by Lt. W. S. Pilcher, all of whom stated that they were "not members of any company" and did not know their charges.[158]

Dutton, William—a Federal prisoner being held at Castle Thunder in the summer of 1863, appealed directly to Confederate Secretary of War James Seddon. If Seddon would give Dutton's case a favorable decision, Dutton promised his heartfelt thanks, and the prayers and blessing of his widowed mother.[159]

Eastman, G. W.—he and John Vellers, two "citizen prisoners," were sent to Castle Thunder on October 7, 1863, in accordance to Special Order No. 211.[160]

Edenborough, Henry, Capt.—a former East India Royal Navy captain, charged with not having the proper credentials, was treated with kindness and courtesy. Edenborough was given good quarters, and his meals were delivered from nearby hotels. He was also at liberty to visit the hotels for his meals, if he chose to do so.[161]

Edwards, John (alias John Tales)—captured as a prisoner of war, but recognized as a deserter from the 3rd Georgia Battalion. He deserted, then took the Oath of Allegiance, and joined the ranks of the enemy. He was confined to Castle Thunder for court martial, and faced either life imprisonment or execution.[162]

Elgin, Elias—both he and Emanuel Elgin (related?) of Company F, 25th Virginia Battalion, were sent by Capt. T. P. Turner from Bell Island to Castle Thunder, with the notation that "charges will be preferred."[163]

Elgin, Emanuel—both he and Elias Elgin of Company F, 25th Virginia Battalion, were sent by Capt. T. P. Turner from Bell Island to Castle Thunder, with the notation that "charges will be preferred."[164]

Eller, Alfred P.—enlisted in Watauga County, North Carolina, on August 5, 1862, as a private in Company I, 58th North Carolina. He was present January-June 1863, and was promoted to Corporal July-September 1863. He deserted on September 20, 1863.[165] Eller was arrested for desertion on September 23, 1863, in Buncombe County, North Carolina, arrived at Camp Holmes near Raleigh on October 10, 1863. Transported to Castle Thunder, he arrived October 12, 1863.[166] He returned to his company on November 12, 1863, and was reduced in rank. He was reported as being confined through February 29, 1864. He returned to duty March-April 1864, and was captured near Marietta, Georgia, on July 28, 1864. He was sent to Nashville, Tennessee, then transferred to Louisville, Kentucky, where he arrived August 5, 1864. He was subsequently transferred to Camp Chase, Ohio, and remained there from August 6, 1864 to December 14, 1864, when he was released after taking the Oath of Allegiance.[167]

Evans, J. B.—had been in Castle Thunder about 10 weeks before he testified at the Congressional Hearings investigating of Captain Alexander and his treatment of prisoners at Castle Thunder.[168]

Fagan, Patrick—of Captain Whitingham's artillery battery, was arrested for striking James Morrissey, "a feeble old man," in the neck. Morrissey fell dead, and Fagan was convicted of manslaughter.[169]

Farmer, John—shot in the arm while attempting to escape from Castle Thunder.[170]

Farwell, Reuben—Private, Company H, 1st Michigan Cavalry, 5'5" tall, black eyes, brown hair, shot in breast and upper right arm at Second Battle of Manassas, wounded at Brandy Station, October 11, 1863. Captured at Wolf Run Shoals, Virginia, and confined at Castle Thunder from March 14–18, 1863.[171]

Fedric, Benjamin F.—of Company D, 15th Virginia Regiment, was recaptured after having escaped from Castle Thunder in the spring of 1863.[172]

Feige, Charles L.—a member of the Maryland Infantry, was tried at New Market for desertion and sentenced to imprisonment for the War. He wished to better his situation and asked to be allowed to join the Confederate Navy.[173]

Fickey, James—a prisoner in Castle Thunder, who was shot and killed. A guard was engaged in an argument with another prisoner. The guard thought he had been insulted and fired at the prisoner. The shot, however, killed James Fickey, who was lounging on the second story awning. The guard was later incarcerated at Castle Thunder.[174]

Finn, Robert—an attorney for the Commonwealth for Morgan County under the "bogus government," was captured on a raid by Major O'Ferrell and arrested, along with citizens of Morgan County and members of the Union League of Western Virginia, Aaron Bechtol, S. M. Shrives, and Joseph S. Wheat. All were sent to Castle Thunder.[175]

Fisher, William—a Yankee being held at Castle Thunder, was released in November of 1863, after taking the Oath of Allegiance to the Confederacy.[176]

Fitch, J. F.—when S. S. Baxter asked Captain Alexander to send Fitch to him, Alexander replied that he "never has been here."[177]

Fitzgerald, William—William wrote to General Winder on June 2, 1863, to plead for himself and his brother. He had been in Castle Thunder over a week, and had not been told what he was charged with.[178] A month later he was still there and so he wrote to President Abraham Lincoln from Castle Thunder on July 4, 1863, to support him in his efforts to restore the union.[179]

Fitzmorrie, Richard—released on parole after giving the Oath of Allegiance, Fitzmorrie was caught, along with Harvey Simmons, attempting to flee to Yankees pickets. He was first sent back to Libby Prison then to Castle Thunder, to await a court martial.[180]

Flannagan, Nat—see Hines, Martin.

Fletcher, Addison—a private in Company D, 49th Virginia Infantry, of Warren County, Virginia, he was court martialed and sent to Castle Thunder on January 6, 1864, for four months. He was paroled at Winchester, Virginia, April 26, 1865.[181]

Folke, George—a free Negro from Suffolk, was charged with carrying information to the enemy. He was placed in Castle Thunder to await trial.[182]

Foran, Edward A.—of the 14th Louisiana Volunteers, he was arrested for trying to sell himself again as a substitute.[183]

Ford, John—of the 25th Virginia Battalion, was sent by authorities at Libby Prison to Castle Thunder after a large-scale escape attempt.[184]

Ford, Samuel H.—born in Savannah, Richland County, Ohio, on October 5, 1839, died May 9, 1883, age 43 years, 7 months, 4 days. Ford came with his parents to DeKalb County, Indiana, in 1847. He enlisted in Company H, 30th Regiment Indiana Volunteers on September 24, 1861. He was badly wounded in the fighting at Pittsburgh Landing, and was furloughed. He rejoined his regiment at Corinth, Mississippi, and participated in the siege of Corinth, and the battles of Stones River and Chickamauga. He was captured at Chickamauga on September 20, 1863, and taken to Richmond, Virginia, where he was confined in Castle Thunder, Belle Island, and Libby Prison. He was sent to the exchange hospital in Annapolis, Maryland, and was carried home on a stretcher by his brother, Dr. Joseph H. Ford, on December 25, 1863. Ford recovered and rejoined his regiment, and continued to serve until the end of the war. At his death, 13 members of his company were present to act as pallbearers. They were members of DeLong Post No. 67, G.A.R., and the funeral rites were conducted according to the ritual of the Grand Army of the Republic.[185]

Forward, _____, Mrs.—arrested by a local provost marshal, Mrs. Forward and her servant were sent to Castle Thunder from Gordonsville on suspicion of disloyalty to the Confederacy.[186]

Fry, _____—a Union Colonel who was reported being kept in irons at Castle Thunder. He was described as greatly emaciated, and living only upon "very coarse, scanty fare in a damp cell. There were rumors that the Confederates planned a private execution of him. A sum of $5,000 in Confederate money was offered if his release could be obtained.[187]

Fulcher, G. G.—a private under sentence of court martial, sent to Castle Thunder on October 7, 1863. Alexander was directed to carry out the sentence "as far as practicable."[188]

Fullerton, Peter—arrived at Castle Thunder on December 15, 1862, from Gordonsville, courtesy of Major Boyle, Provost Marshal, charged with disloyalty to Confederate states.[189]

Gabbert, Harmon G.—a private in Company F, 4th Texas Infantry, was wounded at Antietam, September 17, 1862. He was in guard house under charges during the summer of 1863. Confined at Castle Thunder in spring of 1864 to await sentence of court martial. Paroled at Appomattox on April 12, 1865.[190]

Garlick, A. J.—before being arrested, he had served under Capt. A. H. Peck, Company B, 11th Virginia Regiment. He wanted to get out of Castle Thunder and return to the service because he had an "old gray headed mother and wife and family," with no one to protect them.[191]

Garrack, Patrick—was caught attempting to escape by use of a rope. Garrack had tried to bribe a guard the night before, but the guard reported him, and thus thwarted an excape planned by Garrack and 15 more prisoners.[192]

Garry, H. C.—of Harrison County, western Virginia, was one of 56 citizens taken in a raid on the Baltimore and Ohio Railroad in May 1863. He was put in Castle Thunder and held hostage.[193]

Garvey, Bartholomew—a Virginia citizen who was reportedly imprisoned in Castle Thunder as a Union sympathizer. He had three sons in the Union army. He was living in West Virginia in 1897.[194]

Gaston, Charles R.—sought escape from Castle Thunder by getting General Winder to transfer him to the Navy. He had been sentenced by a court martial to three months in Castle Thunder, and his time would be up on July 18, 1863. He had been a member of the 4th Georgia Regiment, Dole's Brigade, Rhode's Division. At the end of the month, the 15-year-old former farmer wrote Winder again for aid in getting transferred to the navy. He stated that he had served with the Georgia regiment since the beginning of the war. He would have been 13 years old at the time of his enlistment.[195]

Gastreen, John W.—confined in June of 1864 at Castle Thunder as a suspicious character.[196]

Gatrell, Duchett—a citizen of Wester County, western Virginia, was one of 56 citizens taken in a raid on the Baltimore and Ohio Railroad in May of 1863. He and others were confined in Castle Thunder as hostages.[197]

"General"—a slave who claimed he had worked on the battlements and belonged to Mrs. Fanny Marshall of Caroline County, Virginia. He was sent to Captain Richardson at Castle Thunder with instructions to have him confined and taken care of.[198]

Gerbert, George (alias Moore)—Attempted to escape by dressing in a nice suit of clothes and walking out past the guard. He was soon recaptured only a short distance away.[199]

Gilday, Martin—Private Company A, 32nd Battalion, Virginia Cavalry, was sent to Captain Alexander to await the "further order" of the court."[200]

Gilman, Charlotte—a woman held in Castle Thunder for 13 months. She spoke highly of Captain Alexander at the Confederate Congressional hearings.[201]

Glass, W. R.—of Company F, 52nd North Carolina, one of group of deserters sent to Castle Thunder in August of 1863 who were not entitled to the benefit of the Presidential Proclamation because they were arrested carrying arms and they resisted arrest.[202]

Godwin, William H.—of the 63rd Virginia Cavalry, Company A, was arrested for desertion on September 23, 1863, in Buncombe County, North Carolina. He arrived at Camp Holmes near Raleigh on October 10, 1863, then was transported to Castle Thunder, where he arrived October 12, 1863.[203]

Goldstein, Jacob—arrested for passing counterfeit money.[204]

Goodman, G. W.—of the 25th Virginia Battalion, was sent by authorities at Libby Prison to Castle Thunder after a large-scale escape attempt.[205]

Gormley, John—a soldier who wanted a friend who was a prisoner in Castle Thunder to spend Christmas with him. Gormley made up a story about the prisoner's two imaginary children who had supposedly just died of fever. He begged prison officials to let his friend out to attend the funeral for the children. The detectives discovered the lie and put Gormley with his friend in the same room at Castle Thunder, where they spent the next few months together.[206]

Grant, F. M.—a New Yorker, put in Castle Thunder for refusing to take up arms, and for saying he "didn't care whether the Yankees took the city or not."[207]

Graves, A. J., (Robert J.?), Rev.—a minister who, after a visit North, returned to preach against the war at his church in Orange County, North Carolina. He was arrested at "The Oaks" shortly after a sermon on order of General Winder. He was taken to Castle Thunder for a month. However, he was allowed to post $5,000 bond for his appearance in a trial for treason. At the trial on June 20, 1863, the jury refused to find a true bill of indictment.[208]

Green, Henry—Private, Captain Wright's Company, was arrested and lodged in Castle Thunder for leaving his post and trading with the Yankee prisoners on Belle Isle, contrary to military regulations.[209] He was transferred to Capt. Alexander at Castle Thunder on October 4, 1863, charged with "leaving his post without permission on the night" of October 2, and "trading with Yankee prisoners."[210]

Green, John—a citizen of East Tennessee, he was arrested March 24, 1862, and transferred from Atlanta to Castle Thunder, December 1862.[211]

Gregory, William—enlisted at age 32 on April 24, 1862, in Company G, 54th North Carolina Regiment. He was hospitalized in Richmond on October 3, 1862, with rheumatism, but returned to duty three days later. He was hospitalized again on December 15, 1862. He was reported confined to a Richmond hospital from April 5 through April 22, 1863, with chronic rheumatism. He returned to duty on May 1, 1863, but deserted from camp near Fredericksburg on June 19, 1863. He was apprehended and was reported in a Richmond hospital on October 23, 1863, with a cold. He was transferred to Castle Thunder that same day. He later died in a hospital in Lynchburg, Virginia, on May 23, 1864, from a gunshot wound received while he was attempting to desert.[212]

Griffin, S.—of Company F, 25th Virginia, a guard at Libby Prison, he was arrested and sent to Castle Thunder for trading with Yankee prisoners, in violation of a prison department regulation.[213]

Grogger, Paul—of Company F, 2nd Tennessee Volunteer Infantry Regiment, U.S.A., captured on October 23, 1863, Pattonsville, Scott County, Virginia, and taken to Castle Thunder. He remained there a week or ten days, before being removed to Belle Island. He escaped from the train carrying him to Andersonville Prison, and made his way across the Yadkin River in an attempt to cross the mountains into Tennessee. However, he was captured by a miller on the Little Yadkin River near the road to Morganton. The miller gave him a good breakfast then a member of the home guard escorted him to Salisbury prison. He remained there about 3 months until May 7, 1864, when about 200 were sent to Andersonville on the train. In December 1864, he was sent to a prison in Florence, South

Carolina, from which he made a successful escape. He died in Kansas in 1921 at age 81.[214]

Grovnor, Sidney S — a captain in the United States Secret Service, he was held in Castle Thunder charged with being a spy. He escaped when the prisoners were let out when the Confederates evacuated the city. When his guards stopped to take a drink of whiskey, he escaped and hid until the Union forces entered the city.[215]

Gurphy, James — along with James Burns, he was sent to Castle Thunder by S. Van de Graaff, 2nd Lieutenant, Marine Guard at the C. S. Navy Yard.[216]

Hall, _____ — first name unknown, regiment unknown, died at Castle Thunder November 9, 1862.[217]

Hamilton, James B. — a wealthy, educated Virginia civilian who had taken an oath to support the Union, was arrested in July of 1863 and taken to Castle Thunder. In fall of 1863, transferred to Salisbury, North Carolina, he died there September 15, 1864.[218]

Hancock, James — a prisoner during the winter of 1864–1865, Hancock was believed to be a spy. He tried to escape by pretending to be dead. He was saved from hanging by the end of the war.[219]

Hancock, John — was confined in the dungeon at Castle Thunder, but escaped along with Sidney S. Grover when the Confederates evacuated the city.[220]

Hanna, George A. — reported to be "one of the most dangerous men in this country," having engaged for the past 18 months as an "independent scout and spy" for the enemy. Because he was a resident of the county, and familiar with the territory, he "ought not under any circumstances to be released during the war." Although arrested previously, he had always escaped.[221]

Hardister, _____ — a drummer and private in Company B, 25th Virginia Battalion, sent to Richardson at Castle Thunder charged with stealing.[222]

Harrill, Joseph H. — from Gates County, North Carolina, a private in Co. J, 13th Virginia Cavalry. His commanding officer, Capt. Alex Savage, wrote General Winder to say that Harrill had been wounded in the arm on July 8, 1863. He received a furlough shortly thereafter for days, and at the expiration of the furlough, Harrill had sent to Capt. Savage a "certificate of inability" from a physician. Savage requested that Harrill, "a good & faithful soldier," be released from prison and returned to his company.[223]

Harris, Arnold, Capt. — a Yankee sent to Richmond by Major Mallett.[224]

Harris, J. P. — a member of Company G, 16th North Carolina, Harris reported in himself, but was arrested for desertion at Camp Holmes, near Raleigh, North Carolina, on October 15, 1863.[225]

Harrison, D. T. (or P.?) — Undoubtedly Harrison was disappointed when Captain Joseph W. Coker refused to accept him at the barracks on 24th and Franklin Streets. Coker wrote that he wanted Harrison to remain in the Castle and asked Lieutenant York to prefer charges against him and set up a court martial at once.[226]

Harrow, _____ — noted to be a prisoner at Castle Thunder in a letter from James. B. Hamilton to "Dear Wife," December 1, 1863.[227]

Hart, George H. Mr. — one of five newspaper correspondents confined at Castle Thunder. He and Leonard A. Hendrick (Hendrix) were paroled and sent North, to work for the release of the other reporters being held in Richmond.[228] Hart worked for the New York *Herald*.

Harvey, Ward C. — resigned the office of captain in Company C, 19th Tennessee Regiment in February 1863. He traveled to Virginia to visit relatives. He was sick in bed for about 6 weeks, and after he recovered he started back to the Army. He was arrested in Giles County and sent to Castle Thunder as a "conscript." He stated that he had resigned because of "physical disability," and asked for a "speedy hearing,"[229]

Hastings, Hugh — of Company H, 25th Virginia Battalion, Infantry, was sent to Castle Thunder, along with W. H. Strayton to await trial before a court martial.[230]

Hatch, E. — a Federal lieutenant who escaped and was recaptured on the Rappahannock lines with Lieutenant Masters. Both were placed in the "Greanor" prison (Castle Thunder), in close confinement, but were to be exchanged. If not exchanged, they were to be paroled.[231]

Hatch, I. M. — a Federal agent sent into Confederate territory on September 18, 1864, disguised as a deserter from the Federal army. His purpose was to determine the disposition of Union deserters being held by the Confederacy. He was taken to Petersburg, then to Richmond's Castle Thunder. He was questioned only briefly, and kept for three weeks. He was exchanged along with 137 others by being sent to Lynchburg, then to Abingdon. From there they marched, under guard to the Cumberland Mountains on the Kentucky border, where they were set free.[232]

Haynes, William Joseph P. (R?) — a British subject, who had served in the British Army, was arrested under suspicious circumstances in western Virginia on May 6, 1863, and charged as a suspected spy.[233]

Hefner, John Marcus — a private from Catawba County, North Carolina, enlisted in Company E, 57th North Carolina, on July 4, 1862. He deserted before September 1, 1863, and was listed as under arrest on September 12, 1863, and was court martialed on January 27, 1864. He returned to duty sometime before May 12, 1864. Captured at Cold Harbor on June 6, 1864, he was confined at Point Lookout, Maryland on June 15, 1864, where he died on July 27, 1864. Cause of death was not reported.[234] Hefner was sent from Camp Holmes, North Carolina, to Castle Thunder on September 18, 1863.[235]

Hendrix (Hendrick), Leonard A. — Hendricks was a newspaper correspondent for the New York *Herald*. He and another reporter were released on parole and sent north for the purpose of working for the release of the other reporters being held at Castle Thunder.[236]

Henshaw, Hayward — to fill out a new battalion of mounted soldiers for General Imboden's command, R. Henry Glenn wrote to General Winder to obtain the release of two of his men, Thomas Leonard and Hayward Hinshaw. The letter stated that Major Robert White had permission from the War Department to organize the new battalion.[237] Listed as "H. Henshaw," his name was also on a list with 20 others made by Lt. W. S. Pilcher, with the notation that he had been sent by Col. Page and charges "will be preferred."[238]

Hernandez, H. A. — confined for stealing from a hospital.[239]

Hess (?), Spencer — Private, 25th Virginial Battalion, sent to Castle Thunder for desertion, to be held for trial.[240]

Hide, E. S. — for operating on "forged pay rolls."

Higgins, Daniel — wrote to Captain Booker to obtain his release from prison. He was willing to join any company, although he had rather go into the Navy. Higgins believed that if he were confined any longer imprisonment would "completely prostrate me." A notation on the outside of the prisoner's letter by Major Griswold referred the correspondence to Captain Alexander, and stated that the prisoner had been sent from Charleston some five or six months previously as a deserter.[241]

Hill, Edward — a Yankee being held at Castle Thunder, was released in November of 1863, after taking the Oath of Allegiance to the Confederacy.[242]

Hill, R. D. — of Company F, 1st Tennessee Regiment, was captured with 21 others at Camp Maynard on February 25, 1863. They were first taken to Castle Lightening, where most were discharged. Seven or eight of the prisoners sent to Castle Thunder were also discharged. Hill was not discharged, and he petitioned Captain Alexander to be released so he could rejoin his regiment.[243]

Hill, Thomas — a citizen of Bridgeport, was one of 56 citizens taken in a raid on the Baltimore and Ohio Railroad in May of 1863. He and several others were housed in Castle Thunder as hostages.[244]

Hillard, Bartlett Young. — a private in Company I, 58th North Carolina, arrested for desertion on September 23, 1863, in Buncombe County, North Carolina, arrived at Camp Holmes near Raleigh on October 10, 1863, then was transported to Castle Thunder, where he arrived October 12, 1863.[245] Hillard had enlisted at age 29 in Watauga County, North Carolina, on July 15, 1862. He was reported on furlough January-February of 1863, and returned to duty March-April of that year. He remained on duty until he deserted at Chickamauga, Georgia, September 20, 1863. He was reported present but under arrest November 17, 1863-Feburary 29, 1864. He returned in the spring of 1864 but was captured or deserted to the enemy at Resaca, Georgia, May 15, 1864. Sent as a Federal prisoner to Nashville, he was transferred to Lousiville, Kentucky, and arrived there May 20, 1864. He was then paroled at Camp Morton and transferred for exchange. He reached Bulwar's Wharf on the James River March 23, 1865 for exchange.[246]

Hines, Martin (alias Flannagan, Nat) — arrived at Castle Thunder as Nat Flannagan, of Company B, 5th Texas Regiment, but identified later as Martin Hines, of Company C, 32nd Virginia Regiment. He was released on May 2, 1863, by Special Order No. 109, to join Capt. Coke's Company C, 32nd Virginia.[247]

Hollingsworth, Robert. — a Quaker citizen of Waterford, Loudoun County, Virginia, held as hostage in Castle Thunder, along with a Mr. Williams, for two hostages the United States government held.[248]

Horsefield, C. — of Company D, 5th New

York Heavy Artillery, was captured along with several others by Colonel Mosby's command at Kabletown, near Snicker's Gap, during United States General Hunter's retreat from Lynchburg, Virginia.[249]

Hopkins, Wade—of the 16th North Carolina, was arrested October 13, 1863, charged with desertion.[250] This may be the same person as "W. Hopkins," of Company I, 16th North Carolina, who enlisted in Wake County, North Carolina on November 11, 1863. He was listed as being present until he deserted on March 14, 1864.[251]

Howell, Joseph—on July 1, 1863, this prisoner who was awaiting a court martial was discovered trying to dig his way out. He was put in irons to prevent future attempts.[252]

Howland, George—Captain of *U.S.S. Emily*, held in Libby Prison and Castle Thunder. Letters and memoirs are housed in the New York State Library.[253]

Huffman, Daniel F.—a Private of Company E, 57th North Carolina, he was arrested on September 18, 1863, and sent from Camp Holmes, North Carolina, to Castle Thunder.[254] He was a resident of Catawba County, North Carolina, where he enlisted at age 24 on July 4, 1862. He was wounded at Fredericksburg on December 13, 1862. Huffman was present until he deserted on September 1, 1863. Under arrest and charged with desertion from September to December 1863. He was court martialed about January 27, 1864, and returned to duty on May 1, 1864. He was captured at Winchester, Virginia, on July 20, 1864, and confined at Camp Chase, until exchanged in March of 1864.[255]

Hughes, Joseph C.—a private, Company D, 7th Virginia Infantry, from Giles County, Virginia, who was taken prisoner at Antietam on September 17, 1862. He was confined at Ft. McHenry and later exchanged. He was court martialed on February 20, 1865, and convicted of encouraging insubordination and mutiny. He was ordered to Castle Thunder for two years hard labor, but was released March 29, 1865.[256]

Hussey, John—a delegate from the United States Christian Commission, spent time in Castle Thunder. He was confined in the same room as Mr. Alfred Brengle of Frederick, Maryland. After his release, Hussey wrote a report of the conditions there.[257]

Hutchey, C.—a conscript, arrested and sent to Major J. W. Pegram, Hutchey claimed he belonged to the "Washington artillery," and had been detailed to some department in Richmond.[258]

Hutchins, Alex—a private in Company E, 54th North Carolina Regiment, he lived in Wilkes County, North Carolina, until he enlisted in Lenoir County on August 30, 1864. He did not remain long, but deserted before November 1, 1864. He was arrested near Staunton, Virginia, attempting to join the enemy. He was confined in Castle Thunder, and upon his release, returned to duty. He was captured near Petersburg, Virginia, April 3, 1865, and sent to Fort Monroe, Virginia. He was held by the Federals at Newport News, Virginia, until June 6, 1865, when he was released after taking the Oath of Allegiance. He died at Richmond on July 18, 1865, cause of death not reported.[259]

Hyde, Charles K.—from Augusta County, Virginia, was arrested on September 20, 1862, and confined to Castle Thunder. The Confederate Congress wanted to know what officer arrested this man, and by "what orders."[260]

Icenhour, W. Wilson—a private in Company A, 7th North Carolina, was arrested for desertion on October 3, 1863, in Alexander County, North Carolina, arrived at Camp Holmes near Raleigh on October 10, 1863, then transported to Castle Thunder, where he arrived October 12, 1863. Icenhour was a resident of Alexander County, North Carolina, when he enlisted at age 21 on February 26, 1862. He was present until he deserted on May 27, 1863. He returned to duty on November 7, 1863, but deserted to the enemy about July 17, 1864. He took the Oath of Allegiance to the Federal government at Fort Monroe, Virginia, on July 30, 1864.[261]

Jackson, J. C.—enlisted in Company I, 1st South Carolina Infantry (Hagood's), August 31, 1863. He was under arrest at Castle Thunder on May 1, 1864. Reported wounded and in hospital since October 7, 1864, then A.W.O.L. from December 31, 1864, onward.[262]

Jackson, James E.—a Negro, sent by General Pryon to Castle Thunder, on suspicion that he set fire to the Meadow Bridge on Monday, May 4, 1863.[263]

Jeffries, P. M.—a citizen of Wetzel County, western Virginia, was one of 56 citizens taken in a raid on the Baltimore and Ohio Railroad in May of 1863. He and several others were housed in Castle Thunder and held as hostages.[264]

Jelfs, Charles—arrested as a suspicious character for prowling through the Exchange Hotel with "false" keys.[265]

Jennings, James—arrested for desertion, he took "French leave" from Castle Thunder by jumping from a window on the western side of the building. He was later seen at a cigar store by Detective New, who arrested him and returned him to Castle Thunder.[266]

Johnson, Alphonso F.—a private in Company E, 6th North Carolina, arrested October 9, 1863, at Rutherford, charged with desertion.[267] Johnson enlisted in Mecklenburg County, North Carolina, at age 31 on May 28, 1861. He was promoted to Corporal on June 20, 1861, but reduced in rank on June 30, 1861. Wounded at Sharpesburg, Maryland, on September 17, 1862, he returned to duty with his company during March-May 1863. He deserted on July 23, 1863, but returned to duty with his company on November 11, 1863. He was reported "absent, under arrest" until he deserted again on December 21, 1863.[268]

Johnson, Andrew, Jr.—the nephew of Tennessee Governor Andrew Johnson, was arrested in Tennesse during a raid. He was accused of disloyalty, and sent to Castle Thunder from which he complained of poor food, horrible treatment.[269]

Johnson, E. J.—died of mumps at Castle Thunder on September 23, 1862, and was buried in Oakwood Cemetery.[270]

Johnson, J. C.—Member of the City Battalion, ordered confined in Castle Thunder by Capt. Alexander for "sleeping" at his post.[271]

Johnson, John—a Castle Thunder prisoner, wrote to General Winder for the return of letters from his family. The two or three letters were written in the "Norwegian language," and he did not think there was anyone in the state of Virginia who could read them. He was most anxious to see the letters, since he had had no word from his family since December, six months earlier.[272]

Johnson, Laura J.—a North Carolina woman who turned up in Richmond dazed and disoriented. She was confined at Castle Thunder, but eventually was sent home.[273]

Johnson, Martin Van Buren—of Company E, 6th North Carolina, arrested October 9, 1863, in Rutherford, charged with desertion. Johnson had enlisted in Mecklenburg County, North Carolina, at age 21 on May 28, 1861. He was present up until he deserted on April 1, 1863. He rejoined his company on November 11, 1863, and was reported "in arrest" until he deserted again on December, 21, 1863.[274]

Johnson, Thomas—a member of Courtney's Artillery, was sent along with Benjamin F. Fodric to Castle Thunder by Commander John W. Johnson, in the fall of 1863.[275]

Jones, Daniel—contested being detained by Capt. Alexander in Castle Thunder. He swore he was connected in no way to either the military or naval forces of the Confederacy, and that he was over age 40. Judge Halyburton ruled in his favor, and ordered Jones released.[276]

Jones, John—taken to Castle Thunder in June of 1863, his name was listed with 20 others made by Lt. W. S. Pilcher. All stated that they were "not members of any company," and did not know what charges were against them, although most were deserters.[277]

Jones, John R.—a private in Company C, 18th Virginia Battalion of Artillery, having been duly enlisted in the service of the Confederate States, he deserted the service on or about the 22nd day November 1862. He left his camp and Battery No. 4, Richmond Defences without the permission of his commanding officer, and was afterwards arrested in the city of Petersburg about January 14, 1863. The accused plead not guilty to the charges of desertion. Capt. B. J. Black, Co. C, 18th Battalion, Virginia Heavy Artillery, a witness for the prosecution, testified that the accused had left the camp about the 22nd day of November 1862 without his permission. If Jones had been given a permit to leave Camp, such permit would have passed through Black's hands. Black stated that Jones had escaped from Castle Thunder, but had been arrested. See Appendix II for full text of court martial.[278]

Jones, John W.—of the Purcell Battery, deserted a second time, and was again confined to Castle Thunder.[279]

Jones, Lemuel—a private in Company D, First North Carolina Union Volunteers, captured April 6, 1863. He and six others were sent to get a load of wood. They went ashore at night at Little Fatty Creek and were captured by partisan rangers.[280]

Jones, Martin—of Company I, 12th North Carolina, was arrested in Wake County, North Carolina, on October 11, 1863, for desertion. Sent to Camp Holmes, he arrived there on October 10, 1863, then was transported to Castle Thunder, where he arrived October 12, 1863. Jones claimed he was on furlough.[281] However, *North Carolina Troops, 1861–1865: A Roster*, does not list his name in this company and regiment. He may have given a false name or incorrect regimental number.

Jordan, Daniel J.—no company or regiment given. He was arrested on September 14, 1863, in Catawba County, and was sent to Camp Holmes, where he arrived on September 19, 1863. He was deemed a deserter for refusal to state his regiment.[282]

Jordan, Thomas Jefferson—Colonel or Major of the 9th Pennsylvania Cavalry, detained from returning north under a flag of truce because of charges of atrocities brought by citizens of Sparta, Tennessee. He was captured at Tompkinsville, Kentucky, on July 7, 1862, and with four other members of the 1st Maryland Cavalry, were removed from Libby Prison and put in Castle Thunder.[283]

Kane, Christopher P.—a member of Company C, 96th Pennsylvania Volunteer Infantry, was captured during the summer of 1863, and held for 16 months at Libby, Belle Isle, Castle Thunder, and Andersonville.[284]

Keaton, A. W.—of Company D, First North Carolina Union Volunteers, captured on March 12, 1863, near Elizabeth City, North Carolina, one of six guarding some Negroes who were chopping wood. He was taken to Castle Thunder, where he died March 31, 1863.[285]

Kelley, Robert—of 1st Company, Richmond Howitzers, was arrested and sent to Richmond from Staunton, Virginia.[286]

Kellogg, Spencer (alias Brown)—charged with being a spy and a deserter, he was captured in the latter part of January of 1862 on the Mississippi River in a small boat near Columbus, Kentucky. He claimed he was a deserter from the Federal army, and wanted to join the Confederacy. He was transferred to Island No. 10, and there made sketches of the fortifications and defenses. He was arrested, but escaped to Federal authorities. He was promoted and captured on board the Federal gunboat *Essex*. By the end of July 1863, Kellogg had been in Castle Thunder for about two months, according to Exchange Agent Robert Ould.[287] He was to be given a speedy trial. When tried, he was found guilty of desertion and espionage, and sentenced to hang on September 25, 1863.[288]

Kelly, Alexander W.—a private in Company F, 2nd Tennessee Infantry, he was captured with Capt. David Fry after a bridge-burning mission on November 8, 1861. Confined at Madison, Georgia, Salisbury, North Carolina; Castle Thunder; and Libby Prison. Paroled at City Point on December 28, 1863, Kelly was back with his regiment by June 18, 1864.[289]

Kelly, Daniel H.—a private with Company F, 2nd Tennessee Infantry, enlisted in Green County, Tennessee. Captured with Capt. David Fry after a bridge-burning mission on November 8, 1861. Kelly died in captivity on November 15, 1861, at Richmond.[290]

Kelly, John—was on a list with 20 others made by Lt. W. S. Pilcher, beside which was a notation that indicated he was charged with "aiding & abetting substitution."[291]

Kelly, Robert J.—begged Major Carrington to be released on bail and promised that he would appear at his court martial on any day specified. He said he had been quite sick for several days and wanted to "remain with my wife & family until the appointed day of trial," where he could be cared for properly.[292]

Kenny, Patrick—a civilian who obtained a pass and traveled to Richmond in order to purchase a copper pipe for the distillation of alcohol. He was arrested on the border of Essex County, and his money ($76.50 in silver, and $128 in Confederate notes), was confiscated. He wrote General Winder and asked that his money be given to his wife, Teresa. A notation on the bottom of the letter indicated that Kenney was discharged three days later on January 25, 1864.[293]

Kilgrove, J.—arrested on October 18, 1862, along with Thomas and Robert Oatley, citizens of Henrico County, Virginia, for illegally taking government wood.[294]

Kirby, J. T.—testified at the trial of Captain Alexander on April 15, 1863, that he had been imprisoned for some months as a spy. He declared he was an Englishman, a resident of Niagra, Canada, where he had a wife and children. He came through the lines on business with the government.[295] In a letter to General Winder, Kirby said that the government had offered to send him from the Confederacy under a "flag of truce." He claimed that he could establish his innocence, and that Judge Lyons had said that, although the military authorities had the first right to try him, there was "no evidence to convict me before any court," military or civil, and that he should have been tried within "a reasonable time or discharged." That statement was made on March 11, 1863, two months earlier.[296] Kirby was released from Castle Thunder, along with about 650 Yankee prisoners from Libby Prison, and sent to City Point for transfer.[297]

Keys, William H.—a Marylander, and member of Company B, 25th Virginia Battalion, he had escaped from the guard house at Camp Maynard three times during the two weeks he had been confined while awaiting the decision of a court martial. He had been found guilty of theft while at large, and was recaptured each time "while drunk." It was believed he would desert before his sentence was published, so he was sent to Castle Thunder.[298]

King, George W. — a private, he transferred to Company C, 15th North Carolina Regiment on August 14, 1862. He was present or accounted for until wounded at the Wilderness about May 6, 1864. He returned to duty before November 11, 1864. On December 18, 1864, he was hospitalized in Raleigh with a gunshot wound in his left foot. He was given a 60-day furlough on December 19, 1864. No mention is made in *North Carolina Troops: A Roster* of his arrest for desertion and confinement in Castle Thunder on September 18, 1863.[299]

King, J. W. — see William King

King, William (alias J. W. King) — ordered taken into custody, William King was a "notorious character," to be sent to the officer of General Winder for investigation.[300] A subsequent note described hin as a "desperate character" to be held in custody, along with Charles Renquist.[301] His name was on a list of prisoners to be forwarded to Major Griswold in Richmond. King was a citizen of Westmoreland County, sent to Richmond by the clerk of the 1st Congressional District. King, judged disloyal, had been sent to Richmond under guard, but he escaped and went home. He was believed to be a man of "very bad character."[302]

Kirkendall, William — a member of the Graham Battery, was arrested in Buncombe County, North Carolina, on September 28, 1863, for desertion. Sent to Camp Holmes, he arrived there on October 10, 1863, then was transported to Castle Thunder, where he arrived October 12, 1863.[303]

Knox, H. L., Mrs. — a woman confined to Castle Thunder for "communicating treasonable information to the enemies of the Confederacy."[304]

Koontz, Samuel B. — a farmer from the Mt. Cove district of what is now West Virginia, had served as an officer in the 142nd Virginia Militia. After Virginia left the Union, Koontz remained loyal and agreed to accept a commission as a Union officer. Before he could be administered the oath of office and obtain his commission papers, he was arrested by General John Echols near his home on June 5, 1863. Although Koontz said he was a soldier, he was arrested as a "traitorous Virginian" and sent to Castle Thunder. A year later, he was transferred to Libby Prison, and treated subsequently as a military prisoner rather than a traitor. He is mentioned in a letter from James. B. Hamilton to "Dear Wife," December 1, 1863.[305]

Lacy, Charles R. (alias Lawson) — notorious English pickpocket, burgler, and spy, Lacy died November 9, 1862, at Castle Thunder. He had been confined there for some time. Lacy, who used many aliases, escaped from Castle Goodwin in July, but was caught by Alexander's detectives.[306]

Ladd, ____ — a private in Company E, 25th Virginia Battery, charged with deserting.[307]

Lane, Jim — A free Negro who was captured trying to reach Yankee lines.[308]

Lannon, Michael J. — the commander of the gunboat *Beaufort* asked Captain Alexander to confine Lannon in Castle Thunder "for leaving this vessel without permission."[314]

Laprade, Israel — of Company F, 52nd Virginia, was received at Castle Thunder under a court martial sentence of six months for desertion. Laprade was tried for desertion in a court martial at Kinston, North Carolina, in March of 1864. He was also to be branded with the letter "D" one and a half inches in diameter on his left hip, and to perform six months work on some fortification with a 12-pound ball and a 3-foot chain attached to his left ankle. In addition, he was to forfeit all pay and allowances due him.[309]

Lawton, Hattie H. (alias Mrs. Timothy Webster) — see under Webster, Timothy, Mrs.

Lee, Mary — had baby while in Castle Thunder. She named it Castellina Thunder Lee.[310]

Lee, Solomon J. — enlisted in Guilford County, North Carolina, as a private in Company F, 19th Regiment, North Carolina Troops (Company F, 2nd Regiment, North Carolina Cavalry). He was present from the time of his enlistment on June 17, 1861, until he deserted on April 27, 1863. He was arrested for desertion and confined in Castle Thunder on September 18, 1863.[311]

Lemkens, Thomas — a slave committed to Castle Thunder in July or August 1863, was one of several who claimed to be free.[312]

Lemmon, M. J. — of the Manchester Artillery, and J. Wrenn escaped by digging through the rear wall at Castle Thunder. They were recaptured after a short period of freedom, as they attempted to board a train leaving Richmond. Both were returned to Castle Thunder.[313]

Leonard, Thomas—in order to fill a new battalion of mounted soldiers for General Imboden's command, R. Henry Glenn wrote to General Winder to request the release of two of his men, Thomas Leonard and Hayward Hinshaw. Major Robert White had been given permission from the War Department to organize the new battalion. His name was listed with 20 others made by Lt. W. S. Pilcher, with the notation that there were "no charges."[315]

Lewis, ____—of Tyrrell County, North Carolina, was sent by his neighbors to Richmond to retrieve horses stolen from then during a cavalry raid in 1863. However, instead of retrieving the horses, Lewis was placed in Castle Thunder "upon an accusation by the men who had the horses."[316]

Lineberry, Elbert S.—First Lieutenant, Company A, 2nd Tennessee Infantry, enlisted in Roane County, Tennessee. He resigned due to tuberculosis, after which he was arrested while in civilian's clothes as a spy and a recruiting officer for the Federal army. Held first at Knoxville, he was transferred to Castle Thunder, and held until exchanged on August 26, 1863.[317]

Littleton, Joseph—wrote to Captain Alexander from "Room No. 10" of Castle Thunder, and begged to be transferred to Libby Prison because he was a Federal soldier. He stated he had been captured in Loudon County, Virginia, on Friday "the 25th day of Sept." [1863] by Copl. White's men.[318]

Lloyd, Henry—was lodged in Castle Thunder on October 29, 1862, as a deserter from the gunboat *Torpedo*.[319]

Logan, James—a deserter from the 25th Virginia Battalion (the City Battalion), jumped off the train on his way to a court martial. He and Bob Ryan, another deserter, were captured by detectives walking calmly about the streets of Richmond.[320]

Lohman, William—charged with treason against the Confederate government, he was listed among those who had escaped during the last days of the war.[321]

Login, John W.—a prisoner in Castle Thunder, when fellow prisoner Henry Avery wrote to Major Carrington to ask that he and two others (John W. Login and Joseph Day) be released to serve in the Confederate service.[322]

Long, G. W.—suspected of being a spy, this Loudoun County man wrote a very long letter to General Winder on June 2, 1863, and described how he had been sent "from post to post" without a trial or hearing, on charges made by an old woman. He had joined the Confederate service in February of 1863, and was "dismissed when our company had fallen back from Leesburg to White Plains." He pleaded for a chance to prove that he was "free of the base charge against me, but loyal...."[323] After having been imprisoned by the Yankees in Old Capitol Prison, he was arrested in Richmond. He begged Captain Alexander in August of 1863 to help him and give him a hearing. He said he would take the "oath, if it was required," and promised to do everything he could for the Confederate government.[324]

Long, Lazarus—one of three workers at the Tredgar Iron Works, captured while attempting to cross over into Federal lines.[325]

Low, John J.—a private, Company C, 2nd Tennessee, who deserted, and was then arrested in Anderson County, Tennessee, for running off slaves and stealing a horse. Confined initially at Castle Thunder, he later was reported to have joined the Confederate Army while a prisoner at Salisbury, North Carolina.[326]

Lugo, C. Orizio (aka, Lugo, Roezio)—a spy from New York who regularly visited Richmond. He stayed at the best hotels and drank the best whiskey. He avoided suspicion until he forgot to pay "an exorbitant bill." In April of 1864, when he again visited Richmond, detectives arrested him and found incriminating documents in his luggage.[327]

Lundy, ____—volunteered on April 24, 1861, and fought in the First Battle at Manassas. He and his Captain "disagreed and he was court martialed" and sent to Castle Thunder. There he remained for two or three months until he became ill and was sent to Hospital No. 13. His father, John Lundy, was a shoemaker. He obtained a contract to make shoes for the government, and he asked General Winder to release his son to come home to Grayson County, Virginia, so that he might help fill the shoe contract.[328]

Lunsford, James—a private in Company C, 30th North Carolina, reported in himself on October 15, 1863, but was still charged with desertion, and sent to Castle Thunder.[329] Lunsford lived in Wilkes County, North Carolina, before he enlisted at Camp Holmes at age 27 on September 23, 1862. He was present until he deserted from a Danville, Virginia, hospital on

March 24, 1863. He returned to duty sometime before January 1, 1864. Lunsford was captured near Spotsylvania Court House May 10–12, 1864, and confined at Point Lookout, Maryland on May 18, 1864. He was then transferred to Elmira, New York, on August 10, 1864, where he was held until he was released on May 29, 1865, after taking the Oath of Allegiance.[330]

Luters, Henry—a private in Company D, First North Carolina Union Volunteers, captured April 6, 1863. He and six others were sent to get a load of wood. They were captured by partisan rangers when they went ashore.[331]

Luton, James—a private in Company D, First North Carolina Union Volunteers, captured April 6, 1863. He and six others were sent to get a load of wood, and when they went ashore at Little Fatty Creek they were captured by partisan rangers.[332]

Manor, William—a member of Company A, 26th Tennessee, he was arrested in Buncombe County, North Carolina, on September 28, 1863, for desertion. Sent to Camp Holmes, he arrived on October 10, 1863, then was transported to Castle Thunder, where he arrived October 12, 1863.[333]

Marr, John H.—a citizen confined to Castle Thunder on a charge of treason.[334]

Marsh, Charles H.—a private, Company D, 1st Battalion Connecticut Cavalry, was captured October 7, 1862, near Haymarket and put in Castle Thunder prison. He wrote on December 1, 1862, to Secretary of War James A. Seddon to ask why he was not being treated as a prisoner of war, and why he has not been exchanged. He said he was a "poor private" without "friends or money." However, General Winder suspected he was a spy, rather than an ordinary soldier. Earlier, Marsh had also written to Mr. Wood, Commissioner of the United States.[335] Captain Alexander noted on a communication that Marsh had been captured on August 9, 1862, at Bull Run, as a Yankee spy, and that he had been brought to Castle Thunder on October 24, 1862.[336]

Martin, Thomas—a private who deserted from E. P. Alexander's Battalion, was confined in Castle Thunder. Capt. W. W. Parker wrote General Winder to claim the $50 reward offered for Martin's arrest.[337]

Mason, Elihu—of Company K, 21st Ohio Volunteers, and a member of the Andrew's Raid to cut communications in Georgia. Mason was captured on April 14, 1862, and held in Atlanta, then transferred to Castle Thunder in December of that year, charged as an "engine thief."[338]

Mason, John M.—of Company K, 7th North Carolina, reported to Col. Sharp, but was still arrested for desertion. He was sent to Camp Holmes on October 10, 1863, and then was transported to Castle Thunder, where he arrived October 12, 1863.[339] Mason was a resident of Iredell County, North Carolina, who enlisted at age 27 on August 12, 1862. He was present or accounted for through October 1864.[340]

Mason, William—a member of the Home Guard of Fairfax County, Virginia, was sent by Major Bridgeford and committed by Captain Alexander on October 10, 1863. He was then conscripted and delivered on Special Order No. 273, dated November 15, 1863.[341]

Masters, _____—a Federal lieutenant who was captured on the Rappahannock lines with Lieutenant E. Hatch. They were placed in the "Greanor" prison (Castle Thunder), in close confinement, but were to be exchanged. If not exchanged, they were to be paroled.[342]

Mattox, C. C.—died of small pox in the prison hospital at Castle Thunder.[343]

May, Nathaniel A.—resided in Guilford County, North Carolina, where he enlisted as a private in Company E, 2nd Regiment, at age 24 on February 24, 1862, for the duration of the war. He was present or accounted for until detailed for hospital duty in Richmond on March 1, 1864. He served as a nurse at Jackson Hospital from about April 1864 until October 1864.[344] May was also arrested for desertion and confined in Castle Thunder on September 18, 1863, according to Captain Alexander's morning report for that day.[345]

McAlister, James—along with Adams and John Shehan, made a rope out of a blanket and were going to escape. They were discovered, and attacked the guard, Frederick F. Wiley, with a shovel, razor, and ball and chain.[346]

McArthur, W. J. D—Commandant Sidney Smith Lee wrote to Brig. Gen. Winder to obtain a release for McArthur, Summers, and Duffey, who were seamen anxious to join the naval service.[347]

McCammon, S. W.—while confined in the dungeon of Castle Thunder for forgery, he attempted to breakout along with Samuel Wyvill. Both were caught.[348]

McCoy, T.—of Company G, 2nd Tennessee, he was captured May 28, 1862, for bridge burning, sent from Atlanta to Castle Thunder.[349]

McClung, Albert G.—a Federal soldier who was home on furlough when captured by Confederate soldiers. He was brought to Castle Thunder and put in the "condemned cell," where he remained for 36 days. He asked Major Carrington for a hearing and wanted to know the charges against him. He also thought he should be treated as a prisoner of war.[350]

McClusky, John—reportedly from Wheate's Battalion, sent from Petersburg, and taken to Castle Thunder in June 1863. He was on a list with 20 others by Lt. W. S. Pilcher. All stated they were "not members of any company," and did not know what charges were against them, although most were deserters.[351]

McDermont, Charles—sentenced by court martial, he escaped from Libby prison hospital, but was caught in Tyler's Row, near Rockett's, by Detective New. New had to chase the escapee and discharged his pistol twice before the prisoner was captured, and taken to Castle Thunder.[352]

McGalliard, R.—of Company F, 38th North Carolina, he was arrested for desertion October 8, 1863, in McDowell County, North Carolina, and taken to Camp Holmes, before being sent to Castle Thunder in Richmond, Virginia.[353] This man is not listed on the roster of Company F, 38th North Carolina.

McGann, Roger—incarcerated for operating on "forged pay rolls."[354]

McGregor, James P.—a prisoner since September 11, 1863, he asked General Winder for a hearing because he did not know what he was charged with. McGregor stated that he had served on the police force under John T. Monroe when he was mayor of New Orleans.[355]

McKim, William F.—born November 18, 1845, in Missouri, the son of William McKim, a native of Scotland, and Marietta Dourexson, a Pennsylvania Quaker. William F. McKim enlisted on June 25, 1861, in Company I, Second Kentucky Infantry of Union Volunteers, and served for the next three years. He took part in campaigns in West Virginia under General Rosecrans. He then served with General U.S. Grant at Fort Donelson, and at Nashville with General Buell. The Second Kentucky Regiment became part of the Fourth Division, Army of the Ohio, under General William E. Nelson. McKim was wounded at Stones River on December 31, 1862, and taken prisoner. He was confined in Castle Thunder and then Libby Prison for three months. Among the last of those exchanged under the cartel agreement, he rejoined his regiment in June of 1863 at Murfreesboro, Tennessee, and took part in the battle of Chickamauga, and the siege of Chattanooga. He mustered out on June 19, 1864, and when the war ended, he moved to Decatur County, Indiana, to farm. He then operated a hotel for three years, and after that a drug and grocery business in Burlington, Boone County, Kentucky. He married Florence Rich of Kenton County, Kentucky, and they had two children.[356]

McNiven, William—employed by William Barrett, who was pretending to be a substitute agent.[357]

Mead, John A.—a private in Company D, First North Carolina Union Volunteers, captured April 6, 1863. He and six others were sent to get a load of wood. When they went ashore at night at Little Fatty Creek, they were captured by partisan rangers.[358]

Meadows, J. W.—of Company A, 23rd North Carolina, one of group of deserters who was sent to Castle Thunder in August of 1863. He was not entitled to the benefit of the Presidential Proclamation because he and the others were caught bearing arms and resisting arrest.[359]

Mehan, James—he admitted he had gone from the Yankee army to the 3rd South Carolina Regiment. He was willing to take the Oath in order to return to South Carolina, where he would work for the government there.[360]

Miller, D. W.—a resident of Cleveland County, North Carolina, he enlisted at age 37 on February 28, 1863, in Company H, 34th Regiment, North Carolina Infantry. He was captured at Falling Waters, Maryland, on July 14, 1863. He was then confined in various field hospitals with diarrhea until released and paroled at City Point, Virginia, on August 24, 1863. He returned to duty on November 18, 1863. In the final days of the war, he was captured on April 2, 1864, near Jarratt's Station, Virginia, and confined at Hart's Island, New York Harbor, on April 7, 1864. He was released on June 17, 1865, after taking the Oath of Allegiance.[361] No mention was made in *North Carolina Troops* of Miller's arrest for desertion and confinement in Castle Thunder on September 18, 1863.[362]

Mills, H.—a citizen of East Tennessee, arrested on March 12, 1862, for disloyalty, he was transferred from Atlanta to Castle Thunder in December of 1862.[363]

Millsaps, John—of Company K, 7th North Carolina, arrested for desertion on October 1,

1863, in Iredell County, North Carolina, he arrived at Camp Holmes near Raleigh on October 10, 1863, then was transported to Castle Thunder, where he arrived October 12, 1863.[364] Millsaps was a resident of Alexander County, North Carolina, who enlisted on February 24, 1862, at age 40. He was captured at Williamsport, Maryland, on September 16, 1862, and confined in Fort Delaware. He was transferred to Aiken's Landing on October 2, 1862, for exchange, which took place on November 10, 1862. He deserted during March and April of 1863, but was later reported "absent sick" from November-December of 1863 until March-April 1864, when he rejoined his company. He continued to be present until he was wounded at Jones' Farm, Virginia, on September 30, 1864. He was reported "absent wounded" from then through October of 1864.[365]

Mitchell, _____ — beaten by other prisoners, and "has been crazy ever since."[366]

Mollen, J. F.— a lieutenant sent from Mobile charged with being a spy. Alexander was ordered to receive him on October 21, 1863.[367]

Molissa, Ali Ben— a "Frenchman by birth," now a deserter from the Federal Army, confined at Castle Thunder for two and a half months prior to December 1863. He had been told that he might be released "by joining any Infantry Regiment in the field," but he refused to do so. He stated that he was "not fit for Infantry service." He then decided he would join the Independent Cavalry Company service in either Louisiana, Mississippi, Alabama, or Texas, and would do so "honorably as I have done in France for 14 years...."[368]

Moore, Robert T.— from the 18th Virginia Battalion, he and five other soldiers were placed in Castle Thunder to await sentence from a court martial.[369]

Morris, C. A.— from the 4th Pennsylvania Cavalry, he was captured and then recognized as a deserter from Company A, 4th Virginia Cavalry. He was transferred from Libby Prison on May 30, 1864, to Castle Thunder to await a court martial for "desertion to the enemy," the penalty for which is death.[370]

Mountcastle, A. B.— of Company F, 25th Virginia, a guard at Libby Prison, who was arrested and sent to Castle Thunder for trading with Yankee prisoners, in violation of a prison rules.[371]

Mullen, William— his name was on a list with 20 others made by Lt. W. S. Pilcher, with the notation his papers were with General Winder. All the men claimed they were "not members of any company" and did not know what they were charged with.[372]

Mulloroney, William— a "boiler maker" who had been working at the Tredegar Iron Works, was confined at Castle Thunder.[373]

Mumford, Henry P.— from Baltimore, confined at Castle Thunder in November of 1862.[374]

Murphy, Mick— of the 10th Virginia Cavalry, imprisoned April 15, 1863, charged with desertion.[375]

Murphy, William H.— captain of the 1st Louisiana, was arrested for acting as a substitute agent and placed in Castle Thunder early in 1863.[376]

Needham, Elizabeth— a woman from Lynchburg who was arrested as a suspicious person.[377]

Newson, James P.— of Company C, 32rd North Carolina Regiment, a guard at Castle Thunder, who got in an argument with Martin Gripp, another soldier of Company F, and fired his musket. Three men were injured, and one, Private Richard Morris, died. Newson was confined to Castle Thunder.[378]

Nichols, Columbus— having recovered from his illness, he was returned to Castle Thunder from the hospital. He begged Captain Winder to release him and send him back to his regiment.[379]

Norman, Amos— of Company K, 53rd North Carolina, arrested October 2, 1863, arrived at Camp Holmes on October 15, 1863, charged with desertion, and sent to Castle Thunder.[380]

Nowery, George— charged with desertion from the 5th Alabama Battalion, was on the list with 20 others made by Lt. W. S. Pilcher.[381]

Oatley, Robert— arrested on October 18, 1862, along with Thomas Oatley and J. Kilgrove, citizens of Henrico County, Virginia, for illegally taking government wood.[382]

Oatley, Thomas— arrested on October 18, 1862, along with Robert Oatley and J. Kilgrove, citizens of Henrico County, Virginia, for illegally taking government wood.[383]

O'Connor, Dennis— testified at the Congressional Investigation. He was one of those who had been put out in the prison yard for exploding powder inside the building.[384]

O'Connor, Thomas— Captain Alexander mentioned at the Congressional Investigation that he had once held Dennis O'Connor's brother, Thomas, in prison.[385]

Odell, G. C.—from Company E, 3rd South Carolina regiment, confined at Castle Thunder on August 19, 1862.[386]

Odell, Samuel—born on October 8, 1834, he was the son of Samuel and Ovela Welch Odell, from East Hartford, Connecticut. The elder Odell was a civil engineer and was one of those who established the boundary between the United States and Canada. Young Samuel was educated there and in Canada. In May 1861, Samuel Odell enlisted in Company A, 5th Connecticut Volunteers for 60 days, and took part in the First Battle of Manassas (First Bull Run). After the 60 days were up, he and his brother Alexander joined Company A of the 8th Connecticut Volunteers, and served with that unit for the next three years and 10 months. Wounded at the Battle of Seven Pines, Samuel Odell was captured near Richmond and confined for six weeks in Castle Thunder before he escaped. He survived the war and married Miss Victoria Bouguenot of Paris, France on February 2, 1868. They had one son and two daughters.[387]

Ogden, R. D'Orsay—"the theatrical *habeas corpus* man of Richmond," ran away but was captured in King George County, and taken to Richmond. On his arrival he was deposited in Castle Thunder, until a court martial disposed of him.[388]

Orr, James—from the 63rd Virginia Cavalry, Company F, was arrested for desertion on September 23, 1863, in Buncombe County, North Carolina. Sent to Camp Holmes near Raleigh on October 10, 1863, he arrived two days later at Castle Thunder.[389]

Osborn, William C.—his name was on a list with 20 others made by Lt. W. S. Pilcher, with the notation that he was charged with desertion, and had been sent from Major Griswold.[390]

Osborne, William P. (alias Peter Duffield)—a member of the crew of the steamer *Richmond*, was requested to be returned to his ship by his commanding officer. Captain Alexander wrote Captain W. G. Winder on June 13, 1863, to send the orders for his transfer.[391]

Page, Henry—a Yankee being held at Castle Thunder, was released in November of 1863, after taking the Oath of Allegiance to the Confederacy.[392]

Palmer, H. C.—of Company D, First North Carolina Union Volunteers, captured March 12, 1863, near Elizabeth City, North Carolina. He was first confined at Castle Thunder, then was transferred to the Confederate States Military Prison to be exchanged by the first flag of truce.[393]

Palmer, James—of Company C, 20th Pennsylvania Cavalry, was captured with several others by Colonel Mosby's command at Kabletown, near Snicker's Gap, during United States General Hunter's retreat from Lynchburg, Virginia.[394]

Palmer, William Jackson, Brig. Gen.—A member of the 15th Pennsylvania Cavalry, Palmer was captured in civilian dress by Confederate forces after the battle of Antietam. After being in Castle Thunder he was exchanged.[395]

Parke, John F.—on October 31, 1862, Parke, of the Richmond Zouaves, was ordered by to be shot for desertion in the face of the enemy. This sentence was carried out a few days later in the backyard at Castle Thunder.[396]

Parker, Henry—a citizen of Parkersburg, was one of 56 citizens taken in a raid on the Baltimore and Ohio Railroad in May of 1863. They were held in Castle Thunder as hostages.[397]

Parker, Pinkney—Company A, 23rd North Carolina, reported in himself but arrested for desertion and taken to Camp Holmes on October 15, 1863, before being sent on to Castle Thunder in Richmond, Virginia, where he arrived the next day.[398] This may be the same man as James P. Parker, a Catawba County, North Carolina, resident who enlisted in Iredell County, North Carolina, on September 6, 1862. He was present until captured at Spotsylvania, Virginia, on May 12, 1864, and confined at Point Lookout, Maryland, on August 10, 1864. He died there on September 18, 1864, of "chronic bronchitis."[399]

Parrish, Henry—a member of Company F, 54th North Carolina, he was one of six deserters brought from Petersburg and put in Castle Thunder in October of 1862.[400] However, according to the listing of Company F, 54th Regiment by Manarin and Jordan, Henry Parrish died at Camp Mangum near Raleigh on June 20, 1862.[401] Either this is an error or the prisoner used a dead man's name.

Parrott, Jacob—a private in Company K, 33rd Regiment Ohio Volunteers, and a member of the Andrew's Raid to cut communications in Georgia, he was captured April 3, 1862. He was held in Atlanta until December of 1862, when he was transferred to Castle Thunder.[402]

Patterson, Robert—of Company F, 57th Virginia, one of group of deserters who was sent to Castle Thunder in August of 1863. They were not entitled to the benefit of the Presidential

Proclamation because they had been arrested bearing arms and resisting arrest.[403]

Payne, J. W.—of Company D, 28th Virginia, was ordered transported under guard to Castle Thunder.[404]

Pearson, Elijah—one of three workers at the Tredgar Iron Works who was captured while attempting to cross over into Federal lines.[405]

Peck, Sam J.—a private in the Goochland artillery, he was confined in Castle Thunder, but was returned to duty by Captain Alexander.[406]

Pendleton, Benjamin—a corporal with Company D, First North Carolina Union Volunteers, captured April 6, 1863. He and six others were sent to get a load of wood. They went ashore at night at Little Fatty Creek and were captured by partisan rangers.[407]

Petrie, E. B.—from Forsyth County, North Carolina, a member of the "order of Heroes," who knew the signs and passwords, was identified as such on a train between Dublin and Lynchburg, Virginia. He was later confined in Castle Thunder.[408]

Pettis, W. H.—a deserter from the Fayette Artillery, he was sent to Captain Alexander by order of Major E. Griswold, to await a court martial.[409]

Phillips, Elijah—a resident of Burke County, North Carolina, he enlisted at age 42 as a private in Company B, 11th Regiment, North Carolina Infantry, on February 1, 1862. He was present or accounted for until he died in a Richmond hospital on September 5, 1864, cause of death not reported.[410] There was no mention of his arrest for desertion and confinement at Castle Thunder on September 18, 1863.[411]

Phillips, J.—one of three workers at the Tredgar Iron Works, captured while attempting to cross over into Federal lines.[412]

Phoenix, John—A slave committed to Castle Thunder in July or August of 1863, was one of several who claimed to be free.[413]

Pickett, Mary Ann, Mrs.—Brigadier General H. A. Wise had Mrs. Mary Ann Pickett, her son, and her two daughters arrested and taken to Castle Thunder, along with her 34 slaves.[414]

Piper, John A.—Company H, 47th Virginia Regiment, was sentenced to hard labor for desertion.[415]

Pielert (?), George—a member of the crew of the C. C. S. *Torpedo*, was sent to Capt. Alexander by Hunter Davidson, of the C. S. Navy, who stated that he had refused to obey the orders of his commanding officer, and "he needs severe punishment."

Pierce, P.—of Company B, 1st Tennessee Regiment, was captured April 25, 1862, for bridge burning. He was sent from Atlanta in December of 1862 to Castle Thunder.[416]

Pitt, Marie E.—according to a letter to Secretary Seddon, she was working in a factory until it closed. Then she was appointed a matron in the General Hospital where she remained until she resigned due to illness. She was arrested at her home in Isle of Wight County and sent to Castle Thunder.[417]

Pittinger, William—a corporal in Company G, 2nd Regiment Ohio Volunteers, he was one of the Andrew's Raid in Georgia. Captured April 14, 1862, and held for engine theft in Atlanta, then transferred to Castle Thunder.[418] Discharged from the service August 14, 1863, because of his weakened condition from imprisonment, he was awarded the Congressional Medal of Honor.[419]

Poindexter, Richard—a slave belonging to Robert Goodman, reclaimed after a list of slaves being held in Castle Thunder was published in August of 1863.[420]

Portice, Uriah—a private in Company B, 54th North Carolina, he was arrested for desertion on October 8, 1863, in McDowell County, North Carolina, and taken to Camp Holmes. Then he was sent to Castle Thunder.[421] Portice, a shoemaker born in Guilford County, North Carolina, who enlisted in McDowell County, North Carolina, at age 54 on March 21, 1862. He was reported A.W.O.L. from July 1862 through February 1863. He was listed as a deserter, but then returned to duty on November 1, 1863. He was hospitalized in Richmond, Virginia, on December 14, 1863, then transferred to another hospital on December 15, 1863. No further information, other than that of his confinement in Castle Thunder.[422]

Powell, John C.—of the 4th Virginia Regiment, looked in vain for some of his company to come and get him out of Castle Thunder. He wrote General Winder to ask him to "look after my case," and send someone to inform his company at Chaffin's Bluff of his plight.[423]

Price, Eleaney—a member of Company G, 37th Regiment, was headed back to his regiment, when he was arrested and put in Castle Thunder. He wrote to Captain D. L. Hudson to get him out.[424]

Price, Linville—a deserter from the 34th North Carolina, and member of the "order of Heroes," he knew the signs and passwords, and was identified as such on a train between Dublin and Lynchburg, Virginia. He was later confined in Castle Thunder.⁴²⁵ Enlisted in Ashe County at age 21 on August 10, 1861, as a private in Company A, 34th Regiment, and was present until he deserted on July 30, 1862.⁴²⁶

Putnam, Fleming— captured at Tunstall's Station, he was charged with acting as a guide to Yankees in their raid near this city.⁴²⁷

Quinn, James— captured while working on the railroad near Fairfax Court House. He had been confined to Castle Thunder since October 1, 1863.⁴²⁸

Ramsey, L. W.— Company A, 54th (?) North Carolina, arrested in Buncombe County, North Carolina, on September 28, 1863, for desertion. Sent to Camp Holmes, he arrived there on October 10, 1863, then was transported to Castle Thunder, where he arrived October 12, 1863.⁴²⁹ His name is not on the roster for North Carolina Regiments 53 through 56.

Rash, John— taken to Castle Thunder in June of 1863, his name was on a list with 20 others made by Lt. W. S. Pilcher, with the notation that he was a member of the "5th Lou. Reg." He was charged with desertion.⁴³⁰

Reddick, William H., Corp.— of Company B, 33rd Regiment Ohio Volunteers, a member of the Andrew's Raid to cut communications in Georgia, was arrested April 18, 1862. Held for theft of a train engine in Atlanta, he was transferred in December of 1862 to Castle Thunder.⁴³¹

Redman, John Thomas— a private in Company E, 54th North Carolina, reported to Col. Sharp, but still arrested for being A.W.O.L.. He arrived at Camp Holmes near Raleigh on October 10, 1863, then was transported to Castle Thunder, where he arrived October 12, 1863.⁴³² Redman was born in Iredell County, North Carolina, on May 31, 1840, where he worked as a farmer until he enlisted at age 21 on March 20, 1862. He was presented through December of 1862, and was reported hospitalized on April 5, 1863, with an unspecified ailment. On August 1, 1863, he was reported A.W.O.L., but he returned to duty on November 8, 1863 (after his confinement in Castle Thunder), and continued to remain with his regiment through October of 1864. He was captured near Farmville, Virginia, on April 6, 1865, and confined at Newport News, Virginia. He was released on June 26, 1865, after taking the Oath of Allegiance. His pension records indicate he as wounded in the chest by an "exploding shell at Cedar Run, Virginia," on June 15, 1863.⁴³³

Reece, William L.— a resident of Haywood County, North Carolina, Reece enlisted at age 25 on June 29, 1861. He deserted on August 29, 1862, returned to duty, but deserted again on March 27, 1863. He was reported under arrest July-August of 1863, and was confined in Castle Thunder September-October of 1863. He was reported under arrest at Weldon during November and December of 1863. He was executed on February 18, 1864, for murdering G. W. Chambers while deserted.⁴³⁴ The execution of William L. Reece was described by two soldiers who witnessed it. "[T]hare was a man Shot yesterday at Weldon. [T]hare was 4 Rigt [regiments] marched up to look at it."⁴³⁵ Another soldier described the execution: "Our Brigade was all marched out in a field to see a man shot. There was twelve men shot at him. He was tied to a stake. I was told four Balls hit him. He deserted and Killed his Cousin.⁴³⁶

Remine, D. W.— born in Virginia in 1837, he moved to Greene County, Tennessee, in 1847. Educated at Limestone Academy and Tusculum College, Remine married Miss Phoebe Keizel from Rockingham County, Virginia in 1858. They had 14 children. Remine was captured and confined in Castle Thunder, Libby Prison, Abingdon, Jonesboro, Greeneville, and Knoxville prisons as an alien enemy because of his strong views on abolition.⁴³⁷

Renn, Lewis— a member of the 5th Virginia Cavalry, he reported in himself, but was arrested for being absent without leave, and sent to Castle Thunder, and arrived there October 16, 1863.⁴³⁸

Renquist, Charles— described as a "desperate character," he was ordered held in custody along with J. W. King (alias William King).⁴³⁹

Rhode, F. C.— a commissary sergeant for Company H, 20th Pennsylvania Cavalry, this Berks County, Pennsylvania, native was captured with several others by Colonel Mosby's command at Kabletown, near Snicker's Gap, during United States General Hunter's retreat from Lynchburg, Virginia. In late December of 1864, Rhode was in Hospital No. 13 with an unspecified illness.⁴⁴⁰

Rielly, John H.— an Irishman from New York, born July 12, 1839, he enlisted on August 12, 1862, as a private in Company A, 170th New York Infantry, and rose to the rank of 1st Sergeant. He served in many of the major battles on the Peninsula, and was captured at Reams Station on August 25, 1864. He was confined at Libby Prison, Castle Thunder, and Belle Island. Rielly stated he weighed 168 pounds when he entered the service, and only 78 pounds when released. He tried to escape from Libby Prison but was recaptured and, in the process, suffered several injuries, including a broken hand. He claimed to have been present at the surrender at Appomattox.[441]

Richardson, Albert— a reporter for the New York *Tribune,* one of five reporters held at Castle Thunder. He and Junius H. Browne remained in Castle Thunder until February of 1864, when they were transferred to Salisbury, North Carolina. From there, the two escaped and made their way to Federal lines in Tennessee.[442]

Richardson, William— of Company A, 63rd Virginia Cavalry, he was arrested for desertion on September 23, 1863, in Buncombe County, North Carolina. He arrived at Camp Holmes on October 10, 1863, then was sent to Castle Thunder, and arrived there October 12, 1863.[443]

Richmond, Allen— the Richmond brothers, William and Allen, farmed near the New River in Raleigh County, Virginia. They joined Company G of the 20th Virginia Infantry. William and Allen had been members of the Virginia militia, but in 1863, they were charged with being pro-Union. After William's property was destroyed, the brothers fought back and were arrested as "disloyal persons" and confined in Castle Thunder.[444]

Richmond, William— see Richmond, Allen.

Rodgers, A. (?)— a private, Company F, 14th Regiment, Louisiana Infantry, was sent to Captain Alexander on September 30, 1863, to be held until Francis Woodson Hancock could prefer charges against him.[445]

Rogers, Dan (alias Riley)— from the 1st Virginia Regiment, he was condemned and sentenced to be shot. However, he escaped from the second floor of the building.[446]

Rogers, David W.— raised the window of his room at Castle Thunder and then climbed out onto the old tobacco drying porch. He used a wire to climb down to the ground. Rogers swung himself to the ground by holding the iron bracket which supported the porch. The sentinel was alerted only after he heard a noise when the prisoner hit the ground.[447]

Rollins, George— arrested in late Octrober, 1862, for breaking into the hat factory of Moore and Hayward.[448]

Rooney, John— a citizen of Patterson County, in western Virginia, was one of 56 citizens taken in a raid on the Baltimore and Ohio Railroad in May of 1863. He and the others were housed in Castle Thunder and held as hostages.[449]

Rowe, Huffman— born in Giles County, Virginia, Rowe moved to Pike, Floyd County, Kentucky, where he enlisted in the Union Army as part of the 39th Kentucky Regiment. He was confined at Castle Thunder where he reportedly died.[450]

Rucker, William P.— a doctor known as a notorious western Virginia renegade, was placed in Castle Thunder under heavy guard after recovering from either an "assumed" or "real" indisposition. Rucker was known to be a spy, and was guarded both day and night.[451]

Ryan, J. C.— of Company C, 3rd Virginia Cavalry, had previously been confined in the soldiers' home, corner of Cary and 7th Streets, and was to be sent back to his company. He jumped out of a third-story window and landed on a shed in the backyard. He was soon recaptured by detectives, and sent to Castle Thunder. He was found to have a forged furlough in his pocket.[452]

Ryan, Bob— A deserter from Capt. Barlow's Company, attempted to escape a felony charge of stealing jewelry from the residence of Mr. Tyler. He was arrested by detectives walking cooly and calmly about the streets of Richmond, along with James Logan, a deserter, who was also taken into custody.[453]

Shehan, John— along with Adams and McAlister, the three made a rope out of a blanket and were going to escape. When discovered, they attacked the guard, Frederick F. Wiley, with a shovel, razor, and ball and chain.[454]

Salisbury, W. H.— a member of Company L, 1st New York Cavalry, he was captured with several others by Colonel Mosby's command at Kabletown, near Snicker's Gap, during United States General Hunter's retreat from Lynchburg, Virginia.[455]

Sayre, T. P.— of Company B, 21st Illinois Volunteers, he was captured along with about a third of his regiment at Chickamauga, taken to Atlanta, then to Castle Thunder. He spent three months in prison in Richmond before being exchanged.[456]

Schultz, John F. W., Mrs.— and the daughter of Mr. and Mrs. Schultz, Mary Schultz-accompanied John F. W. Schultz when he joined Company E, 87th Pennsylvania Volunteer Infantry in the fall of 1861. The women remained with Schultz throughout the war, except when John was confined at Andersonville Prison. The three had been captured at the 2nd Battle of Winchester, Virginia, on June 15, 1863. Mrs. Schultz hid money and an American flag on her person during her incarceration in Castle Thunder. It is not known if the daughter was imprisoned as well. The Schultz family survived the war, and Mrs. Schultz was declared "Mother of the Regiment" at a reunion of the 87th Pennsylvania 20 years after the war. At that time, the family was living in Egg Harbor, Atlantic County, New Jersey.[457]

Scribner, John H.— from Frederick, Maryland, he escaped Castle Thunder along with a free Negro by walking out the front door. Scribner was found in the loft of Head's Livery Stable, corner 18th and Franklin Street. The Negro was located in the Stokes' Jail where Scribner had put him to be sold.[458]

Scott, Anna— a milliner accused of being a spy in the spring of 1863.[459]

Scott, R. Lewis— arrested in Richmond while on his way home on a furlough. All persons in and around Richmond were required to have a pass with a specific destination and purpose stated. Scott had no pass and was arrested as a spy. He was released only after a friend vouched for him.[460]

Seasel, William D.— a citizen of Taylor County, in western Virginia, he was one of 56 citizens taken in a raid on the Baltimore and Ohio Railroad in May of 1863. He was held as hostage.[461]

Shaffer, William— arrested as a deserter from Caskie Rangers, 5th Virginia Cavalry.[462]

Shanks, John— arrested for selling "Union badges" [a sort of uniform] to Negro slaves in the Norfolk, Virginia, area.[463]

Shelton, Charles— of the 5th Regiment, Texas Volunteers, he was tried and sentenced by a court martial to be shot for desertion, but gained a reprieve from President Davis.[464]

Sherman, J. Harvey— After the battle of Chancellorsville in May of 1863, Sherman was reported to have been captured near Winchester and hung by some of Mosby's Rangers. Later it was reported that he was being held in Castle Thunder. Colonel W. Hoffman wrote Col. William Ludlow, the exchange agent, to make inquiries.[465]

Sherman, James H.— had been presumed killed, but after it was learned he had been arrested, he received a letter from the provost marshal's office in Washington, D.C. His wife was subsequently informed.[466]

Shifflett, Benjamin F.— a private, Company D2, 46th Virginia Regiment, he was captured at Roanoke February 8, 1862, and paroled at Elizabeth City February 21,1862. He went A.W.O.L. in December 1862. Caught, he was confined in Castle Thunder for desertion February 1863-April 1863. Captured again at Petersburg June 17, 1864, he was sent to Elmira Prison, where he died of smallpox on June 20, 1864, and was buried Woodlawn National Cemetery.[467]

Shifflett, Leake— a private, Company D2, "Border Guards," 46th Virginia Regiment, he was captured at Roanoke Island February 8, 1862, and paroled at Elizabeth City. He was sick in June 1862, then A.W.O.L. December 1862-January 1863. A reward was offered for his capture. He was confined in Castle Thunder in Feburary 1863. He was wounded in the left hand at Petersburg, in July 1864, and deserted September 21, 1864. He remained absent until pardoned by Lee's amnesty order Febuary 6, 1865. Paroled at Appomattox, he was probably related to Benjamin F. Shifflett.[468]

Shoemaker, B[urris]— Company E, 54th North Carolina, arrested for desertion October 2, 1863, sent to Camp Holmes, then to Castle Thunder in Richmond, Virginia.[469] One of nine members of the Shoemaker family from Iredell County, North Carolina, who enlisted in Company E, 54th North Carolina. Burris enlisted at age 18 on April 19, 1862. He was reported present or accounted for through April 1863. He deserted from camp near Rapidan Station, Virginia, on August 5, 1863. He returned to duty on November 8, 1863, to be captured at Mine Run, Virginia, on November 27, 1863. He was subsequently confined in Old Capitol Prison, Washington, D.C., then transferred to Point Lookout, Maryland, on February 3, 1864. He was paroled about March 16, 1864, and transferred to City Point, Virginia, for exchange. He was again reported A.W.O.L. on May 23, 1864.[470]

Shrives, S. M.— a citizen of Morgan County, and a member of the Union League of Western Virginia, he was captured along with Aaron Bechtol, Joseph S. Wheat, and Robert Finn. Shrives was sent to Castle Thunder charged with aiding and abetting the public enemy, and of being a member of a treasonable organization.[471]

Sigal, James— a slave belonging to Benjamin Temple, reclaimed after a list of slaves being held in Castle Thunder was published in August of 1863.[472]

Sigman, M. D.— resided in Catawba County, North Carolina, where he enlisted in Company A, 18th Regiment, North Carolina Troops, at age 24 on August 14, 1864. He was present or accounted for until he deserted on May 22, 1863. He was apprehended and court martialed and shot for desertion on November 5, 1863.[473] (On the list of prisoners arriving at Castle Thunder on September 18, 1863, Sigman was listed as a member of Company E, 18th North Carolina.[474])

Simmons, George— a deserter from Fort Delaware, and from a Yankee regiment.[475]

Simmons, Harvey— having been released on parole after taking the Oath of Allegiance, he was caught attempting to flee to Yankee pickets along with Richard Fitzmorrie. He was first sent back to Libby Prison then to Castle Thunder, to await a court martial.[476]

Smith, Daniel— a soldier of Company D, 3rd Georgia Cavalry, Gracie's Brigade, Wharton's Division, Wheeler's Command. After being home on furlough, he went to Raleigh, North Carolina, to see his brother in a hospital recovering there from wounds. He had been there only a few hours when he was arrested, his papers taken from him, and he was sent to Camp Holmes and conscripted. He remained at Camp Holmes until August 15 when he was sent to Richmond. He had a hearing before Major Carrington on September 3, 1863, who decided that the prisoner should be sent to his command without delay. Since the hearing, Carrington told Smith that he had received his papers from Raleigh and that he had informed his commander, but Wheeler's cavalry was currently engaged with the enemy, and a letter would take some time to reach them. Under the circumstances, the prisoner asked Alexander to have his case brought to the attention of General Winder, so that he could be released.[477] On September 5, 1863, General John H. Winder ordered Captain Alexander to securely confine "D. Smith, who has been arrested as a spy and sent from Camp Holmes. Smith was not to be released "until further orders from these HdQuarters."[478]

Smith, James— a civilian arrested for selling liquor.[479]

Smith, John— of Company H, 55th North Carolina, arrested for desertion on October 10, 1863, in Alexander County, North Carolina, and taken to Camp Holmes. He was then sent to Castle Thunder in Richmond, Virginia.[480] Smith enlisted at age 33 on November 7, 1862. He deserted on June 15, 1863, while on the march to Pennsylvania. He was brought back under guard to Rapidan Station on November 7, 1863. Court martialed about January 19, 1864, he was sentenced to be shot by a firing squad.[481]

Smith, John E.— a private who was under a sentence by a court martial. On October 7, 1863, Alexander was ordered by General Winder to execute that sentence "as far as practicable."[482]

Smith, W. W.— a private, Company D, 44th Alabama; and P. Dromey (Dromez?), a private in Company B, 9th Alabama; along with Private J. D. White, Company E, 13th Alabama; were sent to Castle Thunder for "exciting a mutiny in the Division." The case was under investigation for possible charges and court martial.[483]

Smith, William— had been in Castle Thunder, but was already discharged on September 30, 1863, when S. S. Baxter asked Captain Alexander to send the prisoner to him.[484]

Snell, G. W.— had been in Castle Thunder about a month when he wrote General Winder on June 7, 1863, requesting a hearing. He claimed to be "nearly blind" and had to get someone else to write the letter for him.[485]

Snider, George H.— a member of the City Battalion, he was ordered confined in Castle Thunder by Capt. Alexander for "sleeping" at his post.[486]

Snidow, William H. H.— a private in Company D, 7th Virginia Infantry, he went A.W.O.L. after October 1864. Court martialed in February, 1865, he was sentenced to Castle Thunder for encouraging insubordination and mutiny. In Libby on April 10, 1865, then sent to Parkersburg, West Virginia. He was still living in 1914.[487]

Snyder, George— a young boy, from Pendleton County, western Virginia, was one of 56 citizens taken in a raid on the Baltimore and Ohio Railroad in May of 1863. He and the others were held in Castle Thunder as hostages.[488]

Soles, W. L., Lieut.— a forger who attempted to obtain the relase of Fleming Brazer with a forged document. The forgery was discovered, and both Brazer and Soles were captured and imprisoned.[489]

Speaks, Richmond— of Company A, 33rd North Carolina, reported in himself at Camp Holmes on October 15, 1863, but still charged with desertion, and sent to Castle Thunder.[490] Speaks was born in Iredell County, North Carolina, but resided in Wilkes County. He enlisted in Iredell County at age 40 on August 20, 1862.

He was present or accounted for through August of 1863 when he was reported A.W.O.L. He returned to duty November-December of 1863, and continued to be present until discharged on September 6, 1864. The reason for his discharge was not reported.[491]

Staples, Martin—was arrested by order of Major J. R. Robertson, of the 32nd Virginia, Battalion of Cavalry.[492]

Strayton, W. H.—of Company H, 25th Virginia Battalion, Infantry, he was sent to Castle Thunder, together with Hugh Hastings, to await trial before a court martial.[493]

Summers, Charles—Commandant Sidney Smith Lee wrote to Brig. Gen. Winder to obtain the release of Summers, McArthur and Duffey, who were seamen anxious to join the naval service. A notation on the back of the letter indicated that Summers had been imprisoned May 22, 1863, on a charge of deserting.[494] His name was on a list with 20 others made by Lt. W. S. Pilcher, with the notation that he was a sailor and had deserted.[495]

Sumner, Amos L.—Company D, 7th Virginia Infantry, took "French furlough" to go home. He was arrested, brought back, tried before a court martial, and sentenced to a term in Castle Thunder.[496] Sumner had dark complexion, hazel eyes, and brown hair. He enlisted May 31, 1861, at Giles Court House. On April 1, 1865, he was a prisoner at Point Lookout. He took the Oath of Allegiance on June 20, 1865.[497]

Taylor, J. L.—of Company K, 46th Virginia Battalion, Infantry, was sent from Staunton, Virginia, to Richmond.[498]

Thacker, Hiram—of member of Company C, 21st North Carolina, was confined for shooting at a citizen in Guilford County, North Carolina.[499] Thacker enlisted in Rockingham County, North Carolina, on June 3, 1861. He was present or accounted for until September-October 1864, when he was reported confined at Richmond. No reason was given. He had returned to duty prior to February 9, 1865, when he was hospitalized at Richmond with a gunshot wound of the left arm. He deserted from the hospital on February 25, 1865.[500]

Thompson, ____—a member of the Arsenal Battalion, deserted just after coming off picket duty near Bottom's Bridge. As was the habit, the Confederate pickets frequently traded with the Yankee pickets. Thompson went over to get some coffee, and kept on going. He was caught, however, and placed in Castle Thunder on suspicion of disloyalty.[501]

Thompson, Andrew J.—a private in Company D, 7th Virginia Infantry, he was promoted eventually to sergeant. Wounded at Williamsburg May 5, 1862, he was detached to conscript duty September-October 1862. He deserted, and was court martialed in February 1865, and convicted for encouraging insubordination and mutiny. He was sent to Castle Thunder. After Richmond fell, he was confined to Libby Prison, and was sent on April 17, 1865, to Cumberland County, Maryland. In spite of the court martial, a comrade remarked, there was "no better soldier."[502]

Tinsley, Samuel S.—a boy not yet 16, was arrested and sent to Castle Thunder when he decided to return with his brother who had been home for a visit and to join the army. He wrote Captain Carrington to allow him to let him go so that he might join his brother's regiment.[503]

Tompkins, J.—citizen of East Tennessee, who was arrested March 11, 1862. He was transferred from Atlanta to Castle Thunder, December 1862.[504]

Tow, Frank M.—of Company D, First North Carolina Union Volunteers, captured on March 12, 1863, near Elizabeth City, North Carolina, one of six guarding some Negroes who were chopping wood. He was taken to Castle Thunder, where he died April 6, 1863.[505]

Trent, G. B.—of Company A, 58th Virginia, one of a group of deserters who was sent to Castle Thunder in August of 1863. These men were not entitled to the benefit of the Presidential Proclamation since they had been caught with weapolns and resisted arrest.[506]

Trout, James—born July 3, 1838, he was the son of Henry Trout, a storekeeper and postmaster in Ridgeville, West Virginia, and Susan A. Myers. James attended school in Front Royal and Romney, West Virginia. He was a clerk for two years on the Chickasaw Nation Reservation in Oklahoma. A delegate to the national convention in Wheeling to form the new state of West Virginia, James Trout was captured and imprisoned for six months in Castle Thunder. After the war, he was sheriff of Hampshire County in 1865, and the first sheriff of Mineral County. He married Miss Susan Jane Caldwell on August 2, 1865, and they had several children.[507]

Tuck, James—a deserter from Captain Reed's company of the City Battalion, was placed in Castle Thunder on July 27, 1863.[508]

Turner, Alfred—a Yankee being held at Castle Thunder, was released in November of 1863, after taking the Oath of Allegiance to the Confederacy.[509]

Turner, Peter—a native of England, went to Augusta, Georgia, to seek work. He worked in a warehouse until August 1862, when he was taken by military guard to Richmond to be placed in Co. G, 4th Regiment, Georgia Infantry. He refused to be enrolled, and was sent to Castle Thunder where he remained for 18 months. To get out of prison, he enlisted as a private, Company G, 14th Virginia Cavalry. He deserted at Wythville, and traveled 18 miles before he was captured at Cloyd's Mountain, May 9, 1864. Reported arrested at New River Bridge, Virginia, May 10, 1864. He was sent to Camp Chase, Ohio, then transferred to Point Lookout, where he was released March 10, 1865, by Presidential order. He had black hair, florid complexion, 5' 7" tall, grey eyes, aged 25.[510]

Tyler, J. H.—a member of Stuart's Horse Artillery. He was charged with desertion, and taken to Castle Thunder.[511]

Tyree, James—when he entered as a prisoner he was dressed nicely in a black suit. Other prisoners set upon him, beat him, and "stripped him to his drawers." The clothing was never found.[512]

Vanburger, Henry—had been in Castle Thunder, but had been discharged by November of 1863, when S. S. Baxter asked Captain Alexander to send the prisoner to him.[513]

Velaquez, Loreta Janeta (alias Lt. Harry T. Buford and/or Mrs. Alice Williams)—See Chapter 8 for more details.

Underwood, Margaret—suspected spy, enlisted as a "substitute" in her boyfriend's regiment.[514] See Chapter 9.

Unknown slave—a slave owned by "Mr. Lum" who was arrested for hauling liquor.[515]

Veller, John—Vellers and G. W. Eastman, two "citizen prisoners," were sent to Castle Thunder on October 7, 1863, in accordance to Special Order No. 211.[516]

Wade, Ebenezer—of Company K, 10th Texas Regiment (?), was in General Hospital No. 13, in November of 1863, unfit for service in the field because of "droopsy of the abdomen." "There is some question as to this man's being a Southerner. The books at the Castle list him as a Yankee."[517]

Walker, Mary E.—a woman doctor who was also Assistant Surgeon, 52nd Ohio Volunteers. She was still being held in June of 1864.[518] See Chapter 8 for more details.[519]

Walker, W. J.—a private, who, along with Private John J. Bowler, was ordered by Major Bossiux to be confined at Castle Thunder to await charges. They may have been members of Company G, 25th Virginia Battalion.[520]

Walls, John—a citizen from east Tennessee, arrested for disloyalty March 25, 1862, and held in Atlanta until transferred to Castle Thunder in December of that year.[521]

Ward, John—listed with 20 others by Lt. W. S. Pilcher, along with the notation his papers were with General Winder. All this group of claimed they were "not members of any company" and did not know what they were charged with.[522]

Warmkin, George—was sent to Castle Thunder December 15, 1862, from Gordonsville, courtesy of Major Boyle, Provost Marshal, charged with disloyalty to Confederate states.[523]

Washington, W. H.—a slave committed to Castle Thunder in July or August of 1863, he was one of several who claimed to be free.[524]

Watson, John J.—reported to be a member of the 12th North Carolina, he was confined for selling passports.[525] However, his name can not be found on the roster for that regiment.

Watson, Lemuel—of Company K, 53rd North Carolina, one of group of deserters was sent to Castle Thunder in August of 1863, who were not entitled to the benefit of the Presidential Proclamation as they had been arrested with weapons and resisted arrest.[526]

Waymack, George—from Manchester, confined on a charge of desertion. He testified at the Congressional investigation about conditions at Castle Thunder.[527]

Webster, Alphonzo C.—alias of Charles W. Brown. He fought on both sides, but was caught and hanged for the murder of two persons, desertion, and horse stealing. It was believed he was a spy.[528] (See Chapter 8.)

Webster, Charles W.—reportedly a citizen from Maryland being held at Castle Thunder in October of 1863. He was to be held until the Federals released non-combatant prisoners they held in custody.[529] D. S. Boyle, Assistant Surgeon, 2nd Miss., General Davis' Brigade, wrote on January 21, 1864, to inquire what had been the disposition of his case.[530]

Webster, Timothy, Mrs. (alias Hattie H. Lawton)—See Chapter 8 for details of this female spy, an agent of the Pinkerton Agency.[531]

Weeks, _____—a citizen of Loudoun or Fauquier counties, Virginia, Mr. Weeks employed V. T. Crawford as his lawyer. Weeks was finally tried and discharged, after being held for four or five months.⁵³²

West, Richard—a Union army deserter, he wrote his brother, Edward West, in Illinois shortly before he died in the Castle Thunder hospital.⁵³³

Wheat, Joseph S.—a member of the "bogus Virginia Legislature," he was captured on a raid by Major O'Ferrell. Wheat was arrested along with other citizens of Morgan County, Virginia, and members of the Union League of western Virginia, including Aaron Bechtol, Attorney Robert Flinn, and S. M. Shrives. All were sent to Castle Thunder.⁵³⁴

Wheeler, Charles N.—enlisted at age 21 in Company G, 30th Indiana Volunteer Infantry. He was captured at Stones River by Texas Rangers, and held at Libby Prison and Castle Thunder for 42 days. He was released on parole September 9, 1864. He was honorably discharged, and reenlisted after a 30-day furlough.⁵³⁵

White, J. D.—a private in Company E, 13th Alabama; Private P. Dromey (Dromez?), of Company B, 9th Alabama; along with Private W. W. Smith, Company D, 44th Alabama, were sent to Castle Thunder for "exciting a mutiny in the Division." The case was under investigation for possible charges and court martial.⁵³⁶

White, R.—citizen of east Tennessee, arrested March 21, 1862, for disloyalty. He was transferred from Atlanta to Castle Thunder, December 1862.⁵³⁷

White, William—a citizen of Ritchie County, western Virginia, was one of 56 citizens taken in a raid on the Baltimore and Ohio Railroad in May of 1863. He and several others were held in Castle Thunder as hostages.⁵³⁸

White, William—confined at Castle Thunder on a charge of treason. He escaped during the final days of the war, as the Confederates evacuated the city.⁵³⁹

White, _____—along with Bowen, another soldier, were charged with shooting two men on Main Street between 6th and 7th. They were sent to Castle Thunder to await court martial.⁵⁴⁰

Whitney, Thomas (or Theo)—was captured and charged with being a spy. When taken, he was in "full Confederate uniform." Captain Alexander stated that Whitney had been confined "in irons about 2 months," and asked that he be given a "speedy trial."⁵⁴¹

Whitt, David—a life-long resident of Granville County, North Carolina, David enlisted at age 23 as a private in Company E, 2nd Regiment, North Carolina, on August 20, 1861. He was present or accounted for until he died of wounds on May 21, 1864. Whitt was incarcerated in Castle Thunder as a deserter on September 18, 1863.⁵⁴²

Wilcox, William T.—a private in Company E, 25th Virginia Battalion, was sent to Castle Thunder charged with theft.⁵⁴³

Wilde, August—a Yankee confined in Castle Thunder who escaped in November 1863.⁵⁴⁴

Wiley, Walter—a slave belonging to Dr. Harding, reclaimed after a list of slaves being held in Castle Thunder was published in August of 1863.⁵⁴⁵

Williams, Robert G.—a resident of Burke County, North Carolina, Robert enlisted at age 22 on February 1, 1862. He was present or accounted for until hospitalized at Farmville, Virginia, on May 10, 1864, with a gunshot wound. He rejoined his company during September or October of 1864. He was captured at Petersburg on March 25, 1865, and confined at Point Lookout, Maryland, until released upon taking the Oath of Allegiance on June 17, 1865.⁵⁴⁶ The listing in *North Carolina Troops* makes no mention of his arrest on September 18, 1863, and his incarceration at Castle Thunder, having been sent from Camp Holmes in North Carolina.⁵⁴⁷

Williams, William—citizen of Waterford, Loudoun County, Virginia, was held as hostage in Castle Thunder, along with fellow Quaker Mr. Robert Hollingsworth, for two hostages the United States government held.⁵⁴⁸

Willing, G.—of Company H, 7th South Carolina Regiment.⁵⁴⁹

Willis, Jacob—an invalid soldier, Willis was taken from Camp Winder to Castle Thunder, and from there to the Mayor's Court. Since no charges accompanied him, he was returned to Castle Thunder.⁵⁵⁰

Willis, John—wrote Captain Alexander that he had been confined in Castle Thunder since August 21, 1863, for a "trifling offence," and asked to be allowed to rejoin his command, Company A, 15th Louisiana.⁵⁵¹

Willis, John—of the 15th Georgia, was arrested, along with friend Jim Cunningham, for trying to sell a furlough.⁵⁵²

Wilson, George—had been sent on April 12, 1863, to a hospital at Petersburg, and remained there until September 16, 1863, when he was arrested and sent to Castle Thunder as a "supposed deserter." He asked that his case be given some attention, and wanted to rejoin his regiment. He stated "I am surely of no use to my country held here as a prisoner, and am anxious to lend all the aid in my power to it and its great and good cause."[553]

Wilson, J.— a Yankee being held at Castle Thunder, who was released in November of 1863, after taking the Oath of Allegiance to the Confederacy.[554]

Wilson, John W.— a member of Company F, 28th Virginia, who had been sick in the hospital and was sent home where he was arrested. The surgeon had told him to stay at home and that he would send the prisoner a discharge, which he failed to do.[555]

Wilson, R. M.— a private detailed as a hospital attendant from Company C, 5th Virginia Regiment, he was sent to Captain Alexander to be confined to the "guard house," for "infringement of military law." Charges were to be preferred against him.[556]

Wilson, William— an Irishman, a citizen of this country for the past two or three years, was arrested by a part of the 15th Virginia Cavalry near Tappahannock about the first of April 1863. He was sent to Castle Thunder. Theodore P. Brigham, of Miller's Tavern, wrote to plead for Wilson's release. Bringham described Wilson as a poor man, who was much needed at home.[557]

Wolfe, Elijah— of the 63rd Virginia Cavalry, Company A, was arrested for desertion on September 23, 1863, in Buncombe County, North Carolina, arrived at Camp Holmes on October 10, 1863, and then was transported to Castle Thunder, where he arrived October 12, 1863.[558]

Wolfe, J. C.— of the 63rd Virginia Cavalry, Company A, was arrested for desertion on September 23, 1863, in Buncombe County, North Carolina, arrived at Camp Holmes on October 10, 1863, then was transported to Castle Thunder, where he arrived October 12, 1863.[559]

Wolfe, John— was committed to Castle Thunder on November 7, 1863, by order of Major Griswold to be held until further orders.[560]

Wolfe, Thomas E.— a boat captain and master of the bark *Texana*, Captain Wolfe was captured when his ship was taken near the mouth of the Mississippi River. He wrote to his wife in Mystic River, Connecticut, on December 13, 1863.[561]

Woodward, Isaac— no regiment or company stated, but he was sentenced to six months hard labor for desertion.[562]

Worrell, T. J.— a private being held in Castle Thunder because he had tried to get out of prison with a "forged" discharge because of disabilities. The forgery was detected and verified by Dr. Leonidas Holt, surgeon at the General Hospital in Columbus, Georgia.[563]

Wrenn, J.— of Battery No. 2, and M. J. Lemmon, of the Manchester Artillery, escaped by digging through the rear wall at Castle Thunder. After only a short period of freedom, they were caught attempting to board a train leaving Richmond, and were returned to Castle Thunder.[564]

Wright, George— a derranged prisoner mentioned several times in the Congressional Investigation of conditions at Castle Thunder.[565]

Wynne(?), William D.— a resolution was passed authorizing the Governor of North Carolina to request that this man be released from Castle Thunder and returned to North Carolina for trial.[566]

Wyvill, Samuel— confined in the dungeon at Castle Thunder after he attempted to escape by removing bricks. He was convicted for forgery involving the loss of thousands of dollars to the Confederate government.[567]

Young, Alexander— an "aged man," from Tennesse, died November 9, 1862, at Castle Thunder.[568]

Yount, George Washington— born and raised in Catawba County, North Carolina, he enlisted as a private in Company F, 38th Regiment, North Carolin Infantry, at age 23 on October 31, 1861. Yount was present until he deserted on June 18, 1863. He returned to duty about September 25, 1863. After being captured near Hanover Court House May 23–24, 1864, he was confined at Point Lookout, Maryland, until he was released about May 13, 1865, after taking the Oath of Allegiance.[569] The service record in *North Carolina Troops, 1861–1865: A Roster*, Volume X, p. 67, makes no mention of his arrest for desertion and subsequent confinement in Castle Thunder on September 18, 1863.[570]

Appendix 2: Transcript of Court Martial of Private John R. Jones[1]

Proceedings of a General Court Martial Convened at Richmond By Virtue of the Following Orders

Head Quarters Richmond
October 11, 1862
General Orders
No. 7

A general Court Martial will assemble in the room on Ninth Street next to the War Department at 10 o'clock A.M. the 13th instant, or as soon thereafter as practicable for the trial of such persons as may be brought before it.
Detail for the Court.

> Major M. B. Hardin, 18th Battln Va. Hvy. Art.
> Capt. C. L. Harrison, 10th Battln Va. Hvy. Art.
> Capt. C. R. Grandy Norf. Lt. Art. Blues
> Capt. G. A. Martin 20th Battln. Va. Hvy. Art.
> Capt. W. G. Andrews, Mout. 9 True Blues
> Capt. J. H. Hendren, 18th Battln. Va. Hvy. Art.
> Lieut. J. G. Organ, 18th Battln. Va. Hvy. Art.

D. L. Smoot is appointed Judge Advocate for the Court.
Should any of the Officers names in the detail be prevented from attending at the time and place specified, the Court will nevertheless proceed to and continue the business before it, provided the number of members present be not less than the minimum prescribed by law, the above being the greatest number that can be convened without manifest injury to the service.

By com of Maj Genl G. W. Smith
Signed Saml. W. Melton
Major and Act. G.

Head Quarters Richmond
October 25, 1862
Special Orders
No. 102

  III. Captain F. Chalmers, Co. A, 19th Battln. Va. Hvy. Art. will relieve Lieut. Smoot as Judge Advocate of the Court now in session.
  Lieut. Smoot will when relieved report to his command for duty.

By order of Maj. Genl. G. W. Smith
Signed J. W. Riely
A.A.G.

Head Quarters Richmond
November 3, 1862
Special Orders
No. 116

  IV. Major R. C. Taylor, P.A.C.S., having reported at these Head Quarters will relieve Capt. Chalmers as Judge Advocate of the Court for Col. Rhett's command.

By comd of Maj. Genl. G. W. Smith
Signed J. W. Riely
A.A.G.

Head Quarters Richmond
January 3, 1863
Special Orders
No. 3

  Capt. W. G. Andrews is hereby relieved as a member of the general Court Martial convened by Genl. Order No. 7 of 1862 from these Headquarters, and will report without delay to his command for duty.

By comd. of Maj. Genl. G. W. Smith
Signed John W. Riely
A. A. G.

Head Quarters Richmond
January 21, 1863
Special Orders
No. 13

  Captain G. A. Martin, 20th Battaln. Va. Hvy. Art. is hereby relieved from duty on the general Court Martial convened and held by Genl. Order No. 7 from these Head Quarters, and will at once report to his command for duty.

By comd. of Maj. Genl. G. W. Smith
Signed W. L. Barton
Major and A.A.G.

11 O'clock A.M. February 5, 1863

The Court met pursuant to the above orders, and adjournments.

Present Major M. B. Hardin, 18th Battln. Va. Hvy. Art.
Capt C. L. Harrison, 10th Battln. Va. Hvy. Art.
Capt C. R. Grandy, Norf. Lt. Art. Blues
Capt J. H. Hendren, 18th Battln Va. Hvy. Art.
Lieut. J. G. Organ, 18th Battln. Va. Hvy. Art.
Major R. C. Taylor, Judge Advocate
Private John R. Jones, Co. C, 18th Battln.Va. Hvy. Art.
the accused also present.

The Judge Advocate having read the orders convening the Court, asked Private John R. Jones if he had any objection to any member named therein to which he replied "I have not."

The Court was then duly sworn by the Judge Advocate, and the Judge Advocate was duly sworn by the presiding Officer of the Court in the presence of the accused.

The following charge and Specification were then read aloud by the Judge Advocate.

Charge — Desertion

Specification — In this that he the said John R. Jones a private in Company "C" 18th Va. Battalion of Artillery, having been duly enlisted in the service of the Confederate States, did desert the service on or about the 22nd day November 1862, by absenting himself from his camp and Battery No. 4, Richmond Defenses, without the leave of his commanding officer and was afterwards arrested in the city of Petersburg on or about the 14 day of January 1863.

This at the camp of the 18th Virginia Battalion of Artillery Battery No. 4, Richmond Defenses, on or about the 22nd day of November, 1862.

Signed B. J. Black
Capt 18th Va. Battalion Art.
Comd Co. "C"

Judge Advocate — Private John R. Jones you have heard the charge preferred against you, how say you guilty, or not guilty?

To which the accused Private John R. Jones pleaded as follows.
To Specification — Not Guilty
To Charge — Not Guilty

Capt. B. J. Black, Co. C, 18th Battln. Va. Hvy. Art., a witness for the prosecution being duly sworn.

Quest. by the Judge Advocate — What do you know of any offence committed by the accused?

Ans. — I am Captain of Co. C, 18th Battln. Va. Hvy. Art., the accused is a private in my company. He left the camp of the 18th Battln. Va. Hvy. Art. Battery No. 4, Richmond Defences, on or about the 22nd day of November 1862 without my permission; if he had been allowed by a permit to leave Camp, such permit would have passed through my hands.

I heard the accused had made his escape from Castle Thunder, and my guard arrested him and brought him to Camp last Monday the 2nd day of February 1863.

A detective officer from Petersburg told me that he had arrested him in Petersburg on or about the 14th day of January 1863, and brought him and put him in Castle Thunder Richmond. He made a statement to me I think without fear, and without hope of reward, as to how he managed to be at large. He said that some eighty men were sent to Jackson's Army from Castle Thunder and that he came out of the prison in the crowd, and when the train went off, he hid and escaped without notice.

The accused was regularly enlisted in my Company as a soldier of the Confederate Army.

The Court then adjourned until 11 o'clock A.M. tomorrow.

11 o'clock A.M., February 6, 1863

The Court met pursuant to adjournment.

>Present — Major M. B. Hardin, 18th Battln. Va. Hvy. Art.
>Capt C. L. Harrison, 10th Battln. Va. Hvy. Art.
>Capt C. R. Grandy, Norf. Lt. Art. Blues
>Capt J. H. Hendren, 18th Battln. Va. Hvy. Art.
>Lieut. J. G. Organ, 18th Battln. Va. Hvy. Art.
>Major R. C. Taylor, Judge Advocate
>Private John R. Jones, Co. C, 18th Battln. Va. Hvy. Art.,
>the accused also present.

W. T. Peterson a detective officer a witness for the prosecution being duly sworn.

Quest. — by Judge Advocate — Do you know anything of the arrest of the accused?

Ans. — I am a detective officer of Petersburg. I arrested the accused in Petersburg sometime in January 1863 at his residence.

I think he was in citizen's dress, I am positive that he had on a citizen's hat.

When I got to his house I asked his wife if he was there, she replied "No." I however went in and found no one in the room, but seeing a closet door move, I went to it and found the accused hid there; I then took him, he behaved quietly, I delivered him to the Provost Marshal of Petersburg.

Quest. — by the accused — Did I or not have on dark blue pants?

Ans. — He did. I cannot say that he had on a uniform Jacket, he may have had it on.

Here the prosecution closed.

Private J. R. Hail, Co. C, 18th Battln., Va. Hvy. Art., a witness for the defense being duly sworn.

Quest — by the accused — What was the condition of my family when you saw them?

Ans. — I saw the family of the accused shortly before he left Camp, and they were in a very destitute condition, with neither house nor provisions of their own. Our first uniform was dark blue pants, and dark blue jacket.

Lieut David Dunbar, 18th Battln. Va. Hvy. Art., a witness for defense being duly sworn.

Quest. — by the accused — Did or not I ask you to allow me to go to Camp with you?

Ans. — I am Ordnance Officer of the 18th Battln. Va. Hvy. Art., I know the accused — last Saturday afternoon as I was going to Camp he came to me, and said he wished to go to Camp but was afraid to go by himself as the guard might arrest him; I took him under my charge, and carried him nearly to camp. I went into a house for a few minutes, and when I came out he was gone. I did not see him again until he was brought to Camp by a guard of the 18th Battln. Va. Hvy. Art. on the next day. I think he had on the uniform he usually wore in Camp.

The accused had no more evidence to produce, and made no defense.

The statements of the parties being thus in possession of the Court, the Court was cleared for deliberation; and having maturely considered the evidence adduced find the accused Private John R. Jones, Co. C, 18th Battln. Va. Hvy. Art. as follows.

Of Specification — Guilty of as much as implies absence without leave.

Of Charge — Not Guilty of desertion but guilty of absence without leave.

And to therefore sentence the said Private John R. Jones, Co. C, 18th Battln. Va. Hvy. Art., to forfeiture of pay for the period of two months, and to six months hard labor with ball and chain.

Approved — The sentence will be duly executed.
G. M. Smith

/signatures/ M. B. Hardin
Maj. 18th Va. Battalion
Pres. Of C. M.
R. C. Taylor
Major and Judge Advocate

Appendix 3: List of Prisoners Sent from Camp Holmes in September 1863

Camp Holmes was a Conscription Camp of Instruction near Raleigh, N.C. On the 4th of September 1863, these prisoners were listed as having been sent by Col. Peter Mallett to Castle Thunder, Richmond, Va., in charge of Lt. Jones.[1] This appendix reproduces the information on one of many transmittal forms listing prisoners who had been arrested in various places and sent to Castle Thunder. Most of the men on this list were arrested for desertion from the Confederate Army. A few Federal deserters are included in this group as well. One prisoner was arrested for "attempting to run the blockade without a pass."

The listing states the prisoner's name, regiment and company, when and where he was arrested, and when he arrived at the camp from which he is being sent to Castle Thunder. Those on the list in Appendix 3 had been arrested all across the state of North Carolina; sent to Camp Holmes near Raleigh; and then sent by Colonel Peter Mallette to serve their sentences or await trial at Castle Thunder. They were under the command of Lieutenant Jones while in transit. Once they arrived, someone at the prison would sign a receipt for the number of prisoners received.

The form was handwritten and sometimes difficult to decipher. These and other reports are part of the records of the Confederate States of America, Department of Henrico, available on microfilm reel #8 Mss3, 67604a, Virginia Historical Society, Richmond, Virginia.

No	Name	Regiment and Company	When and where arrested	When arrived at this Camp	Charges	Remarks
1	J. Q. Britton	6th N.C. Co. D	Sept. 3, Person Co.	Sept. 4, 1863	Desertion	
2	Alex Moss	6th N.C. Co. D	Sept. 3, Raleigh	Sept. 4, 1863	Desertion	
3	Jas. P. Hicks	26 N.C. Co. F	Aug. 16 Burke	Sept. 3, 1863	Desertion	
4	Ransom Herring	11 N.C. Co. D	Sept. 1 Burke	Sept. 3, 1863	Desertion	
5	Wm. Perry	46 N.C. Co. B	Aug. 30 Burke	Sept. 3, 1863	Desertion	
6	J. M. Michaels	16 N.C. Co. E	Aug. 30 Burke	Sept. 3, 1863	Desertion	
7	S. K. Cannon	16 N.C. Co. E	Aug. 30 Burke	Sept. 3, 1863	Desertion	
8	W. W. Smith	58 N.C. Co. H	Aug. 30 Caldwell	Sept. 3, 1863	Desertion	
9	David Ballou	11 S.C. Co. D	Aug. 21 Rutherford	Sept. 3, 1863	Desertion	
10	R. Peeler	6 N.C. Co. E	Aug. 28 Rutherford	Sept. 3, 1863	Desertion	
11	J. A. England	46 N.C. Co. B	Aug. 24 Burke	Sept. 3, 1863	Desertion	
12	L. F. Tacket	41 Ga. Co. A	Aug. 23 Burke	Sept. 3, 1863	Desertion	
13	Jno Tacket	41 Ga. Co. A	Aug. 23 Burke	Sept. 3, 1863	Desertion	
14	J. L. Tacket	41 Ga. Co. A	Aug. 23 Burke	Sept. 3, 1863	Desertion	
15	L. Geeslin	4 Ala. Co. C	Sept. 2 Alamance	Sept. 3, 1863	Desertion	Deserted from Hospital
16	Wm. Clap	16 N.C.—	Sept. 1 Guilford	Aug. 2, 1863	Desertion	Deserted before reaching Regt last Sept 4
17	Melton W. Lamb	22 N.C. Co. F	Sept. 1 Guilford	Aug. 2, 1863	Desertion	
18	Thos. W. Hall	23 N.C. Co. C	Sept. 1 Guilford	Aug. 2, 1863	Desertion	Parole Prisoner

Appendix 4: Morning Report of Captain G.W. Alexander, Sept. 18, 1863

This appendix reproduces information on a list prepared by the officer in charge of the guards at Castle Thunder, Lieutenant Colonel J. L. Ferguson, of the 32nd North Carolina Regiment.[1] Such a list was prepared daily as new prisoners were received. Names were listed with together with place of residence (if a citizen) or company and regiment (if a soldier); the cause of arrest; the date the prisoner was received at Castle Thunder; and the location from which the prisoner came. In the "Remarks" column the disposition of the prisoners was sometimes noted. Some soldiers were to be sent back to their commands; some were to be held until further orders; and some were to be held to await a trial by court martial.

The last seven names on the list show prisoners who were discharged and released, with a notation showing by whose orders the release took place. Also included is the date they were confined to Castle Thunder and the date they were released. Two of these prisoners were blacks, probably runaway slaves who had been captured and held in Castle Thunder.

Had this form been dated September 5, 1863, it would probably have had the names included in Appendix 3, with the addition of more names from other sources. It is typical of reports filled out and approved by Captain G. W. Alexander each day.

If the men had already been sentenced, it became Captain Alexander's duty to see that the sentence was carried out, whether it was 50 lashes to the back with a whip, a 20-pound ball and chain attached to the prisoner's ankles by leg irons, or one of the other punishments common to that time and place.

These and other reports are part of the records of the Confederate States of America, Department of Henrico, Microfilm reel #8 Mss3, 67604a, Virginia Historical Society, Richmond, Virginia.

	Cause of Arrest	By Whom	Citizen or Soldier	When Confined	When Released	Remarks
C. J. Cash, Co. A, 38 Ga.	Desertion	Capt. Alexander	Sol.	Sept.		Sent from Camp Holmes, N.C.
L. D. Murphy, Co. G, 25 S.C.	Desertion	Capt. Alexander	Sol.	Sept. 18		Sent from Camp Holmes, N.C.
Danl. Huffman, Co. E, 57 N.C.	Desertion	Capt. Alexander	Sol.	Sept. 18		Sent from Camp Holmes, N.C.
J. M. Hefner, Co. E, 57 N.C.	Desertion	Capt. Alexander	Sol.	Sept. 18		Sent from Camp Holmes, N.C.
Geo. Yount, Co. F, 38 N.C.	Desertion	Capt. Alexander	Sol.	Sept. 18		Sent from Camp Holmes, N.C.
M. Sigman, Co. E, 18 N.C.	Desertion	Capt. Alexander	Sol.	Sept. 18		Sent from Camp Holmes, N.C.
Elijah Phillips, Co. B, 11 N.C.	Desertion	Capt. Alexander	Sol.	Sept. 18		Sent from Camp Holmes, N.C.
Robt. Williams, Co. B, 11 N.C.	Desertion	Capt. Alexander	Sol.	Sept. 18		Sent from Camp Holmes, N.C.
S. Lee, Co. F, 2 N.C. Cav.	Desertion	Capt. Alexander	Sol.	Sept. 18		Sent from Camp Holmes, N.C.
T. Edmonds, Co. B, 2 N.C. Cav.	Desertion	Capt. Alexander	Sol.	Sept. 18		Sent from Camp Holmes, N.C.
W. Anderson, Co. F, 47 N.C.	Desertion	Capt. Alexander	Sol.	Sept. 18		Sent from Camp Holmes, N.C.
H. S. Williams, Co. B, 37 N.C.	Desertion	Capt. Alexander	Sol.	Sept. 18		Sent from Camp Holmes, N.C.
D. W. Miller, Co. H, 34 N.C.	Desertion	Capt. Alexander	Sol.	Sept. 18		Sent from Camp Holmes, N.C.
Steph. Roberts, Co. E, 16 Ga.	Desertion	Capt. Alexander	Sol.	Sept. 18		Sent from Camp Holmes, N.C.
J. C. Floyd, Palmetta 8 Shooter	Desertion	Capt. Alexander	Sol.	Sept. 18		Sent from Camp Holmes, N.C.
H. M. Waters, Palmetta 8 Shooter	Desertion	Capt. Alexander	Sol.	Sept. 18		Sent from Camp Holmes, N.C.
J. C. Jameson, 4 Penn. Cav.	Yankee	Capt. Alexander	Sol.	Sept. 18		Sent from Camp Holmes, N.C.
W. Sansing, Co. I, 38 N.C.	Deserter	Capt. Alexander	Sol.	Sept. 18		Sent from Camp Holmes, N.C.
G. W. King, Co. C, 15 N.C.	Deserter	Capt. Alexander	Sol.	Sept. 18		Sent from Camp Holmes, N.C.
Adam Dry, Co. A, 27 N.C.	Deserter	Capt. Alexander	Sol.	Sept. 18		Sent from Camp Holmes, N.C.
J. A. Duncan ?, Co. E, 2 N.C.	Deserter	Capt. Alexander	Sol.	Sept. 18		Sent from Camp Holmes, N.C.
N. A. May, Co. E, 2 N.C.	Deserter	Capt. Alexander	Sol.	Sept. 18		Sent from Camp Holmes, N.C.
David Whitt, Co. E, 2 N.C.	Deserter	Capt. Alexander	Sol.	Sept. 18		Sent from Camp Holmes, N.C.
Lee Siegel, Co. E, 2 N.C.	Federal Deserter	Capt. Alexander	Sol.	Sept. 18		Sent from Petersburg
Henry Deakfeman (?), Co. E, 2 N.C.	Federal Deserter	Capt. Alexander	Sol.	Sept. 18		Sent from Petersburg
C. Breadlin (?), Co. E, 2 N.C.	Federal Deserter	Capt. Alexander	Sol.	Sept. 18		Sent from Petersburg
T. Widner, Co. E, 2 N.C.	Federal Deserter	Capt. Alexander	Sol.	Sept. 18		Sent from Petersburg
David L. Hendricks, Co. E, 11 Va.	to be sent to command	Capt. Alexander	Sol.	Sept. 18		Sent from Petersburg
Burrell Brown, Co. E. 57 Va.	Desertion					Sent by Maj. Boyle
F. J. Pickral, Co. E. 57 Va.	Desertion	Capt. Alexander	Sol.	Sept. 18		Sent by Maj. Boyle
J. McPherson, Co. R. I. Cav.	Yankee deserter	Capt. Alexander	Sol.	Sept. 18		Sent by Maj. Bridgeford
J. Martin, Co. H, I Cav.	Yankee deserter	Capt. Alexander	Sol.	Sept. 18		Sent by Maj. Bridgeford
J. J. Gaye, 125 Penn.	Yankee deserter	Capt. Alexander	Sol.	Sept. 18		Sent by Maj. Bridgeford

Name	Charge			Date	Disposition
James McCarter, Battery ?	Desertion	Capt. Griswold	Sol.	Sept. 18	To be sent to command
Thos. F. Moseby, Fayette Art.	Desertion	Capt. Griswold	Sol.	Sept. 18	To be sent to Maj. Griswold
R. Forbes, Fayette Art.	Desertion	Capt. Griswold	Sol.	Sept. 18	To be sent to Maj. Griswold
C. T. Brown, Co. K, 20 Va.	Desertion	Capt. Griswold	Sol.	Sept. 18	To be sent to Maj. Griswold
J. Lewis, Co. K, 9 Va. Cav	Desertion	Capt. Griswold	Sol.	Sept. 18	To be sent to Maj. Griswold
J. Sebree ?, Co. F, 47 Va.	Desertion	Capt. Griswold	Sol.	Sept. 18	To be sent to Maj. Griswold
J. A. Gowan (?), Co. B, 15 Va. Cav	Desertion	Capt. Griswold	Sol.	Sept. 18	To be sent to Maj. Griswold
James Myers, Co. G, 5 La.	Desertion	Capt. Griswold	Sol.	Sept. 18	To be sent to Maj. Griswold
J. B. Miller			Sol.	Sept. 18	Until Further orders
M. Yeolothall ?			Sol.	Sept. 18	Until Further orders
W. Miller			Sol.	Sept. 18	Until Further orders
John Cotrall	Deserted from Anderson's works		Sol.	Sept. 18	Until Further orders
Geo. C. Morgan	Attempting to run the blockade without pass		Sol.	Sept. 18	Until Further orders
Jas. Schoff, Co. G, 5 La.	Attempting to run the blockade without pass		Sol.	Sept. 18	Until Further orders
K. L. Shepard, Co. G, 5 La.	Attempting to run the blockade without pass		Sol.	Sept. 18	Until Further orders
Joseph Colwell	Detailed to work with new ___ on Shell. _ e		Sol.	Sept. 18	Until Further orders
J. M. Wilson		Gen. Winder	Sol.	Sept. 18	Until further orders
Geo. Macar		Maj. Linsworth	Sol.	Sept. 18	
Capt. A. Galle, Co. I, 10 La.	Paroled Prisoner	Maj. Linsworth	Sol.	Sept. 18	
Chas. Libbers, Co. A, 40 Va.		Maj. Linsworth	Sol.	Sept. 18	
Joe Jackson, Richmond F ___		Maj. Linsworth	Negro	Sept. 18	Papers on file at Maj. Griswold's office
Druiunsen? Simpson, 32 N.C.	To be sent to command	Maj. Linsworth	Soldier	Sept. 18	
Samuel Edwards, 5 N.C.	To be sent to command	Maj. Linsworth	Soldier	Sept. 18	
R. C. West, 47 N.C.	To be sent to command	Maj. Linsworth	Soldier	Sept. 18	
J. P. McMachael, 43 N.C.	To be sent to command	Maj. Linsworth	Soldier	Sept. 18	
Edwd. Rose, 47 N.C.	To be sent to command	Maj. Linsworth	Soldier	Sept. 18	
David Holland, Latham's N.C. Baty.	To be sent to command	Maj. Linsworth	Soldier	Sept. 18	
M. T. Lamb, 2nd N.C.	Desertion	Maj. Linsworth	Soldier	Sept. 18	To be ct. Martialed
S. C. Rock, Goochland Art.	*Discharged*	Maj. Linsworth	Soldier	Sept. 18	
J. Shinard		Capt. Alexander	Negro	Aug. 19	Sept. 18 Delivered on special order 224

W. B. Brooks	Maj. Griswold		Sept. 15	Dschd by order of Gen. Winder
Henry Brisbee	Capt. Alexander	Negro	Aug. 20	Dschd on special order 225
Park Eagan	Capt. Alexander		Sept. 17	Delrd by order of Gen. Winder
Fred'ke Mohn	Capt. Alexander		Sept. 8	Delrd on special order 224
Wm. Dawson	Capt. Alexander		Sept. 8	Delrd on special order 224
J. F. Chambers	Capt. Alexander		Sept. 16	Delrd to ??????

Appended & respectfully submitted
G. W. Alexander
Officer of the Guards

J. L. Ferguson
Lt. Col., 32nd N.C. Regt.

Appendix 5: The Military Prison Keepers of the Late Southern Confederacy, in the Van of the Democratic Party

Full text of a pamphlet published by the National Republican Congressional Executive Committee, 1876. See Chapter 19 for a discussion of this pamphlet.

Reputed the possessor of average intelligence, with some knowledge of United States politics and political parties, and having no axe or other edge tool that requires application to either Republican or Democratic grindstone, I think I may claim ability to write of matters germane to the politics of to-day — matters yet young in the Past — free from fear of being charged with bias.

For something more than a year the partisan Republican papers have urged, with more or less vehemence, that the South did not "accept the situation" in good faith; and although the Democratic and Independent — apparently synonymous terms — papers have with perfect unanimity ridiculed this assertion as partisan claptrap unworthy the name of drivel, and denounced its employment as intended to keep in existence a sectional bitterness that caused the Rebellion, it is my purpose in this article to relate *facts* not of a character to strengthen the position of the parties of the second part in this controversy.

Four years spent in a vast and bloody civil war, to my mind, is a fact not likely to lessen the bitterness that caused such conflict. On the contrary, when the Rebellion terminated, so greatly enhanced was the ill feeling of the South, that even the rare magnanimity of Grant and the United States Government had no appreciable effect in way of its diminution.

And it should not be forgotten that the major percent of present white voters South are men who were much too young to be of military value during the Rebellion, and who, as a matter of fact, never burnt powder in favor of the Southern Confederacy, but who, though physically unequal to military service, had sufficient mental maturity to acquire the pernicious political theories of Jefferson Davis, Toombs, Yancey, and other eminent in the same political school, accompanied by the thorough contempt the Southron of ante-Rebellion time expressed for the people inhabiting all other sections of this broad country.

For some time past appearances have been such as to justify the conclusion, that by far the greater number of the present white voters of the South have only learned caution from the result of the Rebellion. They are manipulated by politicians similar to those who precipitated the Rebellion and their

Congressional representation is largely composed of the very men by whom their fathers were led to crushing defeat, and devastation brought upon their section.

These facts warrant the opinion that the greater number of white voters South do *not* believe the Lost Cause *lost*, but *do* believe the first step essential to its resuscitation to be the regaining of political supremacy for their section, which as they hold, a national Democratic success in 1876 would be preliminary to. Caution is prolific of hypocrisy, and the caution enforced by the result of the Rebellion seems wonderfully fertile of such offspring, as witness the ardent love for the Union now professed by Southern Democratic politicians, who, up to a few years ago, were life-long advocates of a political doctrine that was a constant menace to the perpetuity of this same Union at present so much esteemed by them. Now, any person confiding enough to believe that these Southern Democratic political leaders, so closely resembling the Bourbons of Europe as regards learning and forgetfulness, were induced by the disastrous result of their Rebellion, and while the recollection of their overthrow was of yesterday, to forever cast away the political theories that caused that Rebellion, knows little of human nature, and must necessarily believe in the leopard's ability to change its spots; for belief of the latter is far less nonsensical than belief of the former matter.

Concede these premises — as conceded they must be — and the South's non-acceptance of the situation in good faith, as charged by partisan Republican papers, appears reasonably probable; and I now shall state a few facts that seem to the *apropos* of the foregoing.

When the Amnesty bill was before the present House of Representatives, the Republican Members proposed to exclude Jefferson Davis from its operation for two, alleged good, reasons, namely: First, that he was cognizant of the cruel treatment of Federal prisoners of war by Confederate military prison keepers, and did not interpose his authority to ensure humane conduct on the part of those barbarians; and, second, that he had not asked for, and did not desire restoration to citizenship of the United States. These reasons were strenuously combated by the Democratic Members, and especially so by those from the South, who left nothing untried in attempted refutation of the reason first described in this paragraph; and the substance of their efforts was an assertion that Jefferson Davis did not personally know the keepers of the Confederate military prisons, and absolutely knew nothing of their cruel treatment — if there was cruel treatment — of Federal prisoners-of-war; and they were quite as emphatic in contradiction of the second reason.

It is a matter of general recollection that, immediately after the failure of the Amnesty bill, Jefferson Davis indulged his propensity for appearing in type by publication of a letter, in which he unequivocally stated that he did not desire restoration to citizenship of the United States, and broadly insinuated that, had the bill passed, he would not have availed himself of its benefit, thereby placing his Democratic Congressional friends in rather ridiculous position.

It has been shown that the second reason urged by the Republican Members for excluding Jefferson Davis from the benefit of the Amnesty bill, was proved, by Davis himself, a well-taken objection.

Now let us examine what, if any, foundation in fact the first reason has for basis.

One of the many significant occurrences due to and swiftly succeeding the political upheaval of 1875, was the advent at Washington, as publisher of a Democratic weekly paper, of a man from the South possessing an unpleasant history. This man, up to about the commencement of the Rebellion movement, had experienced moderate success as an adventurer of low type; but, on date of inception of hostilities, through too energetic exercise of his marvelous capacity for description, was in every respect stranded, and generally detested in such parts of the country as had been his field of peculiar operation. The Rebellion was a fortunate event for this man, as it created a demand for just such ability, the possession and use of which had previously brought him in general disrepute, and he rapidly passed through all the irregular and disreputable grades of its service — such as pirate, spy, blockade runner, and would-be abductor — until, by his unscrupulous activity, attracting the notice of a prominent Confederate military official known as "Hog" Winder, he was made a military-prison keeper, and placed in charge of Castle Thunder, Richmond, Va. While there, by bad treatment of Federal prisoners-of-war, and the ownership of a man-killing bloodhound that he maintained at Castle Thunder as additional protection against the escape of those imprisoned, his former bad name became much worse. It is known that, subsequent to his keepership of Castle Thunder, he was employed in similar capacity at the Confederate military prisons of Danville, Va., and Salisbury, N.C., where his reputation for brutality to Federal prisoners-of-war was still further increased, and that, finally, he was dishonorably dismissed [from] the Confederate military service. Now, Jefferson Davis knew, so far as concerned the Southern Confederacy, what this man's career up to the time he was made keeper of Castle Thunder, had been; and, while this man was such keeper, Jefferson Davis had him under his immediate notice. Those assertions the friends of Jefferson Davis can not disprove; and it seems to me safe to assume that knowing so much of this man, Jefferson Davis knew something of his conduct while in charge of the military prisons of Danville and Salisbury; and there can hardly be a doubt that Jefferson Davis knew this man as dishonorably dismissed from the Confederate military service. For the benefit of those who may not credit the assertion that Jefferson Davis knew this man, and knew him intimately, I made the following statement.

Since September, 1875, this man has frequently exhibited a letter addressed to him by Jefferson Davis, from Memphis, Tenn. The letter was wholly in the handwriting of Mr. Davis, and such a communication was as warm and time-tried friends write to one another. It was designed to give this man standing in the esteem of Southern Democratic Senators and Representatives at Washington, to the end that their financial and other aid might be gained to maintain his weekly paper. In that letter Jefferson Davis certifies to the valuable service this man rendered the Confederacy, and assures him that he holds a high place in his esteem. I feel justified in adding that between September 1875 and the date of the debate on the Amnesty bill, nearly all, if not all of the Southern Democratic Senators and Representatives of the present Congress saw this letter; and yet during the pendency of the Amnesty bill, more than a few of these Southern Democratic Representatives rose in their places and denied that Jefferson Davis knew Confederate military prison keepers, or had knowledge of cruelties practiced by them on Federal prisoners-of-war. Now, it appears to me, that having previously seen this remarkable letter from Jefferson Davis to one of the worst, if not the worst of all the Confederate military-prison keepers, these Southern Democratic Congressmen, in denying the first reason assigned by Republican Members for excluding Jefferson Davis from the benefit of the Amnesty bill, either were suffering from epidemic short memory, or, politely writing, "misapprehended *fact*" "by a large majority."

The foregoing shows — and I challenge its disproval — that Jefferson Davis knows and esteems one of the most infamous of those who were Confederate military prison keepers, and this fact justifies the assumption that he knows and esteems others who served the Confederacy in like capacity. And perhaps he considers the late Capt Wirz, of Andersonville notoriety, a martyr, as his friend, the Confederate military-prison keeper at Castle Thunder, Danville, and Salisbury, and present publisher of a Democratic weekly newspaper, does.

As another fact showing that Jefferson Davis knows and highly regards his former Confederate military-prison keeper of Castle Thunder, Danville, and Salisbury, the bloodhound owner, etc., it is proper to state that the letter written by Jefferson Davis, after the failure of the Amnesty bill, in which he stated that he did not desire restoration to citizenship of the United States, appeared in the columns of the Democratic weekly papers published at Washington by this former Confederate military-prison keeper, who boasts, and caused the insertion of the boast in a great number of newspapers using "patent insiders," that he posses the original of this letter written by Jefferson Davis, and has refused $1,000 for it.

But there is other evidence in support of the first reason that the Republican Members urged for not restoring Jefferson Davis to citizenship of the United States.

Brigadier General Winder, *alias* "Hog" Winder, Provost Marshal General of the Southern Confederacy, who, if living, probably would be the Democratic Representative of some Virginia district, in the present House, having control of the Confederate military prisons as a part of his office, was regarded in Richmond, Va., an intolerable brute, and several earnest efforts were made by prominent Confederate gentlemen to effect his removal. This General Winder selected men of his own character as military-prison keepers, and the more brutal their treatment of Federal prisoners-of-war the higher their appreciation by General Winder. Thus encouraged, his military-prison keepers each sought to exceed the other in bad treatment of those placed in their power by the fortunes of war, and their excesses resulted in the movement looking to Winder's removal from an office, the maladministration of which was considered, by every humane Southron, a disgrace to the Confederacy. The facts against Winder were effectively displayed, yet Jefferson Davis refused to remove him, and he held the position until the end of the Rebellion. It will be seen that Jefferson Davis knew the character of Winder, and he must have known that the subordinates of such a man would be no better than their superior. However, the man who was keeper of the Confederate military prisons of Castle Thunder, Danville, and Salisbury, and who maintained a bloodhound to run down and kill escaping Federal prisoners-of-war; the same man now publisher of a Democratic weekly paper at Washington, and who possesses the friendship of Jefferson Davis, has essayed, through the columns of his Democratic weekly paper, to show his former chief, General Winder, a paragon of humanity, and perhaps he was, viewed from the Confederate military-prison keeper's standpoint — the roof of Castle Thunder, or the Stockade of Andersonville, for instance.

Now, if what has been stated to show that the first reason urged by Republican Members of Congress for denying amnesty to Jefferson Davis does not conclusively establish that reason as true, I do not know of what conclusive proof must consist!

There does not seem to me any "situation acceptance" in what I have thus far presented; and, animated by desire to make extensive search for that interesting but apparently rare something — I hardly know what to term it — I shall begin anew. Some three months ago this former Confederate military-prison keeper and present publisher of a Democratic weekly paper at Washington, having, with the assistance of his remarkable letter from Jefferson Davis, made the acquaintance of the Southern Democratic Members of the present House, actuated by several motives, gave a banquet, which, according to first-class Democratic authority, was attended by more than seventy Democratic Congressmen, every one of whom, in all probability, knew the infamous history and character of their entertainer. A question suggests itself: Did these seventy or more Democratic Representatives, in the fraternizing with one of the scum of the late Southern Confederacy, evince any particular "acceptance of the situation?"

I do not know whether or not Mr. L. Q. C. Lamar, Representative and Senator-elect from Mississippi, attended that banquet, and I do not care to venture a guess; but I do know of that distinguished gentleman what follows: Mr. Lamar is the best extant specimen of the converted secessionist, and he has neglected no opportunity to speak in eloquent depreciation of sectional animosities, and protestation of his unalterable love for that Union, that his political love a few years ago, the southern Confederacy, sought to destroy. In cases like that of Mr. Lamar, the meaning of actions and words has peculiar application. The sincerity of a politician always is largely discounted, while that of those graduated from the Southern Confederacy school finds few takers among the voters who, a few years ago, were compelled to purge that institution with the bayonet. I know of no action on the part of Mr. Lamar inconsistent with his present profession of devotion to the Union, but, a few weeks ago, the former Confederate military-prison keeper and present publisher of a Democratic weekly paper at Washington, had a payment of several hundred dollars (about $500) to make on his newspaper, and a short time before that payment was due, he told one of the most reliable Democrats of Washington that Mr. Lamar had pledged him that necessary money. This payment was made, and, as the former military-prison keeper did not possess five dollars of cash or credit in the city of Washington, or elsewhere, it looks very much as though Mr. Lamar had kept his pledge. Now, if the political needs of Mr. Lamar require such an instrument as this most infamous of all former Confederate military-prison keepers, it is very clear that Mr. Lamar's acceptance of the situation lacks the important element of sincerity, and somewhat justifies the belief, expressed by many, that he is a wily hypocrite.

The former Confederate military-prison keeper and present publisher of a Democratic weekly paper at Washington, has been particularly active since his arrival at the Capital, in making himself known to prominent Democrats both South and North, though mainly of the former section. During the Congressional recess of last Summer, he left this city for the avowed purpose of visiting the widely-respected Democratic Senator Bayard. His object in making that visit was to raise money; and since his return Senator Bayard has been this former Confederate military-prison keeper's candidate for the Democratic Presidential nomination, and received abundant advocacy in his Democratic weekly paper, all of which looks as though the former Confederate military-prison keeper got the money he went in search of at the time of his visit. I am aware that there is something of conjecture in so much of the foregoing as relates to Senator Bayard, and equally aware that I digress in having allusion to him in this article, but, knowing that the former Confederate military-prison keeper enjoys the reputation of doing nothing gratuitously, I state it for the purpose of showing, that either the Senator made an unfortunate disbursement, or is less fastidious in the selection of political means than hitherto supposed to be. The statements contained in this article are a few of the Southern Democratic surface indications at the Capital, and if they do not indicate insincerity on the part of Southern Democrats in Congress, so far as regards acquiescence in the result of the Rebellion, they indicate nothing. For the first time since the Winter of 1860–61 the Southern wing of the Democratic party is prominent in our National legislature, and coincidental with this appearance our more recent political history began its repetition. Having on the basis of mutuality of material interest, effected an alliance with the Western Democracy, the Southern political leaders propose to regain their former sectional political supremacy; and, that regained, what is likely to follow? Not a prophet, or son of a prophet, is required to perceive that obliteration from the statute books, or virtual nullification of all Republican party legislation tending to the repression of evils inimical to the integrity of the Union, is certain to follow; which accomplished, *the Southern Separate Nationality idea will be found not killed at Appomattox in 1865*. It will be remembered that Henry A. Wise asserted that the fatal mistake of the Southern Rebellion was secession from the Union, and it now looks as though the Southern political leaders ultimately intend to test the Wise theory. In their greed for power the Northern Democratic Representatives are wholly subservient to their Southern colleagues, and the facility with which they are bent to Southern political purposes is painfully suggestive of ante-Rebellion time. Just now the world is being treated to the extraordinary spectacle of the partisan investigation of the stewardship of the party that prevented the desertion of the Union, by a Democratic House of Representatives largely composed of, and wholly controlled by the very men who sought to destroy the Union, and who owe their present political prominence to the magnanimity of the same party that every Republican party official and invariably the shout is prompted by some former Rebel, at present Southern Democratic Congressman, and uttered from the mouth of his Northern Democratic tool. The Democratic party may rest assured, however, that the people would much rather trust the Government of thieves who fought for and saved the life of the Union, than to men who call themselves honest and fought to kill the Union. But there is sufficient warning against trusting a Democratic party, controlled by Southern political leaders, with the country in the vast military cemeteries scattered over this land, where repose thousands of the victims of Rebellion indulged in by a Democratic party identical with the one now seeking power.

In this article I have had extended reference to Jefferson Davis, and I wish to do him the justice of stating that he is far too honorable to be a hypocrite. Rebel he still is, and he does not profess to be anything else and, in not otherwise professing, he exhibits an honesty worthy of emulation by the majority of Southern Democratic Representatives, and Southern politicians generally.

The name of the former Confederate military-prison keeper and present publisher of a Democratic weekly paper at Washington is withheld for the purpose of preventing a flood of Southern Democratic sympathy in his favor that would tend to protract the existence of a Washington nuisance.

I have only to add that the perpetuity of the Union now appears the great issue of the approaching Presidential canvass.

An affidavit to the truth of the foregoing will be placed in the possession of the National Republican Congressional Executive Committee at Washington, D.C.

Notes

DHP = Department of Henrico Papers.
N.R. = *The War of the Rebellion: A Compilation of the Official Records of the Union and Confederate Navies*
O.R. = *The War of the Rebellion: A Compilation of the Official Record of the War of the Union and Confederate Armies.*

Introduction

1. Neil November, "I Remember When...," unidentified newspaper clipping from files of the Valentine Museum, Richmond, Virginia.

2. Bernard J. Henley, "Col. George W. Alexander: The Terror of Castle Thunder," *Richmond Literature and History Quarterly*, Vol. 3 (2) (Fall, 1980), p. 48.

3. Loreta Janeta Velazquez, *The Woman in Battle: A Narrative of the Exploits, Adventures and Travels of Madame Janeta Velazquez, Otherwise Known as Lieutenant Harry T. Buford, Confederate States Army* (Richmond, Va.: Dustin, Gilman & Co., 1876), picture is facing p. 278.

4. [R.D.W.], "Old Castle Thunder: Death of Colonel Alexander, Who Was Superintendent of This Prison. The Splendid Dog Nero. History of the Noble Specimen of a Lordly Canine Race—Alexander as a Dramatist and Actor—How He Managed Those Under Him," Richmond *Daily Dispatch*, 3 March 1895." The Richmond *Daily Dispatch* will be hereinafter cited as "Old Castle Thunder."

5. Henley, p. 48.

6. *Ibid.*

7. "The Camera and Pen Recall Bygone Days: A Weekly Pictorial Series of Events in Richmond's Past," *The Richmond News Leader*, March 30, 1935.

8. Committee to enquire into Treatment of Prisoners at Castle Thunder, *Evidence taken before the Committee of the House of Representatives, appointed to enquire into the Treatment of Prisoners at Castle Thunder* (Richmond: House of Representatives, 1863), p. 6; Alan Lawrence Golden, "Castle Thunder: The Confederate Provost Marshal's Prison, 1862–1865," (Typescript, Master's thesis, University of Richmond, 1980), p. 11, 27.

9. Golden, p. 12.

10. Henley, pp. 48–49.

11. "A Brave Confederate. Death of Col. George W. Alexander at Laurel Md. Quite Close of a Notable Career. Sketch of Dashing Exploits on the Water and Land—The Daring Plan to Capture the Pawnee—Bold Escape from a Military Prison—Other Experiences," *Baltimore Sun*, 22 February 1985. Hereinafter cited as "A Brave Confederate."

1. Around the World with the United States Navy

1. [R.D.W.], "Old Castle Thunder," *Richmond Dispatch,* 3 March 1895; "A Brave Confederate," *Baltimore Sun*, 22 February 1895.

2. Jean A. Sargeant, ed. *Stones and Bones, Tombstone Inscriptions of Prince George's County, Maryland.* "Ivy Hill Cemetery, Laurel, Mary-

land" (Bowie, Md.: Prince George's County Genealogical Society, Inc., 1984), p. 484.

3. United States Government, Bureau of the Census, 1880 Federal Census of Population, Maryland, National Archives film #T9-0501, page 290C.

4. Excerpts from Ruth J. Walther, *Happenings in ye Olde Philadelphia 1680–1900* (Philadelphia, PA: Walther Printing House, 1925), online at www.ushistory.org/philadelphia/philadelphia.html.

5. Lonnie R. Speer, *Portals to Hell* (Mechanicsville, PA: Stackpole Books, 1997), p. 94; Alan Lawrence Golden, "Castle Thunder: The Confederate Provost Marshal's Prison, 1862–1865," typescript, Master's Thesis, University of Richmond, 1980, p.28.

6. Personal communication, Rebecca Livingston, Old Military and Civil Records, Textual Archives Services Division, National Archives and Records Administration, Washington, D.C., March 20, 2003; acceptance of his appointment can be found in Record Group 45, Records Collection of the Office of Naval Records and Library, Acceptances of Appointments of Officers.

7. Mark Boatner III, *The Civil War Dictionary*, revised ed. (New York: Vintage Books, 1991), pp.6–7 cites several members of the Alexander family from Georgia. Golden, "Castle Thunder: The Confederate Provost Marshal's Prison, 1862–1865," p. 28, lists Washington, Georgia, as the birthplace of George Washington Alexander, the subject of this work, which is in error.

8. Search for name "George W. Alexander," through paid subscription allowing the use of the online facilities of Ancestry.com.

9. Results of search for Civil War Service Records of "G. W. Alexander," online at Ancestry.com, March 10, 2003.

10. [R.D.W.], "Old Castle Thunder" *Richmond Dispatch,* 3 March 1895; and "A Brave Confederate," *Baltimore Sun,* 22 February 1895.

11. Edward W. Callahan, ed. *List of Officers of the United States and of the Marine Corps Z(1775–1900).* New York: L. R. Hammersly and Co., 1901, p. 19.

12. *Ibid.,* pp. 19–20.

13. James C., Bradford, ed. *Captains of the Old Steam Navy* (Annapolis, Md.: Naval Institute Press, 1986), pp. 3–4.

14. *Ibid.*

15. *Ibid.,* p. 5–7.

16. *Regulations of the Navy of the United States,* 1973 edition, "Section X—Assistant Engineers," extracted and forward via e-mail to Frances H. Casstevens by Glenn Helm, Navy Department Library, 805 Kidder Breese Street, S. E., Washington Navy Yard, Washington, D.C., 20374-5060, March 27, 2003.

17. "Records of Officers," Microfilm Publication M330, Roll 8, information extracted by Rebecca Livingston, Old Military and Civil Records, Textual Archives Services Division, National Archives and Records Administration, Washington, D.C., March 20, 2003; Callahan, *List of Officers of the United States and of the Marine Corps from 1775 to 1900,* p. 19.

18. "Proud Beginnings: The History of Warrant Officers in the U.S. Navy," Naval Historical Center, Washington, D.C., online at www.history.navy.mil/trivia/trivia4–5b.htm.

19. *Ibid.*

20. *Ibid.*

21. Personal communication, Rebecca Livingston, Old Military and Civil Records, Textual Archives Services Division, National Archives and Records Administration, Washington, D.C., March 20, 2003.

22. "Records of Officers, Microfilm Publication M330, Roll 8, information extracted by Rebecca Livingston, Old Military and Civil Records, Textual Archives Services Division, National Archives and Records Administration, Washington, D.C., March 20, 2003.

23. Peter Booth Wiley, *Yankees in the Land of the Gods: Commodore Perry and the Opening of Japan* (New York: Viking, 1990), pp. 55–56.

24. "Ships of Commodore Perry's Squadron," www.baxleystamps.com/litho/ships.html.

25. John R. Roberson, *Japan Meets the World: The Birth of a Superpower* (Brookfield, Conn.: The Millbrook Press, 1998), pp. 75–76.

26. *Ibid.,* p. 77.

27. James I. Mooney, *Dictionary of American Naval Fighting Ships*, Vol. 4, (Washington, D.C.: U.S. Government Printing Office, 1969), p. 387–388; Wiley, *Yankees in the Land of the Gods,* p. 119.

28. *Register of the Navy of the United States for 1853,* p. 129, Xerox copy furnished by the Old Military and Civil Records, Textual Archives Services Division, National Archives and Records Administration, Washington, D.C.

29. M. C. Perry, *Narrative of the Expedition to the China Seas and Japan, 1852–1854* (Mineola, N.Y.: Dover Publications, Inc., 2000), p. 81. (Originally titled Francis L. Hawks, *Narrative of the Expedition of an American Squadron to the*

China Seas and Japan, Performed in the Years 1852, 1853, and 1854; under the Command of Commodore M. C. Perry, United States Navy, by Order of the Government of the United States (Washington, D.C.: Beverley Tucker, Senate Printer, 1856).

30. Mooney, pp. 387–388.
31. Wiley, *Yankees in the Land of the Gods,* pp. 122–123.
32. *Ibid.,* pp. 121–122.
33. M.C. Perry, *Narrative of the Expedition to the China Seas and Japan, 1852–1854,* p. 81.
34. Mooney, pp. 387–388.
35. Marius B. Jansen, *The Making of Modern Japan* (Cambridge, Mass.: Harvard University Press, 2000), 277.
36. Rhoda Blumberg, *Commodore Perry in the Land of the Shogun* (New York: Lothrop, Lee & Shepard Books, 1995), pp. 17–18.
37. Robert W. Love, Jr. *The History of the U.S. Navy.* Vol. 1. (Harrisburg, PA: Stackpole Books, 1992), p. 206.
38. Blumberg, p. 22, citing Matthew C. Perry, *Narrative of the Expedition,* abridged and edited by Sidney Wallach (New York: Coward-McCann, Inc., 1952), p. 53.
39. Blumberg, pp. 14–17.
40. *Ibid.,* p. 18.
41. *Ibid.*
42. Roberson, p. 79.
43. *Ibid.,* p. 78.
44. Blumberg, pp. 30–31.
45. *Ibid.*
46. *Ibid.*
47. Roberson, p. 80.
48. Mooney, pp. 387–388.
49. "Records of Officers," Microfilm Publication M330, Roll 8, information extracted by Rebecca Livingston, Old Military and Civil Records, Textual Archives Services Division, National Archives and Records Administration, Washington, D.C., March 20, 2003.
50. U.S. Navy Art Collection, Washington, D.C.; U.S. Naval Historical Center Photograph, Photo #: NH 1310-KN.
51. "Ships of Commodore Perry's Squadron," online at www.baxleystamps.com/litho/ships.html.
52. *Ibid.*
53. "Dictionary of American Fighting Ships," at http://cssvirginia.org/vacan3/crew/susque/.
54. *Statutes at Large, 35th Congress, 1st Session,* "Joint Resolution #10," May 11, 1858, p. 369.
55. "Ships of Commodore Perry's Squadron," online at www.baxleystamps.com/litho/ships.html.
56. "Records of Officers," Microfilm Publication M330, Roll 10, information extracted by Rebecca Livingston, Old Military and Civil Records, Textual Archives Services Division, National Archives and Records Administration, Washington, D.C. March 20, 2003; Callahan, *List of Officers of the United States and of the Marine Corps from 1775 to 1900,* p. 19.
57. "Fulton," *Dictionary of American Fighting Ships,* online www.hazegray.org/danfs/steamers/fulton2.htm.
58. "Records of Officers," Microfilm Publication M330, Roll 10, information extracted by Rebecca Livingston, Old Military and Civil Records, Textual Archives Services Division, National Archives and Records Administration, Washington, D.C. March 20, 2003; Callahan, *List of Officers of the United States and of the Marine Corps from1775 to 1900,* p. 19.
59. *Ibid.*
60. *Greenfield Democrat,* 3 May 1861, p. 2, c. 1

2. Sailing for the Confederacy

1. "Old Castle Thunder," *Richmond Dispatch,* 3 March 1895.
2. "A Brave Confederate," *Baltimore Sun* 22 February 1895.
3. *Ibid.* See also S. Z. Ammen, compl. "Doings of Maryland Boys in Gray, From '61 to '65. Sketches of the War." Baltimore, *The Telegram,* 1879 (part of 180 pages of newspaper clippings were found in a scrapbook of articles which appeared in a Baltimore newspaper in 1879), courtesy of John Wyman.
4. Baltimore *Sun,* July 9, 1861; information from members of the Thomas family, quoted in Charles A. Earp, "The Amazing Colonel Zarvona," *Maryland Historical Magazine* 34 (1939), p. 334.
5. "A Brave Confederate," *Baltimore Sun* 22 February 1895; see also Ammen, "Doings of Maryland Boys in Gray."
6. "Maryland Volunteers," *Richmond Dispatch,* 6 July 1861, page 2.
7. "A Brave Confederate," *Baltimore Sun* 22 February 1895.
8. *Ibid.*
9. *Ibid.*
10. John Letcher to Richard Thomas Zarvona, July 2, 1861, *O.R.,* Ser. II, Vol. 2, p. 399.
11. S. Bassett French, Aide-de-Camp to

Governor of Virginia, Richmond, 3 July 1861, *O.R.*, Ser. II, Vol. 2, p. 399.

12. Ammen, "Doings of Maryland Boys in Gray, From '61 to '65."

13. J. T. Scharf, *History of the Confederate States Navy* (New York: Rogers and Sherwood, 1887), p. 114, cited in Earp, p. 334.

14. "A Brave Confederate," *Baltimore Sun* 22 February 1895; George N. Hollins, *Autobiography of Commodore Hollins, C.S.A.*, *Maryland Historical Magazine* (September 1939), pp.237–239; Professor J. Russel Soley, "Early Operations on the Potomac River." *Battles and Leaders of the Civil War*, Vol. II (Secaucus, N. J.: Castle, 1982), p. 143.

15. Earp, "The Amazing Colonel Zarvona," f22, p. 338.

16. "A Brave Confederate," *Baltimore Sun*, 22 February 1895.

17. Ammen, "Doings of Maryland Boys in Gray."

18. J. P. K. Mygatt to R. B. Lowery, in "Report of Lieutenant Lowery, U.S. Navy, commanding U.S.S. *Thomas Freeborn*, forwarding information regarding the capture of the steamer St. Nicholas," *Official Records of the Union and Confederate Navies in the War of the Rebellion Records*, Ser. I, Vol. 4, p. 549. Hereinafter cited as *N. R.*

19. Charles Worthington to Gideon Welles, July 1, 1861, *N. R.*, Ser. I, Vol. 4, pp. 550–551.

20. Samuel Hinks to G. Welles, July 2, 1861, *N. R.*, Ser. I, Vol. 4, p. 551.

21. George N. Hollis, "Extracts from notes by Commander George N. Hollis, C. N. Navy," *N. R.*, Ser. I, Vol. 4, p. 553.

22. *Ibid.*

23. *Ibid.*, pp. 553–554.

24. *Ibid.*, p. 554.

25. *Ibid.*

26. Scharf, *History of the Confederate States Navy*, p. 114, cited in Earp, "The Amazing Colonel Zarvona," p. 337.

27. Hollis, p. 554.

28. *Ibid.*, pp. 554–555.

29. *Ibid.*, p. 555.

30. *Ibid.*, pp 554–555.

31. "List of the officers and men of the steamer St. Nicholas, under command of Captain George N. Hollins, C. S. Navy, when she captured the prizes *Monticello, Mary Pierce*, and *Margaret* in Chesapeake Bay, June 29, 1861," *N. R.*, Ser. I, Vol. 4, p. 555.

32. "A Brave Confederate," *Baltimore Sun*, 22 February 1895.

33. Baltimore *American*, 9 July 1861; Baltimore *Sun*, 9 July 1861, cited in Earp, "The Amazing Colonel Zarvona," p. 339.

34. Earp, p. 340.

35. Townsend to Edwin Stanton, Secretary of War, February 10, 1863, *O.R.*, Ser. II, Vol. 2, p. 404; Scharf, *History of Confederate Navy*, p. 121, cited in Earp, p. 340.

36. Major General Dix to Edwin Stanton, February 20, 1862, *O.R.*, Ser. II, Vol. 2, p. 390; Extract from record book, State Department, "Arrests for Disloyalty," *O.R.*, Ser. II, Vol. 2, p. 379, cited in Earp, "The Amazing Colonel Zarvona," p. 340.

37. Ft. McHenry Prison Records, www.itd.nps.gov/cwss/fortdetail.cfm?RECNUMBER=545.

38. Major General John H. Dix to Major General G. B. McClellan, September 5, 1861, *O.R.*, Ser. II, Vol. 2, p. 381, also cited in Earp, "The Amazing Colonel Zarvona," p. 341.

39. First Lieutenant G. W. Alexander to Judah P. Benjamin, October 2, 1861, *O.R.*, Ser. II, Vol. 3, p. 725.

40. Ammen, "Doings of Maryland Boys in Gray."

41. Ft. McHenry Prison Records, www.itd.nps.gov/cwss/fortdetail.cfm?RECNUMBER=7; W. W. Morris, "Report of political prisoners taken, released and remaining since March 4, 1861, at Fort McHenry, Md.," *O.R.*, Ser. II, Vol, 2, p. 226.

42. Personal communication from Scott S. Sheads, historian, United States Department of the Interior, National Park Service, Fort McHenry National Monument and Historic Shrine, Baltimore, Maryland, 19 June 2003.

43. Speer, *Portals to Hell: Military Prisons of the Civil War*, p. 221.

44. "A Brave Confederate," *Baltimore Sun*, 22 February 1895.

3. Escape from Fort McHenry

1. Speer, *Portals to Hell: Military Prisons of the Civil War*, p. 221.

2. "Archaeological Treasures at Fort McHenry: An Overview," online at www.nps.gov/fomc/archeology/overview.html.

3. "Fort McHenry — Facts," online at www.bcpl.net~etowner/facts.html.

4. "A Brave Confederate," Baltimore *Sun*, 22 February 1895.

5. Ammen, "Doings of Maryland Boys in Gray."

6. *Ibid.*
7. *Ibid.*
8. "A Brave Confederate," Baltimore *Sun*, 22 February 1895.
9. Ammen, "Doings of Maryland Boys in Gray;" and "A Brave Confederate," Baltimore *Sun*, 22 February 1895.
10. *Ibid.*
11. *Ibid.*
12. "Old Castle Thunder," Richmond *Dispatch*, 3 March 1895.
13. Ammen, "Doings of Maryland Boys in Gray;" and "A Brave Confederate," Baltimore *Sun*, 22 February 1895.
14. "A Brave Confederate," Baltimore *Sun*, 22 February 1895.
15. Ammen, "Doings of Maryland Boys in Gray;" and "A Brave Confederate," Baltimore *Sun*, 22 February 1895.
16. *Ibid.*
17. W. W. Morris, "Report of political prisoners taken, released and remaining since March 4, 1861, at Fort McHenry, Md.," *O.R.*, Ser. II, Vol. 2, p. 226.
18. "An Escape from Fort McHenry," Baltimore *Sun*, 9 September 1861.
19. "The Escape of Lieut. Alexander from Fort McHenry—No More Passes." Baltimore *Sun*, 10 September 1861.
20. Ammen, "Doings of Maryland Boys in Gray;" and "A Brave Confederate," Baltimore *Sun*, 22 February 1895.
21. Speer, *Portals to Hell*, p. 221.
22. First Lieutenant G. W. Alexander to Judah P. Benjamin, October 2, 1861, *O.R.*, Ser. II, Vol. 3, p. 725.
23. Ammen, "Doings of Maryland Boys in Gray."
24. G. W. Alexander, "Attention Marylanders!—Come one, Come all," Richmond *Dispatch,* October 3, 1861, p. 2, col. 4.
25. "Meeting of Marylanders," Richmond *Dispatch*, October 5, 1861, p. 3, col. 1.
26. "Zarvona Zouaves!" Richmond *Dispatch*, October 9, 1861, p. 2, col.6.
27. *Ibid.*
28. "Editor Dispatch," Richmond *Dispatch*, October 23, 1861, p. 3, col. 2.
29. G. Washington Alexander, Captain, "Zarvona Zouaves," Richmond *Dispatch*, November 26, 1861, p. 2, column 6.
30. "Zarvona Zouaves," Richmond *Dispatch*, October 21, 1861, p. 2, col. 4.
31. Ammen, "Doings of Maryland Boys in Gray."
32. *Ibid.*
33. *Ibid.*

4. Assistant Provost Marshal Alexander

1. *O.R.,* Vol. VIII, p. 765, cited in Speer, *Portals to Hell,* p. 94.
2. "Old Castle Thunder," Richmond *Dispatch*, 3 March 1895.
3. *Ibid.*
4. William M. Robinson, Jr., *Justice in Grey: A History of the Judicial System of the Confederate States of America* (Cambridge, Ma.: Harvard University Press, 1941), p. 417.
5. Richmond *Dispatch,* November 4–November 30, 1861, and January 2, 1862, cited in Parker, *Richmond's Civil War Prisons*, p. 6–7.
6. Richmond *Dispatch*, Feb. 24, 1862.
7. Note, *O.R.,* Ser. II, Vol. 8, p. 1004; Harrison, *Prisoners' Mail from the American Civil War* (Dexter, MI: Thompson-Shore, Inc., 1997), pp. 16–105.
8. Speer, *Portals to Hell,*, p. xiv.
9. *Ibid.*
10. Figures are based on those of General C. Ainsworth, U.S. Record and Pension Office, listed in Francis T. Miller, ed. *The Photographic History of the Civil War* (New York: The Review of Reviews Co., 1911) 7:43, 50, cited in Speer, *Portals to Hell,* p. xiv, and footnote 5, p. 341.
11. *Ibid.*; Thomas L. Livermore, *Numbers and Losses in the Civil War* (Boston: Houghton Mifflin, 1901), pp. 6–7.
12. Kenneth Radley, *Rebel Watch Dog: The Confederate States Army Provost Guard* (Baton Rouge, LA: Louisiana State University Press, 1989 *p. 165.*
13. Radley, p. 178.
14. p. Steven H. Gifis, *Law Dictionary* (Woodbury, N. Y.: Barron's Educational Series, Inc., 1975), 93–94.
15. Mark E. Neely, Jr. *The Fate of Liberty* (New York: Oxford University Press, 1991), 7–9, 53, 64–65, 69, 87, cited in Ronald W. Fischer, Jr., "A Comparative Study of Two Civil War Prisons: Old Capitol Prison and Castle Thunder Prison," Master's thesis, Virginia Polytechnic Institute and State University, 1994, p. 9.
16. John B. Robbins, "The Confederacy and the Writ of Habeas Corpus," *Georgia Historical Quarterly* LV (1971): 84–85, 88–89, 92,95–96, cited in Fischer, "A Comparative Study of Two Civil War Prisons," p. 9–10.

17. "An act respecting alien enemies, approved August 8, 1861," *O.R.,* Ser. II, Vol. 2, pp. 1868–1870.
18. "Regulations respecting alien enemies," *O.R.,* Ser. II, Vol. 2, p. 1870.
19. Lou Athey, "Loyalty and Civil Liberty in Fayette County During the Civil War," *West Virginia History,* Vol. 55 (1996) p. 1–24.
20. William B. Hesseltine, *Civil War Prisons: A Study in War Psychology* (Columbus: Ohio State University Press, 1930), p. 55, cited in Speer, *Portals to Hell,,* p. xiv.
21. Radley, p. 1.
22. *O.R.,* Ser. IV, Vol. 1, pp. 106 114, 117, 127–131, cited in Radley, p. 2.
23. *O.R.,* Ser. IV, Vol. II, pp. 202–203, cited in Radley, p. 1.
24. Hudson Strode, *Jefferson Davis, Confederate President* (New York: Harcourt, Brace and Company, 1959), p. 212.
25. Fischer, "A Comparative Study of Two Civil War Prisons," p. 12.
26. Robinson, *Justice in Grey,* p. 416.
27. Joseph Ferguson, *Life Struggles in Rebel Prisons* (Philadelphia: James M. Ferguson, 1865), p. 39, cited in Fischer, p. 13.
28. Strode, p. 212.
29. Sandra V. Parker, *Richmond's Civil War Prisons* (Lynchburg, Va.: H. E. Howard, 1990), p. 6; Speer, *Portals to Hell,* p. 20; Jeffrey, *Richmond Prisons,* p.125.
30. *O.R.,* Ser. IV, Vol. II, pp. 202–203, cited in Radley, p. 1.
31. "General Orders, No. 93, Section 19 — An Act to organize military courts to attend the Army of the Confederate States in the field and to define the powers of said courts," *O.R.,* Ser. IV, Vol. 2, pp. 202–203.
32. *O.R.,* Ser. IV, Vol. 2, pp. 202–203, 248. Also cited in Radley, p. 64.
33. Fischer, "A Comparative Study of Two Civil War Prisons," p. 10.
34. Radley, pp. 200–202.
35. *Ibid.,* pp. 205–209.
36. William Frayne Amann, ed., *Personnel of the Civil War: The Confederate Armies,* Vol. I (New York: T. Yoseloff, 1961). See also Patricia L. Faust and Norman C. Delaney, (eds.), *Historical Times Illustrated Encyclopedia of the Civil War* (New York: Harper & Row, 1986).
37. "Fatal Result," Richmond *Enquirer,* May 27, 1862.
38. Robinson, *Justice in Grey,* 416.
39. Jeffrey, *Richmond Prisons,* pp. 85–89.
40. *O.R.,* Ser. II, Vol. 7, p. 205.
41. Boatner, p. 940–941; Joseph H. Crute, Jr., *Confederate Staff Officers, 1861–1865* (Powhatan, Va.: Derwent Books, 1982), p. 212.
42. Boatner, p. 941.
43. *Ibid.*
44. *Ibid.,* p. 940–941; Joseph H. Crute, Jr., *Confederate Staff Officers, 1861–1865* (Powhatan, Va.: Derwent Books, 1982), p. 212.
45. *The Stranger's Guide and Official Directory for the City of Richmond, Showing the Location of the Public Buildings and Offices of the Confederate, State and City Governments, Residences of the Principal Officers, etc.* (Richmond, Va.: Geo. P. Evans & Co., 1863), p. 12. Hereinafter cited as *The Stranger's Guide.*
46. *Ibid.*
47. *Ibid.*
48. John H. Winder, Order Book, April 14, 1863–October 29, 1863, Museum of the Confederacy, Richmond, Virginia. Hereinafter cited as Winder's Order Book.
49. W. S. Winder, A. A. G. to Capt. G. W. Alexander, Headquarters, Dept. Of Henrico, Richmond, Virginia, October 26, 1863, Winder's Order Book, Museum of the Confederacy.
50. Boatner, p. 941.
51. Parker, p. 11.
52. William C. Harris, *Prison Life in the Tobacco Warehouse at Richmond by a Ball's Bluff Prisoner* (Philadelphia, Pa.: George W. Childs, 1862), p. 129; New York *Times,* 27 Feb 1862, p. 8:4; cited in Speer, *Portals to Hell,* p. 20–21.
53. Note, *O.R.,* Ser. II, Vol. 8, p. 1004.
54. Robinson, p. 416; Parker, pp. 2–3.
55. Emory M. Thomas, *The Confederate State of Richmond* (Austin, Tx.: University of Texas Press, 1971), p. 106. Speer, *Portals to Hell,* p. 19–20.
56. Harrison, *Prisoners' Mail,* p. 85.
57. "Castle Godwin," Richmond *Enquirer,* March 4, 1862.
58. Speer, *Portals to Hell,* p. 20.
59. Richmond *Examiner,* March 2, 1864; "Prison opposite Castle Thunder," photo and written accounts listed at http://mdgorman.com/prison_opposite_castle_thunder.htm.
60. Harrison, *Prisoners' Mail,* p. 85.
61. Michael D. Gorman's list of written accounts of Castle Lightening from various newspapers, online at http://mdgorman.com/castle_lightening.htm.
62. Richmond *Dispatch,* July 2, 16, 24, 31,

and August 2, 1861, cited in Parker, *Richmond's Civil War Prisons*, p. 3.

63. Letter from G. W. Alexander to Archibald Campbell Godwin, May 3, 1862, was listed in the Alexander Autographs Auction Catalogue, April 2001. The purchaser is unknown, per M.D. Gorman, online site at www.mdgorman.com/g_w_alexander_letter.htm.

64. "Castle Godwin," Richmond *Dispatch*, June 11, 1862.

65. Speer, *Portals to Hell*, pp. 20, 89–90.

66. Letter from Lt. Col. ___, 47th Virginia Regiment, Camp Clifton, to Lt. G. W. Alexander, microfilm M331, #3, National Archives, Washington, D.C.

67. Robinson, *Justice in Grey*, 416.

68. "Trial, Sentence, and Execution of Timothy Webster as a Spy," Richmond *Disptch*, April 30, 1862.

69. Richmond *Enquirer*, June 6, 1862.

70. Chronological summary of the military career of G. W. Alexander, 1861–1864, microfilm M331, #3, National Archives, Washington, D.C.

71. *Ibid.*

72. Richmond *Dispatch*, 19 August 1862, and 3 March 1895; Parker, *Richmond's Prisons*, p. 18.

73. Crute, *Confederate Staff Officers*, pp. 212–213.

74. House of Representatives, *Report on the Treatment of Prisoners of War*, p. 1035, cited in Golden, p. 30.

75. *O.R.*, Ser. II, Vol. V, p. 907, cited in Fischer, p. 58.

76. Richmond *Enquirer*, March 22, 1862; Richmond *Dispatch*, February 27, 1862, March 3 and March 6, 1862, cited in Parker, *Richmond's Civil War Prisons*, pp. 7–8.

77. Governor John Letcher to G. W. Randolph, Secretary of War, June 20, 1862, *O.R.*, Ser. II, Vol. 4, p. 781.

78. "To Be Sent Away," Richmond *Dispatch*, July 7, 1862.

79. "Thinning Out," Richmond *Dispatch*, July 11, 1862; "Idle Men," Richmond *Dispatch*, August 8, 1862.

80. "Castle Godwin," Richmond *Dispatch*, August 1, 1862; Richmond *Enquirer*, August 1, 1862.

81. "Grand Exodus of Three Thousand Yankees," Richmond *Dispatch*, August 6, 1862.

82. "The Military District," Richmond *Enquirer*, August 6, 1862.

83. Richmond *Dispatch*, 30 April 1863.

84. Order Book, John Winder to G. W. Alexander, October 9, 1863, Museum of the Confederacy, Richmond, Virginia, cited in Fischer, p. 63.

85. "The Military District," Richmond *Enquirer*, August 6, 1862.

86. "New Lodgings," Richmond *Dispatch*, August 6, 1862.

87. "Castle Thunder," Richmond *Enquirer*, August 12, 1862.

88. "Full," Richmond *Dispatch*, August 14, 1862.

89. "To be Evacuated," Richmond *Dispatch*, August 18, 1862; "To Be Removed," Richmond *Daily Enquirer*, August 18, 1862.

90. Chronological summary of the military career of G. W. Alexander, 1861–1864, microfilm M331, #3, National Archives, Washington, D.C.; "General Orders, No. 25, Prison Series," issued by W. S. , A.A.G., October 27, 1862, *O.R.*, Ser. 2, Vol. 4, p. 928.

91. "Promotion," Richmond *Enquirer*, June 17, 1862, p. 1, col. 7.

5. New Prison Opened in Richmond

1. "Tobacco Warehouses," Richmond *Examiner*, 17 June 1864.

2. "The Prisoners," Richmond *Dispatch*, 8 July 1862.

3. "The Camera and Pen Recall Bygone Days: A Weekly Pictorial Series of Events in Richmond's Past," *The Richmond News Leader*, 30 March 1935.

4. Francis Trevelyan Miller, ed., *The Photographic History of the Civil War*. Part 7: Prisons and Hospitals (New York: Castle Books, 1957), pp. 87, 89, and 199.

5. Henley, "Col. George W. Alexander and the Terror of Castle Thunder," p. 49.

6. Parker, *Richmond's Prisons*, p. 17.

7. *O.R.*, Vol. 8, p. 765, cited in Speer, p. 94.

8. Colonel N. T. Colby, "The 'Old Capitol' Prison," in *The Annals of the Civil War Written by Leading Participants North and South*, 1878; rpt. New York: Da Capo Press, 1994, p. 502–503.

9. "Old Castle Thunder," Richmond *Dispatch*. 3 March 1895.

10. *Ibid.*

11. Personal observation of Brad Hively, a War Between the States provost marshal re-enactor, June 15, 2003, at "Richmond Hill," home of North Carolina State Supreme Court Judge Richmond Mumford Pearson, Yadkin County, North Carolina.

12. *Ibid.*
13. *Ibid.*
14. Richmond *Dispatch*, 3 March 1895; *O.R.*, Ser. II, Vol. 7, 204–205; Parker, *Richmond's Prisons*, p. 18.
15. Galen D. Harrison, *Prisoners' Mail from the American Civil War* (Dexter, MI: Thompson-Shore, Inc., 1997), p. 85.
16. *The New York Times*, 24 May 1865, p. 4:6; Putnam, *Prisoner of War*. P. 28, cited in Speer, p. 95.
17. Harrison, *Prisoners' Mail*, p. 85.
18. W. S. Winder to Captain Turner, November 27, 1862, *O.R.*, Ser. II, Vol. 4, p. 953.
19. Clement Eaton, *A History of the Southern Confederacy* (New York: The Macmillan Company, 1954), p. 272.
20. Van R. Otey to Captain G. W. Alexander, Lynchburg, Virginia, August 15, 1863, DHP.
21. Capt. R. Otey to Captain Alexander, Lynchburg, Virginia, October 16, 1863, DHP.
22. Fischer, p. 26.
23. Richmond *Dispatch*, 1 October 1862, 18 October 1862, 29 December 1862, 27 February 1863, 7 April 1863, 3 May 1864, cited in Fischer, p. 28.
24. "Division of Detective Force," Richmond *Examiner*, April 9, 1863.
25. Speer, pp. 120–121.
26. Surgeon Barton to Maj. Carrington, Hospital No. 13, Richmond, July 21, 1863, DHP.
27. Thomas P. Turner, "Rules and Regulations of the C. S. Military Prisons," National Archives, Record Group 294, cited online at www.mdgorman.com/ prison-rules_and_regulations.htm.
28. *Ibid.*
29. Speer, p. 94.
30. Benjamin F. Booth and Steve Meyer, *Dark Days of the Rebellion: Life in Southern Military Prisons,* revised ed. (Garrison, Ia.: Myer Publishing, 1996), p. 76.
31. George H. Sharpe to Major General Humphries, City Point, September 1, 1864, *O.R.*, Ser. I, Vol. 42, Pt. II, p. 629.
32. Richmond *Dispatch*, 25 July 1862, 16 January 1864, cited in Fischer, p. 48–49.
33. G. W. Alexander to Major Carrington, East District Military Prison, Richmond, October 29, 1863.
34. Boatner, "Henrico, Confed. Dept. Of," p. 393.

6. The Lighter Side

1. Richard Barksdale Harwell, *Brief Candle: The Confederate Theatre,* in *Proceedings of the American Antiquarian Society* (April 1971), rpt. (Worcester, Mass.: Davis Press, Inc., 1971), p. 92–155.
2. *Ibid.*, p. 92.
3. *Ibid.*, pp. 92–93.
4. *Ibid.*, pp. 153–154.
5. *The Southern Illustrated New,* March 28, 1863, cited in Harwell, *Brief Candle: The Confederate Theatre,* pp. 69–70.
6. Capt. G. W. Alexander, lyrics, "The Southern Soldier Boy," Richmond, VA: George Dunn & Company, 1863; Columbia, South Carolina: Julian A. Selby, 1863, copy of the sheet music is in Flowers Collection, Rare Book, Manuscript, and Special Collections Library, Duke University, Durham, North Carolina.
7. Miller, *The Photographic History of the Civil War,* vol. 9. p. 346.
8. Captain G. W. Alexander, "The Southern Soldier Boy,'" sheet music (Richmond, Virginia: George Dunn & Company, 1863. Online, http://memory.loc.gov. Copy in the collection of Historic American Sheet Music, 1850–1920, Duke University, Durham, North Carolina.
9. Captain Alexander, "Dedicated to the Baltimore Light Artillery, CSA," Rare Book and Special Collections Division, Library of Congress. Online, American Memory collection — American Singing: Nineteenth-Century Song Sheets, http://memory.loc. gov.
10. "Old Castle Thunder, " *Richmond Dispatch,* 3 March 1895.
11. "That Big Black Dog Again," Richmond *Whig,* 19 May 1865.
12. "Old Castle Thunder," Richmond *Dispatch,* 3 March 1895.
13. *Ibid.*
14. "Great Dane," online at www.doginformat.com/2-2molossian.htm.
15. "Great Danes," online at www.puppydogweb.com/caninebreeds/grtdanes.htm.
16. "Great Dane," information condensed from Harry Glover, ed., *A Standard Guide to Pure-Bred Dogs,* online at www.renbury.com.au/Great@20Dane. htm.
17. "That Big Black Dog Again," Richmond *Whig,* 19 May 1865.
18. New York *Times,* May 24, 1865, p. 4:6; Putnam, *Prisoner of War in Virginia 1864–5,* p. 28, also cited in Speer, *Portals to Hell,* p. 94.
19. "Old Castle Thunder," Richmond *Dispatch,* March 3, 1895.
20. "A Strange Prisoner," Richmond *Sentinel,* 22 July 1863.
21. Richmond *Enquirer,* 7 June 1864.

7. Life Within the Castle

1. William H. Jeffrey, *Richmond Prisons 1861–1862 From the Original Records Kept by the Confederate Government* (St. Johnsbury, Vt.: The Republican Press, 1893), p. 7. Hereafter cited as *Richmond Prisons*.
2. Jeffrey, *Richmond Prisons*, pp. 44–45.
3. *Ibid.*, p. 45.
4. Speer, picture caption for Castle Thunder, n.p.n.
5. W. Buck Yearns and John G. Barrett, eds., *North Carolina Civil War Documentary* (Chapel Hill, N.C.: The University of North Carolina Press, 1980), p. 121.
6. Richmond *Dispatch*, 20 September 1862, 10, 13, 15 October 1862, 7, 22 and 23 November 1862; Richmond *Enquirer* 22 November 1862; Parker, *Richmond's Prisons*, p. 21.
7. "Sent Away," Richmond *Dispatch*, September 20, 1862.
8. Richmond *Dispatch*, 12 March 1863.
9. *O.R.*, Ser. II, Vol. V, pp. 873, 876, 882, 901, cited in Fischer, pp. 65–66.
10. J. W. Muffley, ed. *The Story of Our Regiment: A History of the 148th Pennsylvania Volunteers* (Des Moines, Iowa: Kenyon Print and Mfg. Co., 1904), p. 373; Richmond *Dispatch*, 3 January 1863, cited in Fischer, p. 25–26.
11. Henry H. Dedrick to wife, Camp Near Hamilton's Crossing, May 25, 1863, Henry H. Dedrick Papers, Virginia Military Institute Archives.
12. E. C. Sanders, Captain Company D, First North Carolina Union Volunteers, to Major General J. G. Foster, New Bern, North Carolina, April 24, 1863, *O.R.*, Ser. II, Vol. 4, pp. 518–519.
13. John McEnter to Brevet Major-General Terry, City Point, November 12, 1864, *O.R.*, Ser. I, Vol. 42, Pt. III, p. 608–609.
14. Richmond *Examiner*, 25 July 1863, *O.R.*, Ser. II, Vol. V, pp. 872–8, 891, 894, 897, 899, and 909; Parker, *Richmond's Prisons*, p. 30–31.
15. Junius Henri Browne, *Four Years in Secessia: Adventures Within and Beyond the Union Lines: Embracing a Great Variety of Facts, Incidents, and Romance of War* (Hartford, Conn.: O. D. Case and Company, 1865), p. 295.
16. *Ibid.*, pp. 295–296.
17. *Ibid.*; Parker, *Richmond's Prisons*, p. 36.
18. Browne, *Four Years in Secessia*, title page.
19. *Ibid.*, p. 295.
20. *Ibid.*, p. 297.
21. *Ibid.*, pp. 296–297.
22. [Unknown], *Ohio Boys in Dixie: The Adventures of Twenty-two Scouts sent by Gen. O. M. Mitchell to Destroy a Railroad; with a Narrative of Their Barbarous Treatment by the Rebels and Judge Holt's Report....*" New York: Miller & Mathews, 1863.
23. J. A. Campbell, Assistant Secretary of War, to Brig. Gen. John H. Winder, Commanding Richmond, Virginia, January 20, 1863, *O.R.*, Ser. II, Vol. 5, p. 816.
24. *Ibid.*, pp. 816–817.
25. *O.R.*, Ser. II, Vol. 5, pp. 830–834.
26. Katharine M. Jones, *Ladies of Richmond: Confederate Capital* (Indianapolis, IN: Bobbs-Merrill, 1962), p. 119.
27. Priscilla Rhoades, "The Women of Castle Thunder," *The Kudzu Monthly*, August 2002, online at www.kudzumonthly.com.
28. Robert Ould to Lieutenant-Colonel Ludlow, January 25, 1863, *O.R.*, Ser. II, Vol. 5, p. 212.
29. Thomas P. Turner to Capt. G. W. Alexander, February 19, 1863, *O.R.*, Ser. II, Vol. 5, p. 883–884.
30. *O.R.*, Ser. II, Vol. 6, p. 324.
31. "Old Castle Thunder," Richmond *Dispatch*, 3 March 1895.
32. Richmond *Dispatch*, 26 June 1863.
33. *O.R.*, Ser. II, Vol. V, p. 872.
34. Parker, *Richmond's Prisons*, p. 32.
35. *O.R.*, Ser. II, Vol. 6, p. 821.
36. *O.R.*, Ser. II, Vol. 6, p. 456.
37. G. W. Alexander to Capt. W. S. Winder, October 28, 1863, *O.R.*, Ser. II, Vol. 6, p. 440.
38. Saml. Burnham, Commissary-Sergeant to Capt. Thomas P. Turner, October 28, 1863, *O.R.*, Ser. II, Vol. 6, p. 440.
39. *Daily Missouri Democrat*, 21 August 1863, p. 1:4, cited in Speer, pp. 125–126.
40. Testimony of Dennis Callahan, Congressional Investigation, *O.R.*, Ser. II, Vol. 5, p. 907; Parker, *Richmond's Prisons*, p. 32.
41. T. P. Sayre, "Prison Life in Richmond," Letter to the Editor *National Tribune*, 13 September 1883.
42. *Ibid.*
43. George H. Sharpe to Major General Humphries, City Point, September 1, 1864, *O.R.*, Ser. I, Vol. 42, Pt. II, p. 629.
44. *O.R.*, Ser. II, Vol. 7, pp. 204, 207.
45. "The Sutler's Post," Richmond *Examiner*, 1 July 1864.
46. Richmond *Examiner*, 10 November 1862.

47. Jas. B. Hamilton, Castle Thunder, to "Dear Wife," December 1, 1863, Hamilton Papers, Virginia Historical Society, Richmond, VA.
48. "A. D. Richardson's Experiences in the Confederacy," in Louis A. Brown, *The Salisbury Prison: A Case Study of Confederate Military Prisons 1861–1865* (Wilmington, NC: Broadfoot Publishing Co., 1992), p.199.
49. E. L. Cox Diary, July 18, 1864, Virginia Historical Society, Richmond, Virginia, cited in Fischer, p. 71.
50. Richmond *Examiner*, 29 June 1864.
51. Speer, p. 38.
52. Michael C. Burns to General Winder, Castle Thunder, July 3, 1863, DHP.
53. E. L. Cox Diary, July 18, 1864, Virginia Historical Society, Richmond, Virginia, cited in Fischer, p. 71.
54. John Hussey to Major General Hitchcock, November 13, 1863, *O.R.*, Ser. II, Vol. 6, p. 513.
55. "Visit to a Confederate Prison," Richmond *Dispatch*, 11 October 1862.
56. "Robbed in Prison," Richmond *Examiner*, 10 November 1862.
57. Richmond *Examiner*, 29 June 1864.
58. "Castle Thunder," Richmond *Whig*, 27 December 1862.
59. S. A. Meredith to Robert Ould, September 16, 1863; First Endorsement, Robert Ould; Second Endorsement, W. S. Winder; Third Endorsement, G. A. Alexander; Fourth Endorsement, Ro. Ould, *O.R.*, Ser. II, Vol. 6, pp. 294–295.
60. "A Mixed Population," Richmond *Enquirer*, 12 June 1863.
61. "Castle Thunder Items," Richmond *Examiner*, 28 July 1863.

8. Spies, Traitors, and Hostages

1. Testimony of Detective William Causey, Congressional Investigation, *O.R.*, Ser. II, Vol. 5, p. 877.
2. "A Mixed Population," Richmond *Enquirer*, 12 June 1863.
3. George Ward Nichols, "The General's Story," *Harper's New Monthly Magazine*. Vol. XXXV (No. CCV) (June 1867), pp. 60–74.
4. *Ibid.*
5. "The 15th Pennsylvania Volunteer Cavalry (The Anderson Cavalry): William J. Palmer–A Biographical Sketch," online www.swcivilwar.com/15PalmerBiography.html; Mark M. Boatner III, *The Civil War Dictionary*. Rev. ed. (New York: Vintage Books, 1987), p. 617–618.
6. Nichols, "The General's Story," pp. 60–74.
7. Robert L. Willett, "Loyal to None," *The Civil War Times*, XLII (April 2003), pp. 43–44.
8. *Ibid.*, p. 44.
9. *Ibid.*, p. 44.
10. *Ibid.*, pp. 44–45.
11. *Ibid.*
12. *Ibid.*
13. *Ibid.*, p. 46.
14. "Attempted Escape," Richmond *Sentinel*, March 30, 1863, p. 2, col. 3; Willett, p. 46.
15. Willett, p. 46.
16. *Ibid.*, p. 47.
17. Wilbur G. Kurtz, Sr., "The Andrews Railroad Raid," *Civil War Times Illustrated*, Vol. 5, No. 1, (April 1966), pp. 8–17.
18. J. Holt, "Report of Judge Advocate-General U.S. Army," *O.R.*, Ser. I, Vol. 10, Pt. 1, p. 630.
19. Boatner, "Andrews' Raid," p. 16.
20. J. Holt, "Report of Judge Advocate-General U.S. Army," *O.R.*, Ser. I, Vol. 10, Pt. 1, p. 630, 634.
21. Boatner, "Andrews' Raid," p. 16.
22. Lou Athey, "Loyalty and Civil Liberty in Fayette County During the Civil War," *West Virginia History*, Vol. 55 (1996) p. 1–24.
23. J. B. Hamilton, Salisbury Prison, N.C., to Col. Tompkins, June 3, 1864, Hamilton Papers, Virginia Historical Society, Richmond, VA.
24. Col. Tompkins, Richmond, VA, to Mrs. J. B. Hamilton, November 27, 1864, Hamilton Papers, Virginia Historical Society, Richmond, VA.
25. Major G. B. Brown, Louisville, KY, to E. M. Stanton, Secretary of War, October 27, 1862, *O.R.*, Ser. II, Vol. 4, pp. 660–661.
26. *Ibid.*
27. Boatner, p. 446
28. Richmond *Dispatch,* 3 November 1862, 31 October 1864, 7 January 1863, 10 March 1864, cited in Fischer, p. 37–38.
29. Richmond *Dispatch*, 26 June 1863, 27 June 1863, 9 July 1863, 18 July 1863, cited in Fischer, p. 39.
30. Rhoades, "The Women of Castle Thunder," *The Kudzu Monthly*, August, 2002.
31. Richmond *Whig*, August 24, 1863, cited in Rhodes, "The Women of Castle Thunder," in *The Kudzu Monthly*, August, 2002.
32. Unidentified newspaper clipping from Valentine Museum, Richmond, VA.

33. Rhoades, "The Women of Castle Thunder," *The Kudzu Monthly*, August, 2002.
34. *Richmond Examiner*, 25 July 1863.
35. Rhoades, "The Women of Castle Thunder" *The Kudzu Monthly*, August, 2002.
36. "Thunder Struck," Richmond *Enquirer*, September 5, 1862.
37. Madame Loreta Janeta Velazquez, *The Woman in Battle* (Richmond, VA: Dustin, Gilman & Co., 1876), p. 278. See also, Katharine M. Jones, "Loreta Janeta Velazquez," in *Ladies of Richmond: Confederate Capital* (Indianapolis, IN: Bobbs-Merrill, 1962), pp. 139–142.
38. *Ibid., Velazquez* pp. 279–280.
39. *Ibid., Velazquez*, pp. 278–279.
40. Priscilla Rhoades, "The Women of Castle Thunder," *The Kudzu Monthly*, August, 2002.
41. "Loreta Velazquez," Jone Johnson Lewis, online Women's History the History Net, http://womenshistory.about.com.
42. Editor, "Book Review of *The Woman in Battle*," *Southern Historical Society Papers*, 1876, cited in Parker, *Richmond's Civil War Prisons*, p. 27.
43. "Going South," Richmond *Dispatch*, 16 July 1863; "Going South," Richmond *Sentinel*, 16 July 1863.
44. *O. R.*, Ser. II, Vol. V, p. 894; also cited online in "The Women of Castle Thunder," *The Kudzu Monthly*, August, 2002.
45. Richmond *Examiner*, 21 July 1863.
46. "Castle Godwin," Richmond *Whig*, 10 March 1862.
47. Richmond *Examiner*, 6 June 1863.
48. Richmond *Examiner*, 25 July 1864, cited in Parker, *Richmond's Civil War Prisons*, p. 26.
49. Charles M. Snyder, *Dr. Mary Walker—The Little Lady in Pants* (New York: Arno Press, 1974).
50. Parker, *Richmond's Civil War Prisons*, p. 26.
51. "Female Yankee Surgeon," Richmond *Sentinel*, 22 April 1864, p. 1, c. 3.
52. *Ibid.*
53. "Miss Walker, The Yankee Surgeoness," Richmond *Examiner*, 29 June 1864.
54. "Wants to Go Home," Richmond *Examiner*, 10 June 1864.
55. Rev. J. L. Burrows, "Recollections of Libby Prison," *Southern Historical Society Papers*, XI (1883), pp. 89–93, cited in Rhoades, "The Women of Castle Thunder," *The Kudzu Monthly*, August, 2002.
56. Jack Davis, Letter to the editor, "Mary Walker Stamp," *Civil War Times Illustrated*, Volume XXIII, No. 5 (September 1984), p. 18.
57. "The Execution To-Day," Richmond *Dispatch*, April 29, 1862, April 30, 1862.
58. Mrs. T. Webster to "My Honorable President," October 13, 1862, *O.R.*, Ser. II, Vol. 4, p. 917.
59. Rhoades, "The Women of Castle Thunder," *The Kudzu Monthly*, August 2002.
60. Donald E. Markle, *Spies and Spymasters of the Civil War,* (New York: Hippocreme Books, Inc, 1994), 188.
61. David R. Ryan, ed. *A Yankee Spy in Richmond* (Mechanicsburg, Penn: Stackpole Books, 1996), pp. 44–45. Cited in Rhoades, "The Women of Castle Thunder," *The Kudzu Monthly*, August 2002.
62. Edwin M. Stanton to Colonel Ludlow, Fortress Monroe, June 30, 1863, *O.R.*, Ser. II, Vol. 6, p. 62.
63. Colonel Wm. H. Ludlow, at Fortress Monroe, to Edwin M. Stanton, June 30, 1863, *O.R.*, Ser. II, Vol. 6, p. 62.
64. Edwin M. Stanton to Major Turner, Annapolis, June 30, 1863, *O.R.*, Ser. II, Vol. 6, pp. 62–63.
65. Edwin M. Stanton to Major Turner, Judge-Advocate, Annapolis, July 2, 1863, *O.R.*, Ser. II, Vol. 6, p. 74.
66. W. Hoffman, Colonel Third Infantry and Commissary General of Prisons, to Capt. E. M. Camp, Washington, D.C., July 7, 1863, *O.R.*, Ser. II, Vol. 6, p. 89.
67. "Caged Camp Followers," Richmond *Examiner*, July 19, 1864.
68. "Arrival of Prisoners," Richmond *Sentinel*, 8 August 1863.
69. "Slaves Confined in Castle Thunder," Richmond *Examiner*, 21 August 1863.
70. "The Slaves at Castle Thunder," Richmond *Sentinel*, 28 August 1863.

9. General Hospital No. 13

1. *O.R.*, Ser. II, Vol. V, pp. 887, 897, 901, cited in Fischer, p. 59.
2. "The Alexander Hospital," Richmond *Enquirer*, 26 June 1862, p. 2, c. 5.
3. "Hospital Index," Civil War Richmond, online at www.mdgorman.com/hospital_index.htm.
4. "Castle Thunder Hospital," Richmond *Examiner*, 10 November 1862.
5. Robert W. Waitt, Jr., compl., "Confed-

erate Military Hospitals in Richmond," Official Publication #22 (Richmond, Va.,: Richmond Civil War Centennial Committee, 1964).

6. Photograph of General Hospital No. 13, enlarged from photograph taken from Church Hill in Richmond, online at www.mdgorman.com/general_hosptal_13_photo.htm.

7. Robert W. Waitt, Jr., compl., "Confederate Military Hospitals in Richmond," Official Publication #22 (Richmond, Va.,: Richmond Civil War Centennial Committee, 1964).

8. *Ibid.*

9. List of Surgeons, no date, at General Hospital No. 13, online at www.mdgorman.com/gh13_list _of_surgeons.htm.

10. H. H. Cunningham, *Doctors in Gray: The Confederate Medical Service* (1958; rpt. Glouchester, Mass.: Peter Smith, 1970.), pp. 80–82.

11. Rations Issued by Commissary, General Hospital No. 13, Richmond, Virginia, Record Group 109, Chapter IX, Vol. 231, National Archives, Washington, D.C.; Abstract of Provisions Drawn from Commissary, General Hospital No. 13, Richmond, Virginia, Record Group 109, Chap. IX, Vol. 231, National Archives, Washington, D.C., cited in Fischer, pp. 88–89.

12. William A. Carrington to E. S. Gaillard, Medical Director, October 3, 1862, William A. Carrington CSR (M331) No. 16, online at www.mdgorman.com/william_a_carrington_csr_.htm.

13. "The Small-Pox," Richmond *Dispatch*. 1 January 1863.

14. "A Good Disinfectant," Richmond *Dispatch*, 12 January 1863.

15. Richmond *Dispatch*, 24 January 1863.

16. Report of Sick and Wounded, General Hospital No. 13, Richmond, Virginia, Record Group 109, Chap. VI, Vol. 256, National Archives, Washington, D.C.; Richmond *Dispatch*, 5 January 1863; Morning Report, Castle Thunder Prison, March 11, 1864, Record Group 249, Entry 107, Item 858, National Archives, cited in Fischer, pp. 91–92.

17. M. L. Bell, Asst. Surgeon in Charge, to Capt. G. W. Alexander, General Hospital No. 13, Richmond, Nov. 5, 1863, DHP.

18. Richmond *Dispatch,* 9 October 1862; cited in Parker, *Richmond's Prisons,* p. 20; Speer, p. 125

19. Richmond *Sentinel,* 28 October 1863, p. 2, c. 4.

20. Jas. B. Hamilton, Castle Thunder, to "Dear Wife," December 1, 1863, Hamilton Papers, Virginia Historical Society, Richmond, VA.

21. "Death at Castle Thunder," Richmond *Dispatch*, 24 September 1862.

22. M. T. Bell to John H. Winder, November 9, 1863, DHP; M. T. Bell to John H. Winder, November 11, 1863, DHP, both also cited in Fischer, pp. 86–87.

23. "New Hospital for Castle Thunder," Richmond *Examiner,* 3 April 1863.

24. "Hospital and Prison Inspection," Richmond *Examiner,* 30 May 1864.

25. "Statistical Reports of Hospitals in Virginia, 1862–1864," Record Group 109, Ch. 6, Vol. 151, National Archives, Washington, D.C., p. 19, online at www.mdgorman.com/NAR/rg_109,_ch_6,_vol_151, p_19.htm.

26. Report of Sick and Wounded, General Hospital No. 13, Richmond, Virginia, June 2, 1862-January 31, 1864, Record Group 109, Chap. VI, Vol. 230, National Archives, Washington, D.C., cited in Fischer, pp. 89–90.

27. Register of Surgical Cases, General Hospital No. 13, Richmond, Virginia, Record Group 109, Chap. VI, Vol. 467, National Archives, Washington, D.C., cited in Fischer, p. 92.

28. Medical Department Register of Patients, General Hospital No. 13, Richmond, Virginia, Record Group 109, Chap. VI, Vol. 230; Record Book, General Hospital No. 13, Richmond, Virginia, Record Group 109, Chap. VI, Vol. 257; Report of Sick and Wounded, General Hospital No. 13, Record Group 109, Chap. VI, Vol. 256; and Record Book, General Hospital No. 13, Richmond, Virginia, Record Group 109, Chap. VI, Vol. 249, National Archives, Washington, D.C., cited in Fischer, p. 92.

29. Letter from Daniel Meeker to the *Army and Navy Journal,* cited in Speer, p. 122.

10. Escape Attempts

1. Fischer, p. 106.

2. "Prisoner Shot," Richmond *Dispatch,* 25 August 1862.

3. Parker, *Richmond's Prisons,* p. 24.

4. "Recaptured," Richmond *Sentinel,* 27 June 1863.

5. "Proceedings of a general Court Martial convened at Richmond by virtue of the following order — General Orders No. 7," October 11, 1862, microfilm, Department of Henrico Papers.

6. Testimony of Frederick F. Wiley before the *Committee of Congress,* p. 46, cited in Golden, p. 58.

7. "A Delivery from Castle Thunder," Richmond *Enquirer,* 19 November 1862, p. 2, c. 4.

8. *Ibid.*
9. "Recaptured," Richmond *Dispatch,* 9 October 1862, cited in Fischer, p. 106.
10. "Attempt to Escape from Prison," Richmond *Dispatch,* 17 October 1862.
11. "Escape," Richmond *Sentinel,* 26 November 1863, p. 2, c. 2.
12. Richmond *Dispatch,* 5 January 1863, cited in Fischer, p. 1
13. "Stray Prison Birds Recaptured," 18 April 1863, Richmond *Examiner,* 18 April 1863.
14. "Castle Thunder Items," Richmond *Examiner,* 4 April 1863.
15. Richmond *Daily Whig,* 6 April 1863.
16. "Killed While Attempting to Escape," Richmond *Examiner,* 7 April 1863, p. 1
17. "A Man Shot," Richmond *Sentinel,* 7 April 1863, p. 2, col. 3.
18. "Killed While Attempting to Escape," Richmond *Examiner,* 7 April 1863.
19. "Once More in Confinement," Richmond *Examiner,* 21 July 1863.
20. Richmond *Dispatch,* 9 October 1862; cited in Parker, *Richmond's Prisons,* p. 20; Speer, p. 125
21. "Attempted Escape," Richmond *Sentinel,* 2 July 1863.
22. "Attempt to Mine Out," Richmond *Sentinel,* 1 October 1863.
23. "Castle Thunder," Richmond *Sentinel,* 16 November 1863.
24. Richmond *Dispatch,* 16 and 21 November 1863, cited in Fischer, p. 108.
25. Browne, *Four Years in Secessia,* p. 299.
26. *Ibid.*
27. "Restless," Richmond *Sentinel,* 20 May 1863.
28. "Attempt to Escape From the Castle," Richmond *Examiner,* 21 May 1863.
29. "An Impudent Scamp," Richmond *Enquirer,* 14 August 1863.
30. "Escape of Prisoners—Sentinel Killed," Richmond *Whig,* 23 October 1863.
31. *Ibid.*
32. Richmond *Whig,* 3 November 1863.
33. "Broke Jail," Richmond *Sentinel,* 15 April 1863, p. 2, c. 2.
34. "Castle Thunder," Richmond *Sentinel,* 14 November 1863, p. 1, c. 7.
35. "Deserters Recanting." Richmond *Sentinel,* 28 April 1864, p. 1, c. 6.
36. "The Winder Guards," Richmond *Examiner,* 16 May 1864.
37. "Ready for Work," Richmond *Dispatch,* 6 July 1863.
38. "Rewarded," Richmond *Examiner,* 21 May 1864.
39. Richmond *Examiner,* 28 May 1864.
40. J. L. Burrows, "Recollections of Libby Prison," *Southern Historical Society Papers* XI (1883), pp. 92–93; see also Fischer, p. 109.
41. Burrows, "Recollections of Libby Prison," pp. 91–92.
42. Richmond *Dispatch,* May 31, 1862.
43. "Caught Again," Richmond *Examiner,* July 26, 1862.
44. "A Sooty Dodge," Richmond *Enquirer,* June 19, 1862, p. 1, col. 7.
45. Richmond *Examiner,* 11 February 1864.
46. D. T. Van Buren, by order of Major General Dix, to Lt. Col. Martin Burke, commander at Fort Lafayette, December 2, 1861, *O.R,* Ser. II, Vol. 2, p. 165; Zarvona to William H. Seward, Secretary of States, December 22, 1861, January 9, 1862, *O.R.,* Ser. II, Vol. 2, pp. 386–387, also cited in Earp, "The Amazing Colonel Zarvona," p. 341.
47. E. D. Townsend to General L. Thomas, February 27, 1862, *O.R.,* Ser. II, Vol. 2, p. 394; Lt. Col. Burke to General Thomas, March 5, 1862, *O.R.,* Ser. II, Vol. 2, p. 395; Thomas to Burke, February 28, 1862, *O.R.,*Ser. II, Vol. 2, p. 394; W. W. Morris to Brig. Gen. L. Thomas, September 28, 1862, *O.R.,* Ser. II, Vol. 2, p. 399. also cited in Earp, "The Amazing Colonel Zarvona," p. 341.
48. First Lieutenant Charles O. Wood to Lieut. Col. M. Burke, Fort Lafayette, New York Harbor, April 22, 1862, *O.R.,* Ser. II, Vol. 2, pp. 396–397; Earp, "The Amazing Colonel Zarvona," p. 341.
49. Scharf, p. 121.
50. *O.R.,* Ser. II, Vol, 2, pp. 411–412; *O.R.,* Ser. II, vol 4, pp. 774–776; Earp, "The Amazing Colonel Zarvona," p. 341.
51. E. D. Townsend to Lieut. Col. Martin Burke, Washington, D.C., June 27, 1862, *O.R.,* Ser. II, Vol. 2, p. 397–398.

11. *Cruel and Unusual Punishment vs. Standard Fare*

1. "Defense of Captain Alexander," pp. 55–58, cited in Golden, p. 96; *O.R.,* Ser. II, Vol. V, pp. 916–919.
2. Thomas P. Lowery, "The Sperryville Outrage," *Civil War Times Illustrated* No. 1, Vol. XXXVIII (March 1999), p. 26; Rhoades, "The Women of Castle Thunder" *The Kudzu Monthly,*

August 2002; and [R.D.W.] "Old Castle Thunder," Richmond *Dispatch,* 3 March 1895.

3. Henley, "Col. George W. Alexander, The Terror of Castle Thunder," p. 49.

4. Testimony of Detective William Causey before the *Committee of Congress,* p. 9, cited in Golden, p. 97; *O.R.,* Ser. I, Vol, 5, p. 877.

5. Lowery, "The Sperryville Outrage," *Civil War Times Illustrated* No. 1, Vol. XXXVIII (March 1999), p. 26. A good picture of prisoners in jackets can be seen in an article by Thomas P. Lowery, "The Sperryville Outrage," and Speer, p. 313.

6. Speer, pp. 319–320

7. Richard F. Hemmerlein, *Prisons and Prisoners of the Civil War* (Boston: Christopher Publishing House, 1934), p. 78.

8. Hemmerlein, p. 77

9. *Ibid.,* p. 78.

10. Speer, p. 319.

11. Hemmerlein, p. 78.

12. Speer, p. 319.

13. J. E. Schaffer, "Treatment of Prisoners at Castle Thunder, Richmond, Va.," *O.R.,* Ser. II, Vol. 5, p. 878.

14. Hemmerlein, pp. 79–80.

15. Speer, p. 319.

16. Hemmerlein, pp. 78–79.

17. "Proceedings of a general Court Martial convened at Richmond by virtue of the following orders — General Orders No. 7, the trial of Private John R. Jones, charged with desertion," Mss3, 67604a, Virginia Historical Society, Richmond, Virginia, hereinafter referred to as DHP.

18. "General Orders, No. 19," Petersburg, Virginia, March 5, 1863, Confederate States Army, Department of Henrico Papers, 1861–1864, DHP.

19. *Ibid.*

20. *Ibid.*

21. "General Orders, No. 12, Petersburg, March 7th, 1864, Before a General Court Martial, Convened at Kinston, North Carolina," electronic edition, online, courtesy of the University of North Carolina at Chapel Hill, Documenting the American South, http://docsouth.unc.edu/imls/csaarmy/csaarmy.html.

22. *Ibid.*

23. *Ibid.*

24. Testimony of V. T. Crawford before the *Committee of Congress,* p. 28, cited in Golden, p. 98; *O.R.,* Ser. II, Vol. 5, p. 895.

25. "Old Castle Thunder," Richmond *Dispatch,* 3 March 1895.

26. Speer, p. 316.

27. Testimony of Detective Robert B. Crow before the *Committee of Congress,* p. 11, cited in Golden, p. 97; *O.R.,* Ser. II, Vol. 5, p. 879.

28. "Old Castle Thunder," Richmond *Dispatch,* 3 March 1895.

29. Testimony of John Caphart, Congressional Investigation, *O.R.,* Ser. II, Vol. 5, p. 876; *Committee of Congress,* p. 7.

30. [R.D.W.] "Old Castle Thunder," Richmond *Dispatch,* 3 March 1895.

31. Lewis Parrish, Master commanding, to Capt. Geo. Alexander, January 25, 1864, DHP.

32. Testimony of Dennis O'Connor, Congressional Investigation, *O.R.,* Ser. II, Vol. 5, pp. 896–897; also cited in Parker, *Richmond's Prisons,* p. 30.

33. "Shot at and Wounded," Richmond *Examiner,* 8 April 1863.

34. Speer, p. 318.

35. Colonel N. T. Colby, "The 'Old Capitol' Prison," in *The Annals of the Civil War Written by Leading Participants North and South,* 1878; rpt. (New York: Da Capo Press, 1994), p. 504.

36. Testimony of John Adams, Congressional Investigation, *O.R.,* Ser. II, Vol. 5, p. 902.

37. Testimony of Detective John Caphart before the *Committee of Congress,* pp. 5–6, cited in Golden, p. 98; *O.R.,* Ser. II, Vol. 5, p. 874.

38. Miller, *Photographic History of the Civil War,* Vol.7, p. 199.

39. Testimony of William Causey, before the *Committee of Congress,* pp. 8–9, cited in Golden, p. 99; *O.R.,* Ser. II, Vol. 5, p. 877.

40. Miller, *Photographic History of the Civil War,* Vol.7, p. 199.

41. Golden, p. 96.

42. J. Holt, Judge Advocate-General, "No. 1. Report of the Judge Advocate-General U.S. Army." March 27, 1863 *O.R.,* Ser. I, Vol. 10, Pt. 1, pp. 630–634.

43. *Ibid.,* pp. 632–633.

44. *Ibid.,* pp. 630–634.

45. "Petition from the survivors of Andrews' party who took the engine on the Georgia State Railroad in April last, to Major-General Bragg, commanding Department No. 2," Atlanta Jail, August 17, 1862, *O.R.,* Ser. I, Vol. 10, Pt. 1, pp. 635–636.

46. J. Holt, Judge Advocate-General, "No. 1. Report of the Judge Advocate-General U.S. Army." March 27, 1863 *O.R.,* Ser. I, Vol. 10, Pt. 1, pp. 630–634.

47. "The Execution of Spencer Kellogg," Richmond *Sentinel,* 26 September 1863.

48. Richmond *Dispatch*, 18, 19, 20 February 1864, cited in Fischer, p. 113–114.
49. *O.R.*, Ser. II, Vol. 7, pp. 93–94, cited in Fischer, p. 79.
50. Richmond *Dispatch*, 5 October 1863, 6 November 1863, cited in Fischer, pp. 79–80.
51. "Castle Thunder Items," Richmond *Examiner*, 9 April 1863.
52. Boatner, pp. 6–7.
53. Gary W. Gallagher, ed. *Fighting for the Confederacy* (Chapel Hill, N.C.: The University of North Carolina Press, 1989), p. 191.
54. *Ibid.*, p. 192.
55. *Ibid.*, pp. 192–193.
56. Henley, "Col. George W. Alexander, The Terror of Castle Thunder," p. 50.
57. *Ibid.*

12. The Congressional Investigation

1. Parker, *Richmond's Prisons*, pp. 28–31; Speer, pp. 124–125.
2. House of Representatives, *Report on the Treatment of Prisoners of War*, p. 1035.
3. Speer, p. 164.
4. "Castle Thunder," Richmond *Sentinel*, April 7, 1863.
5. Parker, *Richmond's Prisons*, pp. 28–31; Speer, p. 124.
6. Radley, p. 236.
7. *Ibid.*, p. 72, citing *O.R.*, Ser. II, Vol, 5, pp. 871–924.
8. Emory M. Thomas, *The Confederate State of Richmond* (Austin, Texas: University of Texas Press, 1971), p. 106
9. "Resolution of the C. S. House of Representatives adopted April 4, 1863," *O.R.*, Ser. II, Vol. 5, p. 886.
10. *Journal of the Confederate Congress*, Sixty-eighth day, Monday, April 6, 1863, online at http://memory.loc.gov.
11. "Treatment of Prisoners in Castle Thunder, Richmond, Virginia, Evidence taken before the committee of the House of Representatives of the Confederate States appointed to inquire into the treatment of prisoners at Castle Thunder," *O.R.*, Ser. II, Vol. 5, pp. 871–924, hereinafter stated as "Evidence."
12. *Ibid.*
13. Congressional Investigation, *O.R.*, Ser. II, Vol. 5, p. 873.
14. Webb Garrison, *The Encyclopedia of Civil War Usage* (Nashville, TN: Cumberland House, 2001), p. 37; Testimony of T. G. Bland, Congressional Investigation, *O.R.*, Ser. II, Vol. 5, p. 873.
15. Testimony of Warden Baldwin T. Allen, Congressional Investigation, *O.R.* Ser. II, Vol. 5, p. 888.
16. Testimony of Detective George W. Thomas, Congressional Investigation, *O.R.*, Ser. II, Vol. 5, p. 882.
17. Testimony of Detective J. F. Schaffer, Congressional Investigation, *O.R.*, Ser. II, Vol. 5, p. 878.
18. Testimony of William Causey, Congressional Investigation, *O.R.*, Ser. II, Vol. 5, p. 872.
19. Testimony of Baldwin T. Allen, Congressional Investigation, *O.R.*, Ser. II, Vol. 5, p. 888.
20. Testimony of T. J. Kirby, Congressional Investigation, *O.R.*, Ser. II, Vol. 5, p. 891.
21. Testimony of Detective J. F. Schaffer, Congressional Investigation, *O.R.*, Ser. II, Vol. 5, p. 872.
22. Testimony of John Caphart, Congressional Investigation, *O.R.*, Ser. II, Vol. 5, p. 874.
23. Testimony of Robert B. Crow, Congressional Investigation, *O.R.*, Ser. II, Vol. 5, p. 873.
24. *Ibid.*, p. 879.
25. Testimony of T. G. Bland, Congressional Investigation, *O.R.*, Ser. II, Vol. 5, p. 873.
26. Testimony of Detective George W. Thomas, Congressional Investigation, *O.R.*, Ser. II, Vol. 5, p. 883.
27. Testimony of Warden Baldwin T. Allen, Congressional Investigation, *O.R.*, Ser. II, Vol. 5, p. 887.
28. *Ibid.*, p. 889.
29. Testimony of Henry Edenborough, Congressional Investigation, *O.R.*, Ser. II, Vol. 5, p. 901.
30. Testimony of T. G. Bland, Congressional Investigation, *O.R.*, Ser. II, Vol. 5, p. 873.
31. Testimony of John Caphart, Congressional Investigation, *O.R.*, Ser. II, Vol. 5, p. 874.
32. Testimony of Detective George W. Thomas, Congressional Investigation, *O.R.*, Ser. II, Vol. 5, p. 884.
33. Testimony of Detective J. F. Schaffer, Congressional Investigation, *O.R.*, Ser. II, Vol. 5, p. 872.
34. Testimony of T. G. Bland, Congressional Investigation, *O.R.*, Ser. II, Vol. 5, p. 873.
35. Testimony of Stephen B. Childrey, Congressional Investigation, *O.R.*, Ser. II, Vol. 5, p. 886.
36. Testimony of Baldwin T. Allen, Congressional Investigation, *O.R.*, Ser. II, Vol. 5, p. 888.

37. Testimony of T. J. Kirby, Congressional Investigation, *O.R.*, Ser. II, Vol. 5, p. 891.
38. Testimony of John Shehan, Congressional Investigation, *O.R.*, Ser. II, Vol. 5, p. 893.
39. Testimony of Marion C. Riggs, Congressional Investigation, *O.R.*, Ser. II, Vol. 5, p. 897.
40. Parker, *Richmond's Prisons*, pp. 28–31; *O.R.*, Vol. 5, pp. 894, 901; Speer, p. 124–125.
41. Testimony of Dennis O'Connor, Congressional Investigation, *O.R.*, Ser. II, Vol. 5, p. 896.
42. Testimony of William Causey, Congressional Investigation, *O.R.*, Ser. II, Vol. 5, p. 872.
43. Testimony of Detective Schaffer, Congressional Investigation, *O.R.*, Ser. II, Vol. 5, p. 879.
44. Testimony of Robert B. Crow, Congressional Investigation, *O.R.*, Ser. II, Vol. 5, p. 873.
45. Testimony of T. G. Bland, Congressional Investigation, *O.R.*, Ser. II, Vol. 5, p. 873.
46. Testimony of Dennis O'Connor, Congressional Investigation, *O.R.*, Ser. II, Vol. 5, p. 897.
47. Testimony of T. J. Kirby, Congressional Investigation, *O.R.*, Ser. II, Vol. 5, p. 891.
48. Testimony of Detective George W. Thomas, Congressional Investigation, *O.R.*, Ser. II, Vol. 5, p. 882.
49. Testimony of John Shehan, Congressional Investigation, *O.R.*, Ser. II, Vol. 5, p. 893.
50. Testimony of Baldwin T. Allen, Congressional Investigation, *O.R.*, Ser. II, Vol. 5, p. 888.
51. Testimony of William Campbell, Congressional Investigation, *O.R.*, Ser. II, Vol. 5, p. 895.
52. Testimony of T. J. Kirby, Congressional Investigation, *O.R.*, Ser. II, Vol. 5, p. 890.
53. Testimony of John Shehan, Congressional Investigation, *O.R.*, Ser. II, Vol. 5, p. 894.
54. Testimony of Marion C. Riggs, Congressional Investigation, *O.R.*, Ser. II, Vol. 5, p. 897.
55. Testimony of T. G. Bland, Congressional Investigation, *O.R.*, Ser. II, Vol. 5, p. 873.
56. Testimony of John Caphart, Congressional Investigation, *O.R.*, Ser. II, Vol. 5, p. 874.
57. Testimony of T. G. Bland, Congressional Investigation, *O.R.*, Ser. II, Vol. 5, p. 880–881.
58. Testimony of Stephen B. Childrey, Congressional Investigation, *O.R.*, Ser. II, Vol. 5, p. 886.
59. Testimony of Baldwin T. Allen, Congressional Investigation, *O.R.*, Ser. II, Vol. 5, p. 889.
60. Testimony of T. G. Bland, Congressional Investigation, *O.R.*, Ser. II, Vol. 5, p. 881–882.
61. Testimony of Dr. Lunday, Congressional Investigation, *O.R.*, Ser. II, Vol. 5, p. 889.
62. Testimony of Detective J. F. Schaffer, Congressional Investigation, *O.R.*, Ser. II, Vol. 5, p. 879.
63. Testimony of Detective George W. Thomas, Congressional Investigation, *O.R.*, Ser. II, Vol. 5, p. 883.
64. Testimony of Baldwin T. Allen, Congressional Investigation, *O.R.*, Ser. II, Vol. 5, p. 887.
65. Testimony of Detective George W. Thomas, Congressional Investigation, *O.R.*, Ser. II, Vol. 5, p. 884.
66. Testimony of Baldwin T. Allen, Congressional Investigation, *O.R.*, Ser. II, Vol. 5, p. 887.
67. Testimony of Stephen B. Childrey, Thomas, Congressional Investigation, *O.R.*, Ser. II, Vol. 5, p. 886.
68. Statement by Captain Alexander, in Testimony of Stephen B. Childrey, Congressional Investigation, *O.R.*, Ser. II, Vol. 5, p. 887.
69. Testimony of John Adams, Congressional Investigation, *O.R.*, Ser. II, Vol. 5, p. 902.
70. Testimony of John Shehan, Congressional Investigation, *O.R.*, Ser. II, Vol. 5, p. 894.
71. Testimony of William Causey, Congressional Investigation, *O.R.*, Ser. II, Vol. 5, p. 878.
72. Testimony of John Adams, Congressional Investigation, *O.R.*, Ser. II, Vol. 5, p. 902.
73. Testimony of Robert Crow, Congressional Investigation, *O.R.*, Ser. II, Vol. 5, p. 879.
74. *Ibid.*
75. Testimony of Stephen B. Childrey, Thomas, Congressional Investigation, *O.R.*, Ser. II, Vol. 5, p. 886.
76. Testimony of William F. Watson, Congressional Investigation, *O.R.*, Ser. II, Vol. 5, p. 904, cited in Robinson, *Justice in Grey*, p. 417, footnote 117.
77. Testimony of T. G. Bland, Congressional Investigation, *O.R.*, Ser. II, Vol. 5, p. 881.
78. Testimony of George W. Thomas, Congressional Investigation, *O.R.*, Ser. II, Vol. 5, p. 883.
79. *Ibid.*
80. Testimony of Baldwin T. Allen, Congressional Investigation, *O.R.*, Ser. II, Vol. 5, p. 887.
81. Testimony of T. J. Kirby, Congressional Investigation, *O.R.*, Ser. II, Vol. 5, p. 890.
82. Testimony of John Shehan, Congressional Investigation, *O.R.*, Ser. II, Vol. 5, p. 894.
83. Testimony of Charlotte Gilman, Congressional Investigation, *O.R.*, Ser. II, Vol. 5, p. 894.

84. Testimony of Marion C. Riggs, Congressional Investigation, *O.R.*, Ser. II, Vol. 5, p. 899.
85. Testimony of Robert Crow, Congressional Investigation, *O.R.*, Ser. II, Vol. 5, p. 879.
86. Testimony of George W. Thomas, Congressional Investigation, *O.R.*, Ser. II, Vol. 5, p. 883.
87. Testimony of T. J. Kirby, Congressional Investigation, *O.R.*, Ser. II, Vol. 5, p. 892.
88. Testimony of Marion C. Riggs, Congressional Investigation, *O.R.*, Ser. II, Vol. 5, p. 898.
89. Testimony of John Caphart, Congressional Investigation, *O.R.*, Ser. II, Vol. 5, pp. 874–875.
90. Testimony of T. G. Bland, Congressional Investigation, *O.R.*, Ser. II, Vol. 5, p. 873.
91. Testimony of T. J. Kirby, Congressional Investigation, *O.R.*, Ser. II, Vol. 5, p. 891.
92. Greenlee Davidson to Capt. G. W. Alexander, Camp Maury, near Milford, April 26, 1863, *O.R.*, Ser. II, Vol. 5, p. 916.
93. Greenlee Davidson to Capt. G. W. Alexander, Camp Maury, near Milford, April 26, 1863, *O.R.*, Ser. II, Vol. 5, p. 916; John H. Winder to Captain Alexander, April 28, 1864, *O.R.*, Ser. II, Vol. 5, p. 916.

13. The Verdict

1. G. W. Alexander, "Captain Alexander's Defense," *O.R.*, Ser. II, Vol. 5, pp. 916–917.
2. *Ibid.*, p. 919.
3. *Ibid.*, p. 917.
4. *Ibid.*
5. *Ibid.*
6. *Ibid.*
7. *Ibid.*, p. 918.
8. *Ibid.*, pp. 918–919.
9. *Ibid.* p. 919.
10. *Ibid.*
11. *Ibid.*, p. 918.
12. *Ibid.*, p. 919.
13. "Old Castle Thunder," Richmond *Dispatch*, 3 March 1895.
14. John H. Winder to Captain Alexander, April 28, 1863, *O.R.*, Ser. II, Vol. 5, p. 916.
15. *Journal of the Confederate Congress*, Ninetieth Day, Friday, May 1, 1863, Volume 6, p. 476, online at http://memory.loc.gov.
16. First Minority Report on the Management of Castle Thunder, *O.R.*, Ser. II, Vol. 5, pp. 920–922.
17. The Majority Report, May 1, 1863, signed by William R. Smith of Alabama, Augustus R. Wright of Georgia, and Daniel C. De Jarnette of Virginia, *O.R.*, Ser. II, Vol. 5, pp. 919–920, cited in Robinson, *Justice in Grey*, p. 417.
18. *O.R.*, Ser. II, Vol. V, pp. 919–924; see also Fischer, p. 60.
19. Parker, *Richmond's Prisons*, p. 33.
20. First Minority Report on the Management of Castle Thunder, *O.R.*, Ser. II, Vol. 5, pp. 920–922.
21. Robinson, *Justice in Grey*, p. 417.
22. "First Minority Report," Congressional Investigation, *O.R.*, Ser. II, Vol. 5, pp. 920–921.
23. *Ibid.*, p. 921.
24. *Ibid.*, p. 922.
25. *Ibid.*
26. "Second Minority Report," Congressional Investigation, *O.R.*, Ser. II, Vol. 5, p. 923.
27. *Ibid.*, pp. 923–924.
28. *Ibid.*, p. 923.
29. *Ibid.*, pp. 923–924.
30. *Ibid.*, p. 924.
31. Robinson, *Justice in Grey*, p. 417.
32. Parker, *Richmond's Prisons*, p. 33.

14. The Washington Adventure

1. G. W. Alexander to Capt. William S. Winder, A.P. Marshal office, Richmond, Virginia, May 8, 1863, DHP.
2. Golden, p. 31; *O.R.*, Ser. II, Vol. 5, pp. 749–750.
3. Edwin M. Stanton to Col. A. B. Jewett, June 6, 1863, *O.R.*, Ser. II, Vol. 5, p. 749.
4. *Ibid.*, pp. 749–750.
5. *Ibid.*, p. 750.
6. *Ibid.*
7. Daniel Moran, "Civil War Spy: The War's Most Dangerous Combatant," Aldie's Civil War Daily, online at www.us-civilwar.com/aldie/spies.html.
8. W. S. Fish to E. M. Stanton, Baltimore, Maryland, June 9, 1863, *O.R.*, Ser. II, Vol. 5, p. 768.
9. J. B. Jones, *A Rebel War Clerk's Diary of the Confederate States Capital*, ed. Howard Swiggett, I, p. 178, cited in Thomas, *The Confederate State of Richmond*, p. 106.
10. *Ibid.*

15. Under Fire Again

1. "Returned to Duty," Richmond *Examiner*, 1 September 1863.

2. "Castle Thunder," Richmond *Sentinel*, 12 September 1863.
3. "City Council," Richmond *Sentinel*, 3 October 1863.
4. Speer, p. 125.
5. "Union and Confederate Correspondence, Orders, etc. Relating to Prisoners of War and State from June 11, 1863 to March 31, 1864 — #18," *O.R.*, Ser. II, Vol. 6, pp. 431–432.
6. Richmond *Sentinel*, 10 November 1863, p. 1, c. 3.
7. Richmond *Sentinel*, 11 November 1863.
8. Richmond *Dispatch*, 17, 18, 19 December 1863, cited in Fischer, p. 61.
9. Richmond *Enquirer*, 16 December 1863; Parker, *Richmond's Prisons*, p. 58.
10. "Malfeasance in Office," Richmond *Sentinel*, 9 December 1863.
11. [R.D.W.], "Old Castle Thunder," Richmond *Dispatch*, 3 March 1895.
12. "Malfeasance in Office," Richmond *Sentinel*, 18 December 1863, p. 1, c. L.
13. Fischer, p. 61.
14. Parker, *Richmond's Prisons*, p. 58.
15. Richmond *Sentinel*, 15 February 1864.
16. Richmond *Dispatch*, 15 February 1864, cited in Fischer, p. 61.
17. [R.D.W.], "Old Castle Thunder," Richmond *Dispatch*, 3 March 1895.
18. *Ibid*.
19. Parker, *Richmond's Prisons*, p. 59
20. *Ibid*.; see also Fischer, p. 61.
21. *O.R.*, Ser. I, Vol. 11, Pt. III, Vol. 33, Vol., 36, Vol. 51, cited in Golden, p. 34.
22. Golden, p. 35.
23. *O.R.*, Ser. I, Vol. 11, Pt. III, p. 107; *O.R.*, Ser. I, Vol. 33, p. 768; *O.R.*, Ser. I, Vol. 36, p. 804; *O.R.*, Ser. II, Vol. 7, pp. 204–207; cited in Parker, *Richmond's Prisons*, p. 59.
24. *O.R.*, Ser. II, Vol. 7, pp. 206–207; Golden, p. 34.
25. *O.R.*, Ser. II, Vol. 7, pp. 206–207; Golden, p. 34.
26. "Rules and Regulations for the Government of Castle Thunder," a broadside in the collection of the Virginia State Library, Richmond, Virginia, cited in Fischer, pp. 44–45.
27. *O.R.*, Ser. II, Vol. 7, pp. 204–205; Golden, p. 35.
28. Golden, p. 35.
29. Browne, *Four Years in Secessia*, pp. 298–299.
30. *O.R.*, Ser. II, Vol. 7, pp. 204–7.

16. 1864

1. Brigadier General J. H. Winder, "Special Order #37," in "the February 15, 1864, notation concerning vouchers refers to Alexander's personal papers.
2. Pay voucher issued to G. W. Alexander, April 1, 1864, Microfilm M331, #3, National Archives, Washington, D.C.
3. "Danville Prison," online at www.wtvzone.com/civilwar/danville.html.
4. Patricia B. Mitchell, "'Truly Horrible' Danville Civil War Prisons," *The Pittsylvania Packet*, Pittsylvania Historical Society (Spring 1993), pp. 12–13.
5. Samuel S. Boggs, *Eighteen Months a Prisoner under the Rebel Flag* (Livington, Ill.: privately published, 1887), cited in Mitchell, "'Truly Horrible' Danville Civil War Prisons," p. 12.
6. Abner Small, 16th Maine Volunteer Regiment, cited in "Danville Prison," online at www.wtv-zone.com/civilwar/danville.html. See Abner Ralph Small, *The Road to Richmond: The Civil War Memoirs of Major Abner R. Small of the Sixteenth Main Volunteers, together with the diary that he kept when he was a prisoner of war*, with an introduction by Earl J. Hess (New York: Fordham University Press, 2000).
7. Small, *The Road to Richmond*, pp. 168–169.
8. *O.R.*, Ser. II, Vol. 7, p. 227, cited in Louis A. Brown, *The Salisbury Prison: A Case Study of Confederate Military Prisons 1861–1865* (Wilmington, NC: Broadfoot Publishing Co., 1992), p. 190.
9. Radley, p. 165.
10. "Interrogation Statements," Record Group 249, Entry 131, National Archives, Washington, D.C.; Richmond *Dispatch*, 19, 20 July 1864, 24 August 1864.
11. "Castle Thunder," Richmond *Sentinel*, 14 April 1864; "The Castle," Richmond *Whig*, 14 April 1864.
12. "Castle Thunder Items," Richmond *Examiner*, 7 May 1864.
13. Browne, *Four Years in Secessia*, pp. 315–361, cited in Yearns and G. Barrett, *North Carolina Civil War Documentary*, p. 121.
14. Chaplain A. W. Magnum, "Salisbury Prison," in Walter Clark, ed. *Histories of the Several Regiments and Battalions from North Carolina in the Great War, 1861–1865, Written by Members of the Respective Command*, Vol. 5, (Goldsboro, N.C.: Nash Brothers, 1901), p. 745.

15. Magnum, "Salisbury Prison," p. 745.
16. Robert E. Eberly, Jr. "Prison Town," *Civil War Times Illustrated*, No. 1, Vol. XXXVIII (March 1999), pp. 30–31.
17. Booth and Meyer, *Dark Days of the Rebellion*, p. 87
18. *Ibid.*, p. 95.
19. Mangum, "Salisbury Prison," pp. 745–772.
20. *Ibid.*, 746–747
21. *Ibid.*, p. 747
22. Eberly, pp. 30–31.
23. George B. Kirsch, "Bats, Balls, and Bullets: Baseball and the Civil War." *Civil War Times Illustrated* No. II, Vol. XXXVII (May 1998), pp. 32–33.
24. "Salisbury Confederate Prison," online at www.ci.salisbury.nc.us/prison/csprison1.htm.
25. Mangum, "Salisbury Prison," p. 751.
26. Brown, *The Salisbury Prison*, p. 190; "Prison Personnel Commandants," online at www.salisburyprison.org; Salisbury Confederate Prison Association, "Prison History," online at www.salisburyprison.org.
27. "Prison Personnel Commandants," online at www.salisburyprison.org.
28. Brown, *The Salisbury Prison*, p. 29.
29. Mangum, p. 748.
30. *Ibid.*, p. 751.
31. *Ibid.*, p.752.
32. Booth and Meyer, p. 95.
33. *Ibid.*
34. *Ibid.*
35. Mangum, "Salisbury Prison," pp. 751–752.
36. *Ibid.*, p. 752.
37. Browne, *Four Years in Secessia*, cited in Yearns and Barrett, p. 121.
38. Jeffrey, *Richmond's Prisons*, p. 157.
39. Small, *The Road to Richmond*, p. 164–165
40. *Ibid.*, p. 165.
41. *Ibid.*, p. 66.
42. Booth and Meyer, *Dark Days of the Rebellion*, p. 95–96.
43. Jeffrey, *Richmond's Prisons*, p. 154.
44. Small, *The Road to Richmond*, p. 166.
45. *Ibid.*
46. "A. D. Richardson's Experiences in the Confederacy," cited in Brown, *The Salisbury Prison*, pp. 198–199.
47. Jeffrey, *Richmond's Prisons*, p. 154.
48. Mangum, "Salisbury Prison," pp. 751–752.
49. Jeffrey, *Richmond's Prisons*, p. 158.

50. "A.D. Richardson's Experiences in the Confederacy," cited in Brown, *The Salisbury Prison*, pp. 198–199.
51. Brown, "The Salisbury Prison," p. 31.
52. Jeffrey, *Richmond's Prisons*, p. 155.
53. Carolina *Watchman*, 25 July 1864; diary William Francis Tiemann, Rowan County Public Library, p. 13, cited in Brown, *The Salisbury Prison*, p. 31.
54. Brown, *The Salisbury Prison*, p. 30.
55. *O.R.*, Ser. II, Vol. 7, p. 401–402.
56. "List of Officers and Attachees at the Confederate States Military Prison, Salisbury, N.C.," Salisbury *Watchman*, June 18, 1864, p. 1.
57. *Ibid.*
58. G. W. Alexander to Col. John Withers, Salisbury, N.C., June 11, 1864, *O.R.*, Ser. II, Vol. 7, p. 227.
59. *Ibid.*
60. Cleve Horton Cox, "Salisbury: The Confederate Prison of General Stoneman, 1860–1865," typescript, n.d., Rowan Public Library, Salisbury, North Carolina; "New Commandant of the Prison," Salisbury *Watchman*, 18 June 1864.
61. "New Commandant of the Prison," Salisbury *Watchman*, 18 June 1864.
62. Mangum, "Salisbury Prison," pp. 753–754.
63. *O.R.*, Ser. II, Vol. 7, pp. 674–675, cited in Louis A. Brown, *The Salisbury Prison: A Case Study of Confederate Military Prisons 1861–1865*, p. 190.
64. Brown, *The Salisbury Prison*, p. 74–75.
65. Browne, *Four Years in Secessia*, p. 318–319.
66. Mangum, "Salisbury Prison," pp. 751–752.
67. *Ibid.*, pp. 751–752.
68. *Ibid.*, pp. 752–753.
69. *Ibid.*, p. 753.
70. Small, *Road to Richmond*, pp. 167–168.
71. Booth and Myer, *Dark Days of the Rebellion*, p. xi, viii.
72. "The Court-martial of Major John H. Gee, Commandant Salisbury Confederate Prison," online at www.geocities.com/ageeford2002/index.html.

17. The Final Months of the War

1. "Castle Thunder Items," Richmond *Examiner*, 30 June 1864.
2. Lt. Col. Archer Anderson to General Braxton Bragg, Richmond, Va, June 6, 1864,

"Inspection report for the week ending May 31," *O.R.*, Ser. II, Vol. 7, p. 205.

3. *Ibid.*

4. Boatner, p. 940–941.

5. "Hospital and Prison Inspection," *Richmond Examiner*, 30 May 1864.

6. Lt. Col. Archer Anderson to General Braxton Bragg, Richmond, Va., June 6, 1864, "Inspection report for the week ending May 31," *O.R.*, Ser. II, Vol. 7, pp.205–206.

7. "Castle Thunder Items," *Richmond Examiner*, 30 June 1864.

8. Lt. Col. Archer Anderson to General Braxton Bragg, June 6, 1864, *O.R.*, Ser. II, Vol. 7, p. 206.

9. *Ibid.*

10. *Ibid.*

11. *Ibid.*

12. C. McRae Selph, Assistant Adjutant and Inspector General, to Col. R. H. Chilton, Richmond, Va., June 6, 1864. *O.R.*, Ser. II, Vol. 7, pp. 204–205.

13. "Chronological List of Military Career of George W. Alexander," Microfilm M331, #3, National Archives, Washington, D.C.

14. Boatner, "Gardner, William Montgomery," p. 323.

15. *O.R.*, Ser. II, Vol. 7, p. 1169, cited in Brown, *The Salisbury Prison*, p. 190,

16. Boatner, p. 323.

17. Lieutenant General R. S. Ewell to Col. W. H. Taylor, Richmond, Va., July 11, 1864, *O.R.*, Ser. I, Vol. 40, Pt. III, pp, 764–765.

18. "To Go to Salisbury," Richmond *Examiner*, 15 July 1864.

19. Boatner, "Barton, Seth Maxwell," p. 48–49.

20. George W. Alexander to Gen. S. Cooper, Hdqrs. Barton's Brigade, near Fort Gilmer, November 28, 1864. Personal papers of G. W. Alexander, on Microfilm M331, #3, National Archives, Washington, D.C.

21. Crute, *Confederate Staff Officers, 1861–1865*, p. 212.

22. Boatner, p. 940–941.

23. Franklin *Repository* (Chambersburg, Pa.), 22 February 1865.

24. John C. Breckinridge, Secretary of War, to Col. R. Ould, March 8, 1865, *O.R.*, Ser. II, Vol. 8, p. 368.

25. Robert Ould to John C. Breckinridge, Secretary of War, March 8, 1865, *O.R.*, Ser. II, Vol. 8, p. 368.

26. E. O. C. Ord to General Rawlings, March 9, 1865, *O.R.*, Ser. I, Vol 46, Pt. II, p. 905.

27. Harrison, *Prisoners' Mail from the American Civil War*, p. 94.

28. "A Remarkable Case," Richmond *Whig*, 12 April 1865.

29. Edward A. Pollard, "The Evacuation and Fall of Richmond," in Greeley, Horace, *The American Conflict: A History of the Great Rebellion in the United States of America, 1860-'64; Its causes, incidents, and results; intended to exhibit especially its moral and political phases, with the drift and progress of American opinion respecting human slavery, from 1776 to the close of the War for the Union*. Vol 2. Hartford: O. D. Case & Company; Chicago: Geo. & C. W. Sherwood, 1865–1866. America, 1865, p.273.

30. Pollard, pp. 274–275.

31. A. A. and Mary Hoehling, *The Day Richmond Died* (New York: A. S. Barnes and Company, Inc., 1981), p. 114; 1st Regimental Reserves Report, Virginia Militia Infantry, April 2, 1865, Virginia Historical Society, Richmond, Virginia, cited in Fischer, p. 115–116.

32. Pollard, p. 277.

33. C. A. Dana to Edwin M. Stanton, Richmond, Va., April 5, 1865, *O.R.*, Ser. I, Vol. 46, Pt. III, p. 97.

34. Hoehling, pp. 211, 236.

35. *Ibid.*, 236, cited in Fischer, p. 116.

36. C. A. Dana to Edwin M. Stanton, Richmond, Va., April 5, 1865, *O.R.*, Ser. I, Vol. 46, Pt. III, p. 97.

37. Richmond *Whig*, 10 April 1865.

38. "Mr. Theodore C. Wilson's Despatches," New York *Herald*, 13 April 1865.

39. "That Big Black Dog," Richmond *Whig*, 1 May 1865.

40. "President Lincoln Enters Richmond, 1865." EyeWitness — history through the eyes of those who lived it. Online at www.ibiscom.com (2000).

41. "Delivered Themselves Up," Richmond *Whig*, 18 April 1865.

42. "Paroled," Richmond *Whig*, 19 April 1865.

43. R. A. Brock, *The Appomattox Roster*, (1887, rpt. New York: Antiquarian Press, Ltd., 1962).

44. *O.R.*, Ser. III, Vol, 5. Pp. 531–532.

45. "The Printing of the Paroles," online at www.nps.gov/apco/chtparol.htm.

18. After the Surrender

1. John T. Trowbridge, *The South: A Tour of its Battle-fields and Ruined Cities, a Journal Through the Desolated States, and Talks with the*

People; Being a Description of the Present State of the Country — Its Agriculture — Railroads — Business and Finances..., (Hartford: Connecticut: L. Steebins, 1866), p. 153.

2. "Libby Prison Now and Then," Dedham *Gazette,* 20 May 1865, pg. 1, col. 3.

3. "Empty Prisons," Richmond *Whig,* 31 May 1865.

4. Richmond *Whig,* 19 May 1865.

5. Burrows, Rev, J. L. "Recollections of Libby Prison." *Southern Historical Society Papers,* Vol. XI, Richmond, Va., Feb.-March, 1883, No. 2 & 3, pp. 90–91.

6. Richmond *Whig,* 19 May 1865; Speer, *Portals to Hell,* p. 287.

7. Richmond *Whig,* May 19, 1865.

8. Putnam, *A Prisoner of War in Virginia, 1864–5,* pp. 28–29.

9. *Herald and Torch Light* [Hagerstown, Maryland], 27 September 1865.

10. Parker, *Richmond's Prisons,* pp. 67–68; "Blood Hounds!" Broadside, Virginia Historical Society; Fischer, pp. 116–117.

11. Richmond *Whig* 9 May 1865.

12. Putnam, *A Prisoner of War,* p. 29; New York *Times,* May 24, 1865, p. 4, col. 6. Parker, *Richmond's Prisons,* p. 68, cited in Speer, p. 287.

13. "The Key of Castle Thunder," Richmond *Whig,* 1 May 1865.

14. "Northeast Auctions August 19–20, 2000, Lots 1–125," *Maine Antique Digest,* cited in Rhoades, "The Women of Castle Thunder," *The Kudzu Monthly,* August 2002.

15. "Arrest of the Late Provost Marshal of Richmond," Richmond *Whig,* 16 May 1865.

16. New York *Times,* July 14, 1865, cited in Hesseltine, *Civil War Prisons,* p. 238.

17. New York *Tribune,* 11 July, 12 August, and 22 August 1865.

18. Boatner, p. 942; Hesseltine, *Civil War Prisons,* pp. 237–238.

19. *National Intelligencer,* August 20, 1865, cited in Hesseltine, pp. 239–240.

20. *O.R.,* Ser. II, Vol. 8, pp. 785–789, also cited in Hesseltine, *Civil War Prisons,* pp. 240–241.

21. *O.R.,* Ser. II, Vol. 8, p. 776, cited in Hesseltine, *Civil War Prisons,* p. 244.

22. *O.R.,* Ser. II, Vol. 8, pp. 790–791, 773–774, cited in Hesseltine, *Civil War Prisons,* p. 244.

23. *O.R.,* Ser. II, Vol. 8, p. 796–798, 815, 817, 819–20, 834, cited in Hesseltine, pp. 245–246.

24. P. Cashmyer to Col. N. P. Chipman, October 12, 1865, *O.R.,* Ser. II, Vol. 8, pp. 764–765.

25. *Ibid.,* p. 765.

26. J. Holt, Judge Advocate General, to E. M. Stanton, Secretary of War, November 3, 1865, *O.R.,* Ser. II, Vol. 5, pp. 782–783.

27. *O.R.,* Ser. II, Vol. 8, pp. 552–553; also cited in Hesseltine, p. 246.

28. *O.R.,* Ser. II, Vol. 8, pp. 782–783, 881, 956–960; also cited in Hesseltine, p. 246.

29. *O.R.,* Ser. II, Vol. 8, pp. 926–928, and note; also cited in Hesseltine, p. 246.

30. Speer, *Portals to Hell,* p. 293.

31. Hesseltine, pp. 247–248.

32. James D. Richardson, ed. *A Compilation of the Messages and Papers of the Presidents, 1789–1897,* Vol. 6 (Washington, D.C.: Government Printing Office, 1896–1899), pp. 310–312.

33. Avery Craven, *Reconstruction: The Ending of the Civil War* (New York: Holt, Rinehart, Winston), 1968), p. 88–89.

34. Richardson, James, D., pp. 310–312.

35. *Special Presidential Pardons for Confederate Soldiers: A Listing of Former Confederate Soldiers Requesting Pardon from President Andrew Johnson,* 2 vols. (Signal Mountain, Tenn.: Mountain Press, 1999).

36. "Historical Survey of U.S. Amnesty," United States Army Military History Institute, Reference Branch, Carlisle, Pennsylvania.

37. "Major Turner's Escape: How the ex-Commandant of Famous Libby Prison Fled to Cuba. His Experiences told by Himself," New York *Times,* 7 July 1895, online at: www.mdgorman.com/NYC-Papers/new_york_times_771895.htm.

38. *Ibid.*

39. Jubal Anderson Early, *Lieutenant General Jubal Anderson Early, C.S.A.: Autobiographical Sketch and Narrative of the War between the States* (Philadelphia; London: J. B. Lippincott Company, 1912), picture on page facing p. 464.

40. "Major Turner's Escape: How the ex-Commandant of Famous Libby Prison Fled to Cuba. His Experiences told by Himself," New York *Times,* 7 July 1895, online at: www.mdgorman.com/NYC-Papers/new_york_times_771895.htm.

41. "Old Castle Thunder," Richmond *Dispatch,* 3 March 1895.

19. 1870–1890

1. House of Representatives, Report No. 65, *Report on the Treatment of Prisoners of War by Rebel Authorities During the War of the Rebellion,*

40th Congress, 3rd Session, (Washington: GPO, 1869), p. 21.

2. "Arrival and Departure of Prisoners," Richmond *Sentinel*, 6 May 1863.

3. "Treatment of Prisoners," *Southern Historical Society Papers*, Vol. 1, No. 3 (March 1876), pp. 216–218.

4. "Treatment of Prisoners," *Southern Historical Society Papers*, Vol. 1, No. 3 (March 1876), pp. 216–218.

5. "Discussion of the Prison Question," *Southern Historical Society Papers*, Vol. III, No. 4 (April 1877), pp. 187–214.

6. John Mack Faragher, ed., *Encyclopedia of American History* (New York: Henry Holt and Company, 1998), p. 36.

7. Schlessinger, Arthur M., Jr., ed., *The Almanac of American History* (New York: G. P. Putnam and Sons, 1883), p. 321.

8. *Journal of the Senate of the United States of America*, Vol. 67, which can be seen online at the Library of Congress site, American Images: A Century of Lawmaking for a New Nation: U.S. Congressional Documents and Debates, 1774–1875.

9. Newspapers in the Library of Virginia's database. See catalog card at http://eagle.vsla.edu/cgi-bin/newspaper.gateway?authority=0003-77080conf=010000++.

10. Wilhelmus Bogart Bryan, *Bibliography of the District of Columbia being a list of books, maps, and newspapers, including articles in magazines and other publications to 1898* (Washington: Government Printing Office, 1900), pp.178, 201.

11. Online catalogue of the American Antiquarian Society, http://www.americanantiquarian.org; and http://catalog.mwa.org.

12. "The Late John C. Proctor, *The Evening Star* 14 July 1876.

13. *The military-prison keepers of the late Southern Confederacy in the van of the Democratic Party*. Washington, D.C.: National Republican Congressional Executive Committee, 1876, 8 pages, microfiche, The Library of Virginia, Richmond, Virginia.

14. *Ibid.*

15. "A Brave Confederate," Baltimore *Sun*, February 22, 1895; Robert E. L. Krick, *Staff Officers in Gray: A Biographical Register of the Staff Officers in the Army of Northern Virginia* (Chapel Hill, N.C.: University of North Carolina Press, 2003), p. 59.

16. United States Government, Bureau of the Census, 1880 Federal Census of Population, Maryland, National Archives film #T9–0501, page 290C.

17. "Old Castle Thunder," Richmond *Dispatch*, 3 March 1895.

18. "Monument Avenue," online at www.monumenthouse.com/richmond/monument.

19. "A Brave Confederate," Baltimore *Sun*, 22 February 1895; "Old Castle Thunder," Richmond *Dispatch*, 3 March 1895.

20. "Residents of Laurel, Maryland, Taken from Special Canvass made by Ross & Fairall, August 1894," in Gertrude Poe, ed. *Laurel, Maryland: Souvenir Historical Booklet. 1870 Centennial 1970* (Privately published by the City of Laurel, Maryland, 1970), pp. 29–39; Susan G. Pearl, Historian, Prince George's County Historical Society, to Frances H. Casstevens, in personal communication via e-mail March 22, 2003, and March 29, 2003.

21. "Prince George's County, Maryland, Directory—1878," online version at www.ls.net/~newriver/md/pg1878.htm.

Epilogue

1. "Richmond Since the War," *Scribner's Monthly, an illustrated magazine for the people*, Vol. 14, No. 3 (July 1877), p. 303.

2. Christopher Silver, "The Ordeal of City Planning in Postwar Richmond, Virginia: A Quest for Greatness," *Journal of Urban History*, Vol. 10, No. 1 (November 1983), pp. 33–60.

3. "Richmond Since the War," *Scribner's Monthly, an illustrated magazine for the people*, Vol. 14, No. 3 (July 1877), p. 303.

4. "The Old and New," Richmond *Dispatch*, 30 June 1894.

5. "Richmond Since the War," *Scribner's Monthly, an illustrated magazine for the people*, Vol. 14, No. 3 (July 1877), pp. 303–305.

6. "Location of 'Castle Thunder,'" Richmond *News Leader*, 30 March 1946.

7. Parker, *Richmond's Prisons*, p. 68.

8. Krick, *Staff Officers in Gray: A Biographical Register of the Staff Officers in the Army of Northern Virginia*, p. 290.

9. Obituary of Richard (Zarvona) Thomas, *The St. Mary's Beacon*, March 25, 1875, v12:23, p. 2, c4; Earp, "The Amazing Colonel Zarvona," p. 342.

10. Earp, "The Amazing Colonel Zarvona," p. 343.

11. Obituary of Richard (Zarvona) Thomas, *The St. Mary's Beacon*, March 25, 1875, v12:23,

p. 2, c4.; Obituary, Baltimore *Sun*, 26 March 1875.

12. Personal communication via e-mail from Beatrix B. Hardy, France-Merrick Deputy Director for the Library, Maryland Historical Society to Frances H. Casstevens, June 30, 2003.

13. "A Brave Confederate," Baltimore *Sun*, 22 February 1895; "Old Castle Thunder," Richmond *Dispatch*, 3 March 1895.

14. Susan G. Pearl, Historian, Prince George's County Historical Society, to Frances H. Casstevens, personal communication via e-mail March 22, 2003; Sargeant, Jean A., ed. *Stones and Bones, Tombstone Inscriptions of Prince George's County, Maryland* (Bowie, Md.: Prince George's County Genealogical Society, Inc., 1984), p. 484.

15. Sons of Confederate Veterans, Maryland Line Camp #1741, "Maryland Confederate Burial Sites in Prince George's County," online at www.mdscv.org/mdline08.htm.

16. Prince George's County, Maryland, Wills, CM 816, CR 11293, pp. 236–238. Maryland Archives, Annapolis, Maryland.

17. Bureau of the Census. Twelfth Census of the United States, Census Microfilm Records: Delaware, District of Columbia, Maryland, 1900. Baltimore County, Maryland, Roll 616, Book 1, page 240a. Online at www.genealogy.com.

18. "Incident of the War of the Rebellion: How a Confederate Officer Escaped from a Union Prison," New York *Times*, 23 February 1895, p. 3, c. 7.

19. Correspondence from Bob Marks, Commander, Maryland Line Camp 1741, Sons of Confederate Veterans, and Quartermaster of the Maryland Division, Sons of Confederate Veterans, June 30, 2002.

Appendix 1

1. Testimony of Frederick F. Wiley, Congressional hearings, *O.R.*, Ser. II, Vol. 5, p. 910.

2. Richmond *Dispatch*, 30 April 1863.

3. Reeves Addcock to Major, Castle Thunder, 2nd Floor, no date. Confederate States of America, Department of Henrico Papers, 1861–1864, Mss3, 67604a, Virginia Historical Society, Richmond, Virginia. Hereinafter cited as DHP.

4. Richmond *Sentinel*, 30 March 1865.

5. William A. Allen to Capt. G. W. Alexander, June 30, 1863, DHP.

6. List of Prisoners sent from Camp Holmes (Conscript Camp of Instruction) near Raleigh, N.C., on the 16th of October 1863, by Col. Peter Mallett to Castle Thunder, DHP.

7. Manarin and Jordan, *North Carolina Troops*. Vol. VI, p. 108.

8. Richmond *Enquirer*, 5 September 1862; J. A. Campbell to Brig. Gen. J. H. Winder, December 16, 1862, *O. R.*, Ser. II, Vol. V, p. 787.

9. "The Slaves at Castle Thunder," Richmond *Sentinel*, 28 August 1863.

10. "Prisoners from Western Virginia," Richmond *Examiner*, 11 May 1863.

11. "The Slaves at Castle Thunder," Richmond *Sentinel*, 28 August 1863.

12. *O.R.*, Ser. I, Vol. 43, Pt. III, p. 79.

13. John Atkinson to Gen. Winder, Richmond, May 9, 1863, DHP.

14. William L. Aughinbaugh, Journal, 1862–1863, Schoff Civil War Collection, William L. Clements Library, the University of Michigan, Ann Arbor, Michigan.

15. Henry Avery to Major Carrington, Castle Thunder, November 20, 1863, DHP.

16. "The Slaves at Castle Thunder," Richmond *Sentinel*. 28 August 1863.

17. Richmond *Dispatch*, 30 April 1863.

18. R. Henry Glenn to Capt. N. Stark, June 6, 1863, and list of prisoners made by W. S. Pilcher after visit to Castle Thunder, June 5, 1863, DHP.

19. List of Prisoners sent from Camp Holmes near Raleigh, N.C., on the 12th of October 1863, by Col. Peter Mallett to Castle Thunder, DHP.

20. H. T. Barton to Capt. Alexander, General Hospital, No. 13, October 25, 1863, DHP.

21. G. W. Lee, Commander Military Post, Atlanta Ga, to Brigadier-General Winder, December 3, 1862, *O.R.*, Ser. II, Vol. 5, p. 777–778.

22. "2nd Tennessee Infantry Regiment, U.S.A.: Complete Roster," compiled from information in the National Archives, online at: http://home.cinci.rr.com/secondtennessee/roster.html.

23. G. W. Lee, Commander Military Post, Atlanta Ga, to Brigadier-General Winder, December 3, 1862, *O.R.*, Ser. II, Vol. 5, p. 777–778.

24. Charles T. Barnes to Maj. Carrington, Castle Thunder, January 21, 1864, DHP.

25. Richmond *Dispatch*, 20 September 1862.

26. Timothy Barrett to General Winder, Richmond, November 26, 1863, letter from Capt. John J. Revena, DHP.

27. Richard Barry to Captain Stark, Castle Thunder, June 1, 1863, DHP.
28. Obituary of Alonzo J. Barton, the *Baron Shield*, Baron County, Wisconsin, 19 October 1888.
29. List of Deserters arrested in 1st Cong. District, unsigned, December 12, 1863, DHP.
30. Richmond *Dispatch*, 31 October 1864, cited in Fischer, p. 38.
31. Rhoades, "The Women of Castle Thunder," *Kudzuu Monthly*, August 2002.
32. Capt. Thomas R. Thornton to Capt. Richardson, January 14, 1864, DHP.
33. Letter to Gen. John H. Winder, February 28, 1864, DHP.
34. Brigadier General J. D. Imboden, indorsement on bottom of letter from Lt. J. R. Nunn, Provost Marshal to Governor William Smith, Harrisburg, Va., March 30, 1864, *O.R.*, Ser. II, Vol. 6, pp. 1119–1120.
35. "At the Castle," Richmond *Examiner*, 9 June 1864.
36. Levi Bennett to Brig. Gen. J. H. Winder, Castle Thunder, January 11, 1864, DHP.
37. *O.R.*, Ser. I, Vol. 10, Pt. 1, pp. 630–636; G. W. Lee, Commander Military Post, Atlanta, Ga., to Brigadier-General Winder, December 3, 1862, *O.R.*, Ser. II, Vol. 5, p. 777–778.
38. Manarin and Jordan, *North Carolina Troops*, Vol. XIII, p. 507.
39. Query posted on 15 April 2000, and 11 December 1999, to Ancestry Message Boards by Steve Peters.
40. Richmond *Dispatch*, 22 November 1862, 25 November 1862, cited in Fischer, p. 30.
41. "Escape of Prisoners—Sentinel Killed," Richmond *Whig*, 23 October 1863.
42. "Murder at Castle Thunder," Richmond *Sentinel*, 23 October 1863.
43. Richmond *Sentinel*, 25 March 1863, p. 2, c.3.
44. Lucian L. _____, Capt. Company G, 25th Virginia Battalion, to Commandant, Castle Thunder, January (or June) 10, 1864.
45. Richmond *Dispatch*, 10 September 1862.
46. List of Prisoners sent from Camp Holmes (Conscript Camp of Instruction) near Raleigh, N.C., on the 12th October 1863, by Col. Peter Mallett to Castle Thunder, DHP.
47. "Cases at the Castle," Richmond *Examiner*, 4 June 1864.
48. W. N. Starke, "Union Correspondence, Orders, etc. Relating to Prisoners of War and State from December 1, 1862 to June 10, 1863," Sixth Endorsement, May 13, 1863, *O.R.*, Ser. II, Vol. 5, pp. 518–520.
49. I. J. Wistar to Major-General Butler, Fort Magruder, February 8, 1864, *O.R.*, Ser. I, Vol. 33, p. 144.
50. "An Impudent Scamp," Richmond *Enquirer*, 14 August 1863.
51. Benjamin F. Butler to Robert Ould, December 25, 1863, *O.R.*, Ser. II, Vol. 6, p. 756.
52. Richmond *Enquirer*, 16 December 1862.
53. "South Carolina 1st (Hagood's) Infantry Regiment, Company I (After Reorganization)," online listing www.researchonlne.net/sccw/rosters/1sthagi2.htm.
54. Rutherford B. Hayes Presidential Center, Civil War Soldier Database, online www.rbhayes.org/databases/soldiers/soldiers/452.htm.
55. Obituary for Simon Broseus, submitted by Linda B. Myers, Perry County, Ohio, Obituaries, online at www:kneller.com/records/obituaries/0002.htm.
56. Richmond *Sentinel*, 9 April 1864, p. 2, c. 4.
57. List of Prisoners sent from Camp Holmes near Raleigh, N.C., on the 12th of October 1863, by Col. Peter Mallett to Castle Thunder, DHP.
58. Manarin and Jordan, *North Carolina Troops*, Vol. IV, p. 57.
59. List of Prisoners sent from Camp Holmes (Conscript Camp of Instruction) near Raleigh, N.C., on the 16th October 1863, by Col. Peter Mallett to Castle Thunder, DHP.
60. "2nd Tennessee Infantry Regiment, U.S. A.: Complete Roster," compiled from information in the National Archives, online at: http://home.cinci.rr. com/secondtennessee/roster.html.
61. Rutherford B. Hayes Presidential Center, Civil War Soldier Database, online www.rbhayes.org/databases/soldiers/soldiers/465.htm.
62. "Put in the Castle," Richmond *Sentinel*, 26 May 1864.
63. "Prisoners from Western Virginia," Richmond *Examiner*, 11 May 1863.
64. Browne, *Four Years in Secessia*, pp. 295–306.
65. Parker, *Richmond's Prisons*, p. 36.
66. *Ibid.*; Browne, *Four Years in Sesessia*, p. 304.
67. *O.R.*, Ser. I, Vol. 10, Pt. 1, pp. 630–636; G. W. Lee, Commander Military Post, Atlanta, Ga., to Brigadier-General Winder, December 3, 1862, *O.R.*, Ser. II, Vol. 5, p. 777–778.
68. Richmond *Examiner*, 10 November 1862.
69. Manarin and Jordan, *North Carolina Troops*, Vol. III, p. 568.

70. George W. Burke to General Winder, Castle Thunder, February 23, 1863, DHP.

71. R. Henry Glenn to Capt. N. Stark, June 6, 1863, and list of prisoners made by W. S. Pilcher after visit to Castle Thunder, June 5, 1863, DHP.

72. Manarin and Jordan, *North Carolina Troops,* Vol. VII, p. 483.

73. R. Henry Glenn to Capt. N. Stark, June 6, 1863, and list of prisoners made by W. S. Pilcher after visit to Castle Thunder, June 5, 1863, DHP.

74. List of Prisoners sent from Camp Holmes near Raleigh, N.C., on the 12th October 1863, by Col. Peter Mallett to Castle Thunder, DHP; and Manarin and Jordan, *North Carolina Troops,* Vol. V, p. 98.

75. 2nd Lieut. S. Van de Graaff to Capt. Alexander, CS Navy Yard, June 12, 1863, DHP.

76. Richmond *Examiner,* 14 March 1863.

77. Michael C. Burns to General Winder, Castle Thunder, July 3, 1863, DHP.

78. "Roster of Company G personnel—Emmett Guards," from "17th Virginia Infantry" by Lee A. Wallace, Jr. Online at http://stevegibson0.tripod.com/co.__g.htm.

79. List of Prisoners sent from Camp Holmes near Raleigh, N.C., on the 16th of October 1863, by Col. Peter Mallett to Castle Thunder, DHP.

80. Manarin and Jordan, *North Carolina Troops,* Vol. XIII, p. 288–289.

81. "Castle Thunder," Richmond *Examiner,* 17 June 1864.

82. Manarin and Jordan, *North Carolina Troops,* Vol. VI, p. 39.

83. Richmond *Examiner,* 14 March 1863.

84. "Killed While Attempting to Escape," Richmond *Examiner,* 7 April 1863, p. 1.

85. Testimony of William Campbell, Congressional Investigation, *O.R.* Ser. II, Vol. 5, pp. 894–895.

86. "Changed Sides," Richmond *Examiner,* 23 June 1864.

87. Oscar R. Hough, Adjutant, to Capt. G. W. Alexander, Richmond, October 2, 1863, DHP.

88. "Escape of Prisoners—Sentinel Killed," Richmond *Whig,* 23 October 1863; *Weekly Standard,* Raleigh, N.C., 28 October 1863.

89. Jno. A. Carper to General Winder, Castle Thunder, June 15, 1863, DHP.

90. Richmond *Sentinel,* April 7, 1863; "Killed While Attempting to Escape," Richmond *Examiner,* 7 April 1863, p. 1.

91. "Sent Away to Salisbury," Richmond *Examiner,* 4 August 1864.

92. "Put in the Castle," Richmond *Sentinel,* 26 May 1864.

93. "Released from the Castle," Richmond *Sentinel,* 2 June 1864.

94. Major John D. Munford to Maj. I. H. Carrington, Richmond, December 24, 1864, *O.R.,* Ser. II, Vol. 7, pp. 1268–1269.

95. John A. Castleman to Brig. Gen. John H. Winder, Richmond, June 14, 1863, DHP.

96. "Castle Thunder," Richmond *Examiner,* 17 June 1864.

97. "Trading with Yankees," Richmond *Enquirer,* 9 October 1863.

98. "The Slaves of Castle Thunder," Richmond *Sentinel,* 28 August 1863.

99. "Escape of Prisoners—Sentinel Killed," Richmond *Whig,* 23 October 1863.

100. William G. Cutler, *History of the State of Kansas,* Biographical Sketches, Part 7, Riley County, online www.kancoll.org/books/cutler/riley/riley-co-p7.htm.

101. "Escaped," Richmond *Whig,* 6 April 1865.

102. Richmond *Sentinel,* 9 April 1864, p. 2, c. 4.

103. Edwin L. Ferguson, *Sumner County, Tennessee in the Civil War,* privately published, 1972, online at www.rootsweb.com/~tnsumner/sumnfg4.htm.

104. "Escape of Prisoners—Sentinel Killed," Richmond *Whig,* 23 October 1863.

105. List of Prisoners sent from Camp Holmes near Raleigh, N.C., on the 16th October 1863, by Col. Peter Mallett to Castle Thunder, DHP; Manarin and Jordan, *North Carolina Troops,* Vol. XIII, p. 289.

106. "Prisoners from Western Virginia," Richmond *Examiner,* 11 May 1863.

107. Luke Conley to Major Carrington, no date, DHP.

108. R. Henry Glenn to Capt. N. Stark, June 6, 1863, and list of prisoners made by W. S. Pilcher after visit to Castle Thunder, June 5, 1863, DHP.

109. Richmond *Whig* 12 April 1865.

110. Receipt for prisoner, signed by G. W. Alexander, May 11, 1863, DHP.

111. Query placed by Tom Cooper, online http://homepages.rootsweb.com/~south1/powquery.htm.

112. "Josiah Copley," in J. H. Beers & Co., *Armstrong County, Pennsylvania: Her People, Past and Present,* pp. 301–324.

113. Charles Cotton to Gen. Winder, General Hospital No. 13, September 28,1862, DHP.

114. Benj. F. Butler to Robert Ould, Fort Monroe, Va., February 4, 1864, *O.R.*, Ser. II, Vol. 6, p. 119.

115. J. H. Cowdery to Maj. Carrington, Room No. 10, no date (1864?), DHP.

116. Richmond *Dispatch*, 5 Februrary 1864, cited in Fischer, p. 30.

117. "Hospital Fracas," Richmond *Sentinel*, 5 October 1864.

118. "Refused to do Militia Duty," Richmond *Dispatch*, 17 May 1864.

119. "Prisoners from Western Virginia," Richmond *Examiner*, 11 May 1863.

120. *Ibid*.

121. F. W. Hancock to Capt. Alexander, Feb. 4, 1863, DHP.

122. R. Henry Glenn to Capt. N. Stark, June 6, 1863, and list of prisoners made by W. S. Pilcher after visit to Castle Thunder, June 5, 1863, DHP.

123. Jim Cunningham and John Willis to General John H. Winder, General Hospital No.13, Ward B, Sept. 24, 1863, DHP.

124. Theodore T. Barham, Capt. Cavalry to Genl. Winder, no date, DHP.

125. Testimony of Baldwin T. Allen, Congressional Investigation, *O.R.*, Ser. II, Vol. 5, p. 888.

126. "North Carolina Civil War Troop, Wilson County, Company C, 43rd Regiment," submitted by Jo Webb to http://ftp.rootsweb.com/pub/usgenweb/nc/wilson/military/c-43rd.txt. See also, Manarin and Jordan, *North Carolina Troops,* Vol. X, p. 317.

127. "Deaths at the Castle," Richmond *Examiner*, 11 May 1863.

128. _____ to Capt. J. W. Richardson, C. S. Barracks, Richmond, February 1, 1864, DHP.

129. Henry Avery to Major Carrington, Castle Thunder, November 20, 1863, DHP.

130. William Daymond to Lt. C. W. Murdaguh [sic], Castle Thunder, May 16, 1863, and C. W. Murdaugh to Capt. G. W. Alexander, Powhatan Hotel, Richmond, May 17, 1863, DHP.

131. Richmond *Dispatch*, 18, 19, 20 February 1864, cited in Fischer, pp. 113–114.

132. Castle Thunder," Richmond *Sentinel,* 14 November 1863, p. 1, c. 7.

133. *History of Scott County, Iowa* (Chicago: Interstate Publishing Co., 1882), cited on Ancestry Message Board for Scott County, Iowa, by Deborah Geischer.

134. Van R. Otey to Captain G. W. Alexander, Lynchburg, Virginia, August 15, 1863, DHP.

135. James S. Legon, Jr., Clerk at C. S. Military Prison, to Major Carrington, Richmond, January 23, 1864, DHP.

136. Robert K. Krick, "The Ninth Virginia Cavalry," online www.9thvirginia.com/coi.htm.

137. List of Prisoners sent from Camp Holmes near Raleigh, N.C., on the 12th October 1863, by Col. Peter Mallett to Castle Thunder, DHP.

138. Manarin and Jordan, *North Carolina Troops*. Vol. XIII, p. 289.

139. List of Prisoners sent from Camp Holmes near Raleigh, N.C., on the 12th October 1863, by Col. Peter Mallett to Castle Thunder, DHP.

140. Manarin and Jordan, *North Carolina Troops*. Vol. XIII, p. 290.

141. Richmond *Dispatch*, 30 April 1863.

142. Richmond *Dispatch*, 19 August 1862.

143. W. G. Dollar to "Dear Brother," Castle Thunder, Richmond, January 15, 1864, DZHPZ.

144. Richmond *Dispatch,* 20 September 1862.

145. Frank B. Doran to Secretary of War, Salisbury, N.C., August 18, 1864, *O.R.*, Ser. II, Vol. 7, pp. 610–611.

146. List of Prisoners sent from Camp Holmes near Raleigh, N.C., on the 12th October 1863, by Col. Peter Mallett to Castle Thunder, DHP; and Manarin and Jordan, *North Carolina Troops,* Vol. IV, p. 310.

147. John W. Carter, Capt., to Captain Alexander, Richmond, August 31, 1863, DHP.

148. John _____, to Surgeon C. D. Rice, in charge of hospital, Howard's Grove Hospital, Richmond, Va., August 24, 1863, DHP.

149. List of Prisoners sent from Camp Holmes near Raleigh, N.C., on the 16th October 1863, by Col. Peter Mallett to Castle Thunder, DHP; and Manarin and Jordan, *North Carolina Troops,* Vol. IX, p. 58.

150. Manarin and Jordan, *North Carolina Troops,* Vol. VIII, p. 13; "Morning Report of Capt. G. W. Alexander," September 18, 1863, DHP. See Appendix 4.

151. List of Prisoners sent from Camp Holmes near Raleigh, N.C., on the 12th October 1863, by Col. Peter Mallett to Castle Thunder, DHP.

152. Sidney Smith Lee, Commandant, to Brig. Gen. John H. Winder, Drewry's Bluff, Va., May 28, 1863, DHP.

153. R. Henry Glenn to Capt. N. Stark, June

6, 1863, and list of prisoners made by W. S. Pilcher after visit to Castle Thunder, June 5, 1863, DHP.

154. Manarin and Jordan, *North Carolina Troops*, Vol. III, p. 423; "Morning Report of Capt. G. W. Alexander," September 18, 1863, DHP. See Appendix 4.

155. Charles Dunham to Gen. John A. Winder, Castle Thunder, Richmond, May 7, 1863, DHP.

156. Obituary of William J. Dunlap, from Clarion, Pennsylvania, newspaper dated Thursday, August 12, 1915, found in the belongings of Grace Stover Byner, online at www.krepps.net/williamjdunlap.htm.

157. Arthur Dutertre to Gen. Winder, October 1, 1863, DHP.

158. R. Henry Glenn to Capt. N. Stark, June 6, 1863, and list of prisoners made by W. S. Pilcher after visit to Castle Thunder, June 5, 1863, DHP.

159. William Dutton to James A. Seddon, August 13, 1863, Record Group 249, No. 966, Box 11, National Archives, Washington, D.C., cited in Fischer, p. 95.

160. Capt. T. P. Turner to Capt. G. W. Alexander, Richmond, October 7, 1863, DHP.

161. Richmond *Examiner*, 25 July 1863, *O.R.*, Ser. II, Vol. V, pp. 872–8, 891, 894, 897, 899, and 909; Parker, *Richmond's Prisons*, p. 30–31; Testimony of Henry Edenborough, Congressional Investigation, *O.R.*, Ser. II, Vol. 5, p. 901.

162. "Cases at the Castle," Richmond *Examiner*, 4 June 1864.

163. Capt. T. P. Turner to Capt. Alexander, Bell Island, October 14, 1863, DHP.

164. *Ibid.*

165. Manarin and Jordan, *North Carolina Troops*, Vol. XIV, p. 390.

166. List of Prisoners sent from Camp Holmes near Raleigh, N.C., on the 12th October 1863, by Col. Peter Mallett to Castle Thunder, DHP.

167. Manarin and Jordan, *North Carolina Troops*, Vol. XIV, p. 390.

168. "Statement of J. B. Evans," *O.R.*, Ser. II, Vol. 5, p. 915.

169. Richmond *Dispatch*, 7 October 1862, also cited in Fischer, p. 29.

170. Richmond *Dispatch*, 25 August 1862.

171. "Reuben Farwell," online, http://jefferson.village.virginia.edu/fdw/volume2/price/memoranda/annotations/farwell10.htm.

172. Commander John W. Johnson to Capt. Alexander, November 2, 1863, DHP.

173. Charles L. Feige to General Winder, Castle Thunder, July 3, 1863, DHP.

174. Richmond *Dispatch*, 5 February 1864.

175. Brigadier General J. D. Imboden, indorsement on bottom of letter from Lt. J. R. Nunn, Provost Marshal to Governor William Smith, Harrisburg, Va., March 30, 1864, *O.R.*, Ser. II, Vol. 6, pp. 1119–1120.

176. "Castle Thunder," Richmond *Sentinel*, 14 November 1863, p. 1, c. 7.

177. S. S. Baxter to Capt. Alexander, November 11, 1863, DHP.

178. William Fitzgerald to General Winder, Castle Thunder, June 2, 1863, DHP.

179. Letter from William Fitzgerald to President Abraham Lincoln, Castle Thunder, Richmond, July 4, 1863, Abraham Lincoln Papers, Library of Congress, Washington, D.C., available online at http://memory.loc.gov.

180. Richmond *Examiner*, April 8, 1863.

181. "49th Virginia Infantry Regiment, Company D, Warren Blues," online www.49thvirginiainfantry.com

182. "Prison Items," Richmond *Dispatch*, 1 May 1863.

183. Richmond *Dispatch*, 20 September 1862.

184. Richmond *Dispatch*, 22 November 1862, 25 November 1862, cited in Fischer, p. 30.

185. Obituary of Samuel H. Ford, *Waterloo [Indiana] Press*, 17 May 1883, copied and submitted to the Ancestry Message Board for DeKalb County, Indiana by Arlene Goodwin, Auburn, Indiana.

186. Richmond *Dispatch*, 10 March 1864, cited in Fischer, p. 38.

187. Geo. H. Sharp to Maj. Gen. George G. Meade, January 18, 1865, *O.R.*, Ser. I, Vol 46, Pt. II, p. 171.

188. W. S. Winder, A.A.G, to Capt. G. W. Alexander, Richmond, October 7, 1863, Winder's Order Book, Museum of the Confederacy, Richmond, Va.

189. Richmond *Enquirer*, 16 December 1862.

190. "4th Texas Volunteer Infantry Regiment, Company F — Mustang Grays," online at www.texas-brigade.com/4texrostercof.htm.

191. A. J. Garlick to Gen. Winder, Castle Thunder, July 3, 1863, DHP.

192. "Attempt to Escape From the Castle," Richmond, 21 May 1863.

193. "Prisoners from Western Virginia," Richmond *Examiner*, 11 May 1863.

194. Query regarding Bartholomew Garvey posted to the Ancestry Message Board by Kelley LaSalle on February 17, 1999.

195. Charles R. Gaston to General Winder, Castle Thunder, July 1, 1863; and July 30, 1863, DHP.

196. "Castle Thunder," Richmond *Examiner*, 17 June 1864.

197. "Prisoners from Western Virginia," Richmond *Examiner*, 11 May 1863.

198. Capt. Hough to Captain Richardson, December 23, 1863.

199. "Recaptured," Richmond *Sentinel*, 27 June 1863, p. 2, c. 4.

200. John H. Cassin, Captain & Provost Marshall to Capt. G. W. Alexander, Military Court, Dept. of Virginia & N. Carolina, Richmond, September 21, 1863, DHP.

201. *O.R.*, Ser. II, Vol. 5, p. 894.

202. Van R. Otey to Captain G. W. Alexander, Lynchburg, Virginia, August 15th, 1863, DHP.

203. List of Prisoners sent from Camp Holmes near Raleigh, N.C., on the 12th October 1863, by Col. Peter Mallett to Castle Thunder, DHP.

204. Richmond *Enquirer*, 5 September 1862.

205. Richmond *Dispatch*, 22 November 1862, 25 November 1862, cited in Fischer, p. 30.

206. Richmond *Dispatch*, 27 December 1862, cited in Fischer, p. 28–29.

207. "Put in the Castle," Richmond *Sentinel*, 26 May 1864.

208. *Weekly Standard*, Raleigh, N.C., 24 June 1863; cited in Fischer, p. 20, as Rev. Robert J. Graves.

209. "Unlawful Trading," Richmond *Examiner*, 5 October 1863.

210. Capt. T. P. Turner to Capt. Geo. W. Alexander, October 4, 1863, DHP.

211. G. W. Lee, Commander Military Post, Atlanta, Ga., to Brigadier-General Winder, December 3, 1862, *O.R.*, Ser. II, Vol. 5, p. 777–778.

212. Manarin and Jordan, *North Carolina Troops*, Vol. XIII, p. 311.

213. "Trading with Yankees," Richmond *Enquirer*, 9 October 1863.

214. Thomas W. Moore, ed. *The Memoirs of Paul Grogger—2nd Tennessee Volunteer Infantry Regiment (USA): From all my Heart a Union Man*, reproduced online http://home.cinci.rr.com/secondtennessee/grogger.htm.

215. "Escaped," Richmond *Whig*, 6 April 1865.

216. 2nd Lieut. S. Van de Graaff to Capt. Alexander, CS Navy Yard, June 12, 1863, DHP.

217. Richmond *Examiner*, 10 November 1862.

218. Hamilton Family Papers, Virginia Historical Society, Richmond, Virginia; Lou Athey, "Loyalty and Civil Liberty in Fayette County During the Civil War," *West Virginia History*, Vol. 55 (1996) p. 1–24.

219. Burrows, "Recollections of Libby Prison," pp. 92–93.

220. "Escaped," Richmond *Whig*, 6 April 1865.

221. Brig. Gen. Thos. Echols to Charles J. Stringfellow, Headquarters, Dept. Of Va., September 28, 1863, DHP.

222. R. H. Gilliam to Capt. L.W. Richardson, February 12, 1864, DHP.

223. Capt. Alex Savage to Gen. Winder, Camp near Culpepper C. H., Oct. 29, 1863, DHP.

224. Richmond *Dispatch*, 17 October 1862.

225. List of Prisoners sent from Camp Holmes near Raleigh, N.C., on the 16th October 1863, by Col. Peter Mallett to Castle Thunder, DHP.

226. Captain J. W. Coker to Lt. York, Barracks 24th & Franklin Streets, October(?) 2, 1863, DHP.

227. Hamilton Family Papers, Virginia Historical Society, Richmond, Va.

228. Browne, *Four Years in Secessia*, pp. 304.

229. Ward C. Harvey to General Winder, Castle Thunder, June 11, 1863, DHP.

230. Major S. J. Bossieux to Captain Richardson, February 25, 1864, DHP.

231. "Secure," Richmond *Enquirer*, 8 August 1862.

232. John McEntee to Brevet Major General Terry, City Point, November 12, 1864, *O.R.*, Ser. I, Vol. 42, Pt. III, p. 608–609.

233. George Moore to General Winder, May 14, 1864; G. W. Alexander notes, May 14, 1863, DHP.

234. Manarin and Jordan, *North Carolina Troops*, Vol. 14, p. 152.

235. "Morning Report of Capt. G. W. Alexander," September 18, 1863, DHP. See Appendix 4.

236. Browne, *Four Years in Secessia*, pp. 304.

237. R. Henry Glenn, Ordnance Bureau, Col. Gorgas' office to Gen. J. H. Winder, May 27, 1863, DHP.

238. R. Henry Glenn to Capt. N. Stark, June 6, 1863, and list of prisoners made by W. S.

Pilcher after visit to Castle Thunder, June 5, 1863, DHP.

239. Richmond *Dispatch*, 19 August 19, 1862.

240. Oscar R. Hough, Adjutant, to Capt. G. W. Alexander, Richmond, October 2, 1863, DHP.

241. Richmond *Enquirer,* 5 September 1862.

242. Daniel Higgins to Capt. Booker, Castle Thunder, April 27, 1863, DHP.

243. Castle Thunder," Richmond *Sentinel*, 14 November 1863, p. 1, c. 7.

244. R. D. Hill, to Captain Alexander, May 14, 1863, DHP.

245. "Prisoners from Western Virginia," Richmond *Examiner*, 11 May 1863.

246. List of Prisoners sent from Camp Holmes (Conscript Camp of Instruction) near Raleigh, N.C., on the 12th October 1863, by Col. Peter Mallett to Castle Thunder, DHP.

247. Manarin and Jordan, *North Carolina Troops,* Vol. 14, p. 391.

248. G. W. Alexander to Capt. William S. Winder, Richmond, May 8, 1863, DHP.

249. John Hussey to Major General Hitchcock, Washington, D.C., November 13, 1863, *O.R.*, Ser. II, Vol. 6, pp. 513–514. See also "William Williams House," The Waterford Foundation, online at www.waterfordva.org/tour/second7.html.

250. Major John D. Munford to Maj. I. H. Carrington, Richmond, December 24, 1864, *O.R.,*Ser. II, Vol. 7, pp. 1268–1269.

251. List of Prisoners sent from Camp Holmes (Conscript Camp of Instruction) near Raleigh, N.C., on the 16th October 1863, by Col. Peter Mallett to Castle Thunder, DHP.

252. Manarin and Jordan, *North Carolina Troops*, Vol. VI, p. 87.

253. "Attempted Escape," Richmond *Sentinel,* 2 July 1863; Richmond *Dispatch,* 2 July 1863.

254. Captain George Howland Papers, Collection #13637. Manuscripts and Special Collections, New York State Library, Room 3045, Cultural Education Center, Albany, New York 12230.

255. "Morning Report of Capt. G. W. Alexander," September 18, 1863, DHP. See Appendix 4.

256. Manarin and Jordan, *North Carolina Troops,* Vol. 14, p. 153.

257. Bruce Young, "Company D Historical Roster," online at: http:/;/home.socal.rr.com/bayoung/history.htm.

258. John Hussey to Major General Hitchcock, Washington, D.C., November 13, 1863, *O.R.*, Ser. II, Vol. 6, pp. 513–514.

259. Capt. John Avis to Major J. W. Pegram, Office of Provost Marshal, Staunton, January 28, 1864, DHP.

260. Manarin and Jordan, *North Carolina Troops*, Vol. XIII, p. 291.

261. *Journal of the Congress of the Confederate States of America 1861–1865,* Vol. 5, p. 418, online version http://memory.loc.gov.

262. List of Prisoners sent from Camp Holmes (Conscript Camp of Instruction) near Raleigh, N.C., on the 12th October 1863, by Col. Peter Mallett to Castle Thunder, DHP; Manarin and Jordan, *North Carolina Troops,* Vol. IV, p. 413.

263. "South Carolina 1st (Hagood's) Infantry Regiment, Company I (After Reorganization)," online listing www.researchonlne.net/sccw/rosters/1sthagi2.htm.

264. "Arrival and Departure of Prisoners," Richmond *Sentinel,* 6 May 1863; see also Fischer, p. 36.

265. "Prisoners from Western Virginia," Richmond *Examiner*, 11 May 1863.

266. Richmond *Enquirer* September 5, 1862.

267. Richmond *Dispatch*, October 9, 1862.

268. List of Prisoners sent from Camp Holmes (Conscript Camp of Instruction) near Raleigh, N.C., on the 16th October 1863, by Col. Peter Mallett to Castle Thunder, DHP.

269. Manarin and Jordan, *North Carolina Troops,* Vol. IV, p. 323.

270. *O.R.*, Ser. II, Vol. 6, p. 294, September 16, 1863; Examination of Andrew Johnson, Jr., July 31, 1863, Record Group 249, Entry 131, National Archives, Washington, D.C., cited in Fischer, p. 20–21.

271. Richmond *Dispatch*, 24 September 1862.

272. Richmond *Examiner*, 9 April 1863.

273. John Johnson to Gen. John H. Winder, Castle Thunder, Richmond, Va., July 4, 1863, DHP.

274. Richmond *Examiner,* 25 July 1863.

275. List of Prisoners sent from Camp Holmes (Conscript Camp of Instruction) near Raleigh, N.C., on the 16th October 1863, by Col. Peter Mallett to Castle Thunder, DHP; Manarin and Jordan, *North Carolina Troops, 1861–1865,* vol. IV, p. 323.

276. Commander John W. Johnson to Capt. Alexander, November 2, 1863, DHP.

277. Richmond *Sentinel*, 16 December 1863, p. 1, c. 6.
278. R. Henry Glenn to Capt. N. Stark, June 6, 1863, and list of prisoners made by W. S. Pilcher after visit to Castle Thunder, June 5, 1863, DHP.
279. "Proceedings of a general Court Martial commenced at Richmond by virtue of the following orders — General Orders No. 7," Richmond, October 11, 1862, DHP.
280. Richmond *Examiner,* April 9, 1863.
281. W. N. Starke, "Union Correspondence, Orders, etc. Relating to Prisoners of War and State from December 1, 1862 to June 10, 1863," Sixth Endorsement, May 13, 1863, *O.R.*, Ser. II, Vol. 5, pp. 518–520.
282. List of Prisoners sent from Camp Holmes (Conscript Camp of Instruction) near Raleigh, N.C., on the 12th October 1863, by Col. Peter Mallett to Castle Thunder, DHP.
283. *Ibid.*
284. Richmond *Dispatch*, 17 October 1862; *O.R.*, Ser. II, Vol. 4, pp. 660–661.
285. "Schuylkill County Civil War POWs," online www.pacivilwar.com/schuylkillcaptured.html. See also letter dated 1/3/1864 from C. P. Kane which was published in the *Miner's Journal.*
286. E. C. Sanders, Captain Company D, First North Carolina Union Volunteers, to Major General J. G. Foster, New Bern, North Carolina, April 24, 1863, *O.R.*, Ser. II, Vol. 4, pp. 518–519.
287. Capt. John Avis to Major J. W. Pegram, Office of Provost Marshal, Staunton, January 28, 1864, DHP.
288. Robert Ould to Lt. Col. William H. Ludlow, Richmond, July 31, 1863, *O.R.*, Ser. II, Vol. 6, pp. 119, 161–162; W. Hoffman to Commodore W. D. Porter, Washington, August 12, 1863, *O.R.*, Ser. II, Vol. 6, p. 196.
289. Richmond *Whig*, cited in Stern, *Secret Missions of the Civil War*, pp. 119–120; "The Execution of Spencer Kellogg," Richmond *Sentinel*, 26 September 1863; John H. Winder, Order Book, September 5, 1863, October 21, 1863, cited in Fischer, pp. 23–24; Richmond *Dispatch*, 26 September 1863.
290. "2nd Tennessee Infantry Regiment, U.S.A.: Complete Roster," compiled from information in the National Archives, online at: http://home.cinci.rr.com/secondtennessee/roster.html.
291. *Ibid.*

292. R. Henry Glenn to Capt. N. Stark, June 6, 1863, and list of prisoners made by W. S. Pilcher after visit to Castle Thunder, June 5, 1863, DHP.
293. Robert J. Kelly to Maj. Carrington, Room No. 7, no date but probably 1864, DHP.
294. Patrick Kenney to Genl. Winder, Castle Thunder, January 22, 1864, DHP.
295. Richmond *Dispatch*, 18 October 1862, cited in Fischer, p. 17.
296. Testimony of J. T. Kirby, Congressional Investigation, *O.R.*, Ser. II, Vol. 5, p. 889–890.
297. J. T. Kirby to Brig. Gen. J. H. Winder, Castle Thunder Prison, May 1, 1863, DHP.
298. Richmond *Sentinel*, May 25, 1863, p. 2., c. 2.
299. Lt. J. W. Beard to Capt. G. W. Alexander, September 21, 1863, DHP.
300. "Morning Report of Capt. G. W. Alexander," September 18, 1863, DHP. See Appendix 4; Manarin and Jordan, *North Carolina Troops*, Vol. V, p. 529.
301. Maj. E. Griswold to Capt. Alexander, Richmond, December 15, 1863, DHP.
302. Maj. E. Griswold to Capt. Alexander, Provost Marshal's office, Richmond, December 16, 1863, DHP.
303. List of Deserters arrested in the 1st Cong. District, unsigned, December 12, 1863, DHP.
304. List of Prisoners sent from Camp Holmes (Conscript Camp of Instruction) near Raleigh, N.C., on the 12th October 1863, by Col. Peter Mallett to Castle Thunder, DHP.
305. Richmond *Dispatch*, 7 January 1863, cited in Fischer, p. 38.
306. Lou Athey, "Loyalty and Civil Liberty in Fayette County During the Civil War," *West Virginia History* 55 (1996), pp. 1–24; Hamilton Papers, Virginia Historical Society, Richmond, Va.
307. Richmond *Examiner*, 26 July 1862, and 10 November 1862
308. H. T. Miller to Capt. Richardson, Camp Seddon, February 25, 1864, DHP.
309. "Castle Thunder," Richmond *Sentinel*, 14 April 1864; Richmond *Whig*, 14 April 1864.
310. "Castle Thunder," Richmond *Sentinel*, 14 April 1864; Richmond *Whig*, 14 April 1864; "General Orders, No. 12, Petersburg, March 7th, 1864, before a General Court Martial, Convened at Kinston, North Carolina," online at UNC-CH, Documenting the American South, http://docsouth.unc.edu/imls/csaarmy/csaarmy.html.

Hereinafter cited as General Orders No. 12, March 7, 1864.

311. Richmond *Examiner,* 21 July 1863.

312. Manarin and Jordan, *North Carolina Troops,* Vol. II, p. 145; "Morning Report of Capt. G. W. Alexander," September 18, 1863, DHP. See Appendix 4.

313. "The Slaves at Castle Thunder," Richmond *Sentinel.* 28 August 1863.

314. "Stray Prison Birds Recaptured," 18 April 1863, Richond *Examiner,* 18 April 1863.

315. William Sharp to Capt. G. W. Alexander, Gunboat "Beaufort," Richmond, October 5, 1863, DHP.

316. R. Henry Glenn, Ordnance Bureau, Col. Gorgas' office to Gen. J. H. Winder, May 27, 1863, DHP; R. Henry Glenn to Capt. N. Stark, June 6, 1863, and list of prisoners made by W. S. Pilcher after visit to Castle Thunder, June 5, 1863, DHP.

317. Governor Zebulon B. Vance to Jefferson Davis, Raleigh, March 9, 1864, *O.R.,* Ser. I, Vol. 51, Pt. II, p. 108.

318. "2nd Tennessee Infantry Regiment, U.S.A.: Complete Roster," compiled from information in the National Archives, online at: http://home.cinci.rr.com/secondtennessee/roster.html.

319. Joseph Littleton to Capt. Alexander, Castle Thunder, Room No. 10, no date (probably October of 1863), DHP.

320. Richmond *Dispatch,* October 30, 1862.

321. "Committals at Castle Thunder," Richmond *Dispatch,* 2 July 1863.

322. "Escaped," Richmond *Whig,* 6 April 1865.

323. Henry Avery to Major Carrington, Castle Thunder, November 20, 1863, DHP.

324. G. W. Long to Gen. Winder, Castle Thunder, June 12, 1863, DHP.

325. G. W. Long to Capt. Alexander, August 3, 1863, DHP.

326. "Running the Blockade," Richmond *Whig,* 14 November 1864.

327. "2nd Tennessee Infantry Regiment, U.S.A.: Complete Roster," compiled from information in the National Archives, online at: http://home.cinci.rr.com/secondtennessee/roster.html.

328. Richmond *Dispatch,* 24 April 1863, 19 April 1864, cited in Fischer, p. 23.

329. John Lundy, shoemaker, to General Winder, July 13, 1863, DHP.

330. List of Prisoners sent from Camp Holmes (Conscript Camp of Instruction) near Raleigh, N.C., on the 16th October 1863, by Col. Peter Mallett to Castle Thunder, DHP.

331. Manarin and Jordan, *North Carolina Troops,* Vol. VIII, p. 347.

332. W. N. Starke, "Union Correspondence, Orders, etc. Relating to Prisoners of War and State from December 1, 1862 to June 10, 1863," Sixth Endorsement, May 13, 1863, *O.R.,* Ser. II, Vol. 5, pp. 518–520.

333. W. N. Starke, "Union Correspondence, Orders, etc. Relating to Prisoners of War and State from December 1, 1862 to June 10, 1863," Sixth Endorsement, May 13, 1863, *O.R.,* Ser. II, Vol. 5, pp. 518–520.

334. List of Prisoners sent from Camp Holmes (Conscript Camp of Instruction) near Raleigh, N.C., on the 12th October 1863, by Col. Peter Mallett to Castle Thunder, DHP.

335. "Cases at the Castle," Richmond *Examiner,* 4 June 1864.

336. C. H. Marsh to Mr. Wood, Commissioner of the United States, October 25, 1862, *O.R.,* Ser. II, Vol. V, pp. 774–777.

337. *O.R.,* Ser. I, Vol. 10, Pt. 1, pp. 630–636; Charles H. Marsh to James A. Seddon, Castle Thunder, December 2, 1862, *O.R.,* Ser. II, Vol. 5, p. 776–777; G. W. Alexander, December 8, 1862, *O.R.,* Ser. II, Vol. 5, p. 777.

338. Wm. W. Parker, Capt. Lt. Atly, Col. E. P. Alexander's Battalion, to General Winder, camp near Bean Station, December 18, 1863, DHP.

339. *O.R.,* Ser. I, Vol. 10, Pt. 1, pp. 630–636; G. W. Lee, Commander Military Post, Atlanta, Ga., to Brigadier-General Winder, December 3, 1862, *O.R.,* Ser. II, Vol. 5, p. 777–778.

340. List of Prisoners sent from Camp Holmes (Conscript Camp of Instruction) near Raleigh, N.C., on the 12th October 1863, by Col. Peter Mallett to Castle Thunder, DHP.

341. Manarin and Jordan, *North Carolina Troops, Vol. IV,* p. 509.

342. G. W. Alexander to Major J. Carrington, December 11, 1863, DHP.

343. "Secure," Richmond *Enquirer,* 8 August 1862.

344. "Deaths at the Castle," Richmond *Examiner,* 11 May 1863.

345. Manarin and Jordan, *North Carolina Troops,* Vol. III, p. 427.

346. "Morning Report of Capt. G. W. Alexander," Richmond, Va., September 18, 1863, DHP.

347. Testimony of Frederick F. Wiley, Congressional hearings, *O.R.*, Ser. II, Vol. 5, p. 910.
348. Sidney Smith Lee, Commandant, to Brig. Gen. John H. Winder, Drewry's Bluff, Va., May 28, 1863, DHP.
349. Richmond *Dispatch*, 30 October 1862.
350. G. W. Lee, Commander Military Post, Atlanta, Ga., to Brigadier-General Winder, December 3, 1862, *O.R.*, Ser. II, Vol. 5, p. 777–778.
351. Albert G. McClung to Major Carrington, Castle Thunder Prison, November 23, 1863, DHP.
352. R. Henry Glenn to Capt. N. Stark, June 6, 1863, and list of prisoners made by W. S. Pilcher after visit to Castle Thunder, June 5, 1863, DHP.
353. Richmond *Dispatch*, 30 October 1862.
354. List of Prisoners sent from Camp Holmes (Conscript Camp of Instruction) near Raleigh, N.C., on the 16th October 1863, by Col. Peter Mallett to Castle Thunder, DHP.
355. Richmond *Enquirer*, 5 September 1862.
356. James P. McGregor to Gen. Winder, Castle Thunder No. 10, Richmond, November 20, 1863, DHP.
357. "William F. McKim," from *Kentucky: A History of the State*, 7th ed. (Boone County, KY: Perrin, & Kniffin, 1887), posted to Ancestry Message Board for Kentucky by Sandi Gorin.
358. Richmond *Dispatch*, September 20, 1862.
359. W. N. Starke, "Union Correspondence, Orders, etc. Relating to Prisoners of War and State from December 1, 1862 to June 10, 1863," Sixth Endorsement, May 13, 1863, *O.R.*, Ser. II, Vol. 5, pp. 518–520.
360. Van R. Otey to Captain G. W. Alexander, Lynchburg, Virginia, August 15, 1863, DHP.
361. James Mehan to Gen. Winder, Castle Thunder, June 4, 1863, DHP.
362. Manarin and Jordan, *North Carolina Troops*, Vol. IX, p. 328.
363. "Morning Report of Capt. G. W. Alexander," Richmond, Va., September 18, 1863, DHP.
364. G. W. Lee, Commander Military Post, Atlanta Ga, to Brigadier-General Winder, December 3, 1862, *O.R.*, Ser. II, Vol. 5, p. 777–778.
365. List of Prisoners sent from Camp Holmes (Conscript Camp of Instruction) near Raleigh, N.C., on the 12th October 1863, by Col. Peter Mallett to Castle Thunder, DHP.

366. Manarin and Jordan, *North Carolina Troops*, Vol. IV, p. 509.
367. Testimony of John Caphart, Congressional Investigation, *O.R.*, Ser. II, Vol. 5, p. 876.
368. Winder's Order Book, October 21, 1863, Museum of the Confederacy, Richmond, Va.
369. Ali Ben Molissa to Brig. Gen. John H. Winder, General Hospital 13, Richmond, December 14, 1863, DHP.
370. "Prison Items," Richmond *Dispatch*, 1 May 1863.
371. "A Black Sheep Among Them," Richmond *Examiner*, 31 May 1864.
372. "Trading with Yankees," Richmond *Enquirer*, 9 October 1863.
373. R. Henry Glenn to Capt. N. Stark, June 6, 1863, and list of prisoners made by W. S. Pilcher after visit to Castle Thunder, June 5, 1863, DHP.
374. J. B. Anderson to Gen. J. H. Winder, Tredgar Iron Works, Nov. 3, 1863, DHP.
375. Richmond *Examiner*, 10 November 1862.
376. Notation on back of Richard Barry's letter of June 1, 1863, referred to Murphy, DHP.
377. Richmond *Dispatch*, 6 February 1862, cited in Fischer, p. 30.
378. Richmond *Enquirer*, 5 September 1862.
379. "Another Shooting Affair," Richmond *Sentinel*, 5 October 1863.
380. Columbus Nichols to Capt. Winder, Castle Thunder, July 1, 1863, DHP.
381. List of Prisoners sent from Camp Holmes (Conscript Camp of Instruction) near Raleigh, N.C., on the 16th October 1863, by Col. Peter Mallett to Castle Thunder, DHP.
382. R. Henry Glenn to Capt. N. Stark, June 6, 1863, and list of prisoners made by W. S. Pilcher after visit to Castle Thunder, June 5, 1863, DHP.
383. Richmond *Dispatch*, 18 October 1862, cited in Fischer, p. 17.
384. *Ibid.*
385. Testimony of Dennis O'Connor, Congressional Investigation, *O.R.*, Ser. II, Vol. 5, p. 896.
386. Captain Alexander, Congressional Investigation, *O.R.*, Ser. II, Vol. 5, p. 897.
387. Richmond *Dispatch*, 19 August 1862.
388. Samuel Odell, article from *The History of Greene County, Missouri*, published in 1883, submitted to the Ancestry Message Board for Greene County, Missouri, by "Webmaster."

389. *Weekly Standard*, Raleigh, N.C., 2 November 1864.

390. List of Prisoners sent from Camp Holmes (Conscript Camp of Instruction) near Raleigh, N.C., on the 12th October 1863, by Col. Peter Mallett to Castle Thunder, DHP.

391. R. Henry Glenn to Capt. N. Stark, June 6, 1863, and list of prisoners made by W. S. Pilcher after visit to Castle Thunder, June 5, 1863, DHP.

392. G. W. Alexander to Capt. W. L. Winder, Richmond, June 13, 1863, DHP.

393. Castle Thunder," Richmond *Sentinel*, 14 November 1863, p. 1, c. 7.

394. W. N. Starke, "Union Correspondence, Orders, etc. Relating to Prisoners of War and State from December 1, 1862 to June 10, 1863," Sixth Endorsement, May 13, 1863, *O.R.*, Ser. II, Vol. 5, pp. 518–520.

395. Major John D. Munford to Maj. I. H. Carrington, Richmond, December 24, 1864, *O.R.*, Ser. II, Vol. 7, pp. 1268–1269.

396. George W. Nichols, "The General's Story," *Harper's New Monthly Magazine,* Vol. XXXV (No. CCV) (June 1867), pp. 60–74.

397. Richmond *Dispatch*, 31 October 1862, cited in Fischer, p. 113.

398. "Prisoners from Western Virginia," Richmond *Examiner*, 11 May 1863.

399. List of Prisoners sent from Camp Holmes (Conscript Camp of Instruction) near Raleigh, N.C., on the 16th October 1863, by Col. Peter Mallett to Castle Thunder, DHP.

400. Manarin and Jordan, *North Carolina Troops*, Vol. VII, p. 152.

401. Richmond *Dispatch*, 30 October 1862.

402. Manarin and Jordan, *North Carolina Troops*, Vol. XIII, p. 303.

403. *O.R.*, Ser. I, Vol. 10, Pt. 1, pp. 630–636; G. W. Lee, Commander Military Post, Atlanta, Ga., to Brigadier-General Winder, December 3, 1862, *O.R.*, Ser. II, Vol. 5, p. 777–778.

404. Van R. Otey to Captain G. W. Alexander, Lynchburg, Virginia, August 15th, 1863, DHP.

405. S. A. Shinn, Special Orders, Lynchburg, Va., October 3, 1863, DHP.

406. "Running the Blockade," Richmond *Whig*, 14 November 1864.

407. G. W. Alexander to Major Carrington, East District Military Prison, Richmond, October 29, 1863.

408. W. N. Starke, "Union Correspondence, Orders, etc. Relating to Prisoners of War and State from December 1, 1862 to June 10, 1863," Sixth Endorsement, May 13, 1863, *O.R.*, Ser. II, Vol. 5, pp. 518–520.

409. Jno. B. Williams and Thos. McGill, Report of Detectives, November 1864, *O.R.*, Ser. IV, Vol. 3, p. 816.

410. Maj. E. Griswold to Capt. Alexander, Provost Marshal Office, Richmond, Sept. 30, 1863, DHP.

411. Manarin and Jordan, *North Carolina Troops*, Vol. V, p. 29.

412. "Morning Report of Capt. G. W. Alexander," Richmond, Va., September 18, 1863, DHP.

413. "Running the Blockade," Richmond *Whig*, 14 November 1864.

414. "The Slaves at Castle Thunder," Richmond *Sentinel*, 28 August 1863.

415. Richmond *Dispatch*, 3 November 1862, cited in Fischer, p. 38.

416. Richmond *Sentinel,* 9 April 1864, p. 2, c. 4.

417. G. W. Lee, Commander Military Post, Atlanta, Ga., to Brigadier-General Winder, December 3, 1862, *O.R.*, Ser. II, Vol. 5, p. 777–778.

418. Marie E. Pitt to Secretary of War Seddon, Castle Thunder, December 30, 1864, cited in Alberta Jane Parker, "Molly Pitt, that 'dangerous & traitorous character,' My Great-Grandmother," *Heritage Quest* No. 41 (July/August 1992), pp. 51–53.

419. *O.R.*, Ser. I, Vol. 10, Pt. 1, pp. 630–636; G. W. Lee, Commander Military Post, Atlanta Ga., to Brigadier-General Winder, December 3, 1862, *O.R.*, Ser. II, Vol. 5, p. 777–778.

420. Pittenger, William. Scrapbook, 1887. Schoff Civil War Collection. William L. Clements Library, the University of Michigan, Ann Arbor, Michigan.

421. "The Slaves of Castle Thunder," Richmond *Sentinel*, 28 August 1863.

422. List of Prisoners sent from Camp Holmes (Conscript Camp of Instruction) near Raleigh, N.C., on the 16th October 1863, by Col. Peter Mallett to Castle Thunder, DHP.

423. Manarin and Jordan, *North Carolina Troops*, Vol. XIII, p. 267.

424. John C. Powell to Gen. Winder, Castle Thunder, June 16, 1863, DHP.

425. Eleaney Price to Captain D. L. Hudson, November 1, 1863, DHP.

426. Jno. B. Williams and Thos. McGill, Report of Detectives, November 1864, *O.R.*, Ser. IV, Vol. 3, p. 816.

427. Manarin and Jordan, *North Carolina Troops*, Vol. IX, p. 261.
428. "Arrival and Departure of Prisoners," Richmond *Sentinel,* 6 May 1863.
429. James Quinn to Right Reverend Bishop McGill, Castle Thunder, Room No. 7, November 14, 1863, DHP.
430. List of Prisoners sent from Camp Holmes near Raleigh, N.C., on the 12th of October 1863, by Col. Peter Mallett to Castle Thunder, DHP.
431. R. Henry Glenn to Capt. N. Stark, June 6, 1863, and list of prisoners made by W. S. Pilcher after visit to Castle Thunder, June 5, 1863, DHP.
432. *O.R.,* Ser. I, Vol. 10, Pt. 1, pp. 630–636; G. W. Lee, Commander Military Post, Atlanta, Ga., to Brigadier-General Winder, December 3,1862, *O.R.,* Ser. II, Vol. 5, p. 777–778.
433. List of Prisoners sent from Camp Holmes (Conscript Camp of Instruction) near Raleigh, N.C., on the 12th October 1863, by Col. Peter Mallett to Castle Thunder, DHP.
434. Manarin and Jordan, *North Carolina Troops*, Vol. XIII, p. 293.
435. Manarin and Jordan, *North Carolina Troops*, Vol. VII, p. 415.
436. L. S. Wright to B. and E. Wright, February 19, 1864, Wright Family Papers, cited in Manarin and Jordan, *North Carolina Troops*, Vol. VIII, p. 560–561.
437. John L. Stuart, of Company D, 49th North Carolina, to Mrs. M. A. Harper, February 22, 1864, Stuart Papers, cited in Manarin and Jordan, *North Carolina Troops*, Vol. VIII, footnote 1218, p. 561.
438. "D. W. Remnine," *Goodspeed's History of Greene County, Tennessee*, published 1887, contributed to the Ancestry Message Board for Greene County, Tennessee, by the Greene County TNGenWeb host.
439. List of Prisoners sent from Camp Holmes (Conscript Camp of Instruction) near Raleigh, N.C., on the 16th October 1863, by Col. Peter Mallett to Castle Thunder, DHP.
440. Maj. E. Griswold to Capt. Alexander, Provost Marshal's office, Richmond, December 16, 1863, DHP.
441. Major John D. Munford to Maj. I. H. Carrington, Richmond, December 24, 1864, *O.R.,*Ser. II, Vol. 7, pp. 1268–1269.
442. Statement by Rielly, for *The Hall of Memories of the Veterans of G.A.R. Post 20,* online http://lincoln.lib.niu.edu/498R/keith/rielly 4.html. This statement contained a number of inconsistencies, such as his weight at release which varied in the statements and subsequent transcription from 73 to 78.
443. Parker, *Richmond's Prisons,* p. 36.
444. List of Prisoners sent from Camp Holmes (Conscript Camp of Instruction) near Raleigh, N.C., on the 12th October 1863, by Col. Peter Mallett to Castle Thunder, DHP.
445. Lou Athey, "Loyalty and Civil Liberty in Fayette County During the Civil War," *West Virginia History*, Vol. 55 (1996), pp. 1–24; Major I. H. Carrington, Commissioner, to Captain W. S. Winder, A. A. G., "Report #246, William and Allen Richmond," September 11, 1863, National Archives, Record Group 109, Washington, D.C.
446. F. W. Hancock to Capt. Alexander, September 30, 1863, DHP.
447. Richmond *Dispatch,* 17 October 1862; Richmond *Enquirer*, October 21, 1862.
448. Richmond *Dispatch,* 21 October 1862, cited in Fischer, p. 107.
449. Richmond *Dispatch,* 30 October 1862, cited in Fischer, p. 18.
450. "Prisoners from Western Virginia," Richmond *Examiner*, 11 May 1863.
451. Information from query placed by Hugh B. Hall, Jr., to the Ancestry Message Board for Giles County, Virginia, on May 23, 1999.
452. Richmond *Dispatch*, 29 September 1862, and Richmond *Enquirer*, 5 September 1962.
453. "Prodigious Leap," Richmond *Sentinel,* 22 April 1864, p. 1, c. 3.
454. "Committals at Castle Thunder," Richmond *Dispatch*, 2 July 1863.
455. Testimony of Frederick F. Wiley, Congressional hearings, *O.R.,* Ser. II, Vol. 5, p. 910.
456. Major John D. Munford to Maj. I. H. Carrington, Richmond, December 24, 1864, *O.R.,* Ser. II, Vol. 7, pp. 1268–1269.
457. T. P. Sayer, "Prison Life at Richmond," *National Tribune,* 13 September 1883.
458. Information submitted by Dennis Brandt to the Ancestry Message Board for Atlantic County, New Jersey, on April 9, 2002.
459. "Recaptured," Richmond *Sentinel*, 10 September 1864.
460. Richmond *Whig*, 10 March 10, 1863; Richmond *Examiner*, June 6, 1863.
461. R. Lewis Scott to Mrs. C. Harper Anderson, Clifton, Texas, February 10, 1892, Virginia Historical Society, Richmond, Virginia, cited in Fischer, p. 22.

462. "Prisoners from Western Virginia," Richmond *Examiner*, 11 May 1863.
463. Richmond *Examiner*, November 10, 1862.
464. Fischer, p. 17.
465. Richmond *Dispatch*, September 15, 1862.
466. W. Hoffman to Col. William H. Ludlow, Washington, D.C., June 3, 1863, *O.R.*, Ser. II, Vol. 5, p. 736–737.
467. Henry B. Todd, Capt., Provt. Marshal, to James H. Sherman, Washington, D.C., June 5, 1863, DHP.
468. "Shiflets and the Civil War: 'Border Guards' Co. D, 46th Reg. Infantry," online www.shifletfamily.org/War/CW/46th.htm.
469. "Shiflets and the Civil War: 'Border Guards' Co. D, 46th Reg. Infantry," online www.shifletfamily.org/War/CW/46th.htm.
470. List of Prisoners sent from Camp Holmes (Conscript Camp of Instruction) near Raleigh, N.C., on the 16th October 1863, by Col. Peter Mallett to Castle Thunder, DHP.
471. Manarin and Jordan, *North Carolina Troops*, Vol. VIII, p. 294.
472. Brigadier General J. D. Imboden, indorsement on bottom of letter from Lt. J. R. Nunn, Provost Marshal to Governor William Smith, Harrisburg, Va., March 30, 1864, *O.R.*, Ser. II, Vol. 6, pp. 1119–1120.
473. "The Slaves of Castle Thunder," Richmond *Sentinel*, 28 August 1863.
474. Manarin and Jordan, *North Carolina Troops*, Vol. VI, p. 319.
475. "Morning Report of Capt. G. W. Alexander," Richmond, Va., September 18, 1863, DHP.
476. Richmond *Examiner*, 10 November 1862.
477. Richmond *Examiner*, 8 April 1863.
478. Daniel Smith to Capt. G. W. Alexander, Castle Thunder, October 5, 1863, DHP.
479. John H. Winder to Capt. G. W. Alexander, Richmond, Sept. 5, 1863, Winder's Order Book, Museum of the Confederacy, Richmond, VA.
480. Richmond *Dispatch*, 20 September 1862.
481. List of Prisoners sent from Camp Holmes (Conscript Camp of Instruction) near Raleigh, N.C., on the 16th October 1863, by Col. Peter Mallett to Castle Thunder, DHP.
482. Manarin and Jordan, *North Carolina Troops*, Vol. XIII, p. 51.
483. W. S. Winder, A.A.G, to Capt. G. W. Alexander, Richmond, October 7, 1863, Winder's Order Book, Museum of the Confederacy, Richmond, Va.
484. John _____, to Surgeon C. D. Rice, in charge of hospital, Howard's Grove Hospital, Richmond, Va., August 24, 1863, DHP.
485. S. S. Baxter to Capt. Alexander, November 11, 1863, DHP.
486. G. W. Snell to Genl., Castle Thunder, June 7, 1863, DHP.
487. Richmond *Examiner*, April 9, 1863.
488. Bruce Young, "Company D Historical Roster," online at: http:/;/home.socal.rr.com/bayoung/roster3.htm
489. "Prisoners from Western Virginia," Richmond *Examiner*, 11 May 1863.
490. "An Impudent Scamp," Richmond *Enquirer*, 14 August 1863.
491. 16th October 1863, by Col. Peter Mallett to Castle Thunder, DHP.
492. Manarin and Jordan, *North Carolina Troops*, Vol. IX, p. 132–133.
493. List of Prisoners sent from Camp Holmes (Conscript Camp of Instruction) near Raleigh, N.C., on the Martin Staples to Gen. Winder, June 22, 1863, DHP.
494. Major S. J. Bossieux to Captain Richardson, February 25, 1864, DHP.
495. Sidney Smith Lee, Commandant, to Brig. Gen. John H. Winder, Drewry's Bluff, Va., May 28, 1863, DHP.
496. R. Henry Glenn to Capt. N. Stark, June 6, 1863, and list of prisoners made by W. S. Pilcher after visit to Castle Thunder, June 5, 1863, DHP.
497. David E. Johnston, *The Story of a Confederate Boy in the Civil War*, pp. 103–104.
498. Bruce Young, "Company D Historical Roster," online at: http:/;/home.socal.rr.com/bayoung/roster3.htm.
499. Capt. John Avis to Major J. W. Pegram, Office of Provost Marshal, Staunton, January 28, 1864, DHP.
500. "Castle Thunder," Richmond *Examiner*, 17 June 1864.
501. Manarin and Jorday, *North Carolina Troops*, Vol. VI, p. 638.
502. "Deserted to the Enemy," Richmond *Enquirer*, 13 June 1864.
503. Bruce Young, "Company D Historical Roster," online at: http:/;/home.socal.rr.com/bayoung/ roster3.htm.
504. Samuel S. Tinsley to Maj. Carrington, Castle Thunder, October 7, 1864, DHP.

505. G. W. Lee, Commander Military Post, Atlanta, Ga., to Brigadier-General Winder, December 3, 1862, *O.R.*, Ser. II, Vol. 5, p. 777–778.

506. E. C. Sanders, Captain Company D, First North Carolina Union Volunteers, to Major General J. G. Foster, New Bern, North Carolina, April 24, 1863, *O.R.*, Ser. II, Vol. 4, pp. 518–519.

507. Van R. Otey to Captain G. W. Alexander, Lynchburg, Virginia, August 15, 1863, DHP.

508. Information on James Trout from a biography published in *History of Keyser, West Virginia*, by William Wolfe, and submitted to the Ancestry Message Board for Mineral County, West Virginia, by Patti McDonald on 9 Sept 1999.

509. "Castle Thunder Items," Richmond *Examiner*, 28 July 1863.

510. Castle Thunder," Richmond *Sentinel*, 14 November 1863, p. 1, c. 7.

511. Letter to Maj. J. C. Turner, Judge Advocate, May 8, 1864, from __ Galloway, recommending the release of Peter Turner, from National Archives, reproduced in "Roster of the 14th Kentucky Cavalry, C.S.A.," online http://morgans_men.tripod.com/14thkycav2.htm.

512. Richmond *Examiner,* April 9, 1863.

513. Testimony of John Caphart, Congressional Investigation, *O.R.*, Ser. II, Vol. 5, p. 875.

514. S. S. Baxter to Capt. Alexander, November 11, 1863, DHP.

515. Richmond *Examiner,* 25 July 1864.

516. Richmond *Dispatch,* 19 August 1862.

517. Capt. T. P. Turner to Capt. G. W. Alexander, Richmond, October 7, 1863, DHP.

518. William T. Bell, Asst. Surg. To Major Gen. J. H. Winder, Richmond, November 10, 1863, DHP.

519. "Wants to go home," Richmond *Enquirer,* 10 June 1864.

520. Richmond *Examiner,* 10, and 29 June, 1864.

521. Lucian L. _____, Capt. Company G, 25th Virginia Battalion, to Commandant, Castle Thunder, January (or June) 10, 1864.

522. G. W. Lee, Commander Military Post, Atlanta, Ga., to Brigadier-General Winder, December 3, 1862, *O.R.*, Ser. II, Vol. 5, p. 777–778.

523. R. Henry Glenn to Capt. N. Stark, June 6, 1863, and list of prisoners made by W. S. Pilcher after visit to Castle Thunder, June 5, 1863, DHP.

524. Richmond *Enquirer,* 16 December 1862.

525. "The Slaves at Castle Thunder," Richmond *Sentinel,* 28 August 1863.

526. Richmond *Examiner,* 20 November 1862.

527. Van R. Otey to Captain G. W. Alexander, Lynchburg, Virginia, August 15, 1863, DHP.

528. Testimony of George W. Waymack, Congressional Investigation, *O.R.*, Ser. II, Vol. 5, p. 912.

529. Willett, "Loyal to None," *Civil War Times Illustrated*, Vol. XLII, No. 1 (April 2003); Richmond *Sentinel*, 11 April 1863.

530. Robert Ould, Agent of Exchange to Brig. Gen. S. A. Meredith, Richmond, October 2, 1863, *O. R.*, Ser. II, Vol. VI, p. 339.

531. D. S. Boyle, Asst. Surg., to "Dear Sir," Camp near Orange, 2nd Miss. Regiment, January 21, 1864, DHP.

532. *O.R.*, Ser. II, Vol. 4, p. 917, December 13, 1862; Richmond *Dispatch*, 29 and 30 April 1862, for notice of execution of Timothy Webster.

533. Testimony of V. T. Crawford, Congressional Investigation, Ser. I, Vol. 5, p. 895.

534. Harrison, *Prisoners' Mail from the American Civil War*, p. 85.

535. Brigadier General J. D. Imboden, indorsement on bottom of letter from Lt. J. R. Nunn, Provost Marshal to Governor William Smith, Harrisburg, Va., March 30, 1864, *O.R.*, Ser. II, Vol. 6, pp. 1119–1120.

536. "St. Joseph County, Michigan, Civil War Veterans Biographies," online at http://members.tripod.com/~tfred/vet82-90.html.

537. John _____, to Surgeon C. D. Rice, in charge of hospital, Howard's Grove Hospital, Richmond, Va., August 24, 1863, DHP.

538. G. W. Lee, Commander Military Post, Atlanta, Ga., to Brigadier-General Winder, December 3, 1862, *O.R.*, Ser. II, Vol. 5, p. 777–778.

539. "Prisoners from Western Virginia," Richmond *Examiner*, 11 May 1863.

540. "Escaped," Richmond *Whig*, 6 April 1865.

541. Richmond *Sentinel*, 25 March 1863, p. 2, c.3.

542. G. W. Alexander to Maj. Carrington, Richmond, October 26, 1863, DHP.

543. Manarin and Jordan, *North Carolina Troops*, Vol. III, p. 430; "Morning Report of Capt. G. W. Alexander," Richmond, Va., September 18, 1863, DHP.

544. Capt. Hough to Capt. Richardson, Richmond, January 24, 1864, DHP.

545. "Escaped," Richmond *Sentinel*, 26 November 1863, p. 2, c. 2.
546. "The Slaves of Castle Thunder," Richmond *Sentinel*, 28 August 1863.
547. Manarin and Jordan, *North Carolina Troops*, Vol. V, p. 32.
548. "Morning Report of Capt. G. W. Alexander," Richmond, Va., September 18, 1863, DHP.
549. John Hussey to Major General Hitchcock, Washington, D.C., November 13, 1863, *O.R.*, Ser. II, Vol. 6, pp. 513–514. See also "William Williams House," The Waterford Foundation, online at www.waterfordva.org/tour/second7.shtml.
550. Richmond *Dispatch*, 19 August 1862.
551. "No Charge," Richmond *Dispatch*, 6 August 1863.
552. John Willis to Captain Alexander, October 4, 1863, DHP.
553. Jim Cunningham and John Willis to General John H. Winder, General Hospital No. 13, Ward B, September 24, 1863, DHP.
554. George Wilson to Major Carrington, Castle Thunder, March 18, 1864, DHP.
555. "Castle Thunder," Richmond *Sentinel*, 14 November 1863, p. 1, c. 7.
556. John W. Wilson to General Winder, Castle Thunder, Richmond, Va., October 18, 1863, DHP.
557. J. K. McLean, surgeon in charge of 2nd Division, to Capt. Alexander, September 26, 1863, DHP.
558. Theo. P. Brighan to M.M. R. H. Garnett, Miller's Tav[ern], April 23, 1863, DHP.
559. List of Prisoners sent from Camp Holmes near Raleigh, N.C., on the 12th October 1863, by Col. Peter Mallett to Castle Thunder, DHP.
560. *Ibid.*
561. Receipt for prisoner, signed by G. W. Alexander, November 7, 1863, DHP.
562. Galen D. Harrison, *Prisoners' Mail from the American Civil War*, p. 86.
563. Richmond *Sentinel,* 9 April 1864, p. 2, c. 4.
564. T. J. Worth to Dr. Holt, May 12, 1863, and Dr. Leonidas Holt to Captain Alexander, May 20, 1863, DHP.
565. "Stray Prison Birds Recaptured," Richmond *Examiner*, 18 April 1863.
566. Testimony of T. G. Bland, Congressional Investigation, *O.R.*, Ser. I, Vol. 5, pp. 880–881; Testimony of Stephen B. Children, Congressional Investigation, *O.R.*, Ser. I, Vol. 5, p. 886. Testimony of Baldwin T. Allen, Congresional Investigation, *O.R.*, Ser. I, Vol. 5, p. 889.
567. *Weekly Standard*, Raleigh, N.C., 16 December 1863.
568. Richmond *Dispatch*, 30 October 1862.
569. Richmond *Examiner*, 10 November 1862.
570. Manarin and Jordan, *North Carolina Troopos*, Vol. X, p. 67.
571. "Morning Report of Capt. G. W. Alexander," Richmond, Va., September 18, 1863, DHP.

Appendix 2

1. Confederate States of America, Department of Henrico, Miscellaneous Papers, Reel #8, Mss 3, 67604a, Virginia Historical Society, Richmond, Virginia.

Appendix 3

1. Confederate States of America, Department of Henrico, Miscellaneous Papers, Reel #8, Mss 3, 67604a, Virginia Historical Society, Richmond, Virginia.

Appendix 4

1. Confederate States of America, Department of Henrico, Miscellaneous Papers, Reel #8, Mss 3, 67604a, Virginia Historical Society, Richmond, Virginia.

Bibliography

Newspapers

Daily Missouri Democrat, 21 August 1863.
Franklin *Repository* (Chambersburg, Penn), 22 February 1865.
Greenfield Democrat, 3 May 1861.
Herald and Torch Light (Hagerstown, Maryland), 27 September 1865.
National Tribune, (Washington, D.C.), 23 December 1893.
New York *Herald*, 13 April 1865.
New York *Times,* 23 February 1895, p. 3, col.7; 7 July 1895.
Richmond [Virginia] *Daily Dispatch*.
Richmond [Virginia] *Enquirer*.
Richmond [Virginia] *Examiner*.
Richmond [Virginia] *Whig*.
Salisbury [North Carolina] *Watchman*.
The Telegram, (Baltimore, Maryland) 1879.
The Sun [Baltimore, Maryland], 22 February 1895.
The Evening Star [Washington, D.C.], 14 July 1876.
Weekly Gazette [Washington, D.C.].
Weekly Standard [Raleigh, North Carolina].

Journals and Periodicals

Harper's Weekly
Southern Historical Society Papers
West Virginia History

Primary Sources

Published Public Records

Committee to Enquire into Treatment of Prisoners at Castle Thunder, *Evidence taken before the Committee of the House of Representatives, appointed to enquire into the Treatment of Prisoners at Castle Thunder,* Richmond, Va.: House of Representatives, 1863.
Confederate States of America. Army. Department of North Carolina. "General Orders, No. 12. Petersburg, March 7th, 1864. Before a General Court Martial, Convened at Kinston, North

Carolina." Electronic ed., University of North Carolina at Chapel Hill Libraries, Documenting the American South, http://docsouth.unc.edu/imls/csaarmy/csaarmy.html.

House of Representatives, Report No. 65, *Report on the Treatment of Prisoners of War by Rebel Authorities During the War of the Rebellion*, 40th Congress, 3rd Session. Washington: GPO, 1869.

Journal of the Congress of the Confederate States of America, 1861–65, 7 vols. Washington: GPO, 1904.

Goldsborough, W. W. *The Maryland Line in the Confederate Army, 1861–1865*. Baltimore, Md.: Press of Guggenheim, Weil, & Co., 1900.

Manarin, Louis H., ed. *Richmond at War: The Minutes of the City Council, 1861–1865*. Chapel Hill: The University of North Carolina Press, 1966.

Regulations of the Navy of the United States, 1863 edition.

"Residents of Laurel, Maryland, Taken from Special Canvass made by Ross & Fairall, August 1894," in Gertrude Poe, ed. *Laurel, Maryland: Souvenir Historical Booklet. 1870 Centennial 1970*. Privately published by the City of Laurel, Maryland, 1970.

Special Presidential Pardons for Confederate Soldiers: A Listing of Former Confederate Soldiers Requesting Pardon from President Andrew Johnson. 2 vols. Signal Mountain, Tenn.: Mountain Press, 1999.

The Stranger's Guide and Official Directory for the City of Richmond, Showing the Location of the Public Buildings and Offices of the Confederate, State and City Governments, Residences of the Principal Officers, etc. Vol. 1, No. 1 (October). Richmond, Va.: George P. Evans & Co., 1863.

United States Naval War Records Office. *Official Records of the Union and Confederate Navies in the War of the Rebellion*. 27 vols. Washington: GPO, 1894–1922.

United States War Department. *War of the Rebellion: A Compilation of the Official Records of the Union and Confederate Armies*. 128 vols. Washington: GPO, 1880–1901.

Unpublished Public Records, Microfilm and Online Sources

Prince George's County, Maryland. Wills. Maryland Archives, Annapolis, Maryland.

United States Bureau of the Census. *Tenth Census of the United States, 1880*. National Archives Microfilm T9-0501, page 290C.

United States Bureau of the Census. *Twelfth Census of the United States, 1900*. Microfilm Records: Delaware, District of Columbia, Maryland, 1900. Baltimore Couty, Maryland, Roll 616, Book 1, p. 240a. Online at www:genealogy.com.

Manuscripts, Diaries, Letters, and Other Unpublished Sources

Aughinbaugh, William L., Journal, 1862-1863, Schoff Civil War Collection. William L. Clements Library, The University of Michigan, Ann Arbor, Michigan.

"Blood Hounds!" Broadside, Virginia Historical Society, Richmond, Virginia.

Carrington, Isaac Howell, Papers. Duke University Libraries, Durham, North Carolina.

Confederate States of America, Department of Henrico Papers, 1861–1864, reel #8, Mss3, 67604a, Virginia Historical Society, Richmond, Virginia.

Chivers, Stephen D. "'Numerous and Insurmountable Obstacles': John Henry Aulick on the Far China Station." A History Honors Thesis. U.S. Navy Academy, Annapolis, Maryland, 2001.

Civil War Soldiers Database, Rutherford B. Hayes Presidential Center, Fremont, Ohio.

"Claim of Samuel B. Koontz, 1866." Adjutant General's Records, Militia, Fayette County, West Virginia, State Archives, Charleston, West Virginia.

Cox, Cleve Horton. "Salisbury: The Confederate Prison of General Stoneman, 1860–1865." Typescript, n.d.

Cox, E.L., Diary. Virginia Historical Society, Richmond, Virginia.

Dedrick, Henry H., Papers, Virginia Military Archives, Lexington, Virginia.

Fischer, Ronald W. *A Comparative Study of Two Civil War Prisons: Old Capitol Prison and Castle Thunder Prison*. Unpublished Master's thesis, Virginia Polytechnic Institute and State University, 1994.

Golden, Alan Lawrence. "Castle Thunder: The Confederate Provost Marshal's Prison, 1862–1865." Typescript, Master's thesis, University of Richmond, 1980.

Hamilton Family Papers, Virginia Historical Society, Richmond, Virginia.

Historic American Sheet Music, Rare Books, Manuscripts and Special Collections, Duke University, Durham, North Carolina.

Howland, Captain George. Howland Papers, Collection #13637. Manuscripts and Special Collections, New York State Library, Room 3045, Cultural Education Center, Albany, New York.

Lincoln, Abraham, Papers, Library of Congress, Washington, D.C.

Moore, Thomas W., ed. "The Memoirs of Paul Grogger — 2nd Tennessee Volunteer Infantry Regiment (USA): From All My Heart A Union Man." Southern Historical Collection, University of North Carolina at Chapel Hill, North Carolina.

Pittenger, William. Scrapbook, 1887. Schoff Civil War Collection. William L. Clements Library, The University of Michigan, Ann Arbor, Michigan.

U.S. War Department. Record Group 249, National Archives, Washington, D.C.

U.S. War Department. Record Group 109, National Archives, Washington, D.C.

"Rules and Regulations for the Government of Castle Thunder." Broadside, Virginia State Library, Richmond, Virginia.

Scott, R. Lewis, letter to Mrs. C. Harper Anderson, Clifton, Texas, February 10, 1892, Virginia Historical Society, Richmond, Virginia.

Selected Records of the War Department Relating to Prisoners of War — Fort McHenry Military Prison. National Archives, Washington, D.C., microfilm No. 596, Roll 96.

Tiemann, William Francis, Diary. Rowan County Public Library, Salisbury, North Carolina.

Winder, John H. Order Book, April 14, 1863–October 19, 1863, Eleanor Brockenbrough Library, Museum of the Confederacy, Richmond, Virginia.

Published Diaries and Memoirs

Abbott, A. O. *Prison Life in the South: at Richmond, Macon, Savannah, Charleston, Columbia, Charlotte, Raleigh, Goldsborough, and Andersonville, During the Years 1864 and 1865.* New York: Harper & Brothers, Publishers, 1866.

The Annals of the Civil War Written by Leading Participants North and South, 1878; rpt. New York: Da Capo Press, 1994.

Boggs, Samuel S. *Eighteen Months a Prisoner under the Rebel Flag* (Lovington, IL: privately published, 1887).

Booth, Benjamin F., and Steve Myer. *Dark Days of the Rebellion or Life in Southern Military Prisons giving a Correct and Thrilling History of Unparalleled Suffering, Narrow Escapes, Heroic Encounters, Bold Achievements, Cold-blooded Murders, Severe Tests of Loyalty and Patriotism.* 1897, rpt. Revised edition, Garison, Iowa: Meyer Publishing, 1996.

Browne, Junius Henri. *Four Years in Secessia: Adventures Within and Beyond the Union Lines: Embracing a Great Variety of Facts, Incidents, and Romance of the War.* Hartford, Conn.: O. D. Case and Company, 1865.

Clark, Walter, ed. *Histories of the Several Regiments and Battalions from North Carolina in the Great War, 1861–1865, Written by Members of the Respective Commands.* 5 vols. Goldsboro, N.C.: Nash Brothers, 1901.

Early, Jubal Anderson. *Lieutenant General Jubal Anderson Early, C.S.A.: Autobiographical Sketch and Narrative of the War between the States* (Philadelphia; London: J. B. Lippincott Company, 1912).

Ferguson, Joseph. *Life Struggles in Rebel Prisons.* Philadelphia: James M. Ferguson, 1865.

Gallagher, Gary W., ed. *Fighting for the Confederacy: The Personal Recollections of General Edward Porter Alexander.* Chapel Hill, N.C.: The University of North Carolina Press, 1989.

Greeley, Horace. *American Conflict: A History of the Great Rebellion in the United States of America, 1860–'64. Its Causes, Incidents, and Results; Intended to Exhibit Especially Its Moral and Political phases, with the Drift and Progress of American opinion Respecting Human Slavery, From 1776 to the Close of the War for the Union.* 2 vols. Hartford: O. D. Case & Company; Chicago: Geo. & C. W. Sherwood, 1865–1866.

Harris, William C. *Prison Life in the Tobacco Warehouse at Richmond by a Ball's Bluff Prisoner.* Philadelphia, Pa.: George W. Childs, 1862.

Hawks, Francis L. *Narrative of the Expedition of an American Squadron to the China Seas and Japan, Performed in the Years 1852, 1853, and 1854; under the Command of Commodore M. C. Perry, United States Navy, by Order of the Government of the United States.* Washington, D.C.: Beverley Tucker, Senate Printer, 1856.

Jeffrey, William H. *Richmond Prisons 1861-1862 From the Original Records Kept by the Confederate Government.* St. Johnsbury, Vt.: The Republican Press, 1893.

Johnston, David E. *The Story of a Confederate Boy in the Civil War.* Portland, Oregon: Glass & Prudhomme Co., 1914.

Muffley, J. W., ed. *The Story of Our Regiment: A History of the 148th Pennsylvania Volunteers.* Des Moines, Iowa: Kenyon Print and Mfg. Co., 1904.

Perry, Commodore M. C. *Narrative of the Expedition to the China Seas and Japan, 1852-1854.* 1856, rpt. Mineola, N.Y.: Dover Publications, Inc., 2000.

Putnam, George Haven. *A Prisoner of War in Virginia 1864-5.* 3rd ed. 1912, rpt. New York: G. P. Putnam's Sons, 1914.

Small, Harold Adams, ed. *The Road to Richmond: The Civil War Memoirs of Major Abner R,. Small of the Sixteenth Main Volunteers, together with the diary that he kept when he was a prisoner of war, with an introduction by Earl J. Hess.* New York: Fordham University Press, 2000.

Trowbridge, John T. *The South: A Tour of its Battle-fields and Ruined Cities, a Journal Through the Desolated States, and Talks with the People; Being a Description of the Present State of the Country—Its Agriculture—Railroads—Business and Finances...,* (Hartford: Connecticut: L. Steebins, 1866), p. 153.

Unknown. *Ohio boys in Dixie: The Adventures of Twenty-two Scouts sent by Gen. O. M. Mitchell to Destroy a Railroad; with a narrative of their barbarous treatment by the Rebels and Judge Holt's report....* New York: Miller & Matthews, 1863.

Velazquez, Loreta Janeta. *The Woman in Battle.* Richmond, Va.: Dustin, Gilman & Co., 1876.

Secondary Sources

Books

Amann, William Frayne, ed. *Personnel of the Civil War.* 2 vols. New York: T. Yoseloff, 1961.

Beers, J. H. & Co. *Armstrong County, Pennsylvania: Her people, past and present, embracing a history of the county and a genealogical and biographical record of representative families.* Chicago, Ill: J. H. Beers & Co., 1914, rpt. Butler, Pa.: Mechling Associates, 1998.

Blumberg, Rhoda. *Commodore Perry in the Land of the Shogun.* New York: Lothrop, Lee & Shepard Books, 1985.

Bradford, James C., ed. *Captains of the Old Steam Navy.* Annapolis, Md.: Naval Institute Press, 1986.

Brock, R. A. *The Appomattox Roster.* 1887, rpt. New York: Antiquarian Press, Ltd., 1962.

Brown, Louis A. *The Salisbury Prison: A Case Study of Confederate Military Prisons 1861-1865.* Revised edition. Wilmington, NC: Broadfoot Publishing Company, 1992.

Bryan, Wilhelmus Bogart. *Bibliography of the District of Columbia being a list of books, maps, and newspapers, including articles in magazines and other publications to 1898.* Washington: Government Printing Office, 1900.

Callahan, Edward W., ed. *List of Officers of the United States and of the Marine Corps from 1775 to 1900; comprising a complete register of all present and former commissioned, warranted, and appointed officers of the United States Navy and of the Marine Corps, regular and volunteer.* New York: L. R. Hammersly and Co., 1901.

Craven, Avery. *Reconstruction: The Ending of the Civil War.* New York: Holt, Rinehart, Winston, 1968.

Crute, Joseph H., Jr. *Confederate Staff Officers, 1861–1865.* Powhatan, Va.: Derwent Books, 1982.

Cunningham, H. H., *Doctors in Gray: The Confederate Medical Service,* 1958, rpt. Glouchester, Mass.: Peter Smith, 1970.

Cutler, William G., A. T. Andreas, and Thelma Carpenter. *History of the State of Kansas, Containing a Full Account of its Growth from an Uninhabited Territory to a Wealthy and Important State.* Chicago: A. T. Andreas, 1883.

Eaton, Clement. *A History of the Southern Confederacy.* New York: The Macmillan Company, 1954.

Faragher, John Mack, ed. *Encyclopedia of American History.* New York: Henry Holt and Company, 1998.

Faust, Patricia L., and Norman C. Delaney, eds. *Historical Times Illustrated Encyclopedia of the Civil War.* New York: Harper & Row, Publishers, 1986.

Ferguson, Edwin L. *Sumner County, Tennessee in the Civil War.* Privately printed by the author, 1972.

Ford, Annette Gee, ed., compl. *The Captive: Major John H. Gee, Commandant of the Confederate Prison at Salisbury, North Carolina, 1864–1865: A Biographical Sketch with Complete Court-Martial Transcript.* Salt Lake City, Utah: Utah Bookbinding Co., 2000.

Garrison, Webb. *The Encyclopedia of Civil War Usage.* Nashville, Tn.: Cumberland House, 2001.

Garrison, Webb. *Southern Tale: A treasury of Stories from Virginia, North Carolina, South Carolina, Georgia, Florida, Alabama, Kentucky, Tennessee and Mississippi.* New York: Galahad Books, 1997.

Gifis, Steven H. *Law Dictionary.* Woodbury, N. Y.: Barron's Educational Series, Inc., 1975.

Hall, Richard. *Patriots in Disguise: Women Warriors of the Civil War.* Reprint ed. New York: Marlow & Co., 1994.

Harrison, Galen S. *Prisoners' Mail from the American Civil War.* Dexter, Mich.: Thompson-Shore, Inc., 1997.

Hammerlein, Richard F. *Prisons and Prisoners of the Civil War.* Boston: Christopher Publishing Co., 1934.

Harwell, Richard Barksdale. *Brief Candle: The Confederate Theatre.* Worcester, Mass.:Davis Press, Inc., 1971.

Hesseltine, William B. *Civil War Prisons: A Study in War Psychology.* Columbus: Ohio State University Press, 1930, rpt. New York: Frederick Ungar Publishing Co., 1964.

Hoehling, A. A., and Mary Hoehling. *The Day Richmond Died.* New York: A. S. Barnes and Company, Inc., 1981.

Jansen, Marius B. *The Making of Modern Japan.* Cambridge, Mass.: Harvard University Press, 2000.

Jones, Katharine M. Jones, *Ladies of Richmond: Confederate Capital.* Indianapolis, IN: Bobbs-Merrill, 1962.

Kautz, August V. *The 1865 Customs of Service for Officers of the Army,* 1866, rpt Mechanicsville, Penn.: Stackpole Books, 2002.

Krick, Robert E. L. *Staff Officers in Gray: A Biographical Register of the Staff Officers in the Army of Northern Virginia.* Chapel Hill, NC: The University of North Carolina Press, 2003.

Livermore, Thomas L. *Numbers and Losses in the Civil War,* Boston: Houghton Mifflin, 1901,.

Love, Robert W., Jr. *The History of the U.S. Navy.* 2 vols. Harrisburg, PA: Stackpole Books, 1992.

Manarin, Louis H., and Weymouth T. Jordan, eds. *North Carolina Troops, 1861–1865: A Roster.* 14 vols. Raleigh, N.C.: North Carolina Department of Archives and History, 1966.

Miller, Francis Trevelyan, ed. *The Photographic History of the Civil War.* 10 Vols. New York: Castle Books, 1957.

Mooney, James L. *Dictionary of American Naval Fighting Ships.* 8 Vols. Washington, D.C.: U.S. Government Printing Office, 1959–1981.

Neely, Mark E., Jr. *The Fate of Liberty.* New York: Oxford University Press, 1991.

Parker, Sandra V. *Richmond's Civil War Prisons.* Lynchburg, Va.: H. E. Howard, Inc., 1990.

Peters, J. T., and H. B. Carden. *History of Fayette County, West Virginia.* Charleston, W.Va.: Jarrett Printing, 1926.

Radley, Kenneth. *Rebel Watchdog: The Confederate States Army Provost Guard*. Baton Rouge, La.: Louisiana State Univ. Press, 1989.
Richardson, James D., ed. *A Compilation of the Messages and Papers of the Presidents, 1789–1897*, 10 vols. Washington, D.C.: Government Printing Office, 1896–1899.
Roberson, John R. *Japan Meets the World: The Birth of a Superpower*. Brookfield, Conn.: The Millbrook Press, 1998.
Robinson, William M., Jr. *Justice in Gray*. Cambridge, Mass.: Harvard University Press, 1941.
Sargeant, Jean A., ed. *Stones and Bones, Tombstone Inscriptions of Prince George's County, Maryland*. Bowie, Md.: Prince George's County Genealogical Society, Inc., 1984.
Scharf, J. T. *History of the Confederate States Navy*. New York: Rogers & Sherwood, 1887.
Schlesinger, Arthur M., Jr., ed. *The Almanac of American History*. New York: G. P. Putnam's Sons, 1983.
Sheads, Scott Sumpter, and Daniel Carroll Toomey. *Baltimore During the Civil War*. Linthicum, Md.: Toomey Press, 1997.
Snyder, Charles M. *Dr. Mary Walker—The Little Lady in Pants*. New York: Arno Press, 1974.
Strode, Hudson. *Jefferson Davis, Confederate President*. New York: Harcourt, Brace and Company, 1959.
Thomas, Emory M. *The Confederate State of Richmond: A Biography of the Capital*. Austin, Texas.: University of Texas Press, 1971.
Wiley, Peter Booth and Korogi Ichiro. *Yankees in the Land of the Gods: Commodore Perry and the Opening of Japan*. New York: Viking, 1990.
Yearns, W. Buck, and John G. Barrett, eds. *North Carolina Civil War Documentary*. Chapel Hill, N.C.: The University of North Carolina Press, 1980.

Articles and Pamphlets

Ammen, S. Z., compl. "Doings of Maryland Boys in Gray, from '61 to '65. Sketches of the War." Baltimore, *The Telegram*, 1879 [part of 180 pages of newspaper clippings were found in a scrapbook of articles which appeared in a Baltimore newspaper in 1879].
[Anonymous] "The Military-Prison Keepers of the Late Southern Confederacy, in the Van of the Democratic Party." Washington, D.C.: National Republican Congressional Executive Committee, 1876. 8 pages, Microfiche, Fiche 31 PG 52, Library of Virginia, Richmond, Virginia.
Athey, Lou. "Loyalty and Civil Liberty in Fayette County during the Civil War." *West Virginia History*, Volume 55 (1996), pp. 1–24.
Burrows, Rev, J. L. "Recollections of Libby Prison." *Southern Historical Society Papers*. Vol. XI, Richmond, Va., Feb.–March, 1883, No. 2 & 3, pp. 84–93.
Colby, Colonel N. T. "The 'Old Capitol' Prison," in *The Annals of the Civil War Written by Leading Participants North and South*, 1878; rpt. New York: Da Capo Press, 1994, p. 502–512.
Earp, Charles A. "The Amazing Colonel Zarvona." *Maryland Historical Magazine* 34(1939), pp. 334–443.
Eberly, Robert E., Jr. "Prison Town." *Civil War Times Illustrated*. No. 1, Vol. XXXVIII (March 1999), pp. 30–33.
Henley, Bernard J. "Col. George W. Alexander: The Terror of Castle Thunder." *Richmond Literature and History Quarterly*. 3(2) (Fall 1980), pp. 48–50.
Hoffert, Sylvia D. "Heroine or Hoaxer? Madame Loreta Velazquez wrote a controversial memoir disclosing her activities as a double agent and brave soldier during the Civil War." http://womenshistory.about.com/library/prm/blheroinehoaxer1.htm.
Hollins, George N. "Autobiography of Commodore George N. Hollis, C. S. A." *Maryland Historical Magazine* (September 1939), pp. 235–243.
"Incident of the War of the Rebellion: How a Confederate Officer Escaped from a Union Prison," New York *Times*, 23 February 1895, p. 3, c. 7.
Kirsch, George B. "Bats, Balls, and Bullets: Baseball and the Civil War." *Civil War Times Illustrated* No. II, Vol. XXXVII (May 1998), pp. 30–37.

Kurtz, Wilbur G., Sr. "The Andrews Railroad Raid." *Civil War Times Illustrated*, No. 1, Vol. 5.

Lowery, Thomas P. "The Sperryville Outrage." *Civil War Times Illustrated* No. 1, Vol. XXXVIII (March 1999), pp. 24–29.

Mangum, William Preston III. "Prison Chaplain and Historian." *Civil War Times Illustrated*. Volume XXXII, No. 5, p. 114.

Mitchell, Patricia B. "'Truly Horrible' Danville Civil War Prisons," *The Pittsylvania Packet,* Pittsylvania Historical Society. Spring 1993, pp. 12–13.

Nichols, George W. "The General's Story." *Harper's New Monthly Magazine,* Vol. XXXV, No. CCV (June 1867), pp. 60–74.

Parker, Alberta Jane Parker. "Molly Pitt, that 'dangerous & traitorous character,' My Great-Grandmother." *Heritage Quest* No. 41 (July/August 1992), pp. 51–53.

"President Lincoln Enters Richmond, 1865." EyeWitness — history through the eyes of those who lived it. Online at www.ibiscom.com (2000).

[R.D.W.] "Old Castle Thunder: Death of Colonel Alexander, Who Was Superintendent of This Prison. The Splendid Dog Nero. History of the Noble Specimen of a Lordly Canine Race — Alexander as a Dramatist and Actor — How he Managed Those Under Him," *Richmond Dispatch,* 3 March 1895.

Rhoades, Priscilla. "The Women of Castle Thunder." *The Kudzuu Monthly* August 2002. (April 1966), pp. 8–17.

"Richmond Since the War." *Scribner's Monthly, an Illustrated Magazine for the People.* Vol. 14, No. 3 (July 1877), 303–312.

Robbins, John B. Robbins, "The Confederacy and the Writ of Habeas Corpus," *Georgia Historical Quarterly.* LV (1971).

Silver, Christopher. "The Ordeal of City Planning in Postwar Richmond, Virginia: A Quest for Greatness." *Journal of Urban History.* 10, No. 1 (November 1983), pp. 33–60.

Soley, J. Russel, Professor. "Early Operations on the Potomac River." *Battles and Leaders of the Civil War,* Vol. II (Secaucus, N. J.: Castle, 1982), p. 143.

"The Old and New." Richmond *Dispatch,* Confederate Reunion Issue, 30 June 1894.

Turner, Thomas P. "Major Turner's Escape. How the ex-Commandant of Famous Libby Prison Fled to Cuba. His Experiences Told by Himself. An Interesting Letter Written by Him from Havana Just After the War to a Friend in Virginia." New York *Times,* 7 July 1895.

Waitt, Robert W., Jr., compl. "Confederate Military Hospitals in Richmond," Official Publication #22. Richmond, Va.: Richmond Civil War Centennial Committee, 1964.

Waitt, R. W. Jr., compl. "Libby Prison, Richmond, Virginia." Richmond, Va.: Official Publication #12, Richmond Civil War Centennial Committee, 1861–1865.

Index

Abernathy, J. M., Asst. Surgeon 140
Adams, Commander Henry A. 12
Adams, John 51, 101, 108, 114
Aiken, Albert, farm of 44
Alexander, Edwin Porter 7, 104–105
Alexander, G. W. 7
Alexander, G. Washington 30
Alexander, George Washington: Adjutant 29; Adjutant, Maryland Zouaves 18; actor, author 55; altercation with Herbert 121; assigned to North Carolina 130; Assistant Adjutant General 43; assistant provost marshal 39, 44; attacks guard at Ft. McHenry 27; attends Proctor funeral 162; attitude toward prisoners 109; authority 100; birth 7; body servant killed 38; burial 167; capture of *St. Nicholas* 20, 22; captured 23–25; career, CSA 119; career, U.S. Navy 8–16, 119; carrying Confederate money 126; Castle Godwin 44; character of 116, 156; charged with accepting bribe 129; charged with contempt 129; Charlotte, North Carolina 132; chronology of career 5–6; commandant 47; commission, U.S. Navy 7; correspondence 39–40, 54, 66–67; court martial 129; criticized by Republicans 162, 213–217; Danville, Virginia 132; death 3, 164, 166–167; denied amnesty 157; description, physical 1, 48, 126; discipline at Castle Thunder 156; discipline at Salisbury 141; disposition 115; dog 59, 60; duties, assistant engineer 9; editor of *Sunday Gazette* 3, 162; engineer, first assistant 15; engineer, second assistant 12; escape from Ft. McHenry 26–29, 42, 45, 119; establishes hospital 84–85; female prisoners 79–81; first lieutenant, C.S.A. 18; flight to Canada 159; imprisoned, Ft. McHenry 24; indicted again 129; injured in escape attempt 117; investigated by Congress 105–106, 107–118; leave 14; leave of absence 128; letter of resignation 148; letter to Capt. W. S. Winder 125; lyrics 56–59; major prisoners' battalion 93; marriage 8; move to Castle Thunder 45; moves to Maryland 163; and Mrs. Velazquez 80; naval service record 10; ordered whipping 110; paralysis 163; "pets" 63; picture of 2; plays for stage 56, 150; political prisoner 28; prisoner at Ft. McHenry 25; promotion 15; provost marshal 32; report, 9/18/1863 209–211; resignation 16, 147, 148; returns from Canada 161–162; returns to Richmond 146; Richmond, Virginia 29; rules and regulations 52; Salisbury, North Carolina 133; Salisbury Prison 133; second expedition 22; special duty 15; spy 125, 167; staff at Salisbury Prison 140; statement in his defense 119; statement on bucking 120; statement on shootings 120; suspended from duties 130; talk to tunnelers 92; treatment of prisoners 117, 156; underground cell 119; unveiling of Lee's statue 163; warranted 9; will 167; with Barton's Brigade 148; witness in court martial 148
Alexander, Susie Ashby 27, 80, 84, 87, 167
Alexander Hospital 84
Alien Enemies Act 35, 78
alien enemies, treatment of 102
Allen, Baldwin T., warden 108, 110–113, 116
Allen, 2nd Lt. G. T., Jr. 140
Allen, Capt. H. P. 140
Allen, John 59
amnesty 157–158
Amnesty Act of 1872 161–162
Anderson, Col. Archer 144, 145
Anderson Cavalry 74
Anderson, John, slave 83
Anderson, W., prisoner 210
Andersonville, Georgia 40, 133, 141, 155, 161
Andrews, James G. 77–78, 103
Andrews, Capt. Snowden 30
Andrews, Capt. W. G. 203, 204
Andrews Railroad Raid 77–78
"Angel of Mercy" hospital 121
Ankrum, Aaron 65
Antietam, Maryland 74
Appomattox, surrender at 151
Arkansas Grays 80
Army of Northern Virginia 147, 151–152
Articles of War 36

265

Index

Ashby, Susanna S. 8
Ashton, James, slave 83
Astor House, New York 154
Atlanta, Georgia, jail 103
attitude of guards 116

Bailey, Jim, slave 83
ball and chain 99
Ballou, David, prisoner 208
barrel shirts 98, 111
Barrett, Lieutenant 156
Barrett's factory 46
Barton, C. M. 162
Barton, Brig. Gen. Seth Maxwell 148
Barton, Surgeon 51
Barton's Brigade 147
baseball at Salisbury 135
Bates, Colonel 19
Bates, W. C. 135
Bavarian boar hound 1
Bean, Millie 79
Beaudry, Louis N., editor/prisoner 70
Beauregard, Gen. P. G. T. 15
Bell, M. T., Asst. Surgeon 86–87
Bell, Mary 79
Bell, Molly 79
Belle Isle 41, 44, 51, 54, 156
Belle Isle deaths 87
Bendix, agent 129
Bennett, George 22
Bensinger, Pvt. William 77, 103
Best, B. James, commandant's clerk 140
Black, Capt. B. J. 205
black prisoners 50
black ships 13
Blackiston, Lieutenant 22
Blair, Peter 65
Bland, T. G., hospital steward 108, 110, 112–115
Blankenship, Lewis J., wardmaster 109
blankets for prisoners 65
Boggs, Samuel S., prisoner 132
Bonaparte, Napoleon, quote from 119
Booker, Lt. R. M. 44
Boone, E. D., escapee 92–93
Bossieux, Cyrus, guard 51, 108
Bossieux, Lt. Virginius 51
Botts, John Minor 41
bounty jumper 105
Bradford's Eating Saloon 41
Brady, Nicholas 22
Bragg, Maj. Gen. Braxton 103
Brazer, Fleming, prisoner 92
Breadlin(?), C., prisoner 210
bribes 92
Bridgford, Major, provost marshal 147
Brisbee, Henry 212

Britton, J. Q., prisoner 208
Brooks, W. B. 212
Brown, Burrell, prisoner 210
Brown, C., slave owner 83
Brown, C. T., prisoner 211
Brown, Charles W. (alias Webster) 75
Brown, Maj. G. B. 78
Brown, James, convicted 99
Brown, John 22
Brown, Lewis, prison historian 136
Brown, Lt. R. W. 39
Brown, W. W. 103
Browne, Junius Henri 62, 64, 131, 133
bucking 95, 98, 109, 120
bucking and gagging 109, 111
Buffum, Pvt. Robert 77, 103
Buford, Lt. Harry T. 79–80
Buissere, Louis 22
Bule, D. J. 69
Burns, Michael C. 69
Burrows, the Rev. J. L. 68, 153–154
Byas (or Byzas), John (alias Charles Carroll) 90
Byrd, Pvt. Sutton, murdered guard 93

C.S. Military Prison 44
C.S. Military Prison rules 52
Callahan, Lt. Dennis 67, 93, 109, 151
Cambridge, Maryland 24
camp followers 82
Camp Holmes, prisoners sent from 208
Camp Lee 39, 103
Camp Parole, Annapolis, Maryland 67
Campbell, R. C. 101
Campbell, William, escapee 91, 108, 113, 114
Canadian spy, T. J. Kirby 112, 117
Cannon, S. K., prisoner 208
Caphart, John, guard 101, 102, 108, 110, 111, 113, 116, 117
Carmichael, Lt. Thomas H. 23
Carney, Edward, escapee 92
Carrington, William A., Major 51, 54, 68, 85, 145, 149, 154
Carroll, Charles (alias John Byas) 28, 90–91, 114
Carroll, R. C. 85
Carter, E. E. 85
Cash, C. J., prisoner 210
Cashmyer, Detective 40
Cashmyer, P. 156
Castle Booker 42
Castle Godwin 41–44, 81, 84, 95
Castle Griswold 42

Castle Grizzly 44
Castle Lightning 41, 42, 62
Castle Thunder: 2, 3, 32, 41, 150; capacity 51; demolished 166; description 48–50, 71–73; detectives 51; emptied of prisoners 153; Federal takeover 150, 153; hospital 84–85; key to Castle Thunder 154; last Confederate commander 151; morning report, 9/18/1863 209–212; prisoners 46, 50, 145, 150, 169–202; sanitation 65; slaves in 82; survives fire 150–151; visitors 69
Castle Thunder, Petersburg, Virginia 47, 112
cat-o-nine tails 111
Causey, William, Detective 51, 108, 110, 112
Cavinaugh, P. H. 51
cells, condition of 146
chain gang 98
Chalmers, Capt. F. 204
Chambers, J. F. 212
changes in prison personnel 126
Charlotte, North Carolina 132
Chattanooga, Tennessee, negro jail 102
Cheny, Henry 22
Chesapeake Bay 12, 19
Chicago Sanitary Fair 154
Childrey, Stephen B., commissary 108, 111, 113–115
Chilton, Col. R. H. 146
Chinn, Samuel, slave 83
Chipman, John A., escapee 92
Chipman, Col. N. P. 154
City Alms House 128
City Battalion 53
civilian prisoners 36
Clackner, George W. 41
Clap, Wm., prisoner 208
Clark of Georgia 108
clothing for prisoners 65
Clover Hill Tavern 152
Coan River 19
Cobb, Howell 155
Coggins, Dr. W. W. 70, 84–86, 112
Coke, Capt. 125
Colbert, John 22
Colby, Col. N. T. 101
Cole, Thomas, escapee 92
Coleman, Edward 51
Collier, L. 51
Colwell, Joseph 211
Committee for Public Safety 139
Company D, 20th Virginia 51
Company H, 47th Virginia 30, 42

conditions worsen at Salisbury 141
Cone, Edward 22
Confederate Congress 3, 36
Confederate deserters 50
Confederate guerrillas 103
Confederate money 126
Confederate Secret Service 80
Confederate States Prison 50–51
Confederate War Department 64
Congressional Medal of Honor 78
Conner, J. G., spy 149
conscription laws 37
Cooper, Charles 76
Cooper, Gen. S. 148
Corbatt, Owen 22
Corey, James 51
correspondents, newspaper 63
Cotrall, John 211
cotton factory building 133
counterfeit money 129
Court of Inquiry 130, 148
court-ordered executions 10
Coyner, Hiram 63
crane wounded 60
cartel canceled 161
Craven, Braxton 136
Crawford, V. T., attorney 108
"Crazy Bet" 65
crazy Yankee shot 115
Crew's 41
cross examination of witnesses 117
Crow, Robert B., Detective 51, 100, 108, 110, 112, 114, 115
Cullen, Frederick 65
Cumberland 16
Cunningham, L. 51
Currin, John 22
Curtain, Gov. Andrew 74

Daffin, F. 18
Daley, John 22
Danville, Virginia, prisons 132
Darby, Martin, tied by thumbs 110
Davidson, Greenlee 109, 118
Davidson, Lt. W. W. 50
Davidson College 134
Davis, E. P. (Baxter) 51
Davis, J. S. 51
Davis, President Jefferson 35, 36, 50, 77, 82, 94, 102, 151, 154–155, 161, 162, 165, 214–217
Davis, 2nd Lt. M. C., Jr. 140
Dawson, Wm. 212
Day, S. M. 51
Deakfeman(?), Henry, prisoner 210

Deaton, Spencer, hanging of 104
DeButts, Dr. John 87, 109
Dedrick, Henry 63
De Jarnette of Virginia 108, 121
Delagnel, Major 51
Delaney, Eugene 93
Democratic Party 213–217
Denham, J. 50
Department of Henrico 39, 54
deserters' prison 41
deserters punished 62
desperados 110
detective force 44
diseases, common 86
District of North Carolina 40
Dix, Col. John H. 23
Dix-Hill Cartel 161
Dorsey, D. A. 103
D'Orsey, Richard 56
Downey, Alice 76
Doyle, John, prisoner 109
Duffin, Francis 22
Dugan, Captain 29
Duncan, J. A., prisoner 210
Duncan, James W., trial of 156
dungeon 109, 113
Dunn, Lt. David 206
Dry, Adam, prisoner 210

Early, Gen. Jubal A. 158
East India Royal Navy 111
Eastern District Military Prison 43, 54
Edenborough, Capt. Henry 63, 108, 111
Edmonds, T., prisoner 210
Edo Bay, Japan 11
Edwards, Samuel 211
Edwards, William 65
Egan, Park 212
8th Virginia Infantry 75
Elizabeth City, North Carolina 63
Ellinger, Leon 126
Elliott, Col. Wyatt M. 130
Ely, Alfred, congressman 61
England, J. A., prisoner 208
enlistments, Confederate 34
enlistments, Union 34
entertainment 69
escape plot October 1864 142
escapes: 1862–1863 88; 1864 94
Evans, Ida D. 30
Evans, J. B., prisoner 109
Ewell, Lt. Gen. R. S. 147, 150

Farmer, John, escapee shot 88
Farrar, Dr. 109
Fayette County, Virginia, civilians 78
Federal deserters 50

Federal prisoners 44, 54
Fellon, R. 22
female prisoners 79–82
Ferguson, Lt. Col. J. L. 209, 212
Fillmore, President Millard 11–13
firing squad 62
First Battalion, 2nd class militia 53
First Kanawaha 78
First Manassas, battle of 61
First North Carolina Volunteers 63
First Regiment Reserve Militia 53
Fish, Colonel, provost marshal 126
Fisher, William 93
Fitzgerald, William 51
flag of truce 93
Flannagan, Nat (alias Martin Hines) 125
Florence, T. B. 162
Floyd, J. C., prisoner 210
Folks, Detective 51, 89, 91, 151
Foncin, Jean 26
Forbes, R., prisoner 211
Ford, Annette Gee 143
forged release order 92
Fort Craig, New Mexico 34
Fort Delaware 110
Fort Gilmer 148
Fort Lafayette, New York 23, 95
Fort Lowery 30
Fort McHenry, Maryland 23, 25, 44; guardhouse 24–25
Fort Pulaski 156
Fort Sumter, South Carolina 15
Fortress Monroe 68
Frances, Antonio 22
Francisville, Pennsylvania 7
Franklin Street guardhouse 42
Frazier, G. H. 22
Fredericksburg, Virginia 19
Freeburger, George A., warden 41
Freeman, Capt. C. D., guard 140
French lady 19, 23
Fritz (Fitzpatrick), tavern keeper 126
Fry, Capt. William H. 39
Fuque, Capt. J. A. 140
Fuller, Richard 22
Fulton II 9, 15

Galle, Capt. A., paroled prisoner 210
Galloway, Capt. Swift, 136, 137
Gardner, Brig. Gen. William M. 147, 158
Garibaldi 17
Garnett, Algernon S. 22

Garrack, Patrick, prisoner 92
Gaye, J. J., Yankee deserter 210
Gee, Maj. John Henry 136, 141, 156; trial of 143
Geeslin, L., prisoner 208
General (train engine) 77
General Hospital No. 13 85, 87
Georgeanna 24
Georgetown, Virginia 76
Gerbert, George (alias Moore) 89
Gettysburg, battle at 93
Gibbs, Maj. George C. 33, 136, 156
Gillmore, James 51
Gilman, Miss Charlotte 63, 80, 108, 116
Gilmer, Col. John A. 136, 141
Ginter & Allen 59
Glass, W. R. 50
Godwin, Archibald C. 41, 43, 133, 136, 156
Goldsboro, North Carolina 145
Goodhart, Briscoe 77
Goodman, Robert, slave owner 83
Gowan, J. A., prisoner 211
Grandy, Capt. C. R. 203
Grant, Gen. U. S. 149, 156, 161, 162
Grant's Factory 41
Graves, Thomas T. 151
Greanor, William 45
Greanor's Tobacco Factory 45, 46
Greanor's Tobacco Warehouse 48
Great Libby Prison Escape 95
Great Locomotive Chase 77–78
Green, John 65
Green, Neal 23
greenbacks, trading in 129
Greeley, Horace 161
Griswold, Maj. E. 39, 44
guards 53, 104, 146; attitudes, actions, character 116; bribed 92; desertion 139; imprisoned 113; inexperienced 104

Hail, Pvt. J. R. 206
Hairston, Maj. J. T. W. 38
Hakodate, Japan 14
Hall, Dr. J. W. 134
Hall, Thos. W., prisoner 208
Hamilton, James B. 68, 78, 86
Hamilton, Thomas B. 78
Hammond, Dr. 85
Hampton Roads 16
Hancock, James, faked death 94
handcuffs 99, 117
Hankels, Thomas 65
Hardin, Maj. M. B. 203
Harding, Dr., slave owner 83
Harpers Ferry 126

Harrison, Capt. C. L. 203
Harrow 22, 86
Harwood's Tobacco Factory 42
Hatch, I. M., Union spy 63
Havana, Cuba 158
Hawkins, M. J. 103
Hefner, J. M., prisoner 210
Hemling, Charles 18
Hemmings, Amos 65
Hendren, Capt. J. H. 203
Hendricks, David L., prisoner 210
Henrico County Jail 41, 42
Herbert, Caleb Claiborne 67, 108, 121, 123
Hero (Nero), Alexander's dog 48, 59, 93, 151, 153–154
Herring, Ransom, prisoner 208
Hewitt, John Hill 56
Hicks, Governor 24
Hicks, Jas. P., prisoner 208
Higgins, John M. 41
Hill, Gen. Daniel Harvey 81
Hill, Edward 93
Hill, Richard 80
Hines, Martin 125
Hinks, Samuel 20
Hodge, the Rev. M. D. 42
Holland, David 211
Hollins, Fred H. 22
Hollins, George N., Jr. 22
Hollis, Capt. George W. 20–22
Holt, Judge Advocate General J. 103
Hong Kong 12
Hopkins, E. B. 51
Horner, John 22
"Horse Haven" 60
horse meat 67
Hospital No. 13 51
Hospitals: and staffing 145; inspection 85–86; number of prisoners treated 145; ration 85
Howard, a deserter 105
Howard's Grove 60
Howard's Grove Hospital 86
Howe, Dr. 20
Howell, James, prisoner 91
Hoyt, William D., surgeon 85
Huffman, Danl., prisoner 210
Hughes' Row, Richmond, Virginia 42
Hunt, James P. 22

inflation, food prices 67
inspection, June 1864 146
Irish prisoners 69
issues examined 109
Iverson, Lt. Colonel 156

Jackson, James 51
Jackson, Joe 211

James River 48
Jameson, J. C., Yankee prisoner 210
Japan 10
Jeffrey, William H., prisoner 137, 139
Jennings, James 90, 109
Johnson, President Andrew 157–158
Johnson, Andrew, prisoner 70
Johnson, Gen. Bradley T. 136, 147
Johnson, J. C., guard 104
Johnson, Laura J. 79
Johnston, General 29
Jones, John 77
Jones, John, slave 83
Jones, Pvt. John R.: court martial 99, 203–206; escape 89
Jones, Capt. William L., cashiered 100
Jordan, Maj. Thomas Jefferson 78
Joynes, H. A. 51

Kellogg, Spencer, execution of 103
Kemper, General 53
Kerwin, Captain 22
Key, Francis Scott 26
Key, Frank 29
Keyer, John (alias Wm. Shulta) 95
King, G. W., prisoner 210
Kinston, North Carolina, court martials 99
Kirby, J. T., (T.J.) prisoner 108, 110–113, 116, 117
Kirby's quarters were "best room" 120
Klyne, Jacob 50
Knight, William 103
Knoxville, Tennessee, prison 102
Koontz 86
Korea 13

Lacey, William, escapee 95
Lamar, Senator L. Q. C. 216
Lamb, M. T. 211
Lamb, Melton W., prisoner 208
Laprade, Pvt. Israel 100
Latham, 1st Lt. G. A. 140
La Touche, Lt. 39
Laughlin, James 22
Laurel, Maryland 3, 163
Lawton, Harrie Lewis 82
Lawton, Hattie H., detective 82
Lee, Castellina Thunder 80
Lee, Mary 80
Lee, Gen. Robert E. 3, 93, 151, 161, 163
Lee, S., prisoner 210

leg irons 99
Lemkens, Thos., slave 83
Lemmon, M. J. 90
Letcher, Gov. John 17, 22, 31, 43
Lewis, J., prisoner 210
Lewis, Lt. Warner 39
Libbers, Chas. 211
The Libby Chronicle 70–73
Libby Prison 39, 41, 42, 46, 51, 53, 54, 70, 95, 133, 149–151, 153; hospital 85–86; tunnel 95
Lincoln, President Abraham 31, 151, 155; assassination 158–159
Lincoln, Mary Todd 40
Livingstone, Dr. David 141
Livingstone, Robert Moffat 141
Lookerman, Captain 29
Loudon Rangers 76–77
Ludlow, Col. William H. 82
Lunday (Lundie), Dr. 108, 114
Lyerly, J. L., prison clerk 140
Lyons, James 59

Madam LaForce 19
Madeira 12
Magill, Mrs. Elizabeth 56
Maguire, William H. 65
mail from home 68
Majority Report 106, 122
Mallett, Col. Peter 207
Mallory, Stephen Russell 20
Mangum, the Rev. A. W. 133–136
Manning, Peter 22
Margaret 20
Marks, Captain 30
Marshal, Humphrey, Atty. 69
Martial law 36
Martin, Capt. G. A. 203, 204
Martin, J., Yankee deserter 210
Martin, Sgt. Maj. James 140
Martin, Mike 51
Mary Pierce 20
Mary Washington 20, 23
Maryland Zouaves 18, 22
Mason, Elihu 77–78, 103
Massey, Captain 149
Mattaponi, the Thomas home 17
Mattison, Colonel 154
Maury, John M. 22
May, N. A., prisoner 210
Mayo, Mayor Joseph 18, 59
Mayo, Col. Robert 109
McCarter, James, prisoner 211
McCarthy, John B. 162
McClasher, James, prisoner 109
McClellan, General 23
McCoy, Capt. Henry 136
McDaniel's Negro Jail 41
McHenry, James 26

McKee, Captain, provost marshal 160
McLaughton, James 65
McLean, Wilmer, home of 152
McMachael, J. P. 211
McPherson, J., Yankee deserter 210
Meade, William E., guard 92
Meadows, J. W. 50
Means, Capt. Samuel C. 75–77
Means' Loudon Rangers 75
Mear, Geo. 211
medieval torture methods 107
Merrimac 16
meteor 13
Michaels, J. M., prisoner 208
military offenders 50
military prison keepers 213–217
military prison system 33–34, 44
Miller, D. W., prisoner 210
Miller, E. J. 51
Miller, Hugh 51
Miller, John 65
Miller, W. 211
Minor, Robert D. 22
Minority Report 106, 121–124
Mires, Frank 51
Mitchell, Gen. O. M. 64
Mitchell, Patricia 132
Monticello 20–21
Moore, 2nd Lt. J. A. 140
morbidity, mortality 87
Morfit, Capt. C. 39
Morfitt, Major 145
Mohn, Fred'ke 212
Morgan, Geo. C. 211
Morgan, Brig. Gen. John Hunt 78, 103
Morris, Major 28
Morris, Richard, guard 104
Mosby's Guerrillas 101
Moseby, Thos. F., prisoner 211
Moss, Alex, prisoner 208
Mt. Cove Guards 78
muggers 100, 137
"mule" bread 67
Munn, Sidney 154
Murphy, L. D., prisoner 210
Murray, James 22
Museum of the Confederacy 39
Myers, James 211
Mygatt, J. P. K. 19

Needham, Elizabeth 79
Negro jail 38
Negro prisoners 50
Nero, Bavarian boar hound 48, 59
Nesbit, Doctor 156
network of spies 65
New, Detective 51, 90
New Richmond Theatre 55
New York City 126, 154

Newsome, guard who shot Morris 104
Nineteenth Regiment Virginia 53
9th Pennsylvania Cavalry 78
nitrate beds 60
Norris, W. H. 28
northern prisons, deaths in 160

Oath of Allegiance 65, 93, 151
O'Brien, Captain 153
O'Brien, Tim, escaped jail 93
O'Connor, Dennis, prisoner 108, 112
Offighter, William 63
Ogden, Mr., manager 84
Ohio boys 64
O'Keefe, William 29
Old Capitol Prison, Washington, D.C. 47, 59, 76, 101, 143
Ord, Maj. Gen. E. O. C. 149
Organ, Lt. J. G. 203
Ould, Robert, judge-advocate 65, 69, 70, 108, 149, 161
Owens, Samuel H. 25

Page, Henry 93
Palmer, Brig. Gen. William Jackson 74–75
Palmer & Allison warehouse 41, 46
Palmer's Factory building 41, 48, 50, 91
Parker, Farnie W. 30
Parkhill, Maj. J. H. 39
parole 65, 151
Parrot, Pvt. Jacob 77, 103
Partington, Miss Sallie 56
Patterson, Robert 50
Paulson, G. B., hospital steward 140
Pawnee 16, 18
Peeler, R., prisoner 208
Pegram, Maj. J. W. 39
Pemberton's 41
Perdue, Detective 51, 91
Perry, Commodore Matthew 2, 8–9, 11–14
Perry, William, prisoner 208
Peters, W. J. (alias Palmer) 75
Peterson, W. T., detective 206
Philadelphia, Pennsylvania 7
Phillips, Elijah, prisoner 210
Phoenix, John, slave 83
Pickral, F. J., prisoner 210
Pierpont, Gov. Francis 76
Pinkerton Detective Agency 75, 82
Pinkerton's Female Detective Bureau 82
Pittenger, Cpl. William 77, 103
"plug-uglies" from Baltimore 102

Plymouth 12
pneumonia 112
Poindexter, Richard, slave 83
Point Lookout 19
Pollard, Edward A. 149
Porter, John R. 103
Portsmouth, Virginia 8
Potomac Zouaves 18
Powers, William 22
Powhatan 13
prison population 70, 146, 149
prisoners: care of 65; character of 109, 115; classification of 110; court 69; daily routine 68; died in hospital 145–146; exchange of 63, 149; execution of 103; food for 65; health care 114; kept outside in cold 111; killed 53, 90–91, 114–115; letters from 53; money and valuables taken 145; passes and paroles 152; plight of 61–62; political 65; standard of treatment of 101, 160–161; stockade 136; transfer of 62, 70, 147, 149; treated in hospital 145
prisoners of war 39, 61
prisons, Confederate, list of 33–34
Proctor, John C., editor 162
provost marshal's department 144; duties 37; prison 39; uniform 48
punishment 50, 62–63, 97–107; methods of 121
Putnam, 1st Lt. George D. 60, 154

quarters at Salisbury 137
Quime, Pvt. Thomas R., deserter 100
Quinn, J. L. 18

Radical Republicans 159
Rappahannock 19
rations for soldiers 66, 120
rations for prisoners reduced 67, 145, 146
record books 146
Reddick, Cpl. William H. 77, 103
religion 68
reporters 63
representation, legal 69
retribution 154
Reynolds, Pvt. Henry G. 99
Richardson, A. D. 68, 138, 139
Richardson, Lucian W. 130–131, 144
Richmond: after the war 165–166; citizens of 53; evacuated 149–150; rebuilding of 165–

166; refugees from 149; warehouses burned 150
Richmond City Jail 41
Richmond Theatre 55
Riggs, Marion C., warden 108, 111, 113, 116, 117
Roberts, Steph., prisoner 210
Rock, S. C. 211
Rockett's dock 59
Rogers, E. Law 28
roll call 68
Rose, Edwd. 211
Rose, Frederick A., surgeon 15
Rosenfelt, Simon 126
Ross, E. W. 39
rules and regulations 51
rules, violation of 112
Rusick, John H. 18
Ryan, William A. 18

sailor's punishment 110
St. Nicholas 2; capture 17–22, 45
St. Nicholas affair 28
Salisbury Prison: 3, 42, 60, 78, 147, 156; commandants 136; compared to Andersonville 143; deadline at 136–137; escape from 64, 142–143; food supply 139; guards at 139; number of prisoners 140; prison staff, 1864 140; tunnels at 141; water shortage 138
Sanders, Capt. E. C. 63
Sands, Capt. John 125
Sansing, W., prisoner 210
Saranac 13
Sayre, T. P. 67
Schaeffer, J. F., Detective 51, 108, 110, 112
Schoff, Jas. 211
Schroeder, Charles 22
Scott, Miss Anna 43, 81
Scott's 41
Scully, Daniel 51
Sebree(?), J., prisoner 211
2nd Massachusetts Volunteers 76
Second Virginia Reserve 53
Secretary of the Navy (Confederate) 69
Seddon, Sec. of War James A. 76, 155
Selph, C. McRae, inspector 131, 146
sentinels arrested for taking bribes 90
Shanghai 12
Sharpsburg, Maryland 74
Shehan, John, prisoner 108, 112, 113, 116
Shepard, K. L. 211
Sherman, Gen. William T. 149

Shields, Col. J. C. 39
Shimoda, Japan 14
Shinard, J. 211
Shinn, Robert 158
Shirley, 1st Lt. J. L. 140
Shockoe Cemetery, Richmond 2
Shogun 13
Shulta, William (alias John Keyer) 95
Siegal, Lee, prisoner 210
Sigal, Jas., slave 83
Sigman, M., prisoner 210
Simms, Charles C. 22
Simpson, Druiunsen(?) 211
Simpson, Capt. James Richard 76
Simpson, W. D. 108, 121–122
Sinclair, William 12
Skinner, Thomas 22
Small, Maj. Abner 132–133, 137–138
smallpox 86, 145
Smith (a deaf mute) 51
Smith, of Alabama 108, 121
Smith, Maj. Gen. G. W. 203
Smith, James M. 22
Smith, Kirby 148
Smith, W. W. 208
Smith's Factory 41
Snead, 2nd Lt. C. H. 140
Snead, Capt. E. D. 140
Snead, 2nd Lt. W. R. 140
Snider, George H., guard 104
Soldiers' Fund
Soles, Lt. W. L., forged release 92
solitary confinement 99, 109, 113
South Mountain, battle of 74
Southern Bastille 64
"Southern Soldier Boy" 56, 58
special committee 106
spies 74–77, 149
Spotswood Hotel fire, 1870 165
spread eagle 98
Sprouse, Samuel 51
spy, Union 63
Stanton, Sec. of War Edwin M. 82, 96, 126, 160
Starke, W. N., investigator 109
state prisoners 69
Stevens, R. R. 155
stocks 98
Stockton, Lt. F. D. 140
Stuart, Gen. J. E. B. 38
Summers, Charles 22
Summers, Captain 126
Sunday Gazette 3
Surratt, Mary, execution of 158
sutler's store 67–68
Sutton, Sue B. 30
"Swamp dragons" 149
sweat box 98
sweat house 101, 113

Tacket, J. L., prisoner 208
Tacket, Jno., prisoner 208
Tacket, L. F., prisoner 208
Taliaferro, Sue J. 30
Tatem, Samuel 22
Taylor, Jacob R. 65
Taylor, Maj. R. C. 204
Taylor, William B. 65
Temple, Benj., slave owner 83
Texas (train engine) 77
Tell, M. L., Asst. Surgeon 86
3rd Cavalry Reg., Virginia Vols. 76
35th Virginia Cavalry 76
Thomas, George W., Detective 51, 91, 108, 110–112, 114–117
Thomas, James, landsman 22
Thomas, Richard 17–18, 20, 22, 27, 43
Thompson, Charles 86
Thompson, Joseph 22
Thorburn, Charles E. 22
thumbs, hanging by 98–99
Tilly, William 51
Timberlake, Mr., clerk 151
tobacco warehouses 46
Todd, Lt. David H. 40
Torsch, J. W. 18
Townsend, George Alfred, reporter 150
Treaty of Kanagawa 14
Tredgar Iron Works, survived fire 150, 151, 166
Treanor, Francis T. 65
Trowbridge, John J., writer 153
trysting (thumb hanging) 98–99, 109, 110
tunnel 91–92
Turner, Alfred 93
Turner, Richard R. 155
Turner, Capt. Thomas P. 39, 45, 47, 50–52, 65, 109, 128, 144, 149, 158, 166
Turpin & Brother's tobacco factory 166
21st Ohio Regiment 103
Tynan, John W. 22

Underwood, Margaret 81
Union soldiers, officers 78
United States Navy 2, 66
United States Sanitary Commission 135
U.S.S. *Thomas Freeborn* 19
U.S.S. *Mississippi* 7, 10–13
U.S.S. *Reliance* 19
U.S.S. *San Jacinto* 13–14
U.S.S. *Seminole* 15
U.S.S. *Susquehanna* 12–15

Van Lew, Miss Elizabeth L. 65, 82
Varina 44
Velazquez, Loreta Janeta 2, 79–80
ventriloquist 142
verdict of Congressional Committee 119–124
Vicksburg, Mississippi 64
The Virginia Cavalier 3, 56, 58
Virginia Historical Society 53
Virginia House of Delegates 76
Vowels, Major 93

Walker, Dr. Mary Edwards 81
wall, holes in 90
Wallace, Gen. Lew 155
Walter, Capt. William 8
Ward, Attorney 102, 108
Ward, Captain 20
Warner, Capt. Jackson 39, 109
Warrington, Tennessee 15
Washington, D.C. 125
Washington, George 26
Washington, W. H., slave 83
Waterford Baptist Church 76
Waters, H. M., prisoner 210
Watlington, 1st Lt. R. H. 140
Watson, Lemuel 50
Watson, William F. 109, 115
Watts, George 22
Waymack, George W., prisoner 109
Webster, Alfonzo C. 75–77
Webster, Timothy 42–43, 82
Webster, Mrs. Timothy 43, 81–82
Weitzel, General, headquarters of 151
Wells, Gideon 19
West, R. C. 211
"wharf-rats" from New Orleans 102
Whetmore, Hiram 22
Whetstone Point, Maryland 26
whipping 62, 99, 110, 111
White, Maj. Elijah V. 76
White, Isiah H. 155
Whitlock's factory building 62
Whitlock's Warehouse 48
Whitsett, 2nd Lt. A. M., Jr. 140
Whitt, David, prisoner 210
Widner, T., prisoner 210
Wile, August, escapee 90
Wiley, Frederick F., guard 108
Wiley, Walter, slave 83

Willet, Felix 65
Williams, Mrs. Alice 79
Williams, Daniel W. 22
Williams, H. S., prisoner 210
Williams, James 51
Williams, Robert, prisoner 210
Wilson, a substitute 105
Wilson, Alfred 103
Wilson, J. 93
Wilson, J. M. 211
Winchester, Virginia 79
Winder, Brig. Gen. John H. 36, 38–40, 42–44, 51–52, 54, 62–66, 80, 86, 109, 112, 145; death of 148–149; indicted on conspiracy 155; letter from, in support of 118; military prison keeper 214–215; office 68; order book 39; orders to shoot 114; statement in support of 121; Winder's Legion 93–94
Winder, Richard B. 155–156
Winder, Capt. W. S. 39–40, 155
Winder Guards 93
Wirz, Henry 43, 148, 155–156, 158, 215
Withers, Col. John 140–141
Wollam, John 103
women prisoners 50
Wood, Mark 103
Wood, Mr. 69
Woodbridge, the Rev. 42
wooden horse, punishment on 99
Woolfolk, Captain 105
Wooten, J. H. 51
work release 64
Worthington, Charles 19–20
Wrenn, J. 90
Wright, George 113–114
Wright, Jesse 51
Writ of Habeas Corpus 34–35
Wynn, Mr., doorkeeper 109

Yancey 22
Yankee officers 46
Yeolothall(?), M. 211
Yount, Geo., prisoner 210

Zarvona, Col. Richard Thomas 17–18, 20, 22, 29, 44; attempts to escape 95–96; captured 22–23; death of 166; Ft. McHenry 26, 30; release from prison 166; solitary confinement 30, 166
Zarvona Zouaves 8, 29–30

www.ingramcontent.com/pod-product-compliance
Lightning Source LLC
Chambersburg PA
CBHW060258240426

43661CB00060B/2825